Italian Gothic
Horror Films,
1957–1969

D1592727

Italian Gothic Horror Films, 1957–1969

ROBERTO CURTI

Foreword by Ernesto Gastaldi

McFarland & Company, Inc., Publishers

Jefferson, North Carolina

Library of Congress Cataloguing-in-Publication Data

Curti, Roberto, 1971–
Italian gothic horror films, 1957–1969 /
Roberto Curti ; foreword by Ernesto Gastaldi.
    p.   cm.
Includes bibliographical references and index.

ISBN 978-0-7864-9437-8 (softcover : acid free paper) ∞
ISBN 978-1-4766-1989-7 (ebook)

1. Horror films—Italy—History and criticism.   I. Title.

PN1995.9.H6C877 2015   791.43'61640945—dc23   2015006889

British Library cataloguing data are available

On the cover: Poster art from the 1963 film *Black Sabbath*
(American International Pictures/Photofest)

Printed in the United States of America

*McFarland & Company, Inc., Publishers
Box 611, Jefferson, North Carolina 28640
www.mcfarlandpub.com*

Table of Contents

Foreword by Ernesto Gastaldi   1

Preface   3

Introduction: Gothic, Italian Style   11

Abbreviations   19

THE FILMS   21

Selected Bibliography   201

Index   205

Foreword
by Ernesto Gastaldi

In the late 1950s and early '60s, we used to call it "*cinema di paura*" ("scary cinema").

"We" were young scriptwriters, called on to make up stories set in gloomy crumbling castles, isolated villas, dark crypts and foggy cemeteries packed full with crooked crosses, in the shade of cypress trees just like in an Ugo Foscolo poem—even better if those cypresses were shaken by a howling wind that recalled the echo of wolf packs or the gnashing teeth of damned souls.

In such pleasant places we had to develop characters of young virgins, unaware of the facts of life, who confidently ventured in the woods and cemeteries, without a red hood but with the same appetizing charm that would attract every wolf or werewolf in the area, either on four or two legs.

Usually the directors were established names, with decent curricula, some artistic merit. They probably accepted those films for food, yet they had their share of fun shooting those "scary" movies.

One of the first and best was Riccardo Freda, who shot *I Vampiri* in 1957, starring Gianna Maria Canale, a year ahead of the famous *Horror of Dracula* by Terence Fisher, starring the mythical Christopher Lee.

Freda did not start from Bram Stoker's novel, but he invented a mysterious Paris where women were drained of their blood to preserve the beauty of a duchess through weird practices.

However, it was Fisher's Dracula that unleashed Italian producers, and a hailstorm of vampire movies flooded the screens: vampires popped up everywhere, with a notable preference for musical stage plays. Opera was a typical wallpaper for these films and ballerinas were the bloodsucker's favorite victims. Yet, at the end of the cycle, the poor fangtoothed thing ended up fighting against ... Maciste!

My debut as a writer and assistant director came with *The Vampire and the Ballerina* (*L'amante del vampiro*), by Renato Polselli, where a company of beautiful ballerinas had decided to rehearse their ballet in the icy cold and gloomy castle of Artena—just the perfect place, was it not? Our working hours: from 8 in the morning till midnight. We had skeletons of poor devils, like my co-assistant director, the unforgettable Franco Cirino, demanded. Home-made special effects. If someone had told me I was making a Gothic film I would have laughed.

Some time later I moved from vampires to werewolves. The film was *Werewolf in a Girls' Dormitory* (*Lycanthropus*) by Paolo Heusch, who told me we were making a horror movie. Actually, there was very little horror in it, but the film benefitted from a beautiful b&w as well as the usual naïve young college girls. Looking back at it, well, it was a bit "scary."

It was Riccardo Freda who explained to me that *The Horrible Dr. Hichcock* (*L'orribile segreto del dr. Hichcock*) was a Gothic film, due to its mixture of romance and horror. He shot it in two weeks with two crews working at the same time in a house by a cemetery in via Rubens, in Rome. Freda asked my permission to cut out a final block of 12 pages from the script, the ones that explained the mystery. I feebly objected that this way nobody would understand a thing, and Freda agreed, nodding vigorously. He smiled and said: "That's the beauty of Gothic!"

So, when I finally got to work with Maestro Mario Bava, I knew quite well how it had to be done. *The Whip and the Body* (*La frusta e il corpo*) is undoubtedly a Gothic film, and Bava outdid himself by using colored lights, allowing actors to do more or less what they thought was right, and composing colorful shots of a beauty that are still unparalleled in the genre.

Meanwhile the Gothic had created a solid market, and everyone was looking for more and more intriguing and gruesome stories.

From Sheridan Le Fanu's *Carmilla*, Tonino Valerii and I wrote *Terror in the Crypt* (*La cripta e l'incubo*), which we completed in one night on the terrace of my house, with a continuous supply of coffee on the part of the beautiful Mara Maryl.

Such a marathon was due to the false claim that we had a Gothic script ready to be filmed, which we had made the day before to a producer. At dawn Tonino was so upset that he started singing ramshackle sonnets in rhyme that ended with "sarà forse Rowena che le succhia la vena? / Ma il sospetto più atroce e che si tratti di froce!" ("could it be Rowena that sucks blood from her vein-a? / But the worst suspicion so far is that they both lesbians are").

Very Gothic.

Then came the "giallo." Our coffee supplier Mara Maryl was also my wife, and I wrote a story with four characters just for her, set in an isolated villa—but this time with less horror and more suspense. The result was *Libido*, which also marked the on-screen debut of Giancarlo Giannini. This little black-and-white movie cost 26 million lire and was sold worldwide, gaining a profit of over 400 percent. It also served as a pretext for my degree in economics, with a thesis on the companies which produced prototypes: *Libido*'s commercial success pushed the late Luciano Martino and Mino Loy on the road to Italian "giallo."

But, as they say, that is another story.

With this book, Roberto Curti will take you by the hand through a labyrinth of titles, among vampires, werewolves, witches and other assorted monsters. You will descend with him in the humid dungeons and eerie crypts, walk in the ghoul-infested graveyards ... but also peek into beautiful girls' dormitories and hot alcoves where horrible murders have taken place under magical nights of full moonlight, in a well-documented and engrossing journey.

Like every good vampire hunter, Roberto has done his research and documented his prey by collecting a great deal of vital and exclusive information in the dusty Archive of State and consulting scripts written with rickety old typewriters. In doing so, he has unearthed a small yet invaluable treasure of little lies and big oversights, well-kept secrets and ingenious fabrications, hidden details and secret identities—which is to say, a common practice in the glory days of Italian genre cinema. And I should know it very well, since I used to sign my own scripts with the name Julian Berry!

Bon voyage ... and sweet nightmares!

Preface

It is customary to apply the term "Italian Gothic horror" to a relatively homogeneous number of films, made in Italy during a limited time: not even a decade, from 1957—the year Italy's first true horror movie, Riccardo Freda's *I Vampiri*, was released—to 1966. Such a classification does not comprise the whole of the horror films produced in Italy, but it merely highlights the genre's heyday, with the emergence of its characteristic traits, main personalities and most significant works. However, despite a hiatus due to production and economic reasons—such as the Spaghetti Western phenomenon—more films were produced in the mid-to-late '60s which can also be labeled as Gothic. These works retained the main ingredients of the previous period and even enhanced them beyond the boundaries of genre filmmaking, before a crucial re-shaping of the Gothic imagery took place in the 1970s.

Therefore, I decided to include the films produced and released up to 1969, a year which marked a crucial turning point in Italian society and the film industry as well, with the loosening of morals and the relaxation of censorship after the turmoils of 1968. With the advent of the new decade, the Gothic would take on new elements which radically altered its identity. Besides the commercial explosion of the *giallo*, which paved the way for a number of hybrids, the 1970s saw the rise of nudity as the main selling point of

commercial feature films, and the Gothic was no exception: Its imagery would be frequently used as a pretext to show erotic scenes, and even stretched out to accommodate out-and-out hardcore.

The Gothic horror is usually considered as a genre, but the Italian term *filone* (streamlet) is perhaps more apt when referring to the various undercurrents of the popular Italian movie industry. As Canadian film scholar Donato Totaro explains, "The word *filone* has many meanings in Italian, which expresses the multifarious forms it can take in cinema. Depending on the context (geological, literary, quotidian) it can refer to a loaf of bread, a thread or cord, or the principle vein in a mineral, or to express when something is 'in the tradition of'...."

As Totaro correctly points out, the *filone* "is a better way to account for the fullness/richness of the ... ever-changing Italian film industry, always ready to veer production off into a current popular cycle. From this perspective, the *filone* is more flexible than genre or subgenre, taking in the idea of cycles, trends, currents, and traditions."[1] Therefore, given the way the Italian film industry worked from the mid–1950s onwards, what is perceived as a film genre is actually "a cluster of concurrent streamlets, veins, or traditions"[2]—something which, in the case of the Gothic, would become evident in the 1970s.

The films produced during the late 1950s

and 1960s, however, interpreted the term "Gothic" in the light of rigid parameters. These were shaped by the analogies with foreign horror movies and in accordance with the characteristics of the seventeenth and eighteenth century Gothic novel. That is, as Gothic scholar David Punter wrote, "an emphasis on portraying the terrifying, a common insistence on archaic settings, a prominent use of the supernatural, the presence of highly stereotyped characters and the attempt to deploy and perfect techniques of literary suspense."[3] The term "Gothic" itself was taken in its vague geographical meaning (as a synonym for "Teutonic" or "Germanic," with the faint implication of barbarism associated with it) and the historical one as well (since stories were often set in a blurred, sometimes remote past).

But there was more than that. The stories had to do with the wicked, the unspeakable, the morbid; eroticism was a primary element, in accordance with what was happening in the films and more generally in Italian society of the time; the style was refined, baroque, over-the-top, so as to convey an antirealistic atmosphere; and the films conveyed anxiety rather than sheer horror.

Summarizing, the Gothic films of the 1950s and 1960s featured a number of key elements, most of which would be repeated, although to a lesser degree, in the works of the next decade(s).

1. The films leaned (or at least *pretended* to) on literary sources, often prestigious ones. Just to name a few, Mario Bava's *Black Sunday* (*La maschera del demonio*, 1960) was very loosely based on Nikolai Gogol's story "Viy"; Bava's "The Wurdalak"—in the film anthology *Black Sabbath* (*I tre volti della paura*, 1963)—was an adaptation of a story by Aleksei Tolstoy; Camillo Mastrocinque's *Terror in the Crypt* (*La cripta e l'incubo*, 1964) took inspiration from Joseph Sheridan Le Fanu's *Carmilla*. Many elements were also inherited from the literary Gothic tradition, starting with the settings, which would invariably be old castles or villas, with an emphasis on enclosed spaces such as corridors, secret passages, crypts and so on.

2. The stories covered similar ground, revolving around vampirism and reincarnation, with such frequent elements as the double (or *doppelgänger*) and the avenging spirit returning from the grave. Furthermore, they often took place in the past. Not, mind you, the archaic and vigorous, flamboyant and grim ancient centuries as told by writers such as Ann Radcliffe or Walter Scott—except, perhaps, for the openings of *Black Sunday* and *The Long Hair of Death* (*I lunghi capelli della morte*, 1964, Antonio Margheriti)—but much closer times: mostly the late nineteenth century or even the beginning of the twentieth. A rather stiff scenario, filled with behavioral affectations, summarily defined through set props and costumes, and observed according to a stereotypical perspective.[4] Given the taboo and transgressive nature of the themes that were portrayed, the period setting actually became a trick to overcome the difficulties of developing those themes according to the parameters of realism.

3. With a few notable exceptions—Renato Polselli's pioneering *The Vampire and the Ballerina* (*L'amante del vampiro*, 1960) and Camillo Mastrocinque's *An Angel for Satan* (*Un angelo per Satana*, 1966)—Italian Gothic horror films produced in the 1950s and 1960s took place almost exclusively abroad.[5] This was mainly because of commercial reasons—the same that caused producers, filmmakers and technicians to hide under Anglo-Saxon pseudonyms or cast foreign actors in order to cover the products' Italian origins. Paris (*I Vampiri*), Moldavia (*Black Sunday*), the Netherlands (*Mill of the Stone Women/Il mulino delle donne di pietra*, 1960, Giorgio Ferroni),

England (*Castle of Blood/Danza macabra*, 1964, Antonio Margheriti) and so on were quite obviously not pictured realistically. Rather, they were no man's lands, suspended in time and space, with vague yet recurring traits, as the scene of a nightmare.

4. The look of Italian Gothic horror films was homogeneous, characterized by the recurring use of the same set-pieces and buildings. The style was often experimental, much more so than in other popular film threads of the period, such as the sword-and-sandal epics. The results detached from the mere slavish imitation of foreign models and can be defined as a "creative reworking" of the Gothic staples.

5. An overall analysis of the films produced in the late 1950s and early 1960s shows how the function of Italian Gothic horror was primarily "to unsettle rather than scare, to blur the boundaries between reality and hallucination rather than attacking reality with the irruption of the supernatural."[6] Filmmakers often played on the thin line between dream and waking, perception and suggestion. Suspense had an accessory role—sometimes even a marginal one.[7]

6. The approach to the myths and archetypes of the Fantastic genre on the part of filmmakers was disenchanted, sometimes ironic, often idiosyncratic (most notably in the depiction of the vampiric figures). It marked a neat difference when compared to most horror movies that were being produced during the same period in foreign countries. However, one element which emerges forcefully from the films of the period is the approach towards the macabre: the skulls and skeletons that make the heroines scream in horror, the rat-infested crypts, the cobwebs that stick to clothes and faces. This somewhat naïve imagery was reworked scrupulously, yet with an undisguised detachment. Yet the attention towards funereal practices—coffins, hearses, candles and braziers, solemn funeral processions—emphasized a deeper relationship with death and its social dimension. This went beyond a mere imitation of the foreign models and gave way to a true aesthetic of decay (as much of bodies as places), coupled with the insistence on issues related to necrophilia as well as the fetishistic attention towards the effects of death on the human body.

7. Besides triggering the transgression, the fantastic elements cloaked in new clothes and roles figures that were typical of the melodrama. The scripts revolved around tales of punished or vengeful lovers, betrayed or unfaithful husbands. Horror grew within the fertile basin of marriage, and—be it a vampire movie, a supernatural tale or a mystery plot—immediately affected marital happiness and sexual chemistry. This conveyed a more general idea of crisis and an impatience towards the institution of marriage—monolithic by tradition but in fact increasingly seen as an impediment. Shortly thereafter, in 1965, congressman Loris Fortuna presented a draft law on divorce to the Parliament, and the debate on the issue would become hot. Divorce would be introduced in Italy only as of December 1, 1970, despite a strong opposition on the part of the Catholic parties and movements: the heated political debate led to a 1974 anti-divorce referendum, led by the right-wing Democrazia Cristiana party, which was surprisingly voted down by 59 percent of the national electorate.

8. The figure of the husband as a master, which related to the patriarchal tradition, was counterbalanced by a frequent presence of weak male figures and a shortage of characters related to the archetype of the Byronic hero. It was a paradoxical retaliation, if one thinks that the "rebels in style, nephews of Milton's Satan and brothers of Schiller's Robbers"[8] of the eighteenth and nineteenth cen-

tury Gothic novel were often Italians, as the adventurer Montoni in *The Mysteries of Udolpho* or the monk Schedoni in *The Italian*.

Male figures in Italian Gothic horror are a weird bunch: succubuses, zombies moved by love (as Javutich and Kruvajan in *Black Sunday*), impotent (Mickey Hargitay in *Bloody Pit of Horror/Il boia scarlatto*, 1965, Massimo Pupillo) or sexually deviated, as the eponymous character in Freda's *The Horrible Dr. Hichcock* (*L'orribile segreto del Dr. Hichcock*, 1962). They are deceived, betrayed, ridiculed, humiliated, tortured, murdered—all at the mercy of the fairer sex.

9. With its barbaric, primitive component, Italian Gothic horror was fertile ground for the cultivation of a sexuality open to perversions and morbidity, in the same way in which the Spaghetti Western would act as a laboratory for the portrayal of extreme violence. Eroticism was staged with ambiguity: it was attractive and punitive, both for the audience and the characters. Pleasure and pain, orgasm and death were closely related. Think of the proliferation of sadomasochistic relationships: the two bloodsuckers in *The Vampire and the Ballerina*, the doctor and Margaretha in *The Horrible Dr. Hichcock*, Nevenka and Kurt in *The Whip and the Body* (*La frusta e il corpo*, 1963, Mario Bava). But just as it captured the viewers' impulses, emphasizing their fantasies, the horrific component brought them back with their feet on the ground: catharsis and visual shocks also served as a call to order. The dissipation of beauty took the most spectacular and sensational forms, such as Gianna Maria Canale's on-screen aging in *I Vampiri* and Barbara Steele's in *Black Sunday*.

10. Last, and most important, Italian Gothic Horror was characterized by the centrality of female characters, seen as perturbing elements: witches, vampires, ghosts. This is perhaps its most interesting aspect, as it offers an in-depth view of the mentality towards women in Italy. After World War II, the nation was experiencing a deep sociocultural turmoil due to its quick modernization, with the migration of whole families from the Southern countryside to the big cities of the North: see Luchino Visconti's *Rocco and His Brothers* (*Rocco e i suoi fratelli*, 1960). This, combined with the growing emancipation of women, clashed against the reactionary mentality which still permeated the lower classes, deep-rooted in prejudices and in the patriarchal conception of family. Traces of this conflict can be seen in Gothic Horror films, often in the duality between a "good" (i.e., virginal) and an "evil" (i.e., sexually promiscuous and/or dominating) woman, and were expressed via the common theme of the double or *doppelgänger*.

Italian Gothic horror heroines were an evolution of the *belles dames sans merci* of literature and opera. But they also recalled the cruel queens, usurpers, witches and sorcerers faced by the sword-and-sandal heroes, who also had magic and supernatural powers. Gothic horror almost looked like a negative cast of the *peplum* genre, with its weak and submissive male figures as opposed to oiled musclemen. The sword-and-sandal focused on an overemphasized, almost parodistic image of masculinity: on the contrary, the Gothic was characterized by the representation of women as dominating and enslaving figures, who seduce and kill, attract and repel: a parade of memorable female characters such as the Duchess Du Grand (*I Vampiri*), Princess Asa Vajda (*Black Sunday*), Nevenka Menliff (*The Whip and the Body*), Elisabeth Blackwood (*Castle of Blood*), Muriel Arrowsmith (*Nightmare Castle/Amanti d'oltretomba*, 1965, Mario Caiano)...

The Devil, in Italian Gothic horror, was a woman.

The devil as a woman: The evil Princess Asa Vajda (Barbara Steele) is about to be executed in the opening sequence of Mario Bava's *Black Sunday* (Billy Rose Theatre Division, New York Public Library for the Performing Arts, Astor, Lenox and Tilden Foundations).

This book lists all the Gothic horror films produced and released in Italy between 1957—the year Riccardo Freda's *I Vampiri* (a.k.a. *The Devil's Commandment*) came out— and 1969, based on the film's release date in its home country. Entries include majoritary Italian co-productions with other European countries (such as Alberto De Martino's *The Blancheville Monster*, a 1963 co-production with Spain), since about half of the films made from 1964 to 1968 were co-productions. On the other hand, films which featured a minority Italian participation are not included—a case in point being Amando De Ossorio's *Fangs of the Living Dead* (*Malenka la nipote del vampiro*, 1968), which, even though it was partly financed by Italian money, is actually a Spanish horror film.

Besides out-and-out Gothic films, I included several parodies where the Gothic element is a main feature of the plot, such as Steno's *Uncle Was a Vampire* (*Tempi duri per i vampiri*, 1959) and Marino Girolami's *My Friend, Dr. Jekyll* (*Il mio amico Jekyll*, 1960), which reworked in a comical way such noted horror icons as Dracula and Dr. Jekyll. Such titles are quite important to understand how the Gothic was perceived in Italy at that time.

There are also a few *sui generis* titles which I feel have a distinct Gothic feel, although they are rather odd choices compared to the majority of the titles listed in the book as they did not germinate within the realm of the *filone*, but are rather authorial approximations to the genre: that is the case with Giulio Questi's "Il passo" (1964), Damiano Damiani's *The Witch* (*La strega in amore*, 1966) and Elio Petri's *A Quiet Place in the Country* (*Un tranquillo posto di campagna*, 1968).

On the other hand, I chose not to include sword-and-sandals such as Mario Bava's *Hercules in the Haunted World* (*Ercole al centro della terra*, 1961) and Riccardo Freda's *The Witch's Curse* (*Maciste all'inferno*, 1962). Even though they do feature definite Gothic elements, these films were born and remained part of a different genre, the *peplum*, with rules and characters of its own. Given the Italians' habit of adding ingredients to the recipe, the Gothic and horror elements were the icing on the cake, as were the odd science fiction references in other sword-and-sandal films such as *The Giant of Metropolis* (*Il gigante di Metropolis*, 1961, Umberto Scarpelli) and *Hercules Against the Moon Men* (*Maciste e la regina di Samar*, 1964, Giacomo Gentilomo), for instance.

For the most part, I have elected to list films under the title used for the original American theatrical release. I have made exceptions where referring to films that exist in specific edits that were not originally released

in the U.S. market. For example, *I Vampiri* came out in the United States in a heavily altered version re-titled as *The Devil's Commandment*. This version has since been supplanted on home video by the original "director's cut" titled *I Vampiri*, so it makes better sense to refer to the film by that title, except where references are made to the revised U.S. edit. With regards to some films, while it is true that they were originally released under one title in the United States, they have since become better known by alternate titles in the era of home video. For example, Antonio Margheriti's film *La vergine di Norimberga* (1963) was originally released in the United States as *Horror Castle*, but it is seldom—if ever—referred to as such now. Thus, I have elected to refer to the film under its best known English title: *The Virgin of Nuremberg*.

Each entry features a comprehensive crew and cast list as complete as possible, based on the film's opening and closing credits. Uncredited extras are also listed whenever possible. Regarding the English aliases adopted by crew and cast members, the participants' real names behind their Anglo-Saxon aliases are listed whenever possible, based on the official production records kept at Rome's Archive of State. In many cases, this book sheds light on such pseudonyms for the first time and corrects recurring mistakes that can be found on most databases.

Home video releases are also listed, with preference given to English-friendly Blu-Ray and DVD releases. When a film is mentioned in the text for the first time, its English title comes first (if there was an English language release) followed by the original Italian one and the year, in brackets. The information bits provided throughout the text are the result of a thorough research from a variety of sources such as academic texts and essays and other assorted material—interviews with filmmakers and actors, newspaper reviews—which are listed in the bibliography. Whenever possible, I located and consulted the films' original scripts kept at the Centro Sperimentale di Cinematografia library in Rome.

Finally, the acknowledgments. First of all, I am deeply honored by the presence of Ernesto Gastaldi, the dean of Italian horror film scriptwriters, who kindly agreed to write a foreword, and did it with his unmistakable wit, irony and style. Thanks, *maestro*! Very, very, very, very special thanks to my Maltese cinephile friends Mario and Roderick Gauci, who sifted through the original manuscript with priceless dedication and patience and flushed out my many mistakes. Guys, you were amazing, and I mean it! A huge "Thank you!" goes also to Alessio Di Rocco and Eugenio Ercolani, who did an invaluable research job on some of the most obscure titles in the book and the cast/crew pseudonyms; Steve Fenton, who gave me a great hand in locating, collecting and scanning original posters and stuff; and to fellow McFarland author Tom Lisanti, who kindly helped me locate vital bits of information as well as a number of lovely stills from the New York Public Library.

My most sincere gratitude goes also to the following, all of whom had an important part in the making of this book. I am deeply grateful to you all: Mark Thompson Ashworth, Lucas Balbo, Tom Betts, Davide Cavaciocchi, Francesco Cesari, Chris Fujiwara, Sergio Grmek Germani, Benjamin Halligan, Troy Howarth, Steve Johnson, Frank Lafond, Tommaso La Selva, Stefano Lecchini, Antonio Marchesani, Paolo Mereghetti, Paul Mims, Robert Monell, Domenico Monetti, Frederick Muller, Luca Pallanch, Alberto Pez-zotta, Roberto Poppi, Pete Tombs, Donato Totaro, Tonino Valerii.

To Cristina, my one and only love, my guide, my ray of light in the darkest days.

Notes

1. Donato Totaro, "A Genealogy of Italian Popular Cinema: The Filone," *Offscreen* vol. 15, no. 11, November 2011.
2. Mikel J. Koven, *La Dolce Morte: Vernacular Cinema and the Italian Giallo* (Lanham, MD: Scarecrow Press, 2006), p. 6.
3. David Punter, *The Literature of Terror: A History of Gothic Fictions from 1765 to the Present Day, Vol. 1: The Gothic Tradition* (New York: Routledge, 1996), p. 1.
4. Such an approach sticks to Devendra P. Varma's much-discussed definition of the Gothic as "the surrealistic expression of those historical and social factors which the ordinary chronicle of events in history does not consider significant." Devendra P. Varma, *The Gothic Flame: Being a History of the Gothic Novel in England: Its Origins, Efflorescences, Disintegration, and Residuary Influences* (Metuchen, NY: Scarecrow, 1957, 1987).
5. This marked a significant detachment from the literary sources. Curiously, the "return of the past" evoked by Gothic novels often took place in Italy, from *The Castle of Otranto* to *The Italian*. What is more, the Picturesque, which preluded Romanticism, had Italian origins in such painters as the Lorenese or Salvator Rosa, as the illustrious Mario Praz noted: see Mario Praz, *La carne, la morte e il diavolo nella letteratura romantica* (Milan: BUR Rizzoli, 2008), p. 25. On the other hand, Italian fantastic literature of the 1800s, even though it featured Northern European settings, was closer to home territory, mostly in the North, in Milan or some other province. Antonio Fogazzaro set the story of death and love *Malgari* in Venice, and his masterpiece *Malombra* (brought to the screen in 1917 by Carmine Gallone and, most impressively, in 1942 by Mario Soldati) took place between an anonymous lake (most likely Como) and Milan, while Verga opted for his native Sicily for the impressive Gothic short story *I racconti del castello di Trezza*.
6. Alberto Pezzotta, "Doppi di noi stessi," in Marcello Garofalo, ed., "Sangue, amore e fantasy," *Segnocinema* no. 85, May/June 1997, p. 27.
7. As Italian film historian Teo Mora observed, "its forms shunned the typical climax construction, based on a succession of tense moments." Teo Mora, "Elegia per una donna vampiro. Il cinema fantastico in Italia 1957–1966," in *Storia del cinema dell'orrore, vol. 2* (Rome: Fanucci, 1978, 2002), p. 186.
8. Praz, *La carne, la morte e il diavolo nella letteratura romantica*, p. 61.

Introduction: Gothic, Italian Style

On the Trail of the Gothic: From Silent Films to Melodrama

Italian Gothic on film developed much later than in the rest of Europe and overseas.

In the early days of silent cinema traces of the fantastic can be found in the patterns of melodrama, or reworked within moral or sentimental tales: the initiator was Gaston Velle, a Frenchman of Italian origins, a former traveling magician (like his father, Joseph) who reinvented himself as a director.

Velle arrived at the Cines in Rome after working at the Parisian company Pathé, where he held the role of "director of *féerie*" (that is, an expert in films laced with special effects). His film *Lo spettro* ("The Ghost," 1907) was a ghost story turned into an exemplary moral parable, where ghosts and demons symbolized the accusing conscience. The same happened in other works of the period: *Maschera tragica* ("Tragic Mask," 1911) by Arrigo Frusta (real name Augusto Sebastiano Ferraris) transposed Edgar Allan Poe's "The Masque of the Red Death" to Naples and added to it an optimistic religious conclusion; *Satana* ("Satan," 1912, Luigi Maggi) was most likely an influence on C. T. Dreyer's *Leaves from Satan's Book* (*Blade af Satans bog*, 1920). Nevertheless, although at this point Italian cinema featured a flourishing of "reanimated corpses, resurrecting mummies, strange transplants, invisible men, hypnotists,"[1] it is improper to speak of a Gothic genre.

There was already, however, a tendency to focus on the female characters. *Rapsodia satan-ica* ("Satanic Rhapsody," 1917, Nino Oxilia) was a variation on the Faustian bargain with a female protagonist, while *La vergine dei veleni* ("The Virgin of Poisons," 1917, Enrico Vidali)—a transposition of a novel by Carolina Invernizio with debts to Hawthorne's "Rappaccini's Daughter"—featured a girl turned into an unwitting poisoner by a jealous scientist, who makes her kisses fatal to her hapless lovers. Besides, since the dawn of the silent film the screens were full of *femmes fatales* and their devouring feelings: "She loved him until death—and beyond," is the caption that ends *Ma l'amor mio non muore!* ("Yet my love will never die!," 1913, Mario Caserini). A phrase that sums up one of the *leitmotifs* of the Gothics to come.

While in Germany the season of Expressionism seethed, in Italy the Fantastic slipped primarily towards adventure and farce, with the odd concession to Grand Guignol. Even the lost feature *Il mostro di Frankenstein* (*Frankenstein's Monster*, 1920, Eugenio Testa), produced by and starring Luciano Albertini, was an unlikely hybrid. Albertini had become popular thanks to his character of the strongman Sansone (Samson), while the creature (created by chemistry instead of surgery) was played by Umberto Guarracino, bald and simian in appearance, who had often played Bartolomeo Pagano's opponent in the *Maciste* series. The famous *Maciste all'inferno* ("Maciste in Hell," 1926, Guido Brignone) was also connected to the early *peplum* genre.

Things did not change after the advent of sound.[2] The Fascist regime's dislike towards the

Fantastic is well reported: Italian films had to "spread the civilization of Rome throughout the world as quickly as possible," as Cinecittà's first manifesto proudly proclaimed. The virtual reality as portrayed by Mussolini's film industry would not include nightmares and horrors, but cheerful and reassuring dreams, if not glorious ones. Another key factor was the influential Catholic world: the Centro Cattolico Cinematografico (Catholic Cinematic Centre) reviewed and catalogued all films with an approach characterized by "a kind of double grid of moral–ideological type"[3]—that is, permissive towards propaganda and repressive against everything related to sexuality and morality. With World War II approaching, the Vatican's newspaper *L'Osservatore Romano* exalted propaganda war films while criticizing "the circulation of such films as *Bride of Frankenstein*."[4]

The season of Neorealism clipped the wings to further fantastic digressions in the post-war period. However, even though the Gothic *filone* blossomed with the first stirrings of the nascent genre cinema, in the late 1950s, there were anticipations, ideas, or "ghosts," so to speak, already at the beginning of the previous decade. Such a sedimentation took place on fertile ground, the same that often joined to Italian horror and fantasy literature of the late nineteenth century in an inextricable embrace: that of melodrama, late Romanticism and the serial novel.

That was the case with *Gelosia* (1942, Ferdinando Maria Poggioli), based on the novel *Il marchese di Roccaverdina* by Luigi Capuana: it is the story of a marquis (Roldano Lupi) who becomes a murderer for mad love of a woman and is persecuted by the ghosts of his conscience, which leads him to madness. Even though Poggioli's aim was to describe a society dominated by a superficial morality, and characterized by conventional and suffocating social rules, *Gelosia* displayed the director's stylistical and thematic attention towards the inner self, plus an Expressionist-like emphasis on moods (that caused one reviewer of the period to call Lupi's character "a Dr. Jekyll type"[5]) and great attention to detail—even deformed, excessive, grotesque. These were all characters that became key points of the Gothics to come.

Poggioli's last film, *Il cappello da prete* ("The Priest's Hat," 1944) shared the same themes: it was another novel adaptation, centered on an obsession that results in murder and madness. A penniless Baron (the outstanding Roldano Lupi again) kills a defrocked priest and throws the body in the well, only to be haunted by the sight of the victim's hat: guilt settles in the symbolic shape of an object that accompanies the protagonist to ruin, a Poe-inspired theme that recalls "The Tell-Tale Heart." Poggioli managed to give horrific tones to a typical *feuilleton*: the dissipated villa where the crime happens is a haunted place worthy of the castles that would characterize the Gothic thread of the 1960s.

The third and most important progenitor of Italian Gothic dating to the 1940s had its roots in an important novel of the late nineteenth century. Mario Soldati's *Malombra* (1942) was the second adaptation of Antonio Fogazzaro's novel after the one directed by Carmine Gallone in 1917, and was obviously influenced by the Gothic tradition, from Matthew Lewis to Ann Radcliffe. Soldati used the environment to emphasize the heroine's descent into madness as early as the opening sequence, in which the orphan Marina di Malombra (Isa Miranda) arrives by boat to the huge and lonely mansion on Lake Como, where her uncle will hold her segregated until the marriage of convenience that he has designed for her. Said castle is to *Malombra* as Udolpho's manor was to *The Mysteries of Udolpho*: an imposing place, haunted by sinister rumors linked to a cumbersome past that is impossible to conceal. When Marina insists on settling in a room in the East, overlooking the lake but uninhabited for a long time, the maid asks her to change her mind because "the devil's inside."

The sequence in the darkened room where Marina learns the story of Cecilia—a young woman who was kept segregated by the ancestor of Marina until she ended up mad—synthesizes the paraphernalia of the Gothic novel. The environment is charged with an evocative and hostile power, symbolized by the sound of the wind that penetrates between the window frames, causing the candle's flame to flicker—a striking image captured by Massimo Terzano's fascinating black and white photography. The past retains a looming enchantment, exemplified by the sad story of Cecilia, Marina's doomed predecessor with whom the heroine will eventually identify. Objects are loaded with hidden meanings and arcane powers, such as the spinet on which Cecilia loved to sing and play the same music, obsessively. And, finally, a prohibition is imposed which, once violated, entails the punishment for the offender (the maid who, having dared to play the spinet, heard a sigh in the room). What is more, with this scene Soldati introduces the theme of the double and reincarnation through a volume that Marina voraciously reads, and is hopelessly affected by, which is significantly called *Fantasmi del passato* ("Ghosts of the past").

However, after flirting with the Gothic novel and the ghost story, *Malombra* steps back to embrace the rational. The themes of reincarnation and the double are just an excuse to dwell on the condition of the heroine, who is not the typical damsel-in-distress, but a more complex and ambiguous figure: a woman who is not allowed to live her life and who ends up living someone else's, a victim who in turn will become a murderer, a living woman who identifies herself with a ghost out of suggestion and rebellion. In addition to all this, the oppressive late romantic atmosphere that accompanies this story of *amour fou* does not prevent Soldati from emphasizing the realistic component: the humble servants speak the dialect of the regions where the story takes place.

Malombra proved to be a subterranean influence on Italian Gothic horror films of the 1960s: not only did it patently inspire one of the most atmospheric films of the lot, Camillo Mastrocinque's *An Angel for Satan*, but its restless heroine would be the blueprint on which many of the *filone*'s female characters—*Black Sunday*'s Katia and *The Whip and the Body*'s Nevenka, to name just two—would be more or less patterned.

The ideal continuity between melodrama and the Gothic, in the path of popular cinema, passed through the numerous rivulets of the adventure genre. It started with such prototypes as *La corona di ferro* (1941, Alessandro Blasetti),

and then proceeded through ancient period dramas, swashbucklers and historical dramas. In the 1950s, the thread was represented by cheesy adventure flicks populated with knights and masked swordsmen that were blessed with almost supernatural skills. As was typical of low-budget productions, these films often displayed near-identical plots, sets, props, costumes and extras. Furthermore, they all conveyed a stereotypical view of the past which featured tame Gothic elements, exemplified by secret passages and deadly traps galore.

The relationship between the 1950s/1960s Gothic and the tradition of melodrama was not limited to production values, with the reuse of the same costumes and props. Melodrama was an essential ingredient of the Gothic, although "a subterranean and twisted one ... with its lights and shadows, the taste for the stylization, the attention to female figures, the insistence on the themes of guilt and wickedness."[6] The Gothic *filone* became the paroxistic yet necessary outlet after a thickening of all topics related to erotic, dreamlike, violent components, that could not find a way out during Neorealism: it was the culmination of a growing infiltration of the codes of melodrama in Italian cinema.

Consider the suggestions of *Legend of Love* (*Paolo e Francesca*, 1950, Raffaello Matarazzo) and *The Iron Swordsman* (*Il Conte Ugolino*, 1949, Riccardo Freda). The latter, loosely inspired by a horrific episode described in Dante's *Inferno*, featured blood, torture, magic, and the same setting of the classical Gothic novel: it started and ended in a dungeon, and kept the final horrific twist for the very last shot, where Freda hinted at an off-screen act of cannibalism.[7] *The Iron Swordsman*'s final scene culminates in the close-up of a woman screaming in horror: it is an iconic image that will resonate through the decades, not only in Freda's final film *Murder Obsession* (1981), but also in Dario Argento's *Tenebrae* (*Tenebre*, 1982). A similar atmosphere can be found in the adaptations of Carolina Invernizio's novels such as *Dead Woman's Kiss* (*Il bacio di una morta*, 1949, Guido Brignone) and *La cieca di Sorrento* (1953, Giacomo Gentilomo).

The most vivid progenitor of the Gothic thread was actually a melodrama: *Il Trovatore*, directed in 1949 by Carmine Gallone and based on Giuseppe Verdi's 1853 opera of the same name. *Il Trovatore*, from a libretto by Salvadore Cammarano based in turn on a play by Antonio García Gutiérrez, is, to quote Verdi scholar Julian Budden, "a high flown, sprawling melodrama flamboyantly defiant of the Aristotilian unities, packed with all manner of fantastic and bizarre incident."[8] Gallone's adaptation retains such qualities and transposes them into atmospheric visuals that will become commonplace in the Gothic horror films to come.

The film opens with a panning shot at night on the Palace of Aljafería (recreated with a suggestive miniature: the set-pieces were designed by Gastone Medin), accompanied by the off-screen narration telling the story of the mysterious sickness that caught Count Luna's youngest son. The people believed it was caused by the evil eye directed towards the Count by a gypsy who had been condemned to the stake. Gallone then cuts to a night scene outdoors on a misty moor, showing the arrival of the gypsy at the stake. She is led in a cart, escorted by soldiers and followed by a howling mob armed with torches, and then tied to the stake by the Executioner. Her daughter Azucena, who is watching the punishment from afar, overhears her mother pledging to be avenged. The sequence ends with the image of the burning pyre.

It is a moment that will return many times in 1960s Italian Gothic horror films, from *Black Sunday* to an almost verbatim recreation in Riccardo Freda's *The Witch's Curse* and Antonio Margheriti's *The Long Hair of Death*. When it came to hatching a personal aesthetic of the Gothic, filmmakers would rely on the forms of melodrama, giv-

Il Trovatore (1949, Carmine Gallone), based on Giuseppe Verdi's opera of the same name, features elements that will become commonplace in Italian Gothic horror, such as the burning of the witch in the opening sequence (courtesy S. I. Bianchi).

ing full vent to its antirealist elements, in order to give familiar semblances to the difficult terrain they were venturing into.

Of Excess and Transgression

The emerging of the irrational in Italian Gothic horror movies was seen by many as a compensation against the chains of Neorealism, which had monopolized Italian cinema for over a decade. Popular cinema was in full turmoil, while the Neorealist push was coming to an end and audiences were demanding films that allowed them to dream and to explore transgression. "Neorealism removed the ghosts of the unconscious because it had to, and wanted to deal rationally with quite different nightmares and fears: hunger, unemployment, poverty," as Gian Piero Brunetta noted. "But once that—by the government's will—the most monstrous aspects of the Italian situation would be kept away from the big screen, and at the same time the average standard of living had reached higher standards, it would certainly appear legitimate to start exploring the Fantastic, by using literary and figurative models, rather than psychoanalytic ones."[9]

To put it briefly, the birth of the Gothic horror thread was also the result of a need to escape. However, such a need was somewhat different from that of their foreign counterparts. Hammer Films, with their glittering and licentious Victorian universe of lace and blood, represented a revolt, "a vivid reaction in fact to the dull, repressive 1950s," as David Pirie put it.[10] On the other hand, the Italian way to the Gothic responded to an urgency that arose not from an unbearable deprivation, but from a new-found wealth and the awareness of the new possibilities that it opened up. As renowned Italian film scholar Goffredo Fofi put it, "ghosts, monsters and the taste for the horrible appear when a society becomes wealthy and evolves by industrializing, and are accompanied by a state of well-being which began to exist and expand in Italy only since a few years."[11] Italian Gothic did not germinate from the greyness, but from the light at the end of

the tunnel. It was born from the thrill of transgression, which was finally possible and had to be celebrated on the big screen as well.

As a whole, Italian Gothic Horror films of the 1950s and 1960s reworked—in an original and singular way—the mixture of excess and transgression that had been the basis of their literary counterparts. Excess, in these films, meant not only a more direct approach to horror, but also the presence of a strong emotional element, which was a direct result of the Italian tradition of melodrama. Transgression, on the other hand, was the consequence of the troubled relationship between the movie industry and the board of censors, which in the early 1960s underwent a deep transformation after a new law on censorship was passed in 1962.

The Gothic horror thread allowed filmmakers to deal with "forbidden" topics related to human sexuality, and explore the female body as much as they could: this was before the relaxation of censorship which, by the end of the decade, resulted in nudity and sex being the primary element in commercial films. In a sense, 1960s Gothic Horror was a laboratory of sorts where all the elements that would characterize Italian exploitation cinema in the following decade were tested.

Gothic and the Italian Popular Cinema

Italian Gothic Horror films were firmly rooted in popular cinema. They were made with limited budgets and were aimed at less-than-demanding audiences. Most were designed for foreign consumption, with a frequent resort to co-production deals, whereas box-office performances in Italy were nondescript, if not decidedly marginal. The reliance on co-productions—aided by the 1965 Legge Corona, the economical law that regulated the Italian film industry—allowed producers to benefit from state subsidies and tax rebates, which covered poor box-office takings. However, the Gothic *filone* gave the opportunity to such talented filmmakers as Mario Bava, Riccardo Freda and Antonio Margheriti to helm some of their very best works. It also featured experienced directors who dabbled with it out of necessity, such as Camillo Mastrocinque—a veteran director with a career almost entirely devoted to comedy, who directed a pair of remarkable Gothic flicks near the end of his career, *Terror in the Crypt* and *An Angel for Satan*. The Gothic was also a starting point for many young scriptwriters such as Ernesto Gastaldi, Tonino Valerii and Roberto Natale, who later became directors in their own right.

Most interestingly, the 1960s Gothic trend was part of a wider horror craze, spawned by the Italian release of Terence Fisher's *Horror of Dracula* (1958), which generated not just movies, but also a flood of paperback novels, photonovels, comic books, etc. If anything, Italian Gothic was born under the sign of cynicism. Scripts were written in a hurry, sometimes rearranged on the set, almost always inconsistent not by choice but by sloppiness. Production companies came and went, sometimes lasting only through one film. There was a wily willingness to dissimulation, with ample use of Anglo-Saxon pseudonyms that were barely concealing the very Italian origins of actors and technicians. "Pretend to" was the motto—just like the ghosts of those films pretended to be alive and benevolent (or the living pretended to be dead and malevolent), and witches shaped themselves in the image and likeness of the pure heroines, so as to mislead the hero. Because, as Riccardo Freda realized in front of a movie theater in San Remo where *I Vampiri* was being screened, by watching a young couple turn back and leave after noticing the director's name, horror was not perceived as something *Italian*. In the work of disguise and travesty that underlied the Gothic *filone*, and anticipated what would happen with the Western, one can read the parable of a country that sold its people a deceptive illusion of well-being, and a nation that was a willing victim of a culture of appearances.

The Gothic showed a patent affinity with another genre: the sword-and-sandal. Both were born approximately in the same period—Pietro Francisci's *Hercules* (*Le fatiche di Ercole*) came out in Italy in early 1958—and followed grossly a similar course: the last tiresome examples of the *peplum* were released in 1964 and 1965, when the Western fever was rising high. Both threads had in common the pen of Ennio De Concini, one of the primary architects of the sword-and-sandal's success: De Concini co-scripted Bava's *Black Sunday* as well as Freda's *peplum*/Gothic hybrid *The Witch's Curse*, which at times looks just like a bastardized remake of Bava's film. The sword-and-sandal was the Gothic's opulent and luckier twin: many more films were produced, more substantial box-office takings were achieved, richer production values were employed—at least apparently, due to the use of color and the recycling of sets and footage. Nevertheless, directors, scriptwriters and crews were often the same. The *peplum*'s affinity with the Gothic was so strong that the *filone* boasted such hybrids as *Hercules in the Haunted World* (1961), *Goliath and the Vampires* (*Maciste contro il vampiro*, 1961, Giacomo Gentilomo, Sergio Corbucci) and the aforementioned *The Witch's Curse*.

The *peplum* displayed an enthusiastic easiness in staging monsters and figures pertaining to a horror-related imagery: examples are the flying zombies set off by Licos (Christopher Lee) in *Hercules in the Haunted World*, the faceless army under the command of Kormak the vampire (Jacques Sernas) in *Goliath and the Vampires*, the creatures designed by Carlo Rambaldi for *Medusa Against the Son of Hercules* (*Perseo l'invincibile*, 1963, Alberto De Martino) and the legions of undead of *Rome Against Rome* (*Roma contro Roma*, 1964, Giuseppe Vari). Even the themes and characters of the Gothic would show up over and over in the sword-and-sandal genre, with minor changes: the *doppelgänger* (Gordon Scott facing Kormak disguised as himself in *Goliath and the Vampires*), the mad scientist and his lab (Kormak's in the same film, which also includes petrified victims, reminiscent of *Mill of the Stone Women*), even the use of color filters—most impressively in Bava's movie.

Even the dichotomy between two female models—the wife and the lover, the companion of a lifetime and the one-night stand—was portrayed in a similar way in sword-and-sandal films. In *Hercules*, the titular demigod is divided between Iole and Antinea, while in *Hercules Unchained* (*Ercole e la regina di Lidia*, 1959) a magic potion makes him fall for Queen Onfale (Sylvia Lopez). In *Hercules Against the Moon Men* (*Maciste e la regina di Samar*, 1964, Giacomo Gentilomo) the two female opposites, Selene and Bilis, are played by the same actress (Anna Maria Polani), just like in *Black Sunday*. The same idea, however, was already present in *Ulysses* (1954, Mario Camerini), where Silvana Mangano played both Penelope and Circe—that is, the centripetal force and the centrifugal one, the safety of home against the exotic and sensual adventure.

After the commercial *exploit* of Sergio Leone's *A Fistful of Dollars* (*Per un pugno di dollari*, 1964), producers and distributors were quick to jump onto another, much more fruitful bandwagon. The birth of the Italian Western gave way to new male models that combined the strength of the sword-and-sandal heroes with a new-found amorality, which extended to a renewed attitude towards the opposite sex. It was no longer a matter of chivalry (as for Hercules, Maciste and the like), neither impotence or awe (like so many male Gothic characters): most Western heroes had in common an apathetic indifference, that is "a particular masculine indolence against the sexual possibilities."[12]

The Gothic horror *filone*, then, was in some ways a necessary transition. It marked a discovery of sexuality in Italian cinema, which—due to the inner characteristics of the thread itself—made it the culmination of a dualistic conception of woman as well as overcoming it towards achieving a new complexity. All this was helped by the loosening of censorship that in a few years would lead to the predominance of eroticism on screen.

Dead and Reborn: Italian Gothic After the Mid-1960s

After 1966 the production of Gothic horror films came to a halt. The drying up of the *filone* was a reflection of a broader crisis that affected the whole film industry. The 744 million moviegoers in 1960 (already 75 million less than the peak of 1955) had become just 663 million by 1965. Five years later, in 1970, the number would drop to just 525 million.

Yet the Gothic did not entirely vanish. Its language and characters were already expanding outside the realm of genre production and at times flirting with experimental suggestions, as shown by Giulio Questi's outstanding "Il passo" ("The Step," 1964), Damiano Damiani's fascinating *The Witch* (*La strega in amore*, 1966) and Elio Petri's thought-provoking *A Quiet Place in the Country* (*Un tranquillo posto di campagna*, 1968).

Other Gothic elements, thinned and almost impalpable, were seeping in the folds of the most popular film genre, and the only one that kept rising in spite of the crisis. Soon the Western developed a strong macabre component, which emphasized the genre's funereal aesthetics and iconography, with a particular fetishistic attention to coffins, at least since Sergio Corbucci's *Django* (1966).[13] Films such as *Django the Bastard* (*Django il bastardo*, 1968, Sergio Garrone) and *And God Said to Cain* (*...e Dio disse a Caino*, 1970, Antonio Margheriti), with their almost supernatural avengers, were hybrids of sorts, as was Mario Pinzauti's ramshackle *Ringo, It's Massacre Time* (*Giunse Ringo e... fu tempo di massacro*, 1970). On one hand, this certified the extraordinary ability of the Euro-Western to engulf the most disparate ideas; on the other, it testified to the now-ingrained presence of the Gothic-horrific component in the Italian popular imagery—to the point that *Kill, Baby...Kill!*'s creepy-child-with-the-ball popped up in what looked like a bourgeois drama about conjugal crisis, Marcello Avallone's *Un gioco per Eveline* ("A Game for Eveline," 1971).

When Gothic horror films resurfaced, by the end of the decade, they proved to be a rather different matter. The main themes were still all intact, and filmmakers such as Bava, Freda, Ferroni and Margheriti returned to them, with somewhat diverse approaches and results—even by remaking their own films: Margheriti remade his own *Castle of Blood* in color as *Web of the Spider* (*Nella stretta morsa del ragno*, 1970), while Ferroni helmed a gory reworking of Bava's "The Wurdalak" set in the present in *The Night of the Devils* (*La notte dei diavoli*, 1972).

Yet the boundaries became more blurred and confused, due to the concurring influences and intersections with other threads, as well as the practice on the part of scriptwriters, producers and filmmakers to blend and stuff together various influences in order to create commercially palatable hybrids. On top of it all, however, one thing stood out: eroticism—the key ingredient in 1970s Italian popular cinema.

This, however, is another story. And, perhaps, another book.

Notes

1. Giorgio Placereani, "Historia del cine fantástico italiano," in Javier G. Romero, ed., "Antología del cine fantástico italiano," *Quatermass* 7, November 2008, p. 17.

2. A marginal exception was *Il caso Haller* (1933, Alessandro Blasetti), which told the story of a split personality case in the form of a crime drama: an upright solicitor (Memo Benassi) leads a double life as a criminal and has a relationship with a prostitute. Blasetti's film (which today is sadly lost) was a remake of Robert Wiene's *Der Andere* (1930), based on Paul Lindau's stage drama: however, there are patent similarities with R. L. Stevenson's *The Strange Case of Dr. Jekyll and Mr. Hyde*.

3. Gian Piero Brunetta, *Storia del cinema italiano. Il cinema del regime: 1929–1945* (Rome: Editori Riuniti, 1993), p. 65.

4. *L'Osservatore Romano*, September 7, 1940.

5. Mino Doletti, "Film," January 16, 1943, p. 7.

6. Stefano Della Casa, "Cinema popolare italiano del dopoguerra," in Gian Piero Brunetta, ed., *Storia del cinema mondiale. Vol. III, L'Europa. Le cinematografie nazionali* (Turin: Einaudi, 1999), p. 801.

7. Count Ugolino Della Gherardesca (1220–1289) was locked in a prison with no food in the company of his little sons, and popular credence has it that he devoured his own offspring. Dante introduces him (*Inferno*, Canto XXXII) constantly gnawing an Archbishop's skull. "The big question is whether Dante invented this act of cannibalism or if it had a historical basis.... Of course, my film remains vague: the last wall of Ugolino's prison comes tumbling down and a traveling shot forward stops on Gianna Maria Canale's face as she screams in horror.... According to some interpretations, Dante let us believe there was cannibalism without ever saying that. On the contrary, I believe Dante told it clearly: '...And I,/ Already going blind, groped over my brood / Calling to them, though I had watched them die,/ For two long days. And then the hunger had more/ Power than even sorrow over me,' hunger is stronger than love." Éric Poindron, *Riccardo Freda, un pirate à la camera* (Arles: Institut Lumière/Actes Sud, 1994), p. 195. It must be noted that another, less ghastly interpretation of Dante's verses is that starvation killed Ugolino after he had failed to die of grief.

8. Julian Budden, *The Operas of Verdi: 2. From Il Trovatore to La forza del Destino* (London: Cassell, 1984), p. 59.

9. Gian Piero Brunetta, *Storia del cinema italiano dal neorealismo al miracolo economico: 1945–1959* (Rome: Editori Riuniti, 1993), p. 584.

10. David Pirie, *A New Heritage of Horror: The English Gothic Cinema* (London: I. B. Tauris, 2008), p. xi.

11. Goffredo Fofi, "Terreur in Italie," *Midi-Minuit Fantastique* 7, September 1963, p. 80.

12. Carlos Aguilar, "Lo spaghetti-western. Etica ed estetica di un genere assolutamente europeo," in Roberto Curti, *Il mio nome è Nessuno. Lo spaghetti western secondo Tonino Valerii* (Rome: Un mondo a parte, 2008), p. 109.

13. As Italian film scholar Giorgio Placereani pointed out, though, in the Italian Western coffins "have a utilitarian function. They don't serve for the final rest, as a place where to wait in peace the dissolution of the flesh: rather, they are a hiding place, a means of transport, storage, carriage and home. In the baroque configuration, Catholic and funereal, of the Italian Western, the coffin is some sort of habitable place." "Eurowestern," *Nickelodeon Gazette* 70, 1997, p. 39.

Abbreviations

The following abbreviations are used in the credits list for each entry

Crew

AC	Assistant camera
ACO	Costume assistant
ACON	Assistant continuity
AD	Assistant director
AE	Assistant editor
AMU	Assistant makeup
APD	Production design assistant
ArtD	Art director
B	Boom man
C	Camera
ChEl	Chief electrician
CHOR	Choreographer
CO	Costumes
CON	Continuity
D	directed by
DialD	Dialogue coach/Dialogue director
DOP	Director of photography
DubD	Dubbing director
E	Editor
El	Electrician
GA	Gaffer
Hair	Hairdresser
KG	Key grip
LT	lighting technician
M	Music
MA	Master of arms
Mix	Sound mixer
MU	Makeup
OE	Optical effects
PD	Production designer
PrM	Property manager
S	Story
SC	Screenplay
SD	Set decoration
SE	Special effects
2ndAD	2nd Assistant director
SO	Sound
SOE	Special sound effects
SP	Still photographer
SS	Script supervisor/Script girl
W	Wardrobe

Production

ADM	Administrator
AP	Associate producer
EP	Executive producer
GM	General manager
PA	Production assistant
PM	Production manager
PROD	Produced by
PS	Production supervisor
PSe	Production secretary
PseA	Production secretary assistant
UM	Unit manager

THE FILMS

Films are listed alphabetically within each year

1957

I Vampiri, a.k.a. *The Devil's Command-ment (I vampiri)*

D: Riccardo Freda. S: Piero Regnoli, Rijk Sijö-strom; SC: Piero Regnoli, Rijk Sijöstrom, Riccardo Freda; DOP: Mario Bava (B&W, Cinemascope); M: Roman Vlad, conducted by the author (ed. Titanus); E: Roberto Cinquini; PD, CO: Beni Montresor; ACO: Adriana Berselli; AD: Piero Regnoli; MU: Franco Freda; Hair: Ada Palombi; SO: Mario Mes-sina; SE: Mario Bava (uncredited); C: Corrado Bar-toloni. Cast: Gianna Maria Canale (Gisèle Du Grand/Marguerite Du Grand), Carlo D'Angelo (In-spector Chantal), Dario Michaelis (Pierre Lantin), Wandisa Guida (Lorrette Robert), Angiolo [Angelo] Galassi (Ronald Fontaine), Renato Tontini (Ri-naldo), Charles Fawcett (Lonette's father), Gisella Mancinotti (Schoolgirl), Miranda Campa (Lorrette's Mother), Antoine Balpêtré (Julien Du Grand), Paul Muller (Joseph Signoret); uncredited: Armando An-nuale, Riccardo Freda (Autopsy doctor), Piero Reg-noli (mr. Bourgeois), Emilio Petacci, Barbara Wohl (Lisette), Ronny Holliday (Nora), Joy Holliday (Anita). PROD: Ermanno Donati and Luigi Car-pentieri for Titanus and Athena Cinematografica (Rome); PM: Piero Donati; PA: Claudio Agostinelli. Country: Italy. Filmed at Titanus–Appia Studios (Rome). Running time: 81 min. (m. 2220); Visa n: 23894 (04.03.1957); Rating: V.M.16; Release dates: 04.05.1957 (Italy); 02.1961 (U.S.A.). Distribution: Titanus (Italy); RCIP (U.S.A.); Domestic gross: 125,300,000 lire. Also known as: Lust of the Vampire (U.S.A.), The Vampires (U.K.), Les Vampires (France, 11.27.1957), Der Vampir von Notre-Dame (West Ger-many, 11.28.1958), Los vampiros (Spain). Home video: Image (DVD, U.S.A.—as I vampiri), Sinister Film (DVD, Italy)

Paris, present day. The city is plagued by mys-terious killings which the newspapers claim to be the work of "vampires," as the victims—all women in their twenties—have been completely drained of their blood. Journalist Pierre Lantin investigates, but his involvement in the case be-comes much more personal when his fiancée Lor-rette is kidnapped. The executor of the crimes, a man named Signoret, is arrested: before mysteri-ously dying, he reveals that the culprit is Professor Du Grand, a renowned physician who lives in a gloomy castle with his cousin, the elderly Duchess Marguerite Du Grand. Marguerite's niece, the ravishing Gisèle, is hopelessly in love with Lantin, just like Marguerite had loved his father, but Pierre is strangely repulsed by her. Eventually it turns out that Marguerite and Gisèle are the same person, and the old woman is rejuvenated with the blood of the young victims by her cousin (who in the meantime faked his own death in order to escape the police and continued working in the castle's underground lab). However, the ef-fects of Du Grand's serum are only temporary, and Gisèle ages to her true self before the very eyes of Pierre and the police. Lorrette, who was being held prisoner in the castle, is released just in time.

In his book *The Literature of Terror: A His-tory of Gothic Fictions from 1765 to the Present Day,* David Punter numbers among the essen-tial requirements of the Gothic novel the "com-mon insistence on archaic settings,"[1] or, at least, settings that are not contemporary to the writ-er's: a component which was to be overcome in the genre's subsequent metamorphoses.

Originally, the term "Gothic" was used in lit-

Italian poster for *I vampiri* (author's collection).

erature to designate all things Medieval, or otherwise prior to the seventeenth century, as opposed to "classic," to give an idea of chaos, primitiveness, excess and exaggeration, whereas the other term would indicate order, proportion, purity, simplicity. Celluloid Gothic conformed to the same parameters: it usually opted for a past setting, usually the eighteenth and (more often) nineteenth century, as in Hammer films. The British company would face the present day only in the early Seventies, with somewhat traumatic results—*Dracula A.D. 1972* (1972, Alan Gibson) and *The Satanic Rites of Dracula* (1973, Alan Gibson) come to mind, with their awkward collections of Swingin' London paraphernalia—whereas the Spaniards would soon begin to juggle between past and present (see Amando De Ossorio's *Blind Dead* series).

In Italy things moved in a different direction: with the exception of *Black Sunday* and *Mill of the Stone Women*, the Gothic horror films released between 1957 and 1961 mostly featured contemporary settings. As Riccardo Freda stated about *I Vampiri*, "by placing my film in the

1950s, I avoided costly period recreation, and I made my story more believable. I wanted viewers to leave the theater and think, this might happen today, it might happen here!"[2]

Freda's film is considered the landmark of the Italian Gothic *filone*, and generally speaking this can be considered true. Its genesis is well known: as Freda himself explained to Éric Poindron, the project was born out of a challenge with producers Luigi Carpentieri and Ermanno Donati. "In Italy there were just 'scary' films which were very naive, with a cheap supernatural angle, Carolina Invernizio-style," the director underlined, referring to Italy's most famous *feuilleton* writer of the nineteenth century. "Italian cinema never ventured in the realm of the supernatural, never tried to make something like Murnau's *Faust*, which I still recall vividly ... an extraordinary film. We couldn't even dream to have filmmakers of Murnau's strength,"[3] as Freda bluntly stated. "I did a *fantastique* film as I had done adventure films. Fantastic cinema was a privilege of the Americans and the German Expressionists. And I wanted to prove that we could make fantastic films in Italy," the director recalled. "I explained to Carpentieri that I could write a story in just one day and shoot the film in two weeks. Carpentieri phoned Goffredo Lombardo, who was the biggest film producer, distributor and idiot in Italy. "Freda says he can do a horror film in two weeks..." and Lombardo answered "Well, it's not a big investment, we can try." I dictated the scenario on the magnetophone, wrote the script with Piero Regnoli and we started shooting."[4]

Freda made *I Vampiri* in two weeks indeed, even playing the small role of the coroner who finds out that the victims have been drained of blood. It was a low-budget production, since Lombardo did not care much about the project. Freda and his crew utilized mostly existing sets: "There were the remains of a papier-mache castle abandoned in the heart of the studio. The sets were about to collapse at any moment. [...] The castle's garden was the castle of Titanus studio. [...] The only time we left the studio was to shoot the scene were the body is found in the river. It's the Aniene, a tributary of the Tiber."[5] On the twelfth day of shooting, however, the notoriously bad-tempered director left the set after an argument with the producers—some argue it might have been caused by their wish to change the film into some sort of a police procedural, which in some way happened— leaving his d.o.p. Mario Bava to finish the job.

However, despite the apparently explicit Italian title *I vampiri* ("The Vampires"), Freda ignores or even overthrows the genre's conventions. For one thing, the first apparition of the alleged vampire (who will actually be revealed as a mere *factotum*) played by Paul Muller, is strikingly offbeat. Freda shows the character reflected in the mirror—visible as much to the viewer as to the victim. It is a bold move, as Freda immediately puts it clear that his "vampires" don't have anything to do with the supernatural: the man is dressed in a way that is more suitable for a gangster than to an undead bloodsucker, and he narcotizes the first victim with a chloroform-soaked handkerchief. Furthermore (and most impressively), the romantic-erotic element of vampirization is missing: there is no hypnotic seduction, no sight of sharp teeth

closing over the woman's neck in a bloody kiss. The victims are unceremoniously abducted and drained of their blood in a cold lab, with medical efficiency. "Syringes are more shocking than either vampire's fangs or a bat. I transposed "suction" with "transfusion," as Freda would comment to Poindron. "This kind of vampirism is practiced every day in hospitals but is called transfusion. Therefore I gave my fantastic film a medical nature. Abandoning the Anglo-Saxon imagery, I threw myself headlong into horror [...]. Horror and reality nowadays march side by side."[6]

Freda would return to the subject of vampirism in his autobiography *Divoratori di celluloide* ("Celluloid eaters"): "Vampires do exist and they stir close to us all the time, even though they can't be recognized by their incisors [*sic*], and even if a timely heart attack is enough to make them die. To be a vampire means to live near someone who is much younger than us and 'suck,' without him or her noticing, the best— intelligence, vital spirit and especially freshness—of ideas, feelings, reactions. Woe be it to live with elderly people: they drag you to the abyss of their anxious waiting for death. Hence the modern idea of a vampire which must be objectified, in order to make audiences understand it, through an old woman craving for the blood of a young one."[7]

Since the very first examples of cinematic Gothic, movies took inspiration from its literary forms, with a plagiaristic activity that gave rise to an artificial imagery, filtered by the different sensibility of the twentieth century. Yet, at the same time, cinema ensured that the features, the characters, the atmosphere associated with the Gothic took on a recognizable form and cemented in popular culture. Italian Gothic horror films, though, blossomed in delay, and therefore applied another filtering to the procedure, by drawing on the earlier examples of celluloid Gothic: however, this further elaboration of various models soon exceeded the limits of tracing and helped the *filone* shape an original, unmistakable identity.

I Vampiri is a case in point: released in Italy in April 1957, it predated by a month the English release of Terence Fisher's *The Curse of*

Frankenstein. Only in his following film, the sci-fi/horror hybrid *Caltiki, the Immortal Monster* (*Caltiki il mostro immortale*, 1959), Freda would borrow elements from Hammer films, namely *The Quatermass Xperiment* (1955, Val Guest) with the scientist played by Gérard Herter, who is infected by the deadly blob, goes crazy and escapes from the hospital, a character patently traced off the astronaut played by Richard Wordsworth in Val Guest's film.

However, analyzing the catalogue of influences displayed by *I Vampiri*, it's obvious that Freda harked back to celluloid models which were already very distant in the past, and curiously heterogeneus. The idea of a woman pursuing eternal youth looks back at such classics as *She* (1935, Lansing C. Holden and Irving Pichel), from which Bava took the effect of Gianna Maria Canale's instantaneous aging on camera. "It was Bava's idea," as Freda admitted. "We aged Gianna Maria Canale's face with color make-up. While shooting in b&w, the make-up was invisible. But when Bava placed progressive filters before the camera, the wrinkles and the transformations in her face appeared ... she really looked as if she was decomposing visibly."[8] The trick, already experimented by Rouben Mamoulian in *Dr. Jekyll and Mr. Hyde* (1931), can also be found in the contemporaneous U.S. horror *The Man Who Turned to Stone* (1957, László Kardos), another example of an idiosyncratic, science-based rereading of vampirism (albeit with far worse results than Freda's film). Yet Freda was probably thinking of another famous movie history character, Queen Antinea in G. W. Pabst's *Die Herrin von Atlantis* (1932), played by Brigitte Helm.

The director's refined cinephile culture brought him to contaminate various sources throughout the film. There are elements taken from U.S. horror and science fiction films of the 1930s and 1940s: the mystery subplot recalls *Mystery of the Wax Museum* (1933, Michael Curtiz), while the character of Julien Du Grand refers to the archetypal mad doctor. But Freda also brings in memories of Feuillade's silent serials—starting with the Italian title which recalls *Les Vampires* (1915–16)—and German Expressionism: the notion of a horror strictly

related to technology hints at Fritz Lang's *Dr. Mabuse* films, and the scary Signoret (Paul Muller) is not just a hybrid between Dracula's Renfield and the Frankenstein monster, as some critics have noted, but most of all a perverse contemporary variation on Cesare, the somnambulistic zombie of Robert Wiene's *The Cabinet of Dr. Caligari* (1920). "There was in Germany a current that certainly influenced me more than any other: the vampire film series and then Expressionism, *Nosferatu*, *Der Golem*, Dreyer's film [*Vampyr*], all the fantastic films of that era. It's common saying that movies leave a mark on children, but certainly they made a huge impression on me: I wasn't frightened, I loved them."[9]

The most interesting choice on Freda's part is the reference to Carl Theodor Dreyer's *Vampyr* (1932). For the apparition of the decrepit duchess Du Grand, who hides her octogenarian features behind a black veil, Freda took inspiration from the disturbing old lady (Henriette Gerard) who is responsible for the vampirizations in Dreyer's film: a fact underlined by the name that the Duchess assumes in her juvenile incarnation after she has been injected with the rejuvenating serum— Gisèle, just like the young girl threatened by the old woman in Dreyer's masterpiece. Freda would later use again the image of the veiled old lady in *The Horrible Dr. Hichcock*, where he also recreated one of *Vampyr*'s most celebrated images, that of David Gray laying in his coffin, in the scene where Barbara Steele wakes up in a casket which has a small glass window at face level, just as in Dreyer's film.

Vampyr would become one of the most ransacked works by Italian Gothic films. A curious choice, since Dreyer's is definitely a *sui generis* vampire movie, characterized by a cultured approach to horror, and whose style was based more on atmosphere, expectation and suggestion rather than on shock effects: a style "stretched between form and presence of reality," as noted by Dreyer scholar Sergio Grmek Germani.[10] A key factor in the lasting visual suggestion that *Vampyr* exerted on Italian Gothic horror cinema was perhaps the contribution to the film as (uncredited) set designer on the part of Giulio Cesare Silvagni, the author of inno-vative set-pieces during the silent era for such idiosyncratic Fantastic films as *La Coquille et le clergyman* (1928) by Germaine Dulac.[11]

Besides its cinematic references, *I Vampiri* is also remarkable for its take on literary Gothic. If the character of Duchess Du Grand is a re-reading of the historical Erszebet Bathory, who bathed in the blood of virgins to stay young, one of the film's major influences—as Freda himself acknowledged[12]—was Edgar Allan Poe's short story "The Fall of the House of Usher," with the suggested parallel between the decay-ing, dissipated interiors and the "vampire" played by Gianna Maria Canale. On the other hand, Gisèle's sudden final transformation into her octogenarian self after suffering violent emotions, which make the precarious chemical balance created by Professor Du Grand's para-scientific alchemies collapse, is an obvious nod to the finale of Robert Louis Stevenson's *The Strange Case of Dr. Jekyll and Mr. Hyde*: "We wanted to create a double as terrifying as Mr. Hyde," Freda commented.[13] As in Stevenson's novel, the psychophysical dissociation and split of the social identity is stressed by the contrast between the social norms which the individual rationally forces himself to obey and the pri-mary, irrational impulses that shake him (or, in case of Freda's film, her) from deep within.

But there is more. One of literary Gothic's most noted scholars, Devendra P. Varma, ana-lyzed the role of architecture and places in the Gothic novel in his study *The Gothic Flame* (1957), and suggested an interpretation of the Gothic castle as a psychological symbol of neu-rosis. Varma argues that the manor in ruins—often incongruously so, if we think about the periods in which the stories take place—is often the primary agent of terror which the hero or heroine must confront. However, it remains a *passive* agent, whereas the villain who inhabits it is the active agent, who is born as a supple-ment of the castle itself and whose nature is dictated by the former's origins. In movies, the setting immediately reveals itself as merely pre-textual, as it tends to "a decontextualization which is proper to a state of mind" where "the set-pieces exceed their ornamental function to

form themselves into a metaphor for the sepa-ration of the individual from normality as well as social integration."[14]

I Vampiri's Castle Du Grand is a paradig-matic example of such a metaphor, starting with its tripartite vertical structure: the crypts are the site for unspeakable experiments, while in the tower the damsel-in-distress is held pris-oner, in pure Gothic tradition. The two differ-ent ambients are connected by the huge hall and the staircase where the final transformation of the Duchess takes place. The hall is the cross-road that leads to the castle's hidden spaces, through a pair of secret passages, and it repre-sents "a semantic element which will character-ize all the houses and manors of Italian horror, as if it was an attribute of the antagonist's "power," and a proof of his/her ubiquitous-ness."[15]

In order to better appreciate the formal and thematic weight of the setting—definitely a character in itself in Italian Gothic—it is inter-esting to compare the Du Grand castle designed by Beni Montresor[16] for *I Vampiri* with the set-pieces created by Bernard Robinson for Ham-mer's *Horror of Dracula*. In both films the identification between the character and the en-vironment is immediate. Robinson took inspi-ration from the great architect Sir Edwin Lu-tyens, and avoided all kinds of Gothic clichès such as cobwebs and Expressionist shadows, opting for a baronial splendor—such a radical choice, in stark contrast to the Gothic imagery, that left producers puzzled. If Dracula's manor is the expression of a multisecular power that is perfectly integrated in the environment, self-confident and able to assert itself and dominate the outside world, the Du Grand manor ("more disturbing and closer to us than Dracula's castle in Transylvania" as Freda commented[17]) is no less than an architectural monster, conceived "like a putrefying organic structure, whose stones are corroded and almost falling apart, a metaphorical expansion of its inhabitant,"[18] complete with such bizarre details as the Saint-Jacques tower, a renowned Parisian monument which Freda and Bava turn into the castle's tower with a simple optical trick.

What is more, the castle is incongruously imprinted in the postcard-like Paris that surrounds it, as recreated by Bava in the courtyard of Titanus studios with the help of the d.o.p.'s customary *maquettes*, and therefore immediately hints at Duchess Du Grand's abnormality, her being out of place in the present. "I really don't understand how she can live in a place like this," Pierre's friend says about Gisèle Du Grand; and the hero adds: "I don't know why, but I can't stand neither her nor this castle," unconsciously associating person and place as one whole.

I Vampiri lives on the contrast between the sunny modern-day Paris, and the dusty aristocracy ("A bunch of dried-up mummies is what they are!" as Gisèle admits) that celebrates— and unnaturally perpetuates—itself in the hall of castle Du Grand. There is more than a hint of social criticism in Freda's film, as the castle becomes the offshoot of a decaying noble class which is out of time (see also the relics of the past that adorn the Duchess' bedroom) yet still looks down on the world. While Freda reveals their debauchery—see the columns adorned by grotesque high reliefs, portraying big-nosed demons of uncertain sex—he predates their defeat: a few years later, in *La Dolce Vita* (1960), Federico Fellini would show the blue bloods as impalpable ghosts secluded in their villas, the relics of a past that have been buried alive by the frantic present.

By its nature, the Gothic works on the emotions rather than stressing rational reactions. It enacts vice, violence, perversions; it evokes the specter of social disintegration as replicated in a closed microcosm; it calls into question the very foundations of common life, power, family and sexuality, and hypothesizes their (more or less violent) removal; it plays with the ambiguities related to its fundamental ambivalence, by urging excess and transgression and showing at the same time their jarring effects on the foundations of the community. Finally, it leads the reader (or the viewer) on the edge of the abyss and allows him to look down, where reason would never bring him.

As founded on such pillars, the Gothic lends itself to be modeled on the basis of the commercial strategies used by Italian cinema—that

Duchess Du Grand (Gianna Maria Canale) makes her memorable entry atop a staircase in *I vampiri*. Note the grotesque, big-breasted demon adorning the column (author's collection).

is, as one critic put it, "a textual organization based on attraction."[19] The spectacle that is being staged is not centered on narration, but on the visual appeal itself. Whereas in sword-and-sandal epics the center of the show were the muscular bodies of the bodybuilder heroes, who were called in to perform feats of strength, in Gothic horror films the main point is the "behavioral and sometimes somatic aberration," so as to produce "an aesthetic of the female body and the violence that the monstrous forces apply to it."[20]

But there is more than that: other than a mere object of attraction, the feminine as a whole is the subject, focus and driving force of the story. The female body becomes the incarnation and the main expression of what Sigmund Freud defined as *uncanny*, which is at the core of the Gothic genre: "that class of the frightening which leads back to what is known of old and long familiar."[21] What emerges instead of remaining secret, here, is that ambivalent feeling towards the female—a mixture of seduction and terror, desire and repulsion, the more pronounced if framed in relation to the presence and role of women in Italian culture and tradition.

This is evident in *I Vampiri*. Since the dawn of the silent era, Italian cinema focused on the portrayal of the "multiple female morphology—the *belle dame sans merci*, the ruthless ruler of the destinies of the unfortunates who fell in love with her, the demonic being that emerges from the fears of the collective subconscious of the European male," as film historian Gian Piero Brunetta observed.[22] Silent divas in Italy were priestesses of love who looked as if they came straight out of Gabriele D'Annunzio's novels: they were the epitome of the dominatrix, and the center of a world where overwhelming passions dominated everything and everyone. Female stardom enhanced a typically male imagination, brought to life removed desires, overturned taboos. It was, to quote Brunetta, "an army of tempting Eves, Sirens, Ophelias, Circes, Dianes, Salomés, of flexuous figures with the prehensile lips of a carnivorous flower, and eyes that could kill and paralyze like those of Medusa."[23] Faced with al-most mythical creatures as those portrayed by the likes of Francesca Bertini, Leda Gys and Lyda Borelli, men were reduced to secondary figures, weak and slavish: a situation that was destined to be overturned in the Fascist era, with its virile vision and the advent of such heroes as Maciste.

A similar process accompanied the birth of Italian Gothic cinema, when a noteworthy all-female star-like phenomenon developed. *I Vampiri* and *Black Sunday* are the two key stages in the definition of a changing idea of the feminine. Freda's film was also the last one the director made with his lover Gianna Maria Canale: a former secretary who ended up second at the 1947's Miss Italia beauty contest won by Lucia Bosé (Gina Lollobrigida classified as third), Canale became a film star thanks to Freda, who was struck by her arrogant, glamorous beauty.

Their first work together was 1948's *The Mysterious Rider* (*Il cavaliere misterioso*), where Canale played Baroness Lehmann alongside Vittorio Gassman: the role won her the covers of Italy's most popular film magazines and made the 21-year-old actress a movie star. Her liaison with Freda became a public scandal when the director left his wife and flew with the actress to Brazil, where they made two films, *Guarany* (1948) and *O Caçula do Barulho* (1949). However, Canale did not stand South America and forced Freda to return to Italy: she would be the leading lady in almost all of his following films, including *The Iron Swordsman*, *Sins of Rome* (*Spartaco*, 1953) and *Theodora, Slave Empress* (*Teodora, imperatrice di Bisanzio*, 1954). Then their love story brusquely ended, and Canale's star abruptly faded, until her early retirement from the scenes in 1964.

At the time she made *I Vampiri*, Gianna Maria Canale was not even 30, yet Freda has her play a character not unlike Gloria Swanson's in *Sunset Blvd.* (1950, Billy Wilder)—a woman obsessed with aging, secluded from the outside world, in love with a man much younger than her, served and revered by a cousin/lover/slave. This all conveys the sense of a fading ideal of beauty, that is about to be swept away by another female icon (no wonder Canale initially did not want to star in the film). Three years later, Bava's film (and Fellini's *La Dolce Vita*) would do the rest.

Horror, in *I Vampiri*, has a distinctly sexual undercurrent: the real horrific element in the film is not the idea of draining young women's blood, but the old duchess' love for the handsome photographer Pierre Lantin (Dario Michaelis): that is, the senile passion and the desperate attempt to rejuvenate her sagging flesh and make it desirable, and the implicit repugnance in the thought that the ravishing Gisèle hides a wrinkled, disgusting body. All this is acutely reflected in Beni Montresor's dilapidated castle, with its high ceilings from which worn curtains hang, and its courtyard strewn with withered shrubs and dead leaves blown by the wind. Freda's aforementioned words on the disgust of vampirism come to mind: Italian Gothic horror was born with a penchant for allegories—and very cruel ones indeed.

For all her ambivalence, Gisèle Du Grand is an imposing, dominating figure, who surrounds herself with slaves—a vampirism of the feelings which is a direct nod to the melodrama. Far from being a science-obsessed, asexual mad doctor, Julien Du Grand (Antoine Balpêtré) is hopelessly in love with his cousin, and their relationship is also vampiric in a way—as is the one between Julien and Signoret, whom the doctor controls through drugs: the correspondence between desire and drug addiction will return in *The Horrible Dr. Hichcock*. What is more, the Duchess receives her visitors from a dominant position, peering down the staircase of the castle; later on in the film, Gisèle is sitting in an armchair that looks more like a throne, while the men gather around her like her subjects: her power is based on the ascendancy that she has because of her social and economical position, and she maneuvers her minions according to a strict hierarchical order.

As an out-and-out horror film, however, *I Vampiri* denotes a certain awkwardness. The first part, dedicated to the police investigation after the young girls' disappearances, sticks to a realistic tone: due to the use of syringes on the part of the "vampire," the hero even considers that the crimes might be related to a drug ring—a subplot which will return in Bava's *Blood and Black Lace* (*Sei donne per l'assassino*, 1964) with the character of Marco, played by Massimo Righi. This, among other things, has led some critics to consider *I Vampiri* as "the prehistory rather than the "year one" of Gothic," as it lacks "the organic unity, coherence and self-consciousness that should be recognizable in a founder,"[24] although it is debatable whether this was Freda's intention or the result of the producers' alterations after he left.

It is not until professor Du Grand's fake funeral that the Gothic atmosphere comes to the fore, with the violent contrast between the crypt's trappings and the previous sequences' terse light. Yet *I Vampiri* ends like a standard detective story, with the hero and the commissioner solving the case and walking away from the Du Grand castle just like Humphrey Bogart and Claude Rains in *Casablanca* (1942, Michael Curtiz). A concluding shot by Bava which Freda was not satisfied with, as he had envisaged a much grimmer payoff: "They find the heroine locked inside a crypt, while I had her hanged. I did shoot that sequence. The young actress was suspended in the air and had to fall into some kind of abyss. She wasn't a real actress, [...] she was terrified at the idea of being suspended into the void [...] and the poor thing screamed. I filmed her screams. It was not the cry of an actress but a real scream of horror!"[25]

If *I Vampiri* offers very little to a modern audience in terms of shivers and shocks (and Du Grand is a rather bland mad doctor), it must be underlined that Freda's original project was much more daring, with a surprising reliance on Grand Guignol effects—starting with a shocking opening scene which was actually shot but cut by the producers, and whose only evidence left are a few on-set stills.[26] "My film started with the execution of a murderer played by Paul Muller," as Freda explained. "He was guillotined at dawn by some men in black: the scene was quite shocking, and Bava's black-and-white cinematography underlined its horrific quality. You could see the head fall. After the execution, professor Du Grand [...] purloined the body and the head. And after Frankenstein-like manipulations he gave new life to this dead body."[27]

A fragment of the scene can however be glimpsed in the German trailer for the film, *Der Vampir von Notre Dame*: the camera dollies down from a high-angle long shot while Muller is taken to the guillotine, as an impassive crowd observes under their umbrellas—one figure elegantly posing as a silhouette in the foreground as the camera ends its descent. It is a fascinatingly grim Hitchcockian moment (and one that Freda would later recreate in *The Horrible Dr. Hichcock*'s funeral scene), followed by an elliptical shot of the blade descending.

Judging from these few seconds, had the scene been preserved in the film, our view of *I Vampiri* would possibly be rather different today: not only the idea of opening the story with a gruesome act of violence partly predates *Black Sunday*, but it shows a tendency towards blood and gore that was quite ahead of its time, and delves deeper into the Gothic tradition, with its reference to Mary Shelley's novel. That is even more patent considering another scene that Freda could not film as he wanted (in some interviews he claimed he actually shot it), where Signoret is being questioned at the police station: in the current version, the man suddenly falls unconscious to the floor, whereas originally we could see Signoret's head detaching from the neck, as the reanimated manservant had run out of vital energy. On paper, it looks like another typical Grand Guignol effect, and expresses a certain confidence in handling gruesome effects—a trait which would characterize Italian genre cinema overall in the following decades, and which must also be seen in a few gory effects in Freda's subsequent *Caltiki, the Immortal Monster*.

However, such material was considered too daring and unpleasant by the film's producers and distributors. On the other hand, the version released in North America in 1960 by Jonathan Daniels and Victor Purcell's RCIP and titled *The Devil's Commandment* featured new material written by J. V. Rhems and filmed in New York by Ronald Honthauer (without any assistance, needless to say, on the part of Freda). The result was, to quote Robert Monell, "Laden with absurdly conceived and badly filmed inserts, and missing about a third of its original

footage. [...] it was this heavily doctored property that was marketed through a carefully targeted playoff on the sex and sleaze circuit. To fulfill RCIP's requirements several scenes involving scantily clad starlets in compromising positions were quickly filmed and rushed into a severely edited down assembly."[28]

The inserts include the first and third stalk-and-abduct scenes (the second, featuring Paul Muller, was the only one specifically filmed by Freda and Bava): the opening scene shot by Honthauer has an anonymous actress slowly stripping off her bra and stockings and stepping into a foaming bubble bath before an intruder comes in and assaults her. The first scene from Freda's original footage has *two* silhouettes dumping the woman's body into the river. Besides these jarring continuity non sequiturs, as Monell pointed out, "the real problem with this U.S. version are some of the later inserts, especially the redundant and unerotic 'rape' scene featuring veteran character actor Al Lewis as a horny body double for the lab assistant originally played by Angelo Galassi."[29] Said attempted rape takes place near the end: Lewis (who went on to play Grandpa in CBS's *The Munsters*) rips the blouse off a girl who should remotely look like Wandisa Guida: risibly, the scene is supposed to take place just as—in the original film—the police are descending on Du Grand's castle. Another ill-conceived insert was an awkwardly comic interlude set in an unlikely French bistro (where a bizarre floorshow is taking place) where a maître'd insists that a female client tries their *poulet au grat*. On the other hand, no less than eight scenes were cut from the Italian original.[30] The original edit eventually surfaced overseas for the first time on DVD in 2001, by Image Entertainment, under the title *I Vampiri*.

In its home country, the result was not the commercial success the director had hoped, and according to Freda this was due to its explicitly Italian origin. "I remember I was at the film's premiere in San Remo. Many people entered the theater lobby and stopped to look at the posters and reading the names on them. When they saw mine, they exclaimed: 'My God, but this is an Italian movie!?' and left. Back then, people didn't think Italians were able to make horror films."[31]

Yet things would soon change in just a couple of years, after the release of a foreign film that dealt with vampirism in a much more straightforward and classical manner, and which would prove to be an extraordinary commercial success in Italy as well—Terence Fisher's *Horror of Dracula*.

Notes

1. Punter, *The Literature of Terror, Vol. 1*, p. 1.
2. Poindron, *Riccardo Freda*, p. 260.
3. Riccardo Freda, *Divoratori di celluloide* (Milan: Edizioni del Mystfest, Il Formichiere, 1981), p. 6.
4. Poindron, *Riccardo Freda*, p. 258. The credits in the Italian version also feature, as co-scenarist and scriptwriter, a non-existent Rijk Sijöstrom.
5. Ibid., p. 260.
6. Ibid., p. 258.
7. Freda, *Divoratori di celluloide*, pp. 88–89.
8. Poindron, *Riccardo Freda*, p. 262.
9. Freda, *Divoratori di celluloide*, p. 6.
10. Sergio Grmek Germani, ed., *Carl Theodor Dreyer. L'unica grande passione* (Udine: Cinemazero, 2003), p. 117.
11. "There was a continuous collaboration between the director, the cameraman and the set designer, in order to heighten from the outside the literary–Expressionist content of the film. [D.o.p. Rudolph] Maté asked that Silvagni's drawn sketches indicated all the light-shadow games on which to lean in the camera movements." Renato Giani, "Al vampiro piacquero i decors di Silvagni," *Cinema* 77, December 31, 1951, p. 368.
12. Poindron, *Riccardo Freda*, p. 259.
13. Ibid.
14. Ruben Paniceres, "El gotico italiano. Fantastico y ciencia ficcion," in Jesus Palacios and Ruben Paniceres, eds., *Cara a cara. Una mirada al cine de genero italiano* (Gijon: Semana Negra, 2004), p. 103.
15. Francesco Di Chiara, *I tre volti della paura: il cinema horror italiano (1957-1965)* (Ferrara: UniPress, 2009), p. 69.
16. In 1960, Beni Montresor (Bussolengo, 1926—Verona, 2001) moved to the United States, and started working as an art director and costume designer in theatres throughout the world: New York's Metropolitan, London's Covent Garden, the Paris Opera. He also directed two films, *Pilgrimage* (1972) and *The Golden Mass* (*La Messe dorée*, 1975): the latter was rejected by the Italian censorship commission because of its erotic content and came out in Montresor's native country in a very manipulated version.
17. Poindron, *Riccardo Freda*, p. 260.
18. Mora, "Elegia per una donna vampiro," p. 166.
19. Francesco Pitassio, "L'orribile segreto dell'horror italiano," in Giacomo Manzoli and Guglielmo Pescatore, eds., *L'arte del risparmio: stile e tecnologia. Il cinema a basso costo in Italia negli anni Sessanta* (Rome: Carocci, 2005), p. 34.
20. Ibid.
21. Sigmund Freud, "The Uncanny," in *Writings on Art and Literature* (Redwood City, CA: Stanford University Press, 1997), p. 195.
22. Gian Piero Brunetta, "Cinema muto italiano," in Gian Piero Brunetta, ed., *Storia del cinema mondiale. Vol. III, L'Europa. Le cinematografie nazionali* (Turin: Einaudi, 1999), p. 47.
23. Ibid., p. 49.
24. Riccardo Fassone, ed., *"La stagione delle streghe. Guida al gotico italiano,"* *Nocturno Dossier* 80, March 2009, p. 11.
25. Poindron, *Riccardo Freda*, p. 263.
26. See Stefano Piselli, Riccardo Morlocchi and Antonio Bruschini, *Bizarre sinema! Wildest sexiest weirdest sleaziest films: Horror all'italiana 1957–1979* (Florence: Glittering, 1996), p. 19.
27. Poindron, *Riccardo Freda*, p 262.
28. Robert Monell, "Riccardo Freda," *European Trash Cinema Special* 2, 1997, p. 17.
29. Ibid.
30. For a detailed comparison between the Italian and the U.S. cut *see* Tim Lucas, "Is There Life After Suspiria?," in *The Video Watchdog Book* (Cincinnati, OH: Video Watchdog, 1992), pp. 182–183. Lucas also mentions a nudie version being assembled in the United States, titled *Lust of the Vampire*—the same title as the version that was released in the United Kingdom. However, such a hybrid has remained elusive to this day.
31. Franca Faldini and Goffredo Fofi, eds., *L'avventurosa storia del cinema italiano raccontata dai suoi protagonisti 1960–1969* (Milan: Feltrinelli, 1981), pp. 200–201.

1959

Uncle Was a Vampire (*Tempi duri per i vampiri*)

D: Steno [Stefano Vanzina]. S and SC: Edoardo Anton, Marcello Fondato, Sandro Continenza, Dino Verde, Stefano Vanzina, Renato Rascel, from an idea by Mario Cecchi Gori; DOP: Marco Scarpelli (Ultrascope–Technicolor); M: Armando Trovajoli, Renato Rascel, conducted by Armando Trovajoli; songs by Renato Rascel, Bruno Martino; E: Eraldo Da Roma; PD: Giorgio Giovannini; ArtD: Andrea Tomassi; CO: Ugo Pericoli; C: Pasquale De Santis, Sandro D'Eva; AD: Mariano Laurenti; MU: Eligio Trani; Hair: Gustavo Sisi; SO: Umberto Picistrelli, Mario Amari; AE: Emilio Miraglia. Cast: Renato Rascel [Renato Ranucci] (Baron Osvaldo Lambertenghi), Christopher Lee (Baron Roderico from Frankfurten), Sylva Koscina (Carla), Lia Zoppelli (Letizia), Kai Fischer (Lellina), Franco Scandurra (Prof. Stricker), Carl Very (The hotel's new director), Antje Geerk, Federico Collino (Carla's father), Susanne Loret (Susan, American tourist), Angelo Zanolli, Antonio Mambretti, Ivana Gilli, Franco Giacobini, Fiorella Ferrero, Francesco Tenzi, Lamberto Antinori; *uncredited*: Lia Lena, Rik Van Nutter (Victor, Carla's boyfriend), Mario Cecchi Gori (Notary). *PROD*: Mario Cecchi Gori for Maxima Film, Montflour Film [*U.S. Version–EP*: Joseph E. Levine]; *AP*: Antonio Sarno, Adriano De Micheli; *PM*: Pio Angeletti; *PS*: Umberto Santoni. *Country*: Italy. Filmed at Castello Brown, Portofino (Genoa), Hotel dei Castelli, Sestri Levante (Genoa). *Running time*: 90 min. (m. 3100); Visa n: 30310 (09.24.1959); *Rating*: not rated; *Release dates*: 10.28.1959 (Italy); 1964 (U.S.A., TV). *Distribution:* C.E.I.-Incom (Italy); Embassy Pictures Television (U.S.A., syndication); *Domestic gross:* 385,000,000 lire. *Also known as*: *Hard Times for Dracula, Dracula Is My Uncle, Hard Times for Vampires, My Uncle the Vampire* (U.S.A.), *Les Temps sont durs pour les vampires* (France, August 1962), *Schlechte Zeiten für Vampire* (West Germany). *Home Video*: GI Studios (DVD, U.S.A.), PR Studios (DVD, U.S.A.—double feature w/ *Horror Express*)

Due to his heavy debts, Baron Osvaldo Lambertenghi is forced to sell his ancestral castle. The manor is ingloriously converted into a frivolous five-star hotel and Osvaldo is allowed to go on living there working as a porter. One day, though, Osvaldo receives a visit from his uncle Roderico, who turns out to be a vampire. Osvaldo tries to warn the various guests of the hotel, which only result in his being taken for a madman. Bitten by his uncle, Osvaldo turns into a vampire, and starts preying on the hotel's female guests, who suddenly find him irresistible and seductive. But only the one girl who truly loves him, Lellina, will be able to free Osvaldo from the curse. In the end, uncle Roderico returns home, determined, henceforth, to enjoy sex rather than blood.

Released in Italy in late 1958, *Horror of Dracula* was generally slammed by critics. "The regret for an era when cinema was able to give us such masterworks as *Nosferatu* is still alive, if we think about the laughable grossness of *Horror of Dracula*," wrote the renowned Nino Ghelli, blaming the film's "banal photographical tricks," its "vulgar sadistic suggestions" and its "bloodily stupid sequences."[1] Nevertheless, Fisher's film proved to be a tremendous box-office hit in the country, paving the way for a commercial renaissance of the horror and the fantastic among the public. Yet, Italy's first vampire film was to be a parody.

The use of elements taken from the Gothic and horror tradition for laughs was obviously not unknown to Italian comedies. Ghosts as a comic resource appeared in such films as *Quel fantasma di mio marito* (1950, Camillo Mas-

trocinque) and *La paura fa 90* (1951, Giorgio Simonelli), while in *Ghosts of Rome* (*Fantasmi a Roma*, 1961, Antonio Pietrangeli) a typical ghost story became the instrument for a sharp satire on the Boom. Totò's films often reprised horrific clichés in a mocking way: the Faustian bargain in *Totò al Giro d'Italia* (1948, Mario Mattoli), the staging of a fake afterlife in *47 morto che parla* (1950, Carlo Ludovico Bragaglia), Dante's *Inferno* by way of Gustave Doré's etchings in *Totò all'inferno* (1955, Camillo Mastrocinque), actor Tino Buazzelli's lycanthropic metamorphosis in *Le sei mogli di Barbablù* (1950, Carlo Ludovico Bragaglia), the hilarious night watch at the undead Marquis De Lattanziis (Nino Taranto) in a crypt in *Il monaco di Monza* (1963, Sergio Corbucci). However, especially in the sequence when Totò is hired as a cemetery caretaker in the wonderful *Totò cerca casa* (1949, Mario Monicelli, Steno), one could detect a patent diffidence toward Gothic paraphernalia, accompanied by a healthy, detached irony which was typical of Italian cinema's approach to *all* genres.

In *Uncle Was a Vampire* the deadly charm of Bram Stoker's character is attacked and demolished by Renato Rascel's vaudevillian spirit and director Steno (Stefano Vanzina)'s knack for comedy.[2] Rascel (1912–1991) was an extremely popular vaudeville, film and radio actor, dancer and singer/songwriter who gained international fame in 1957 through his own song *Arrivederci Roma* (which inspired the film *The Seven Hills of Rome*, starring Rascel and Mario Lanza). Vanzina (1917–1988) was a former scriptwriter who had been part of the renowned satiric mag *MarcAurelio* together with such important names as Marcello Marchesi and Federico Fellini. Vanzina had debuted behind the camera in 1949, and over his 40-year career he directed 80 films, mostly comedies: however, he also signed the landmark crime film *Execution Squad* (*La polizia ringrazia*, 1972).

Farce—the treatment reserved to non-native models—enriched itself with new targets thanks to the Gothic: next year it would be the turn of Stevenson's character in Marino Girolami's *My Friend, Dr. Jekyll*. But what is most remarkable about Vanzina's parody, however, is how it high-

Italian *fotobusta* for *Uncle Was a Vampire* (courtesy S. I. Bianchi).

lights what will be one of Italian Gothic's main elements: eroticism. *Uncle Was a Vampire* is packed full with jokes related to the sexual metaphor linked to vampirism: after Osvaldo is transformed into a vampire by his uncle Roderico, he nightly visits the rooms of his castle-turned-into-luxury hotel,[3] bites the female guests and awakens their libido. A visual gag has the dial of a clock that marks the progress of the hours while Osvaldo repeatedly stoops on the neck of scantily dressed women in their nightgown, who greet him with open arms: by morning, we will find out that he has bitten no less than 42 of them, in a vampiric *tour-de-force* that is obviously a double-entendre for an extraordinary sexual performance. The next morning, the ecstatic victims snub their husbands and boyfriends and chase the vampire (who has forgotten every detail of his nightly forays), begging him to "bite" them again.

The metamorphosis of Osvaldo, from romantic and asexual sweetheart to voracious predator who openly winks at the camera, makes him an unsuspecting stud, all the more comically

unlikely given Rascel's lack of the necessary *physique du rôle*; at the same time, it mocks the typical theme of sexual dissatisfaction, a recurring theme in Italian comedies of the time, in a manner not dissimilar from Luciano Salce's *Le pillole di Ercole* (1960) where a sort of miraculous Viagra *ante litteram* turns a meek newlywed (Nino Manfredi) into a sex maniac. "He's not a man, he's more—*much* more" the vampirized ladies sigh, in a stunning anticipation of one of Italian Gothic's most explicit examples of sexual innuendos, Graziella Granata's character in *Slaughter of the Vampires* (1962, Roberto Mauri).

As the titular vampire, Christopher Lee plays his role straight, as Bela Lugosi did when reprising his Dracula role in the Abbott and Costello parodies, as opposed to Renato Rascel's customary grimaces, jokes and double-entendres. *Uncle Was a Vampire* was the first of Lee's forays into the *Belpaese*: in the following years, the actor would be a recurring presence in Italian genre cinema, starting with Mario Bava's *Hercules in the Haunted World* (*Ercole al centro della terra*,

1961), whose working title was, significantly, *Ercole contro il vampiro*—Hercules vs. the Vampire.

Yet, despite Lee's imposing presence, the tone is quite different from typical horror movie parodies. "It's 1959, and you still believe in vampires?" asks Osvaldo in a scene—a most revealing line indeed. In Vanzina's film one can feel the smell of the so-called Boom making its way through a plot that recalls the unpretentious musicals (the so-called *musicarelli*) which were one of the period's most profitable genres, with such titles as Lucio Fulci's *Howlers of the Dock* (*Urlatori alla sbarra*, 1960: "Howlers" was the pejorative term with which the press used to name the young singers who were influenced by rock 'n' roll and gradually detached from Italy's melodic tradition). One such example is the romantic subplot involving Carla (Sylva Koscina) and a "howler," Victor (Rik Van Nutten), who is predictably disliked by the girl's parents.

As seen is Steno's film, 1959's Italy is the total opposite of a Gothic scenario: a sunny, vital, enthusiastic and sexually hungry country, populated by young bullies chasing Nordic beauties, wealthy vacationers and greedy companies whose aim is to buy and reconvert villas, beaches and stretches of land into tourist attractions—along the lines of Bava's *Bay of Blood* (*Ecologia del delitto*, 1971) here. In 1959's Italy there is no room for vampires, as suggested by the Italian title (which translates into "Hard Times for Vampires"): the pompous Baron Roderico is unceremoniously evicted from his castle, his nephew Baron Osvaldo is forced to sell his family's manor, and Roderico finally has to settle for a crypt in Osvaldo's chateau which has been redesigned into a fancy bar. To put it bluntly, if Fisher's vivid color palette pointed at an attack toward Victorian times' hypocritical haughtiness, *Uncle Was a Vampire*'s bright Ferraniacolor unmasks the unlikelihood of a pairing between the Boom's epicurean euphoria and the Gothic's punitive gloom: it is no wonder that in the final scene Roderico finally opens up to a mischievous smile and walks away arm in arm with a pair of curvaceous ladies, while Bruno Martino's contagious song "Dracula cha-cha"[4] accompanies the end credits.

Despite being essentially a silly—but not hollow—comedy, *Uncle Was a Vampire* surprisingly works as a memento for Italian Gothic films to come. The fact is, the rampant, pragmatic Italy of the Boom years does not accommodate the romantic melancholy and the darkly, tormented figures that populate Gothic fiction and films. Unless, as Steno does, they are played for laughs. The present did not look dark and gloomy at all, to audiences of the period: Italy was quickly becoming a modern, civilized country. In 1956 works had started on the construction of the A1 (the so-called "Motorway of the Sun"), Italy's longest motorway which would connect the North and the South of the country (it would open in 1964), the 1960 Rome Olympics would be a prestigious showcase and a huge asset for Italy's tourist economy, while 1961 saw the inauguration of Rome's Fiumicino—Leonardo da Vinci International Airport.

In a country driving at full speed towards urbanization, wealth and consumerism—a condition best exemplified by Dino Risi's masterpiece *The Easy Life* (*Il sorpasso*, 1962)—and where the transition from a rural society to an industrial one is taking place traumatically quickly, the idea of vampirism as "a myth produced by the middle class to explain its own antecedents and its own fears"[5] has no *raison d'être* as it is superseded by the present. To destroy the vampire, the combination of science and religion, as well as rationalism and ethical conformism, are no longer necessary. There is no need of crucifixes, garlic and holy water: the smell of money is enough, as Steno's film explains. The real vampires are the rampant bourgeois like *The Easy Life*'s Bruno Cortona (Vittorio Gassman), who bite—nay, scrounge—and run. The future definitely looked bright—brighter than the sun which turns vampires into dust.

Notes

1. Nino Ghelli, "Dracula il vampiro," *Rivista del Cinematografo* 1, January 1959, pp. 31–32.

2. The U.S. version erroneously credits production manager Pio Angeletti as the director.

3. The film's use of its Ligurian scenario is another example of Italian Gothic's jaunty approach to settings. In the opening scene the camera pans on the notorious

fifteenth century's Castle Brown at Portofino, hinting at the fact that it is the film's setting. Yet, after a dissolve, the rest of the film has the story actually taking place at the Hotel dei Castelli, Villa Gualino, in Sestri Levante: not a real Medieval castle, but an example of Gothic revival of the late nineteenth/early twentieth century (the castle was actually built between 1925 and 1929 and turned into a luxury hotel in 1950).

4. The song turned out a hit. In 1960 Henri Salvador launched a French version, with lyrics by Fernand Bonifay, while Vincente Minnelli's *Two Weeks in Another Town* (1962) featured it as well in a scene where several characters are dancing to it in a hotel suite while Edward G. Robinson is taken away by paramedics after suffering a heart attack. More recently, the song inspired the title of Kim Newman's 1998 dystopian vampire novel *Dracula Cha Cha Cha* (retitled *Judgment of Tears* in the United States), the third book in the *Anno Dracula* series.

5. Punter, *The Literature of Terror*, p. 105.

1960

Atom Age Vampire *(Seddok "l'erede di Satana")*

D: Anton Giulio Majano. *S*: Piero Monviso; *SC*: Gino De Sanctis, Alberto Bevilacqua, Anton Giulio Majano; *DOP*: Aldo Giordani (B&W, 1,85:1—Ferrania Pancro C/7); *M*: Armando Trovajoli, conducted by the author (Ed. Nord Sud); *E*: Gabriele Varriale; *AE*: Elsa Arata; *PD*: Walter Martigli; *APD*: Giuseppe Ranieri; *SD*: Giorgio Gallani; *AD*: Sergio De Pascale; *2ndAD*: Piero Monviso; *C*: Sergio Bergamini; *CHOR*: Marisa Cianpaglia; *MU*: Euclide Santoli; *SE*: Ugo Amadoro; *SO*: Ivo Benedetti; *B*: Osvaldo Capperi; *AMU*: Alma Paciotti, Enrico Mecacci; *Hair*: Fernanda Titta; *SS*: Lina D'Amico. *English version*: *DubD*: Richard McNamara; *Dialogue*: John Davis Hart. *Cast*: Alberto Lupo (Prof. Alberto Levin), Susanne Loret (Jeanette Moreneau), Sergio Fantoni (Pierre Mornet), Franca Parisi (Monique Rivière, Levin's assistant), Andrea Scotti (Gardener), Rina Franchetti [Ester Girgenti] (Nurse), Roberto Bertea (Sacha), Ivo Garrani (Commissioner), Gianni Loti, Tullio Altamura, Gianna Piaz, Francesco Sormano, Nicoletta Varé, Appio Cartei, Bruno Benedetti, Silvano Marabotti, Alfredo Mariotti, Glamor Mora (Dancer) and the "Complesso 5 Diavoli." *PROD*: Mario Fava for Lion's Films (Rome); *PM*: Elio Ippolito Mellino; *PS*: Dino Benedetti; *PSe*: Claudio Sinibaldi. *Country*: Italy. Filmed at Pisorno Studio, Tirrenia. *Running time*: 105 min. (m. 2924); *Visa n*: 32625 (08.11.1960); *Rating*: V.M.16; *Release dates*: 08.19.1960 (Italy); 05.29.1963 (U.S.A.). *Distribution*: Film Selezione (Italy); Manson Distributing, Topaz Film Corporation (U.S.A.); *Domestic gross*: 90,000,000 lire. *Also known as*: Le Monstre au masque (France, 02.02.1963), Seddok—Der Wüger

mit den Teufelskrallen (West Germany, 06.14.1963). *Home video*: Media Target (DVD, Germany), Alpha Video, Sinister Cinema, AFA Entertainment (DVD, U.S.A.), Passworld (DVD, Italy).

After suffering a horrible car accident, night-club stripper Jeanette is persuaded by a mysterious woman to undergo experimental treatment in the hopes of regaining her beauty: professor Levin has developed a method to restore her beauty by injecting her with a special healing serum. However, while performing the procedure with the help of his assistant (and lover) Monique, Levin falls in love with Jeanette. As the treatment proves to be only temporary, Levin determines to save Jeanette's beauty at all costs. Since the doctor gets the serum from young women's glands, he needs to kill for her sake. To do so, Levin injects himself with another serum, which turns him into a ferocious monster, and goes on a killing spree to get the glands he needs. However, Jeanette's ex-boyfriend Pierre starts looking for her, and leads the police onto Levin's tracks...

Released in Italy a mere eight days after *Black Sunday*, Anton Giulio Majano's *Atom Age Vampire* looks as if it belonged to a different decade, in the sense that it is closer to *I Vampiri* in its expunging of supernatural elements in favor of pseudo-scientific ones. The talky script[1] cobbles together a number of cinematic and literary influences that result in a clumsy hybrid which has little in common with Italian Gothic horror films to come.

The story's backbone openly recalls Georges Franju's *Eyes Without a Face* (*Les Yeux sans visage*, 1960, released in Italy several months earlier), with a little bit of *She Demons* (1958, Richard Cunha) thrown in—most likely by coincidence since Cunha's film was never released in Italy—but superimposes other narrative tracks to it. The first part, focusing on a scientist, Prof. Levin (Alberto Lupo with an incongruous platinum blonde hair color), who is obsessed with the idea of restoring beauty to Jeanette (Susanne Loret), a stripper disfigured after a car accident, adheres to Franju's film almost verbatim.

The turning point, however, derails the story in territories inspired by *The Strange Case of Dr. Jekyll and Mr. Hyde*, though a thousand times sillier: in order to develop the necessary courage to kill young women and gather the

Atmospheric Italian poster for *Atom Age Vampire* **(author's collection).**

(unspecified) glands which are essential to heal Jeannette, Levin injects himself with a serum that turns him into some kind of werewolf, and roams at night in seedy areas of the city to kill prostitutes. In the third act, the police investigation takes over—complete with tiresome crime story clichés such as an inspector who just quit smoking and a nosy reporter—denoting an all-too obvious uncertainty towards the fantastic dimension of the story, which leads to a predictable and decidedly unmemorable conclusion.

The film's awkward composite nature is all over the place. Levin's unlikely laboratory recalls the American science fiction B-movies of the period as well as the attempts at actualizing the myth of Frankenstein such as *I Was a Teenage Frankenstein* (1957, Herbert L. Strock); the script calls for a pseudo-scientific explanation for Levin's experiments and references to Hiroshima, including a scene where Alberto Lupo shows the inspector (Ivo Garrani) pictures of horribly disfigured survivors,[2] while the plot twist that has Levin's murders attributed to a gorilla escaped from the zoo is a throwaway nod to Edgar Allan Poe's story "The Murders in the Rue Morgue"; finally, the doctor is given an Igor-like mute assistant named Sasha, whose sole purpose in the movie is seemingly to provide the good doctor with a final comeuppance.

The discomfort in handling the genre's paraphernalia is patent: even the filmmakers are not sure how to define the monster, so much so that a dialogue exchange has Levin allude to his alter ego as "a sort of atomic vampire who wants to heal," a line that offered overseas distributors the inspiration for the memorable U.S. title, definitely more impressive than the very bad—and unexplained—Italian one, *Seddok "l'erede di Satana"* ("Seddok 'Satan's Heir'"). If Levin's pointless man-to-werewolf routine was not silly enough, Alberto Lupo's crude make-up and the use of lap-dissolves in the transformation scenes take the viewer back to early Universal horror films, and make for an unrealistic, grotesque monster.

The theme of the disfigured face—one which would become crucial to Italian Gothic horror films—ends with a reversal of roles that pushes back the story into the classic Gothic stereotypes: Levin turns into the monster in front of his by-now healed beloved, thus re-enacting the classic *Beauty and the Beast* theme: it is a conventional, simplistic vision that Freda had already undermined in the ending of *I Vampiri*, where Beauty turned out to *be* the Beast.

More enlightening, however, is the figure of the mad doctor. Whereas Hammer's Baron Frankenstein was a sort of an antihero for the age of Enlightenment, obsessed by science and ahead of his time, his Italian counterparts are driven by uncontrollable impulses towards their objects of desire. Majano turns the desperate fatherly love that moved Pierre Brasseur in *Eyes Without a Face* into an erotic obsession, and the film itself into a horror-tinged melodrama centered on a case of *amour fou*: in order to keep Jeanette beautiful—hence desirable to his eyes—Levin sets out to "do what no man has ever done for his woman." What is more, the relationship between the doctor, his female assistant Monique (Franca Parisi) and their patient develops into a bizarre love triangle of sorts. "It's not love," though, as Levin confesses to Monique, "it's a sentiment complex, it's only a compulsion if you like.... I want to dominate the girl—to possess her creatively." Similarly, the jarring alchemies that deform the body and behavior are related to sexuality and desire.

Despite its slapdash nature, *Atom Age Vampire* is unexpectedly vital when it comes to dealing with sex. The erotic element is well in evidence as from Jeannette's opening striptease before her lover (Sergio Fantoni)—a sequence tuned in to the same wavelength as the period's sexploitation documentaries and *Mondo* movies. It is no wonder that the film earned a V.M.16 rating from Italy's harsh board of censors. Its box-office takings were modest in its home country, whereas it gained a certain notoriety abroad, where it was released in a truncated version, only 87 minutes long, eighteen minutes less than the original running time: several public domain copies, then, sadly clock in at 69 minutes.[3]

After a career in the movies as scriptwriter and filmmaker that started in the Thirties—his best film being *L'eterna catena* (1951)—Anton Giulio Majano (1909–1994) became one of Italian television's more important directors since its early days in the mid–Fifties, introducing the TV movie concept (the so-called "teleromanzi," then "sceneggiati") in the country with many successful adaptations of popular novels, including *Little Women*, *Crime and Punishment*, *The Citadel*, *The Moonstone*, *The Master of Ballantrae* and others. *Atom Age Vampire* was his penultimate work for the big screen, followed by the Alexandre Dumas adaptation *I fratelli Corsi* (1961).

Notes

1. Among the scriptwriters the name Alberto Bevilacqua stands out. Bevilacqua (1934–2013) would become a renowned author in Italy after the success of his novels *La califfa* (1964) and *Questa specie d'amore* (1966). He also tried his hand at directing, starting with an adaptation of his own novel *La Califfa* in 1970, starring Romy Schneider and Ugo Tognazzi. Bevilacqua also co-scripted two films by Mario Bava, *Black Sabbath* and *Planet of the Vampires* (*Terrore nello spazio*, 1965). Incidentally, several reference books incorrectly claimed *Atom Age Vampire* to be produced by Mario Bava, which it was not: the producer's name, for the company Lion's Films, was Mario *Fava*, an a.k.a. for Elio Ippolito Mellino.

2. Alberto Lupo would deal with the Hiroshima blast again in Roberto Mauri's clumsy *giallo Le notti della violenza* (1965), in which he plays an inspector who investigates a maniac that is attacking prostitutes in a Roman park: the culprit turns out to be a Hiroshima survivor who has been disfigured by atomic radiation.

3. In 2009 animator Scott Bateman released a new version of the film, created by taking the English-language soundtrack and pairing it to animated visuals, with humorous results in the vein of *Mystery Science Theatre 3000*. In 2011 British artist Adam Roberts made *Remake*, a 31-minute, scene-for-scene reshoot of the original … without any of the characters, again using the English language soundtrack. As Roberts explained, "More or less, the shots have been recreated to preserve the framing, focus and moves of *Seddok's* camera—minus its cast. The texture and image quality of the film is intended to evoke the poor quality of films that once circulated on poor 16mm prints, worse VHS tape and now in extremely poor YouTube copies. [...] Remaking is a familiar process, harking back to copies of paintings made in a previous era. This film is an experiment, removing the human presence from the film frame but preserving the effect of human presence. It is a response to Gorky's comment that film is a "kingdom of shadows": he was talking about seeing film images of people as ghosts, preserved eternally on a film of emulsion. I thought to remove these ghosts and see what remains" (www.adamroberts.eu).

Black Sunday (*La maschera del demonio*)

D: Mario Bava. *S:* Mario Bava, based on Nikolai Gogol's short story "Viy"; *SC:* Ennio De Concini, Mario Serandrei [and Mario Bava, Marcello Coscia, Dino De Palma, uncredited]; *DOP:* Mario Bava (B&W, 1,85:1); *M:* Roberto Nicolosi, conducted by Pierluigi Urbini (*U.S. version:* Les Baxter; music coordinator: Al Simms); E: Mario Serandrei; *PD:* Giorgio Giovannini; *SD:* Nedo Azzini; *C:* Ubaldo Terzano; *CO:* Tina Loriedo Grani; *AD:* Vana Caruso; *SO–U.S. version:* Robert Sherwood; *SE:* Mario Bava (special effects; matte paintings—uncredited), Eugenio Bava (sculptor: masks and faces—uncredited); *DialD–U.S. version:* George Higgins III; *DubD–U.S. version:* Lee Kresel; *SS:* Bona Magrini. *Cast:* Barbara Steele (Asa Vajda/Katia Vajda), John Richardson (Dr. Andrej Gorobec), Andrea Checchi (Dr. Chomà Kruvajan), Ivo Garrani (Prince Vajda),

Arturo Dominici (Igor Javutich), Enrico Olivieri (Constantine Vajda), Tino Bianchi (Ivan), Antonio Pierfederici (Priest), Clara Bindi (Innkeeper), Mario Passante (Nikita, the coachman), Renato Terra (Boris), Germana Dominici (Sonya, the innkeeper's daughter). *U.S. version:* George Gonneau (narration). *PROD:* Galatea–Jolly Film (Rome); *PS:* Paolo Mercuri; *PSe:* Armando Govoni. *Country:* Italy. Filmed at Titanus Studios and at Arsoli's Castle Massimo, Rome. *Running time:* 87 min. (m. 2415); Visa n: 32584 (08.05.1960); *Rating:* V.M.16; *Release dates:* 08.11.1960 (Italy); 02.15.1961 (U.S.A.). *Distribution:* Unidis (Italy); AIP (U.S.A.); *Domestic gross:* 139,000,000 lire. *Also known as:* Revenge of the Vampire (UK, June 1968), The Mask of Satan (UK, Home video); Le Masque du démon (France, 03.29.1961); Die Stunde wenn Drakula kommt (West Germany, 09.29.1961), La máscara del demonio (Spain, 10.07.1969). *Home video:* Kino (Blu-ray, U.S.A.), Anchor Bay, Image (DVD, U.S.A.), RHV (DVD, Italy)

Moldavia, 1630. Princess Asa Vajda and her paramour Igor Javutich are sentenced to death for sorcery by Asa's brother. A spiked metal mask is nailed onto her face and she is burnt at the stake. Before dying, Asa puts a curse on her brother's descendants, and a rainstorm extinguishes the flames. Two hundred years later, two doctors— the young Gorobec and his elderly colleague Kruvajan—are traveling in the region. They venture into a ruined crypt and find Asa's tomb: Kruvajan accidentally revives the dead witch with his blood. Gorobec meets princess Katia, Asa's descendant and a dead ringer for the witch, and he falls for her. The revived Asa summons Javutich, and together they exact vengeance. First Asa vampirizes Kruvajan, making him her undead servant and sending him to murder Katia's father. Asa's aim, however, is to take Katia's place after draining her of her blood. Javutich abducts Katia and takes her to his mistress, but the girl's crucifix prevents Asa from going through with her plans. When Gorobec arrives to save the girl, after dispatching the undead Kruvajan, Asa pretends to be Katia, and asks him to stake the vampire. At the last moment, though, Gorobec notices the crucifix on Katia's neck and realizes the truth...

The first few minutes of Mario Bava's feature film debut *Black Sunday* put on a show unmatched in Italian cinema of the time. A woman is stripped, branded with a hot-iron poker on her bare back, then subjected to an unspeakably gruesome torture as an iron mask is nailed directly onto her face. When the executioner starts his terrible hammer blow, rather than leave it to occur off-screen, Bava shows the impact and its aftermath: the shot of the mask applied with a sledgehammer onto the witch's face, with blood spilling abundantly, is a low blow that marks a quantum leap in the representation of violence in movies, even though Bava's original concept was even more gruesome. In the storyboard, he had planned another over-the-top gory detail: the nails piercing from side to side of the stake the witch is tied to.

Something was happening in the portrayal of violence on screen. A few months earlier, cinema-goers had got to see a similar sequence in *Messalina* (*Messalina Venere imperatrice*, 1960, Vittorio Cottafavi), where a Roman slave played by a very young Paola Pitagora was branded: that was nothing, however, compared to *Black Sunday*. Until then, audiences were educated by the unspoken laws of American cinema to witness a clean and polite depiction of violence, both in the way it manifested itself and regarding the object to which it was directed. Here, blatantly and with incredible ferocity, the object of violence was the female body, whom filmmakers at the time were trying by all means to unveil to the audience, even if just a few inches more, despite the opposition on the part of the censorship commissions. In a matter of minutes, Bava had that very body stripped, humiliated, marked by fire and martyred.

There had not been anything like *Black Sunday* before. Certainly not Hammer films, which had introduced a few Grand Guignol elements: *The Curse of Frankenstein* relied mostly on Christopher Lee's make-up as the monster, while the censorship issues that plagued *Horror of Dracula* regarded a few shots near the end, which were removed in order to gain the film a

Princess Asa (Barbara Steele) faces the torture device known as the "Mask of Satan" in the opening scene of Mario Bava's *Black* (Billy Rose Theatre Division, New York Public Library for the Performing Arts, Astor, Lenox and Tilden Foundations).

visa on the part of the BBFC—which instead would ban Bava's film for eight years in the United Kingdom.

Equally significant is the comparison with the opening of *The Hound of the Baskervilles* (1959, Terence Fisher), which narrated the antecedent that caused the family curse around which the film was based: the debauched Sir Hugo chases and kills a peasant girl on the heath, only to be mauled by a hound from hell. Although the addition to Conan Doyle's original story emphasized one of the director's favorite themes—the surfacing of animal instincts that underlie the formal aristocratic ostentation—and introduced an erotic element that was not on paper, Fisher kept violence off-screen, preferring the suggestion of the unseen.

On the contrary, Bava attacked the viewer in the jugular, with images of violence that exceeded even the atrocities staged in Anglo-Amalgamated's "Sadean trilogy"—*Horrors of the Black Museum* (1959, Arthur Crabtree), *Circus of Horrors* (1960, Sidney Hayers) and, naturally, *Peeping Tom* (1960, Michael Powell). Although AIP's Corman/Poe cycle benefitted from the loosening of the Production Code, the results—even when centered on the spectacularization of torture, such as in *The Pit and the Pendulum* (1961, Roger Corman)—were certainly not comparable to the Italian director's work.

Even Alfred Hitchcock's *Psycho*—which came out in British theaters just a week earlier and in American ones (after the June previews) on August 10, the same day *Black Sunday* was released in Italy—stopped way earlier in its depiction of violence, by reducing the Grand Guignol of the shower scene to a matter of suggestion by quick editing and visual illusion. Furthermore, whereas Marion Crane was stabbed to death forty minutes into the film, Steele's torture came just after the lights had gone down, catching everybody unprepared.

Black Sunday also marked a huge step forward with respect to violence as portrayed in the sword-and-sandal genre, which was superficially evoked by the sight of the muscle-bound, bare-chested hooded executioner. In the *peplum* it was the mythological hero who was usually being subjected to torture, and martyrdom was intended to solicit his physical reaction and the display of muscles and virile strength. What is more, sword-and-sandal films portrayed a bloodless violence—naive, baroque but harmless, made up of gadgets as brainy as they were ultimately ineffective. *Black Sunday*'s violence is shocking because scary instruments (hot-irons, spiked masks) *do cause* gruesome effects.

Middle Age inquisitors used to exhibit their tools of torture to the victims, while painstakingly explaining their effects in order to increase the unfortunates' terror. Bava does the same by dilating Asa's execution in a series of 19 shots that, through an elaborate and elegant use of the dolly, follow the "Mask of Satan" from the moment it is picked up by the executioner until it has been nailed to Asa's face. By emphasizing the shot/reverse shot of the mask that moves ominously towards the woman, in a brilliant succession of shots (first Asa's point-of-view shot of the mask approaching, then one from *inside* the approaching instrument), Bava triggers a sense of alarm in the viewer that is accompanied by an anticipation of the payoff—a "reward" that is both awaited and feared.

Time dilation, an emphasis on the aesthetic and graphic effects of violence, the refusal to resort to off-screen: *Black Sunday* already featured—albeit in an embryonic way—the method of representation that would characterize other genres and threads in Italian cinema, from Spaghetti Westerns to *gialli*, starting with Bava's own *Blood and Black Lace* up to Argento and Fulci's films. There is more: with *Black Sunday* Bava staged a "horrific eroticism of the tortured body"[1] which paved the way for a new manner in which to conceive the horror movie. It is no coincidence that among the admirers of *Black Sunday* there were filmmakers such as Jesús Franco and Jean Rollin, who put the connection between horror and eroticism at the heart of their experience in the *fantastique*. Criticism, on the other hand, had easy game to develop theories about this specific issue: according to Carol Jenks, violence is also addressed "towards the audience, a desire to aggress against the very site of vision, the eye

... the spiked mask of Satan is carried forward into the camera to pierce the gaze of the spectator,"[2] with the consequent references to the eye violence in Dario Argento's *Suspiria* (1977) and *Opera* (1987).

If the opening sequence used the vision of the tortured body for the purpose of visual shock, the gradual recomposition of Asa's face, with her eyes reforming in their sockets in close-up, mixes revulsion and erotic fascination. The resurrection that follows, accompanied by the unexpected explosion of the witch's sarcophagus, shows how Bava's tactics consisted in a "reliance on fresh rendering or novel manipulation of traditional images."[3] The killing of Kruvajan, modeled on the murders of the vampire's victims in *Horror of Dracula*, is another shocking moment, which shows how Italian horror exceeded by far Hammer's timid use of gore. The stake was driven off-screen into the vampire's heart in Fisher's film, and the director allowed the audience just a quick shot of the aftermath, with the wood already lodged in the chest (according to the convention borrowed from Hollywood for which the violent act and its consequences should not be shown in the same shot). Here, the viewers were confronted with the sight of a long nail that penetrates the undead's eye. All this happens in close-up, without cuts.

The disruptive quality of violence in *Black Sunday* must have been quite clear even before shooting: according to a 1947 law, in force until the new regulation on censorship which was passed in 1962, film scripts were sent by producers to a Ministerial Commission of Revision which evaluated them prior to shooting, giving an opinion on the content—and sometimes vetoing it. As for *Black Sunday*, the Commission stated that "the script is so stuffed with witches, vampires, skeletons, ghosts, with its complement of murders and dead bodies, that the film about Dracula (*Horror of Dracula*) looks like a children's show when compared to it [...]. The many horrific sequences, for what concerns their gruesome content, may be evaluated only in the finished film." However, *Black Sunday* passed the Board of Censors with a V.M.16 rating[4] but with no cuts at all.

Mario Bava's official directorial debut—after a few titles he had at least partially directed or completed without taking credit, including Riccardo Freda's *Caltiki, the Immortal Monster* and Jacques Tourneur's *The Giant of Marathon* (also 1959)—was offered to the then 45-year-old director of photography by the head of Galatea Film, Nello Santi. Galatea was perhaps the most active company within genre cinema: it had launched the sword-and-sandal fever with Pietro Francisci's two *Hercules* movies (*Hercules*, 1958, and *Hercules Unchained*, 1959), which had been box-office hits in the U.S., and after a not-so-lucky attempt at science-fiction with *Caltiki*, the company was planning to move on to horror films.

Bava's choice was a short story by Nikolai Gogol, "Viy," which he used to tell his children as a macabre fairytale before they went to sleep. Gogol stated that the Viy was a figure taken from Slavic mythology, although the writer's scholars tend to agree it was only part of Gogol's imagination.

First published in 1835 in the short stories collection *Mirgorod*, Gogol's tale was centered on three students—Khaliava, Khoma and Gorobets—who get lost in the wilderness and take refuge by an old hag who turns out to be a witch. At night she visits one of the students, Khoma, leaps on his back and has him gallop all over the countryside before Khoma is set free from the spell. The old woman eventually collapses and turns into a beautiful girl. Some time later, Khoma is called on to watch over a dead woman for three nights and pray over her body at a ruined temple: he finds out that the corpse belongs to the old witch. During the three nights he must fight for his life, as the undead woman summons all the demons from hell, including the eponymous figure. Eventually Khoma dies of fear, while the monsters are taken by surprise by the dawn and are frozen in the windows.

Bava's very first outline—a scant four pages dated September 1959, entitled "Il Vij"—featured a beginning and an epilogue set in the present, where a newlywed couple are caught by a rainstorm while on a trip in the country and take shelter inside a sinister church whose guardian tells them the story of Khoma (Chomà in the script) and the witch. Overall, the story was much closer to Gogol's tale than the finished film would be: the original model would become almost unrecognizable, as Bava himself—always the one to belittle his own work—joked. Although only Ennio De Concini and editor Mario Serandrei are featured as scriptwriters in the credits, the official papers at Rome's State Archives contain a longer list of names: the story is credited to Bava, Serandrei, De Concini, Marcello Coscia and Dino De Palma, while another paper lists also Fede Arnaud, Domenico Bernabei, Walter Bedogni, Lucia Torelli and Maria Nota!

Yet, unlike most of its contemporaries, who adopted (or pretended) bombastic literary ascendances as a decoy, just as with their English pseudonyms, in Bava's case the relationship with Gothic literature was neither instrumental nor predatory, but the result of a true sensibility towards the genre. Besides the effective or nominal models of his works—from Gogol to Tolstoy, up to his last film *La Venere d'Ille* (1978, co-directed with his son Lamberto), based on Mérimée's story—Bava's cinema would be prodigal with literary influences, and reflected the curiosity of an attentive and omnivorous reader, who in his interviews used to quote such pillars of twentieth century fantastic literature as George Oliver Onions and H. P. Lovecraft.

This is not to say *Black Sunday* was not influenced by Hammer's horror hits: the references to *Horror of Dracula* are patent throughout. Bava and De Concini reprised situations (the carriage ride), tricks (the crucifix that burns the vampire's forehead) and characters (the savant priest who helps the hero defeat the witch). However, such references are merely superficial concessions, since Bava's effort radically reinvents horror film imagery. Bava was not a movie buff: he himself admitted it in interviews, and his son Lamberto confirmed it, by describing his father as a compulsive reader. This quality is evident from his following work, filled with literary and figurative references rather than filmic ones, and devoted to carving a visual journey in itself.

Bava's cinephile touches are limited to a few classics. This is the case of Murnau's *Nosferatu*

(1922), explicitly mentioned in the scene of the coach that goes through the woods, which Bava reimagines in a striking slow-motion shot. "By showing it in slow-motion (whereas Murnau speeded it up), Bava underlines his originality when citing a pre-existing iconography," as Bava scholar Alberto Pezzotta observed, "and therefore he establishes with Murnau's classic a dialogue of equals, as only someone who is well aware of his own talent would do."[5] The *Monthly Film Bulletin* reviewer also emphasized the reminiscences of James Whale's *Frankenstein* (1931): "Javutich stomping off like Karloff's Monster through the graveyard; villagers rushing to the rescue with torches; the idyllic lake where the peasant girl watches the abduction of the doctor."[6]

Hammer's Gothic—rigorous, realistic, male-oriented—had little to do with what would be seen on Italian screens from then on. *Black Sunday* marked the entrance in the Italians' dreams of a new, powerful erotic phantasm. In the years of *La Dolce Vita* and the economical Boom, while the so-called "commedia all'italiana" was finally released from (most of) the shackles imposed by the ruling party Democrazia Cristiana in the past decade and was able to scratch at the bottom of the country's aspirations, the Gothic *filone* looked like a timeless bubble, which allowed audiences to shut themselves out of the world and time itself.

Yet the Gothic could not avoid expressing the changes in popular culture and the anxieties that underlied them. One such example was the role of women in Italian society. *Black Sunday* was released in the same year as Fellini's masterpiece and Luchino Visconti's *Rocco and His Brothers*, two films that portrayed opposite female models. *La Dolce Vita*'s most famous scene had the glamorous Anita Ekberg bathing in the Trevi fountain, while Visconti's featured a prostitute (Annie Girardot) who is raped and murdered—that is, the two extremes of the female presence in a male-dominating culture: emancipated and submissive, a tempting mirage and a poor helpless victim. In Bava's film, Barbara Steele turned out to be both: first she was tortured and burned at the stake, then she came back as an avenging seductress.

An extraordinary insight into Italian sexual mores during the period is Pier Paolo Pasolini's report *Love Meetings* (*Comizi d'amore*, 1965), in which the director interviewed common people of different ages, background and social classes, interspersing them with questions to renowned personalities of the cultural world and show business. The results provided the framework of a country divided on many axes (North/South, city/rural, working-class/middle-class) and split between bursts of willing open-mindedness, confusion and misinformation; a country undermined by repression, rooted in patriarchal traditions, prejudices and unwritten rules.

In the late 1950s and early 1960s, Italy was still a discriminatory and sexophobic nation, where even family law established the possibility for man to seek the annulment of marriage in case of his wife's sterility, and not vice versa. In such a *milieu*, virginity was a primary value for the woman just like sexual honor was for the man: "I think the woman is evangelical, angelic, just like Dante meant," was a passer-by's answer to Pasolini's question. Therefore, the blonde Ekberg and the raven-haired Steele— the first Swedish, the second British, with all that geographical origins entail in a limited and gullible male imagery that proceeds by stereotypes and elementary associations—hinted at unthought of erotic possibilities. They embodied a new idea of excess (immoral, sensual, carnal) and transgression.

The image of homegrown divas—Sophia Loren, Gina Lollobrigida, even Claudia Cardinale—was still marked by their roles as working-class women, which on the one hand made them closer to audiences, but on the other were a sort of downsizing, as they reduced their sex-symbol status to everyday life. The foreign movie star who brings havoc to the Eternal City in *La Dolce Vita* and the haughty seductive witch who takes revenge on her persecutors in *Black Sunday* gave the audiences' erotic dreams a new aura of inaccessibility. This fact granted Barbara Steele—who in the States, under contract to Fox, was forced to inactivity since she was not amenable to the reassuring physical types of that era's stars such as Sandra Dee or Debbie Reynolds, before Bava's film made her a star overseas as well[7]—a diva status, and a much greater popularity than any of the films she starred in.

Steele's apparition as Katia in *Black Sunday* is a case in point: dressed in black, standing with two wary mastiffs kept on a leash, she is an otherwordly presence that underlines an idea of inaccessibility and dominion. Asa's power is also based on the idea of control, due to the woman's irresistible sexual lure. Therefore, Kruvajan's vampirization has openly erotic undertones: the camera focuses on Asa's motionless yet pulsating body, her heaving breasts and hands crawling on the edges of the sarcophagus and twitching. It is a language of the body (absent in *I Vampiri*) which refers to sexuality, and which no man can escape—to the point that Bava chooses not to show the vampiric act, instead ending the scene on Kruvajan's POV shot as he bends to kiss the witch's lips, like in a proper love scene destined to end on a fade to black.

In Gogol's "Viy" the crux of the story was the spell of the repellent witch on the young student Khoma: it is one of the things that Bava keeps in the film, revisiting it in a very peculiar manner. Kruvajan's initial fascination before Asa's character has a distinct necrophilic feel, and preludes the man being vampirized.[8] In the final scenes, though, Asa's seductive looks prove an illusion that hides decay and horror, and it is the vision of the woman's bare chest (reduced to a rotten skeleton and horrible to look at) that has Gorobec come to his senses: corruption has lost its attractiveness.

As the lights turned back on, viewers had consumed their transgression according to a predetermined path that brought them back to the starting point: the Gothic *filone* was a basically conservative thread, as was the sword-and-sandal one. And yet, some substantial differences catch the eye. In the finale of *Hercules vs. the Giant Warriors* (*Il trionfo di Ercole*, 1964, Alberto De Martino), the eponymous hero must choose which of the two women clinging to a cliff—both with the face of his beloved Ate (Marilù Tolo)—to save. Once again, it is purity (glimpsed deep in the eyes of the woman) that guides him, bypassing the deception of the witch Pasiphae (Moira Orfei). It is a moment in all respects similar to the ending of Bava's film. Whereas in De Martino's picture Hercules' choice is firm and clear-cut, since the hero is fearless and unblemished, in *Black Sunday* the young male's weakness, his ambiguity and indecision make him falter.

Besides its violent and erotic content, *Black Sunday* displayed a striking conception of the Fantastic. To Bava, this implies the arbitrary breaking of rules: not so much an admission that, if there are rules, they do not belong to the logic of filmic representation, but, more mischievously, the conclusion that it is not the film-maker's obligation to respect them. As he would do in his subsequent efforts, Bava was apparently accepting genre conventions while at the same time more or less subtly subverting them when the audience least expected it. This made him ahead of many of his contemporaries, since it inferred a conception of "reality" ("one of the few words that mean nothing without quotes," as Nabokov observed) which was no longer the same that generated the majority of contemporary horror (and Gothic) cinema, borrowed from the nineteenth century tradition.

This is especially true for spatial coordinates. Castle Vajda, the inn, the cemetery and the crypt where Asa's body is found are part of a microcosm whose inner distances are constantly changing, stretching or contracting depending on who is traveling along. It is a germ of an idea that, consciously or not, goes beyond the hesitation (or rather, the *impasse*) as described by Tzvetan Todorov as the core of the Fantastic. Similarly, as in Gogol's story—with the witch's metamorphosis taking place in an unreal dimension where night seemed to give way to the day: "Then he beheld how, instead of the moon, a strange sun shone there"—Katia's first appearance in the ruins is characterized by a crepuscular light, unlike that of the surrounding environments.

Black Sunday's world is constantly hanging in the balance between illusion and reality—a quality emphasized by Bava's use of the landscape and its relation to the characters. Human feelings—anxiety, fear, uncertainty, hatred, love—are immediately synthesized by the natural context in which they express themselves, and the same goes for human types. Katia's first apparition occurs amid the ruins of an old monastery immersed in the greenery: an iconic Gothic moment if ever there was one. Here, the scenery (ruins as an uncanny effigy are a *tòpos* since *The Castle of Otranto*) is provided with a number of functions: first, it symbolically synthesizes the idea of a gloomy past whose burden oppresses the young woman; furthermore, it suggests a palpable sense of decadence; lastly, it gives the black-clad female figure a timeless quality, so much so that at first the viewer believes the woman to be the revived witch Asa. When the coach carrying Gorobec and Kruvajan moves on after the stop near the crypt and Gorobec's encounter with Katia, the camera pans in the opposite direction: again, and unexpectedly, withered branches pop up in the frame, underlining the proximity and the patency of two worlds—the menacing and malevolent forest and the fairytale-like and enchanted one where the princess belongs—which echo the duality at the film's core.

It is within and from such moments that the Italian Gothic film developed its own mythology and drew its persuasive force, creating an eminently visual imagery by reworking "the iconographic legacy of Italian art and its inclination to recreate gloomy and dreamlike scenarios."[9] Echoes of the turbulent, stormy landscapes painted by Salvator Rosa can be found in *Black Sunday*'s shadowy initial scenes, while the aforementioned monastery ruins—a set which Bava would later reuse in *The Wurdalak*—convey suggestions worthy of another celebrated eighteenth century artist, Giovan Battista Piranesi. Later on, when the ambiguity over her character has dissolved, Katia is associated to the graceful quiet of a marble fountain in her palace's garden; similarly, after her father's death, the sun's rays that penetrate into her room, revealing her sleeping figure, enhance the young woman's innocent sensuality.

A similar discourse can be made for the interiors. *Black Sunday*'s Castle Vajda is characterized by two different types of spaces: visible

Princess Katia Vajda (Barbara Steele), Asa's descendant, appears amid the monastery ruins in *Black Sunday*: an otherwordly presence that underlines an idea of inaccessibility and dominion (courtesy Libreria Eleste).

(accessible) and invisible (secret). The castle contains a hidden double, concealed and kept under an illusory surface and ready to manifest itself again: beneath Javutich's portrait, a maze of corridors and tunnels lead to the crypt where Asa's tomb is situated. It is yet another reference to one of the film's main themes: the present is continually menaced by a past that hangs and waits, ready to take back what belongs to it. This is what happens in one of *Black Sunday*'s most memorable moments: a malevolent, invisible presence emerges from the secret passageway behind the fireplace—the symbolic center of family life—and makes its way through the castle corridors, knocking over chairs and armors in its unstoppable pace.

With its grim and eerie opening—originally to be set in an Inquisition's dungeon, according to the English language script of the film deposited at Rome's CSC library—*Black Sunday* evokes a fear of past times which is typical of Gothic literature, by reworking the awe of the aristocracy which was the basis of the legends on vampires. Through Asa, Bava synthesizes one of the Gothic's fundamental themes: the fear of a "return of the past." Time becomes an obsessive presence, and produces a sense of vertigo and inevitability: just as the barriers between life and death become blurred, the same happens between the past and the present. The returning past takes the form of a curse launched centuries earlier, whose oppressive legacy has an impact on the present.

Asa's curse brings to the fore the image of a barbaric past, which reconnects to the original meaning of the term "Gothic": such an issue was already to be found in the adventure films set in the Middle Ages that were being made in Cinecittà during the 1940s and 1950s, but it reached its peak with Bava's film. Asa and Javutich are noble, and are judged and punished by their peers, yet the memory of their deeds terrifies the common people generations later.

Black Sunday—one of the very few Italian Gothic horror films that features the intervention of a mob of angry townsfolk assaulting the princes' manor to eradicate the curse—was also among the few to capture a sense of belonging to a caste that goes beyond appearances. As An-

drew Mangravite pointed out, "When Prince Javutich of *Black Sunday* croons sadly to his beloved, the moribund princess Asa of the house of Vajda, "We'll live once more as we used to," Bava takes us beyond the nail-scarred faces and cob-webbed hair to a center of true sorrow: a longing for past grandeur and lost love. Asa and Javutich represent the great (and evil) days of Vajda as much as Katia, her hunt-loving brother Konstantin, and her moody father, the "reigning" Prince Vajda, represent its inept, dysfunctional present."[10]

A present of decadence, it must be added, crushed by the weight of memory.

Black Sunday develops another staple element of the genre: the notion of the double, or *doppelgänger*, as expressed by the same actress playing both the virginal heroine and the evil vampire witch. According to Freud, the double also embodies "all the possibilities which, had they been realized, might have shaped our destiny, and to which our imagination still clings, all the strivings of the ego that were frustrated by adverse circumstances, all the suppressed acts of volition that fostered the illusion of free will."[11] Such a "return of the repressed" has its most explicit example in the relationship between Asa and Katia, where the ancestress takes care of her descendant's unspoken inclinations, before taking possession of her identity and replacing her.

The double is associated to a portrait which visually makes this duality clear. Such an element recalls not only the romantic tradition, but also 1940s *film noir* melodramas such as *Laura* (1944, Otto Preminger) and *The Woman in the Window* (1944, Fritz Lang): such portraits are a junction point between the living and the dead, and the means by which the past tries to overwhelm the present and erase it. *Black Sunday* even doubles this visual motif, as Bava juxtaposes Asa's portrait in the salon of Castle Vajda (where it stands near Javutich's portrait) with another painting, kept in the manor's hidden wing, which portrays Asa as a temptress Eve, naked and surrounded by symbols of seduction. It is a wonderful intuition, which not only hints at the theme of female dichotomy that is at the genre's core, but also at an idea of a "hidden" self: the castle's viscera become an embodiment of the subconscious—here, of Katia's pulsions—and its depths.

Faith as a saving force is represented in the film by the crucifix—not Catholic but Orthodox, and paired with a sacred icon—as an instrument of prevention and revelation: it can stop the vampire and reveal her identity when placed on her forehead. What is more, the young hero is helped by a senior priest as a spiritual guide. Overall, religion is a rather tepid presence in *Black Sunday*, and it is most likely that Bava and his co-scriptwriters chose not to meddle with such a topic, in a time when even innocuous references to politics and religion were cut by the censors, filmmakers such as Fellini and especially Pasolini were facing a lot of trouble, and the Vatican was at the forefront in the battle against so-called "immoral" films.

Yet the Catholic mentality is clearly present throughout, albeit declined in a symbolic way. The most disturbing thing in *Black Sunday* is not so much the promise of hell and eternal damnation, as the idea of a seductress who returns from the grave, embodying the lure and the nightmare of a passion that never dies. The witches of Italian cinema would not inspire fear as emissaries of the devil (as in Roger Corman's *The Undead*, 1957) but for the transgression that they embodied, and their "eternal return" would be perceived mainly in a sexual key. Therefore, their inevitable reappearance following their torture and death was not imbibed with the Puritan sense of sin and the historical memory of the burnings of Salem. Rather, it would be the embodiment of a desire that never dies, because once satisfied it is reborn into new objects—like the myth of an endlessly repeatable orgasm which brings with it an equally irrepressible sense of guilt.

It has been written that Italian Gothic was about "the horror of the face [...] as a mask and mirror of the body"[12] and not (yet) about the horror of the body, as post–1968 horror movies would be: the emphasis on the transience of life and the liability of pleasures and beauty reveal the Catholic matrix of a nation (and a cinema) tempted by sin and its representation, but conscious of the price that must be paid for it. The

wrinkles and age spots that appear on the skin of Bava's (and Freda's) wicked heroines are the equivalent of those that ply the portrait of Dorian Gray, and represent the retaliation for a dissolute life. Beauty and sexuality always carry a price to pay. In Italian Gothic, it is the face that suffers the retaliation of time and justice: scarred, pierced, disfigured, worn by pestilential sores and boils. As he did in *I Vampiri*, Bava's camera fascinatedly captures the disintegration of perfection in the ending of *Black Sunday*, with no editing cuts and merely by means of make-up and light tricks, just as it observed the regeneration of beauty, in the extraordinary sequence of Asa's resurrection (which Antonio Margheriti reprised almost verbatim in *The Long Hair of Death*).

If the genre in which he worked prevented him from *auteur* temptations, Bava's predilection for special effects as sleight-of-hand and cinema as a source of wonder showed his affinity with Jean Cocteau. The Sanremese filmmaker must have loved the dreamlike enchanted world created by d.o.p. Henri Alekan for *Beauty and the Beast* (*La Belle et la bête*, 1946), as he took inspiration from it on a number of occasions. For one thing, in *Black Sunday* Bava reworked the scene in Cocteau' film where an invisible presence greets and guides visitors, with the lantern hanging in the air that leads Kruvajan to the crypt. His later films also featured images and scenes inspired by Cocteau: the magic mirror that acts as an interface to other worlds (*Hercules in the Haunted World*), Josette Day gliding forward apparently without touching the ground in the corridors of the castle ("The Drop of Water," in 1963's *Black Sabbath*), the enchanted manor with a corridor of candlesticks clasped by human hands (*Kill, Baby...Kill!*, 1966).

Instead of pointing to the wonder and enchantment in itself, though, Bava used these effects mostly for fright purposes. The director's renowned special tricks aimed at similar pragmatic ends: to carry out their task—to scare the audience—in the most efficient manner possible. However, Bava was also able to consciously inject Surrealist elements in the Gothic imagery, by way of his living statues and dummies (as in "The Drop of Water"), the continuous rebound between living and inanimate matter (such as in *Lisa and the Devil*, 1972) and the use of insignificant objects in a scary manner (as in *Shock*, 1977). Art portrays horror, amplifying it and sometimes exploring its inner fascination, but to Bava it was also the contrary: he used horror to imitate art, as in the image of Asa's eyeless face in the tomb, motionless as an exquisite Venetian porcelain mask—a reminiscence of E.T.A. Hoffmann's uncanny dolls and at the same time a Surrealist image worthy of the living statues in Jean Cocteau's *The Blood of a Poet* (*Le Sang d'un poète*, 1930).

Stylistically, for *Black Sunday* Bava had at his disposal a more reasonable array of resources compared to the rest of his career. Shooting started in June 1960, and lasted seven weeks. In accordance with production manager Massimo De Rita, one week was added to the shooting schedule, so that Bava could enhance the look of the film by employing the dolly in many shots and working carefully on frame composition. Bava was also the d.o.p., and took particular care in the b&w cinematography, "with the dual purpose of creating a tense and visionary atmosphere [...] and to mask the few set pieces that were being used."[13]

The debuting director chose to adopt the sequence shot as a tool to convey the Fantastic element and generate anxiety: examples of this tactic are the emerging of the invisible presence from behind the fireplace and along the corridors of the castle, and the long tracking shot backwards that precedes the innkeeper's daughter's path from the inn to the stable. In the latter shot, the camera is placed almost at ground level so as to frame the little girl from bottom to top, thus emphasizing her loneliness in the surrounding environment and exacerbating the passage from a familiar dimension to a menacing one, through the gradual disappearance of the inn behind her. Similarly, a 360 degree panoramic shot (like the one that reveals the crypt for the first time to its visitors) is employed to sharpen a feeling of threat. The camera itself becomes a character, who is able to see more (or better) than the others and steer their view, as in the scene in the barn, where a traveling shot

shows the graveyard from which Javutich is about to rise, framed through a window.

On *Black Sunday* Bava was rather moderate in his use of the zoom, which would reach a pinnacle in his 1970s films, starting with *5 Dolls for an August Moon* (*5 bambole per la luna d'agosto*, 1970). Even though the zoom serves to bring things closer to the eye, in his subsequent works Bava often paired it to a focus/out-of-focus transition—that is, a pulsion towards the irrational, the oneiric, the abstract. Here, however, the zoom works exclusively as an instrument to heighten the horror, as in Javutich's sudden apparition in Vajda's room. Riccardo Freda praised *Black Sunday*, but later on he often accused Bava of over-using the zoom. "He employed it so much to cause surprise as to insist on a detail, clumsily. Even worse, the use of a zoom instead of a traveling produces an offset of perspective and a loss of illumination."[14] Such a misunderstanding is at the core of the difference between Freda—a filmmaker who firmly stuck to a classical conception of cinema—and Bava, who loved to disrupt and innovate forms, and reach through them the very heart of the Fantastic.

Black Sunday's commercial success was rather limited in Italy, even though it made Steele a popular name. Its popularity was best summed up by a comic sketch of a 1962 anthology film, Camillo Mastrocinque's *I motorizzati* (also produced by Jolly Film) where Ugo Tognazzi plays an overtly impressionable horror movie fan who is terrified by Bava's film, and is then involved in a tragicomic adventure when he finds an apparently dead body in the back seat of his car.[15] Predictably, Italian critics ravaged *Black Sunday*, although some of them pointed out the virtuoso cinematography, whereas the French (such as Fereydoun Hoveida on the prestigious *Cahiers du cinéma*) immediately treated it as a *film d'auteur*, praising the camera's extreme mobility and the way Bava's visual style created a fantastic, even poetic dimension.[16]

Picked up by American International Pictures for U.S. distribution, *Black Sunday* underwent a few notable changes: Roberto Nicolosi's ominous score was replaced with a more ordinary one by Les Baxter—a sign of a less ortho-

U.S. poster for *Black Sunday*: picked up for distribution in 1961 by American International Pictures, the film became AIP's most profitable picture to date as a distributor (Libreria Eleste).

dox approach to the subject matter on the part of the Italians, which led to Sergio Leone's revolutionary use of film score. Released in 1961, it was a hit in the United States, becoming AIP's most profitable picture to date as a distributor: its success paved the way for more Italian Gothic horror to reach the States, and allowed Bava (and Galatea) to continue with their commercial partnership. In the United Kingdom, however, the film was banned until 1968, when it was released in a widely truncated version as *Revenge of the Vampire* (the uncut version surfaced only in 1992).

Gogol's tale was adapted for the screen in 1967 with Konstantin Yershow and Georgi Kropachyov's (*Viy*, a.k.a. *Spirit of Evil*), co-written by the great fantasy director Aleksandr Ptushko, and later in 1990 (*Sveto mesto*, by Djordje Kadijevic). In 1989 Lamberto Bava directed the made-for-TV *La maschera del demonio*, not so much a remake of his father's film

as a reworking of Gogol's story in a contemporary context.[17]

Notes

1. Alberto Pezzotta, "La cosa in sé. Un percorso nei primi e negli ultimi film," in Stefania Parigi and Alberto Pezzotta, eds., *Il lungo respiro di Brunello Rondi* (Rieti: Edizioni Sabinae, 2010), p. 42.

2. Carol Jenks, "The Other Face of Death: Barbara Steele, 'Black Sunday' and the Beginnings of the Italian Horror Film," quoted in Leon Hunt, "A (Sadistic) Night at the Opera," in Ken Gelder, ed., *The Horror Reader* (New York: Routledge, 2000), p. 325.

3. Alain Silver and James Ursini, "Mario Bava: the Illusion of Reality," in Alain Silver and James Ursini, eds., *Horror Film Reader* (New York: Limelight, 2000), p. 95

4. From 1962 onwards, with the new law on film censorship, the V.M.16 rating (forbidden to viewers under 16 years old) was replaced with two different ratings: V.M.14 and V.M.18 (respectively, forbidden to viewers under 14 or 18 years old).

5. Alberto Pezzotta, *Mario Bava* (Milan: Il Castoro, 1995, 2013), p. 41.

6. TM, "The Mask of Satan (Revenge of the Vampire)," *Monthly Film Bulletin* 408, January 1968, p. 100.

7. See David J. Hogan, *Dark Romance: Sexuality in*

the *Horror Film* (Jefferson NC: McFarland, 1997), pp. 164–165. Working with Steele was not easy, according to Bava. On the other hand, the actress recalled, "Lord alone knows I was difficult enough. I didn't like my fangs—I had them changed three times. I loathed my wig—I changed that four times. I couldn't understand Italian. I certainly didn't want to allow them to tear open my dress and expose my breasts, so they got a double that I didn't like at all, so I ended up doing it myself—drunk, barely over eighteen, embarrassed and not very easy to be around." Mark Thomas McGee, *Faster and Furiouser: The Revised and Fattened Fable of American International Pictures* (Jefferson, NC: McFarland, 1996), p. 155.

8. According to Italian critic Francesco Di Chiara, "In films of the period, a love forbidden by the age difference with necrophiliac and adulterous shades—the same would happen with other prohibited practices that will appear in later films—seems to exist only in a supernatural dimension, that of vampirism." As Di Chiara pointed out, the teratomorphic nature of Asa's sexuality is made explicit by the representation of her disfigured face and fleshless body "which associate her seductive power to necrophilia." Di Chiara, *I tre volti della paura*, pp. 60–76.

9. Paniceres, *El gotico italiano*, p. 103.

10. Andrew Mangravite, "Once Upon a Time in the Crypt," *Film Comment* 29, January 1993, p. 50.

11. Sigmund Freud, "The Uncanny," in Sigmund Freud, *Writings on Art and Literature* (Redwood City, CA: Stanford University Press, 1997), p. 143.

12. Pezzotta, "Doppi di noi stessi," p. 26.

13. Simone Venturini, *Galatea Spa (1952–1965): storia di una casa di produzione cinematografica* (Rome: Associazione italiana per le ricerche di storia del cinema, 2001), p. 138.

14. Poindron, *Riccardo Freda*, pp. 280–281.

15. In the scene where Tognazzi leaves the vehicle out of town and goes looking for a place to call the police, the actor is preceded by a tracking shot backwards, from the bottom, similar to the scene in *Black Sunday* where the innkeeper's daughter ventures into the barn. A sign, perhaps, of a sincere tribute to Bava's technique that goes beyond the film's facetious context.

16. Fereydoun Hoveida, "Les grimaces du démon," *Cahiers du cinéma* 119, 1961.

17. The 1989 version of *La maschera del demonio* was produced by Reteitalia and conceived as the first in a series of films about witches entitled "Sabbath." Other films originally produced for the series—which saw the participation of Spain, France and Germany—were *La luna negra* (1989, Pedro Olea) and *Anna Goldin, The Last Witch* (*Anna Göldin, letzte Hexe*, 1989, Gertrud Pinkus). Lamberto Bava's remake was released in the United States as *Demons 5: The Devil's Veil*, even though it had no connection at all with the director's own *Demons* films.

Mill of the Stone Women (Il mulino delle donne di pietra)

D: Giorgio Ferroni. *S:* Remigio Del Grosso, "from the short story of the same name in *Flemish Tales* by Pieter Van Weigen"; *SC:* Remigio Del Grosso, Ugo Liberatore, Giorgio Stegani, Giorgio Ferroni; *DOP:*

Pier Ludovico Pavoni (Eastmancolor); *M:* Carlo Innocenzi; *E:* Antonietta Zita; *PD:* Arrigo Equini; *SD:* Carlo Gentili; *AD:* Giuliano Betti; *2ndAD:* Piero Braccialini; *C:* Angelo Lotti; *AC:* Renato Mascagni; *SO:* Umberto Picistrelli; *MU:* Franco Palombi. [*U.S. version: executive supervisor:* Hugo Grimaldi; *script:* John Davis Hart; *DubD:* Richard McNamara; *French version: D:* Louis Sauvat]. *Cast:* Pierre Brice (Hans von Arnim), Scilla Gabel (Elfie Wahl), Dany Carrel [Yvonne Chazelles du Chaxel] (Liselotte Kornheim), Marco Guglielmi (Ralf), Liana Orfei (Annelore), Herbert Boehme [Herbert A. E. Böhme] (Gregorius Wahl), Wolfgang Preiss (Dr. Loren Bohlem), Olga Solbelli (Selma), Alberto Archetti (Conrad). *PROD:* Vanguard Films (Rome), C.E.C.—Comptoir D'Expansion Cinématographique (Paris); *EP:* Giorgio Venturini [*U.S. version:* Riley Jackson, Robert Patrick; *French version:* Charles Kornel]; *PM:* Giampaolo Bigazzi [*French version:* Lucien Vittet]; *PS:* Piero Ghione, Tommaso Sagone. *Country:* Italy/France. Filmed at Cinecittà Studios. *Running time:* 100 min. (m. 2608); Visa n: 32613 (08.20.1960); *Rating:* V.M.16; *Release dates:* 08.30.1960 (Italy); 01.23.1963 (U.S.A.). *Distribution:* C.D.C. (Italy); Parade Releasing Organization (U.S.A.); *Domestic gross:* 164,000,000 lire. *Also known as: Horror of the Stone Women, The Horrible Mill Women* (U.S.A.), *Le Moulin des supplices* (France, 09.05.1962), *Drops of Blood* (U.K.), *Die Mühle der versteinerten Frauen* (West Germany, 03.23.1962), *El molino de las mujeres de piedra* (Spain), *Doktor Skräck och de förstenade kvinnorna. Home video:* Mondo Macabro (DVD—US), Sinister Film (DVD, Italy), Neo Publishing (DVD, France)

Entrusted with the task of collecting data for a study on Dutch folk art, the young art student Hans von Arnim makes the acquaintance of Wahl, a well-known sculptor and the owner of a famous eighteenth century windmill: inside the mill, Wahl is keeping a gigantic carillon where statues of famous heroines of the past perform a sort of macabre dance. In Wahl's house, Hans meets Elfie, the sculptor's beautiful daughter, who seduces him. One night, while they are together, Elfie apparently dies. Yet, when Hans returns to the mill, everything seems to be normal. After another art student, Liselotte, disappears, Hans and his friend Ralf discover that the statues of the "Mill of the Stone Women" are actually dead women's bodies that Wahl and his assistant Bohlem have killed to keep Elfie (who suffers from an incurable disease) alive with their blood...

The third horror film in a row to be released in Italy in August 1960 after *Black Sunday* and *Atom Age Vampire*, Giorgio Ferroni's *Mill of the Stone Women* is closer to the former, production-wise—that is, an attempt at making a dignified Gothic film with a rather respectable budget (hence the intervention of a French co-producer). The box-office result would be rather disappointing in its home country, but the film proved to be a good success abroad, where it was distributed by Galatea.

Ferroni's film marked the first in a series of typical occurrences in Italian Gothic: even though the credits claimed the script was based on a short story included in the book *Flemish Tales* by a "Pieter Van Weigen," there is no book with such a title, nor a Flemish author by that name, for that matter. A sign of discomfort for being located at the periphery of the empire? Or a bait for the more gullible viewers? According to some critics, the phony literary origin is "a semantic element, although located outside of the text and announced in the threshold of the opening credits, which was considered inevitable [...]: to Italian producers such an origin, albeit fictitious, from a foreign and past text was the warranty of an exoticism that is supposed to attract viewers just as much as the English pseudonyms of the crew members."[1] For distributors, on the other hand, it provided a point of attraction for channeling Gothic films in the wake of Corman's Poe adaptations.

Such a tendency towards counterfeit, however, provided a curious point of contact with the literary tradition: the founder of the Gothic novel, *The Castle of Otranto*, was introduced as a translation of an ancient Italian manuscript—a gimmick destined to become a *tòpos* of the genre. What really matters is the artificiality, the literary source flaunted so as to exhibit illustrious origins and give the film an aura of perceived nobility that set it above contemporary genre products—as was also the case with Bava's *Black Sabbath*.

However, the main inspirations behind such pseudo-literary smoke screen are evident, starting with Dreyer's *Vampyr*. Ferroni celebrated the Danish filmmaker's masterpiece by reworking its themes, suggestions and visual imagery, beginning with the man who rings the bell on the pier where the boat stops in the opening scene. What is more, the titular mill, with its impressive gears in evidence, recalls the one where the vampire's accomplice ends up buried under the flour in Dreyer's film. On the other hand, the scene where Hans' wristband first appears covered in blood and later on immaculate refers to the transfusion sequence in which David Gray hallucinates about the blood that he sees dripping onto his arm.

Other patent influences are Hammer films—the eighteenth century setting, the use of color, the sets (the mad doctor's machinery is patently inspired by Hammer's pseudo-scientific devices, with pumps rising and lowering, level indicators that oscillate crazily and crimson blood flowing in tubes)—and especially *House of Wax* (1953, André De Toth). The latter model is evident in the theme of the titular "stone women," the scenographic display of mannequins looking like they belong in the wax museum in De Toth's film, and the character of Wahl, the mad sculptor who shapes dead bodies as if they were wax statues.

However, the script significantly splits the character of the mad doctor in two: Wolfgang Preiss—who would soon play the eponymous evil genius in Fritz Lang's *The Thousand Eyes of Dr. Mabuse* (*Die 1000 Augen des Dr. Mabuse*, 1960) as well as its follow-ups—is a mere executioner as Wahl's right-hand man Bohlem, who performs blood transfusions on the victims. Which brings us to the film's core: the center of evil, the real element of danger and perturbation is neither the mad sculptor nor his assistant, but the woman whom they serve and protect, and whose life and beauty they try to maintain by any means necessary—another main reference is, obviously, *Eyes Without a Face*. And such a woman is less a victim than a (partially unwilling) source of death and destruction: Wahl's daughter Elfie (Scilla Gabel).

Whereas male vampires showed up in Italian horror films with the customary cape and fangs, things went differently with their female counterparts. That is the case with Elfie, who receives a new artificial youth, obtained through the blood of young women—not always virgins as Countess Bathory demanded, yet suitable to the task. Instead of fangs, blood transfusions do the trick, and work as a horrific element as well as a suggestive and morbid one.

United States poster for *Mill of the Stone Women*.

Mill of the Stone Women draws on the dichotomy between the damsel-in-distress (passive, good, moderately attractive) and the *femme fatale* (luscious and lustful, dangerous, provocative). The raven-haired, aggressively beautiful Elfie is juxtaposed with the dull art student Liselotte (Dany Carrel), who has been in love with the hero Hans (Pierre Brice) since forever. Hans too falls for Liselotte—but only after he has enjoyed the favors of the beautiful Elfie. It is exactly the easiness of seduction that eventually turns him away from the woman. "I loved no one but you ... even if there were others before, who were able to take advantage of my solitude here, and also of my inexperience," Elfie admits, as Ferroni's camera frames Hans from behind, without showing his reaction. Then the woman steps back as the camera moves forward, isolating her in the shot and therefore separating Elfie from her beloved, once and for all. It is an exquisite directorial moment, one of many in Ferroni's elegant film, and one that implicitly underlines a moral male-oriented judgment: better a modest life companion than a passionate lover who could not even offer her virginity.

Yet, in the typical duality of Italian horror films of the period, there is no doubt as to which of the two women is the real focus of attraction for both the director and the audience. At first barely glimpsed by Hans behind a curtain, like an actress who spies on the audience just before her entry on stage, Elfie then shows up from atop a spiral staircase—a dominating figure, holding a greyhound on a leash and a rose in her hand. An appearance nearly as memorable as Barbara Steele's in *Black Sunday*, which on one hand certifies the character's aristocratic grace, and on the other underlines her passion.

Elfie is an evolution of Duchess Du Grand, with whom she has in common a life sustained artificially through someone else's blood. But she is also a step back from the titanically powerful Asa. The pale undead seductress of *Mill of the Stone Women* acts according to the symbolic code of the romantic heroine (note the red rose she leaves every morning on her lover's desk) and adopts an attitude of passive acquiescence in the act of seduction: she gives Hans appointment in her bedroom and welcomes him from her bed. When eventually the man confesses he does not love her, she replies angrily: "And what does that matter? As long as you let me love you, as long as I can always be at your side! Please take me away, far away from here—I would go with you wherever you'd like!" thus implicitly acknowledging the need to find a man who sets her free from enclosure, just like Marina di Malombra (Isa Miranda)

dreamt in Mario Soldati's *Malombra*. Passion is associated with a feverish state, which makes her delirious and submissive at the same time. Elfie moves through the film with the same passivity, seducing men and letting them take her by inertia; similarly, when she finds a girl who is dying for her during a blood transfusion, she does nothing to save the victim from her fate. Curiously enough, it is Dany Carrel (top-billed in the French version) who provides the film's required nude scene, briefly uncovering her breast in a blink-and-you'll-miss-it moment.

Several scholars have underlined the incestuous implications in the film, which nevertheless seem quite lame to this writer. Sure, Wahl is so bound to his daughter Elfie that he sacrifices young women to keep her alive, and gets rid of Bohlem, who asked him to marry his daughter, as if he was a rival; in the end, we even see him blame the whole world for the disgrace that befell the girl. Nevertheless, Wahl is an asexual character, more intent on satisfying his aesthetic taste than prone to lewd impulses when he models and shapes the arms of a voluptuous clay bust. *Black Sunday*, in this sense, featured a much more disturbing, subterranean incestuous vein, such as the scene where Katia's father, revived as a living dead, attacks his daughter who was watching the coffin.

The very first Italian horror film in color, *Mill of the Stone Women* looks no less than luscious. Pier Ludovico Pavoni's outstanding Eastmancolor cinematography recreates Hammer's rich palettes as well as the ethereal atmosphere of Powell and Pressburger's classics, and perfectly fits in with Ferroni's academic and elegant style, which—unlike his contemporaries— rarely, if ever, contemplates abrupt expressive bursts. Color, in *Mill of the Stone Women*, has an essentially decorative function, rather than a dramatic one (such as in Freda's films, for instance). It has been written that Ferroni's work looks more pictorial than cinematic: frame compositions follow an aestheticizing criterion which camera movements try to disturb as little as possible, and images look like paintings— and at times they refer to them. See, for instance, the shot which depicts Elfie in her coffin, surrounded by flowers, a reference to John

Everett Millais' celebrated Pre-Raphaelite painting *Ophelia*.

To emphasize suspense or plot twists, Ferroni systematically adopts short and sudden tracking shots onwards, so as to isolate a detail in close-up, whether it be a necklace dangling from a statue's hand which later disappears, or a half-open door that hides a shocking truth. The effect—aesthetically exquisite—recalls De Toth's use of 3-D in *House of Wax*, and provides a classical, Cartesian conception of space. Every set-piece is immediately revealed to the viewer: the huge gears driven by the windmill's blades, which in turn set in motion the film's clockwork with its display of female mannequins; Wahl's study; the cemetery crypt where Hans thinks he has seen Elfie's lifeless body. Freda, and especially Bava, will go for a quite different, and often though-provoking rendition of the diegetic space in their subsequent works.

The role of sound is particularly significant, as with the carillon which accompanies the macabre parade of the "stone women" mechanism, or the bell that rhythmically signals the timing for blood transfusions: the use of the carillon as a sound *leitmotif* to express horror would soon become a recurring element in Italian Horror (and in other genres as well: see Sergio Leone's Westerns).

However, compared to other Italian horror films of the period, *Mill of the Stone Women* still looks rather timid in its exploring of shock tactics: a full hour passes by before Ferroni sets up a hallucinatory sequence for Hans to lose his grip on reality. However, right from the outset one can detect an attention for the macabre, the funereal, the repellent, suggesting an idea of decay that reflects what lies beneath the seductive features of the enchanting Elfie. The grim self-satisfaction that accompanies the portrayal of the macabre responds to the "accentuation of attractions"[1] that is one of Italian Gothic's main assets. Example? A few minutes into the film, Ferroni ends an elegant sideways tracking shot in Wahl's workshop on the naked torso of a hanged female mannequin, whose most evident feature is its realistically exposed tongue; what is more, the windmill is filled with casts of heads and hands scattered or hung on walls.

Men and mannequins, animated and inanimated objects: the dichotomy that will characterize some of the genre's most extraordinary examples is already in essence in Ferroni's film.[2]

Ferroni (1908–1981) was a veteran of the Italian film industry, who had started in the early 1930s making documentaries for Istituto LUCE. Over the years he worked on both documentaries and fiction films, helming such remarkable efforts as the extraordinary post–World War II film *noir Tombolo* (*Tombolo paradiso nero*, 1948) and the documentary *Vertigine bianca* (1957). His following output—starting with *The Bacchantes* (*Le baccanti*, 1961), a thinking man's sword-and-sandal epic based on Euripides' play—would fall into the realms of genre cinema, often with accomplished results.

Ferroni would return to the horror genre with 1972's *The Night of the Devils*, an impressive remake of Mario Bava's "The Wurdalak" set in modern-day Slovenia.

Notes

1. Pitassio, "L'orribile segreto dell'horror italiano," p. 34.
2. It must be noted that the American version—supervised by Hugo Grimaldi and adapted by John Davis Hart—adds a bombastic, overtly didactic voice-over ("Trouble began with a woman" is the opening line) which detracts from the film's rarefied atmosphere.

My Friend, Dr. Jekyll (*Il mio amico Jekyll*)

D: Marino Girolami. *S* and *SC*: Giulio Scarnicci, Renzo Tarabusi, Carlo Veo, Marino Girolami; *DOP*: Luciano Trasatti (B&W, Ferrania C/7); *M*: Alessandro Derevitzky [Alexandre Derevitsky], conducted by the author (Ed. Firmamento); *E*: Franco Fraticelli; *PD*: Saverio D'Eugenio; *SD*: Luigi Gervasi; *CO*: Giulietta Deriu; *AD*: Romolo Girolami; *C*: Franco Villa; *SO*: Pietro Ortolani, Bruno Moreal; *MU*: Duilio Scarozza; *Hair*: Adriana Cassini; *SS*: Marisa Merci. *Cast*: Ugo Tognazzi (Giacinto Floria), Raimondo Vianello (Prof. Fabius), Abbe Lane (Mafalda De Matteis), Hélène Chanel (Rossana), Carlo Croccolo (Arguzio), Linda Sini (Adelaide), Luigi Pavese (Colonel Rolando), Anna Campori (Clarissa De Matteis), Tina Gloriani (Irma De Sanginto), Elena Fontana (Loredana), Maria Fiè (Mara), Angela Portaluri (Fanny), Dori Dorika (Yvonne Trelati Norcia), Ivana Gilli (Margot), Mimmo Poli (Rupio), Silvio Bagolini (German member of the "young girl's relief" committee), Arturo Bragaglia (Perimetri), Pina

Gallini (surveillant at the finishing school), Leopoldo Valentini (Spanish committee member), Pasquale De Filippo (French committee member), Mirco Testi (Italian committee member), Francesco Tensi (English committee member), Marcello Bonini Olas (second at duel), Enzo Maggio (Night club waiter). *PROD*: Marino Girolami for M.G. Cinematografica, CEI-Incom; *PM*: Pio Angeletti, Jacopo Comin; *PS*: Umberto Santoni, Marino Vaccà; *PSe*: Adriano De Micheli. *Country*: Italy. Filmed at Incir-De Paolis Studios (Rome). *Running time*: 90 min. (m. 2700); Visa n: 31789 (04.28.1960); *Rating*: V.M.16; *Release dates*: 08.11.1960 (Italy); 03.1965 (U.S.A.). *Distribution*: Incei Film (Italy); Union Film Distributors (U.S.A.); *Domestic gross*: 157,000,000 lire. *Also known as*: My Pal Dr. Jekyll (U.S.A.), Casanova Jekill (Spain). *Home video*: none.

Giacinto Floria, the tutor in an Institute of Rehabilitation for ex-prostitutes, is kidnapped every night by Professor Fabius, who is able to transfer his mind into Floria's body, turning him into a sadistic sex maniac. A detective on the case discovers the truth, and releases Floria from Fabius' influence. Floria will then be able to marry his fiancée Mafalda, while the Professor's mind ends up in a monkey in the zoo.

A further clue to the way the Gothic infiltrated into Italian cinema is Marino Girolami's *My Friend, Dr. Jekyll*, a hit-and-miss parody where Stevenson's juxtaposition between good and evil, reason and instinct, is transposed into early twentieth century Italy. It was a scenery of respectability, in a period where the country was governed by a centrist coalition with Giovanni Giolitti as Prime Minister, and Girolami's film replaced the typical Victorian air of repression with a similar facade of bourgeois conformism that hid strong sexual impulses—as evident right from the opening scene, where a luxurious carriage stops at night in a park populated by prostitutes.

Despite the title, there is no Jekyll in sight, although the story revolves around a case of split personality. As played by Ugo Tognazzi—soon to become Marco Ferreri's favorite actor in a series of strikingly vitriolic grotesque comedies, starting with 1963's *The Conjugal Bed* (*Una storia moderna: l'ape regina*)—the story's protagonist Giacinto Floria becomes the unlikely instrument to unveil the repression of the bourgeois society he belongs in. An upright, naive professor who teaches manners to former

prostitutes in an Institute of Rehabilitation—"Remember: there is nothing more indecent than a pair of naked female legs" he tells his class of students, whose legs are all prominently in display—Floria becomes the guinea pig of the lascivious Professor Fabius (Raimondo Vianello, then Tognazzi's comic partner in the duo's popular TV sketches) and his ugly servant Rupio (the unmistakable character actor Mimmo Poli, who ends up "feminized" in one amusing bit). Mildly amusing lewd consequences arise, as the asexual Floria becomes a sex fiend under Fabius' mental control, letting his "primal impulses" go.

Despite the actors' verve, however, *My Friend, Dr. Jekyll* is most notable as a sign of the times than anything else. Once again, as in *Uncle Was a Vampire*, the plot's driving force is sex—a topic which parody allows the filmmakers to deal with in a frank, albeit humorous, manner, with such lines as "Doctor, my inhibitions are broken!" "So what am I gonna do? I'm not a mechanic!" Fabius' mumbo jumbo experiments on a "psychic catalyst" which allows him to transfer his own mind into another person are closer to contemporaneous sci-fi flicks than to Stevenson's novel, and are caused by the urgency to find a woman (or more than one) to satiate the professor's libido. What is more, as in other films of the period, such as Alberto Lattuada's *Sweet Deceptions* (*Dolci inganni*, 1960) and Luciano Salce's *Crazy Desire* (*La voglia matta*, 1962), Girolami embraces the point of view of a mature man who is attracted to underage girls, in a frank—and perhaps unconscious—dismantling of the Gothic's hidden symbols.

Horror clichés are played for laughs, with a predilection for the grotesque. As in many other Italian flicks, monsters belonged to comedy—see Dino Risi's *Opiate '67* (*I mostri*, 1963) or Alberto Sordi as the horrid buck-toothed TV announcer of 1965's *I complessi*—and *My Friend, Dr. Jekyll* is no exception. Professor Fabius, with his bushy eyebrows, buck teeth and lustful gaze, is a caricature from vaudeville, not unlike his more serious counterparts, such as *The Vampire and the Ballerina*'s Walter Brandi and *Atom Age Vampire*'s Alberto Lupo.

My Friend, Dr. Jekyll was distributed in the

UGO TOGNAZZI

REGIA
MARINO GIROLAMI

PRODUZIONE
PROD. CINEMAT. M.G.-CEI INCOM

DISTRIBUZIONE

Il mio amico JEKYLL

con ABBE LANE
HELEN CHANEL

LUIGI PAVESE LINDA SINI ANNA CAMPORI ELENA FONTANA MARA FIE'
con CARLO CROCCOLO E RAIMONDO VIANELLO

The Italian poster for Marino Girolami's spoof *My Friend, Dr. Jekyll* emphasizes the erotic element, represented by female legs on display (courtesy S. I. Bianchi).

United States in 1965, through Union Film Distributors, which had been acquired by Dick Randall via his Associated Screen Distributors' purchase of Sam Fleishmann's shares in the company.

Marino Girolami (1914–1994), one of Italy's most prolific genre directors with 78 titles in three decades, was an ex-prizefighter who ended up at Italy's Centro Sperimentale di Cinematografia: he debuted as an actor in 1940 and later become an assistant director for Mario Soldati, Marcello Marchesi and Vittorio Metz. He debuted behind the camera in 1949 with *La strada buia*, the Italian version of Sidney Salkow's *Fugitive Lady*, followed by a number of tearjerking melodramas and comedy musicals. Through the Sixties and Seventies, Girolami jumped from one genre and *filone* to the other, including the Western—*Between God, the Devil and a Winchester* (*Anche nel west c'era una volta Dio*, 1968) and, most impressively, the crime film—*Violent Rome* (*Roma violenta*, 1975). In his late career he even ventured into hardcore (*Sesso profondo*, 1980) as well as gore, with the infamous cult zombie-cannibal flick *Zombie Holocaust* (*Zombi Holocaust*, 1980).

Girolami was the patriarch in a family of filmmakers, being the father of actor Ennio Girolami and ace action director Enzo G. Castellari, as well as the elderly brother of Romolo Girolami. The latter, who was the assistant director on *My Friend, Dr. Jekyll*, would later become a director on his own under the a.k.a. Romolo Guerrieri, with such titles as *Johnny Yuma* (1966), *The Sweet Body of Deborah* (*Il dolce corpo di Deborah*, 1968) and a number of noteworthy crime films, including *Detective Belli* (*Un detective*, 1969), *La polizia è al servizio del cittadino?* (1973), *City Under Siege* (*Un uomo, una città*, 1974), *Young, Violent, Dangerous* (*Liberi, armati, pericolosi*, 1976) and *Covert Action* (*Sono stato un agente C.I.A.*, 1978).

The Playgirls and the Vampire (*L'ultima preda del vampiro*)

D: Piero Regnoli. S and SC: Piero Regnoli; *DOP*: Aldo Greci (B&W, Ferrania Pancro C/7); *M*: Aldo Piga, conducted by Pier Luigi Urbini (Ed. Campi Nord-Sud); *E*: Mario [Mariano] Arditi; *ArtD*: Giuseppe Ranieri; *AD*: Mario Colucci; *C*: Luigi Allegretti; *MU*: Gaetano Capogrosso; *Hair*: Enzo Amato; *SO*: Pietro Seriffo; *SS*: Vanna Lomery. [*English adaptation*: Peter Riethof]. *Cast*: Lyla Rocco (Vera), Walter Brandi [Walter Bigari] (Count Gabor Kernassy/The Vampire), Maria Giovannini (Katia), Alfredo Rizzo (Lukas), Marisa Quattrini (Ilona), Leonardo Botta (Ferenc/*U.S. version*: Frank), Antoine Nicos (Caretaker), Corinne Fontaine (Magda), Tilde Damiani (Miss Balasz), Erika Di Centa (Erika), Enrico Salvatore (Peasant). *PROD*: Tiziano Longo for Nord Film Italiana; *PS*: Umberto Borsato;

AP: Armando Novelli. *Country*: Italy. Filmed at Castle Odescalchi, Bracciano; Villa Catena, Poli; Palazzo Borghese, Artena (Rome) and at Inter Studio (Rome). *Running time*: 83 min. (m.2750); Visa n: 33364 (11. 19.1960); *Rating*: V.M.16; *Release dates*: 11.28.1960 (Italy); 07.04.1963 (U.S.A.). *Distribution:* Film Selezione (Italy); Fanfare Films (U.S.A.); *Domestic gross*: 72,193,000 lire. *Also known as*: Curse of the Vampire (U.S.A., TV//U.K.), The Vampire's Last Fling, Des Filles pour un vampire (France), Das Ungeheuer auf Schloß Bantry (West Germany, 10.16. 1964). *Home video*: Image (DVD, U.S.A.), Salvation (DVD, U.K.).

When they find out that the road their bus is travelling on has been blocked by a landslide, ballet manager Lucas and his five showgirls—Vera, Katia, Erika, Ilona and Magda—stop by Castle Kernassy. There, Vera senses a strange feeling of familiarity. The castle owner, Count Gabor Kernassy, lends them hospitality—on one condition: at night, no one is to leave their bedrooms. Katia disobeys him, and the next morning she is found dead. Vera notices a painting of Margherita Kernassy, an ancestor of the Count who looks just like her. Vera and the Count fall in love with each other, despite the man's ambiguous and at times inexplicable behavior. After Katia turns up again as a vampire and Vera is attacked in the crypt by the Count, who bites her on the neck, it seems that the Count is actually a vampire: yet the real bloodsucker is actually the Count's undead ancestor, whom his descendant is vainly trying to stop...

Piero Regnoli's *L'ultima preda del vampiro* is a typical example of how Italian Gothic usually had more resonance abroad than in its home country. The success of Hammer productions, which were normally picked up for distribution in the United States by the American majors, caused a frenzy. As English-born producer/distributor Richard Gordon, whose cheap horror and sci-fi flicks (*Corridors of Blood, The Haunted Strangler, Fiend Without a Face*) were distributed worldwide by Metro-Goldwyn-Mayer, explains: "Suddenly every independent distributor in America also wanted similar product and did not much care from where it came. At the same time, European film makers [...] decided to get on the band wagon."[1]

Gordon started scouting for European horror films to release in the States through his own company Gordon Films, Inc. Sometime in 1963 he was invited to a screening of a French language copy of *L'ultima preda del vampiro*, *chez* Janus Films, a New York–based company specialized in importing arthouse material (Bergman, Fellini, Truffaut). The screening was accompanied by the uproarious laughter and yells on the part of Janus' founders Cy Harvey and Bryant Halliday—Fellini it was not. "When it was over, they apologized to me for wasting my time," as Gordon recalls. The very next day Gordon telephoned Janus' agent in Paris, bought the film's rights and prepared an English language version with Peter Riethof. "I was worried about the possibility of a censorship problem with United States Customs which, at the time, had to screen and approve every import," as Gordon pointed out. "As an extra precaution, I brought the film back via a port of entry where rumor had it that the examiners were more lenient than in New York."

Gordon eventually sold the film to Joe Solomon of Fanfare Film: retitled *The Playgirls and the Vampire*, it was launched as a "for adults only" feature and became a success in drive-in theaters and metropolitan grindhouses. It even surfaced in Canada, in both the French and English versions, through Jerry Solway's Astral Films. Eventually Gordon edited another, softer variant, entitled *Curse of the Vampire*, destined to television broadcasting through Seven Arts. In the United Kingdom, however, *Curse of the Vampire* faced the predictable censorship problems with the austere British Board of Film Classification: in October 1963 the film was classified X, with cuts being demanded that, according to Gordon, "would have rendered the picture meaningless." Distributed by Gordon himself through New Realm Pictures in a version that "left little of interest to any audience," not to mention being barely comprehensible, the film circulated as a second feature without making too much of an impression.

The Playgirls and the Vampire was the brainchild of one of Italian cinema's most fascinating personalities. Piero Regnoli (1921–2001) penned more than 100 scripts between 1953 and 1991, mostly popular films of all kind: from sword-and-sandal to Western, from horror to erotic farce, he left no genre untouched. Most surprisingly, given the frequent emphasis on eroticism,

Regnoli had been the film critic of the Vatican's daily newspaper *L'Osservatore Romano*—not exactly the kind of background one imagines for the man who wrote stuff such as *Malabimba* (1979) and *Patrick Still Lives* (*Patrick vive ancora*, 1980). As for Regnoli's directorial career, it can be defined as erratic at best: eleven films in twenty years, covering a number of *filoni* but never rising above mediocrity.

The Playgirls and the Vampire shares all the shortcomings of early Italian low-budget vampire films made in the wake of Hammer's *Horror of Dracula*. The setting is the present day, and references to the typically male-centered British Gothic sit uneasily next to an emphasis on sex and nudity. At first the plot looks like a reworking of a typical comedy routine: a busload of ballerinas and their stingy impresario (the priceless Alfredo Rizzo as the comic relief, in a variation on his dirty old man persona), end up at a gloomy Hungarian manor[2] whose owner (Walter Bigari, under the alias of Walter Brandi, who enjoyed a short-lived notoriety as the "Italian Dracula" after his role in *The Vampire and the Ballerina* and in Regnoli's film) hides a terrible secret.

Much of the film's first half is devoted to the dancers and their negligees, while the homages to the Gothic tradition are few and far between, most notably in a prologue where Regnoli borrows a famous shot from Tod Browning's *Dracula* (1931), the vampire's hand menacingly coming out of a coffin. Yet, in Brandi's hopelessly wooden portrayal, the Count is nothing more than a laughable cypher in cape and fangs. The vampire never becomes the Antichrist-like figure as suggested by Stoker and later Fisher, who, in *Dracula: Prince of Darkness* (1966), would portray an occult ritual that symbolically reverses the resurrection of Christ. In Regnoli's film there is not even a trace of the crucifix as a salvific weapon: daylight and a spiky, strategically placed spear are all that is needed to destroy the monster, whose crumbling to dust is shown through a very crude animation effect.

However, more out of a commercial calculation than by instinct, scriptwriters and filmmakers captured Stoker's point: *Dracula* is a novel about lust, not love (as Francis Ford Cop-

The alluring American poster for *The Playgirls and the Vampire* (1960), released in the United States as an "adults-only" feature by distributor Richard Gordon.

pola would re-interpret it), and, to quote David Pirie, "one of the more appalling things that Dracula does to the matronly women of his Victorian enemies (in the novel as well as in the film) is to make them sensual."[3] Here, the perspective is turned upside down. Whereas in Hammer films the vampire's preys are repressed and prudish—such as the couple portrayed by Charles Tingwell and Barbara Shelley in *Dracula: Prince of Darkness*—in Italian Gothics there is no such problem: the half-dressed, empty-headed,[4] uninhibited dancers of *The Playgirls and the Vampire* are a case in point. The central pivot on which the British models worked is no longer the same: originally the vampire functioned as a catalyst for the liberation of a chaotic and destructive sexual energy, which the forces of good—usually in the shape of a paternal, asexual savant who accompanied the young hero—are called upon to suppress. The vampire here becomes a punitive agent instead.

Compared to most Italian Gothic horror films, the theme of the *doppelgänger* here involves the male protagonist as well: not only the vampire's "last prey" (Lyla Rocco) is the living image of the woman the bloodsucker had loved centuries earlier, but the same actor (Walter Brandi) plays both the vampire and his descendant who vainly tries to release his ancestor from its centuries-old curse. Whereas the vampire is wild and uncontrollable, thirsty for blood and female flesh, his descendant is—as is customary with Italian Gothic's male figures—repressed and tormented, ascetic and abstinent. This is all merely sketched, anyway: as Regnoli knew too well, psychology was not what viewers demanded.

Even more than Renato Polselli in *The Vampire and the Ballerina*, Regnoli had no qualms in getting to the point: sex. The first scene, after an establishing shot of a bus on a country road, starts with a lingering image of a woman adjusting her stockings, amply displaying her legs in the process. *The Playgirls and the Vampire* is less interested in staging scary scenes than in finding pretexts to show the actresses in see-through nightgowns and high heels, no matter how idiotic and far-fetched the plot might sound. Hence the inclusion of Erika Di Centa's

gratuitous strip scene (Di Centa would also appear in the documentary "by night" *Notti nude*, "Naked Nights," 1963)

What is more, the film has at least the merit of showing Italy's very first naked vampire. Actually, Maria Giovannini's curvaceous shapes can only be guessed at, hidden in the shadows, while the camera strategically keeps her nipples off-screen by a matter of inches, at least in the current version. Yet nude scenes were definitely shot, as proven by production stills that show topless ballerinas,[5] hinting at a *nudie* version for foreign markets.

The ending allowed Regnoli an unexpected mixture of eroticism and horror, by showing the female vampire being transfixed in the chest and her blood dripping down her thighs: it is a daring image that not even the black-and-white appeases. Here, Regnoli predated what would become of the Gothic by the turn of the new decade, after the loosening of censorship.

In Italy, *The Playgirls and the Vampire* passed almost unnoticed, even though it was also published as a photonovel in the March 1961 issue of *Malìa—I fotoromanzi del brivido*. The censorship commission gave it a V.M.16 rating because of its "macabre subject matter and its many shocking scenes," with only a brief cut in the aforementioned scene of the nude vampire's nightly visit.

The commission's president explained the decision at length, in a note to the Ministry of Spectacle's undersecretary that reads more like a review, and certainly not a raving one: "*L'ultima preda del vampiro* [...] is a very modest work, devoid of any artistic merit, and despite its title, unable to provoke in the viewer the morbid state of anxiety that normally characterizes this type of product. The few scenes that should give thrills make use of the usual cumbersome ingredients, which are however used in such an unskilled and elementary way as to give the film almost a parodic flavor compared to the wider genre production. However, the Commission—in view of the subject matter's nature, its gloomy setting and intentionally scary (although poorly made) scenes, and with a few cuts of several shots where a well-determined complacency towards eroticism can be found—has decided not to deny the visa, failing to find any evidence that would justify such a measure. The only valid reason to refuse the visa, if that were possible, would be represented by the patent offense to good taste as well as the viewers' intelligence."

Notes

1. Gordon's quotes are taken from his essay featured as an extra on the Salvation DVD of *The Playgirls and the Vampire*.
2. As was customary for the period, the castle was a result of different locations combined: long shots featured Castle Odescalchi in Bracciano, whereas shots of the entrance were filmed at Villa Catena, in Poli (Rome). The interiors were those of the familiar Palazzo Borghese in Artena. Also typically with Italian cinema, the props would also be recycled over and over in other movies: the weird arms-shaped candelabra protruding the walls were to be seen again in Bava's *Kill, Baby...Kill!*, whereas the shield of arms with the "K" of Kernassy on it popped up—this time as a symbol of the Karnstein family—in *Terror in the Crypt*.
3. Pirie, *A New Heritage of Horror*, p. 98.
4. Several lines of dialogue would make many viewers groan for their blatantly sexist attitude and content, especially those regarding the dimwitted Katia.
5. See Stefano Piselli and Roberto Guidotti, eds., *Diva—Cinema 1951–1965* (Florence: Glittering, 1989), p. 88. Curiously, in the scene where the vampire's victim enters her impresario's room, almost frightening him to death, Alfredo Rizzo is shown flipping through *Frolic*, a U.S. girlie magazine with pin-up June Wilkinson on the cover.

The Vampire and the Ballerina a.k.a. *The Vampire's Lover (L'amante del vampiro)*

D: Renato Polselli. S and SC: Renato Polselli, Giuseppe Pellegrini, Ernesto Gastaldi; DOP: Angelo Baistrocchi (B&W, 1,85:1—Ferrania Pancro C/7); M: Aldo Piga, conducted by Piero Urbini (Ed. Campi Nord-Sud); E: Renato Cinquini; AE: Misa Gabrini; PD: Amedeo Mellone; SD: Sandro Schirò; AD: Ernesto Gastaldi; 2ndAD: Paolo Cirino Pomicino; C: Elio Polacchi; AC: Remo Grisanti; SO: Leopoldo Rosi, Raffaele Del Monte; MU: Gaetano Capogrosso; SE: Vampire masks designed by Amedeo Mellone, created by Cesare Gambarelli; Hair: Ottorino Censi; SP: Poletto & Bottini; SS: Giuseppe Pellegrini; CHOR: Marisa Ciampiglia [Ciampaglia]. Cast: Hélène Rémy (Luisa), Tina Gloriani (Francesca), Walter Brandt [Walter Bigari] (Herman), Maria Luisa Rolando (Countess Alda), Isarco Ravaioli (Luca), John Turner [Gino Turini] (Giorgio), Ugo Cragnani [Pier Ugo Gragnani] (The Professor), Brigitte Castor, Lut Maryk, Ombretta Ostenda (Dancer), Bava Sanni (Brigida), Marisa Quattrini (Dancer), Giorgio Braccesi (Doctor), Titti Valeri (Dancer), Stefania Sabatini (Dancer), Franca Licastro (Dancer). PROD: Bruno Bolognesi for Consorzio Italiano Films (Rome); GM: Giulio Niderkorn; PM: Umberto Borsato; PS: Camillo Fantacci; PSe: Antonio Pisani. Country: Italy. Filmed at Palazzo Borghese, Artena (Rome) and at Istituto Nazionale Luce Studios (Rome). Running time: 83 min. (m. 2700); Visa n: 31701 (04.14.1960); Rating: V.M.16; Release dates: 05.23.1960 (Italy); 10.31.1962 (U.S.A.). Distribution: Rome International Films; (Italy); United Artists (U.S.A.); Domestic gross: 98,000,000 lire. Also known as: The Vampire's Lover (U.S.A.), Die Geliebte des Vampirs (West Germany, 12.02.1960). Home Video: Amazon (Instant video, U.S.), NoShame (DVD, Italy)

While a ballet company, engaged in the preparation of a show, is housed inside a villa in the countryside, a young peasant girl is attacked by a vampire. Two dancers, Luisa and Francesca, and Francesca's boyfriend, Luca, visit a ruined castle nearby, which is believed to be uninhabited: however, they discover that a strange woman, Countess Alda, lives with her servant Herman within those walls. During the visit, Luisa is suddenly snatched by a vampire who bites her throat, turning her into his slave. Herman is revealed as the bloodsucker, but it is the Countess who guides him, as she needs blood to retain eternal youth. It is too late to save Luisa, but Luca and the choreographer, Giorgio, get back to the castle to rescue Francesca, who has been abducted by the monsters...

"I immediately grasped the originality of the story: a bit of eroticism, a bit of sentiment, a hint of vulgarity and a happy ending—plus a new ingredient: vampirism. The new ingredient had been added by a box-office hit starring Christopher Lee, *Horror of Dracula*, and producers and distributors jumped headlong and bit the vein, determined to suck each other's blood to the last drop."[1]

As he himself humorously recalls in his autobiography *Voglio entrare nel cinema. Storia di uno che ce l'ha fatta* ("I want to be in the movies: The story of somebody who made it"), Ernesto Gastaldi was rather disenchanted when his acquaintance Renato Polselli phoned him and told him the basic plot of *The Vampire and the Ballerina*: the (immutable) main ingredients of a script (eroticism, sentiment, vulgarity and a happy ending) are the omnipresent *leitmotifs*

CIF- CONSORZIO ITALIANO FILM *présente*

LA MAITRESSE DU VAMPIRE

HELENE REMY · **MARIA LUISA ROLANDO** · TINA GLORIANI · WALTER BRANDI · ISARCO RAVAIOLI · JOHN TURNER ·

REGIE: RENATO POLSELLI

DE MINNARES VAN DE VAMPIER DISTRIBUÉ PAR UNITED ARTISTS

Belgian poster for Renato Polselli's *The Vampire and the Ballerina* (author's collection).

that accompany the scriptwriter's amusing memories of his own days in the Italian movie industry. Yet, Gastaldi perfectly summarizes the insiders' bewilderment when *Horror of Dracula* became a hit, and the subsequent, frantic run at providing audiences with more of the same—a tendency which would characterize Italian genre cinema for the following decades, as the industry moved in an erratic way, following and squeezing a trend until it was dry and then looking for another, and another.[2]

Vampires were the sensation of the moment,

and not only in movies. In April 1960, the prestigious Feltrinelli published an anthology volume edited by Ornella Volta and Valerio Riva, *I vampiri tra noi* ("The Vampires Among Us") which included works by Gauthier, Maupassant, Polidori, Merimée, Lautreámont, Dumas, Hoffmann, Capuana and Poe, plus Gogol's "Viy," Aleksey Tolstoy's *The Wurdalak* (with the title *La famiglia del vurdalak* [*sic*]) and J. Sheridan Le Fanu's *Carmilla*. It would prove to be a major resource for scriptwriters and filmmakers in the following years. On a more mundane level, June 1959 saw the release of a paperback pulp novel entitled *Il vampiro* by a certain "Clay O'Neil": it was the first issue of a new paperback series, *KKK. I Classici dell'Orrore*, published by Edizioni KKK. Another similarly lurid series of pulp novels were *I racconti di Dracula*, curated by Aldo Crudo and published by Editrice Romana Periodici, which started on December 15th, 1959. Vampires were all over the place.

The original script for *The Vampire and the Ballerina* had been written by Giampaolo Callegaris. "It looked rather canine, so Renato and I wrote a second, more incisive one," Gastaldi joked. Too bad he could not do anything about Polselli's trademark bombastic dialogue.

The scriptwriter's recollection of the casting is quite amusing: "Polselli took me to the production offices, squalid, near the Termini Station. We already had the vampire, Walter Brandi, who brought the deal. The vampire's friend will be a big boy from Tuscany (Gino Turini) who put in part of the money. The vampire's victim is Hélène Rémy because we're going to sign a co-production deal with France, the heroine will be Tina (Gloriani) because she's the director's lover, while the hottie vampire's lover is Maria Luisa Rolando, a big-busted *protégé* of the general manager."[3]

Shooting took place at the castle of Artena, owned by prince Borghese, in winter 1959, near Christmas, for three freezing weeks. "Huge halls as icy as tombs, with fireplaces as big as stages, made with marble that's been cold for generations. Deadly drafts came as spears of ice in your back whichever way you turned." Gastaldi quips he did not bother to warn Polselli whenever the director jumped the line: it was too cold to stop and redo the take. The skeletons that decorate the vampire's crypt were real skeletons, as Polselli told an interviewer: "One day, production manager Umberto Borsato told me he had a bargain in his hands. He took me to a cemetery undertaker who wanted to sell us a skeleton for 300,000 *lire*. 'This is a rich man's skeleton,' he told Borsato, who thought it was too expensive. 'Look, he's even got golden teeth!' Borsato replied: 'But we could as well make do with a poor man's skeleton!'"[4]

Overall, *The Vampire and the Ballerina* is a mixed bag—mostly because no one involved seemed to have a clear idea of what to do with a vampire film. Take, for instance, the setting in contemporary Italy. *I Vampiri* managed to bridge the chasm between the nineteenth century conception of Gothic and modern sensibility through a refined visual collage that inserted Du Grand's ultramodern lab, which seemed to come straight out of a science-fiction film, in the dungeons of the castle. On the other hand, Polselli's attempts at grafting the Gothic archetypes onto the present are quite awkward: the camera's initial panning over the placid Lazio countryside, amidst apartment buildings and television antennas, is embarrassing. What is more, the conflict between past and present—which is vital in *I Vampiri*—is rendered in an unconvincingly didactic manner, as Countess Alda declares in a scene: "I don't care for the world you live in—it is not my world."

The filmic influences are patent. *Horror of Dracula* is the stylistic blueprint for such scenes as Rolando's apparition, the carriage driven by the monster and running in the night, or the sequence in which the vampirized Luisa (Rémy) awaits in her room the bloodsucker's visit, while the wind outside whistles among the trees: it is a moment that reworks (yet with a more daring approach) a similar scene in Fisher's film. However, as it had happened with Freda, Polselli and Gastaldi liberally steal from *Vampyr*, most patently in the "premature burial" scene, which is a shot-by-shot rip-off of Dreyer's film. However, although the black-and-white photography is suitably atmospheric, Polselli's technique is crude, as shown by his infringements of the 180-degree rule.

The reworking of the vampire tradition's clichés is also awkward. *The Vampire and the Ballerina* leans on the canon of pointed canines and vampires sleeping in coffins, and stages the bloodsucker's final meltdown in the sun; it even includes a didactic expository sequence in which an elderly professor (Ugo Gragnani) improvises a brief conference on the theme for the benefit of the young protagonists (and the audience as well), explaining vampires' origins, habits and idiosyncrasies as if he was telling a child's tale ("Many years ago—a hundred, two hundred, a thousand ... lived a race of evil men, then the good angel condemned them to bite each other and feed on their own blood"). On the other hand, the use of the cross as a weapon is detached from religious symbolism and implications: in one scene, Isarco Ravaioli and Gino Turini keep the vampire at bay by crossing two candlesticks, just like Professor Van Helsing (Peter Cushing) did in *Horror of Dracula*, but whereas in Fisher's film Van Helsing defeated evil because his faith was firm (and in the later chapters of the saga the scripts often played with the theme of religion as juxtaposed with the vampire's devilish power), Italian *savants* are fairly inexperienced in the field, or better indifferent to a higher moral: what moves them is not faith, but love.

Italian censors gave *The Vampire and the Ballerina* a V.M.16 rating ("forbidden to those under 16 years old": the V.M.18 was introduced in 1962, replacing the V.M.16) because of the "shocking quality of several scenes, in connection with teenagers' mental development." The censorship commission demanded that all close-ups of the vampire's face be cut and the final melting of the vampires be shortened. A few months later, following several seizures demanded by the local authorities, the producer submitted a new version of the film, most likely featuring different edits of the scenes featuring the vampire, with the close-ups replaced by medium or long shots, which passed with a V.M.16 rating and no cuts. Despite all the fuss caused by the film, however, the horrific moments are staged in an unconvincing way: besides the Carnival-like vampire masks that melt like snow in the sun in the final scene, the un-

easiness in dealing with a monster who is perceived only as a macabre icon is evident.

As Polselli recounted, the vampire's meltdown was executed with primitive yet ingenious homemade tricks. "We made a face cast with plaster, then the make-up artist and I molded an adhesive rubber mask over it. Our trick was to put a layer of ash between the plaster and the rubber. A grip suggested we added some maggots, so I put a dozen of them inside the empty eye socket—I got scared myself when I saw the results! The rubber, invested by a projector's hot light, melted and flew in streams, thanks also to a ventilator that we placed by its side, revealing the ash below. The rotating eyes during this transformation were operated through a pump."[5]

Although the disfigured and decaying female face would be one of Italian Gothic's most characteristic elements (and *Black Sunday*'s opening scene, far more shocking than anything in Polselli's film, was passed uncut), the idea of make-up and mutations applied to male actors was still something of a novelty (and Polselli's film, with its ugly wax-modeled masks, only underlines this fact), and something difficult to copy convincingly.

It was not just a matter of low budgets. It rather denoted the inability to metabolize and put on-screen a believable physical and carnal repulsion, and at the same time to feel pity for the monster. Whereas sword-and-sandal films featured bizarre creatures of every shape and size, the Gothic *filone* shunned this kind of thing. According to film historian Teo Mora, it was the absence of figures of folklore that caused horrific make-up to have a marginal importance in the genre.[6] But it was also the consequence of the Gothic leaving aside sword-and-sandal's carefree, prepubescent sense of wonder in order to savor a sense of the forbidden which was just as visceral but definitely more ambiguous and sexually aware.

Understandably, Polselli and Gastaldi were much more interested in the scantily dressed dancers and their choreographies, and especially in the sadomasochistic relationship between the luscious, predatory bloodsucker and her corresponding male. As Gisèle Du Grand did in *I Vampiri*, Countess Alda meets her visitors from a dominant position, looking down at them from the castle's staircase ... and allowing the director to highlight her prominent bust.

Despite her claims of being the prisoner of a "mad servant who's got a passion for his own madness," the Countess is a real man-eater, who has her own lover/slave/butler serve tea to her guests. The male vampire, as played by Walter Brandi, turns into some sort of a succubus, in a striking reversal of Bram Stoker's typical "brides of Dracula" situation—yet the relationship between Alda and Herman is one of mutual dependency. "I, I am your only love. I am yours forever. I am your slave. I belong to you," Herman declares before allowing the countess to bite him, in order for her to preserve her beauty with his blood, in Polselli's riff on one of Italian Gothic's recurring themes, eternal beauty—she regains it while he turns ugly again. "Now it's done. You are a hideous monster again. I need you, but cannot look at you," as Alda sums it up.

This leads *The Vampire and the Ballerina* to develop its own internal logic and coherence, that paradoxically innovates within the genre's trappings and leads to a mind-boggling reversal of clichés: for once, the male vampire drives a stake through the heart of the woman he just vampirized, because, as he claims, "I am and must be the master of my own world!"

Such an approach towards eroticism would characterize Polselli's subsequent *oeuvre*, up to the director's infamous (and truly delirious) output of the following decade, such as *La verità secondo Satana* (1970), *Delirium* (*Delirio caldo*, 1972), *Mania* (1973), *The Reincarnation of Isabel* (*Riti, magie nere e segrete orge nel '300*, 1973), *Oscenità* (1973–1980), etc., before Polselli moved on to out-and-out hardcore by the end of the 1970s. Take the obvious sexual pleasure displayed by Hélène Rémy after she has been bitten in the neck, as the woman caresses her own breast. In another striking moment, the obedience to horror movie imagery—the crucifix hanging from a girl's neck, whose sight stops the vampire from biting her—is annihilated by the context: a close-up of a florid, pulsating female cleavage.

L'amante del vampiro was also published as a photonovel, in the March 1962 issue (no. 14) of *Malìa—I fotoromanzi del brivido*.

Notes

1. Ernesto Gastaldi, *Voglio entrare nel cinema. Storia di uno che ce l'ha fatta* (Milan: Mondadori, 1991), p. 177.
2. Donato Totaro, "A Genealogy of Italian Popular Cinema: the Filone," *Offscreen* vol. 15, no. 11, November 30, 2011.
3. Gastaldi, *Voglio entrare nel cinema*, p. 177.
4. Luca Andolfi, "Renato Polselli tra horror e censura. Conversando con Renato Polselli," in Antonio Tentori and Luigi Cozzi, eds., *Horror Made In Italy* (Rome: Profondo Rosso, 2007), p. 492.
5. Ibid.
6. Mora, "Elegia per una donna vampiro," p. 186.

1961

Werewolf in a Girls' Dormitory (Lycanthropus)

D: Richard Benson [Paolo Heusch]. *S and SC*: Julian Berry [Ernesto Gastaldi]; *DOP*: George Patrick [Renato Del Frate] (B&W, Dupont); *M*: Francis Berman [Armando Trovajoli] (Ed. C.A.M.); *U.S. version*: "The Ghoul in School" sung by Marilyn Stewart and Frank Owens; *E*: Julian Attenborough [Giuliana Attenni]; *PD*: Peter Travers [Piero Filippone]; *SD*: Cesare Monello; *CO*: Walter Cobb [Walter Patriarca]; *AD*: John Farquhar [Giovanni Fago]; *C*: Vittorio Bernini, Ugo Nudi, Emilio Giannini; *AC*: Nello Renzi; *MU*: Raffaele Cristini, Franco Palombi, Emilia Pomilia, Aldo Ascenzi; *Hair*: Anna Fabrizi Panzironi; *W*: Fausta Scotolati; *SO*: Shenson Ray [Aldo De Martino]; *SP*: Pierluigi Praturion; *KG*: Giulio Diamanti; *ChEl*: Bruno Pasqualini; *SS*: Nadia Colby [Giovanni Fago]. *Cast*: Barbara Lass [Barbara Lass-Kwiatkowska] (Priscilla), Carl Schell (Dr. Julian Olcott), Maureen O'Connor [Donatella Mauro] (Sandy), Alan Collins [Luciano Pigozzi] (Walter Jeoffrey), Anni Steinert [Anna Degli Uberti] (Mrs. Sheena Whiteman), Mary McNeeran [Bianca Maria Roccatani] (Mary Smith), Maurice Marsac (Sir Alfred Whiteman), Curt Lowens (Director Swift), Grace Neame [Grazia Fachini] (Leonor MacDonald), Joseph Mercer [Giuseppe Mancini] (Tommy the porter), Anne Marie Avis [Anna Maria Pignataio Aveta] (School girl), Herbert Diamonds [Giuseppe Transocchi] (Police inspector), Mary Dolbek [Francesca Dolbecco], Lauren Scott [Rossana Canghiari], Elisabeth Patrick [Liliana Rondoni] (Miss Schultz), Patricia Meeker [Luciana Fratini] (School girl), Lucy Derleth [Lucia Cera] (School girl), Martha Marker [Marta Melocco] (School girl). *Uncredited*: John

Karlsen (Old man), Giuseppe Transocchi. *PROD*: Royal Film; *PM*: Jack Forrest [Jone Tuzi]; *PS*: Lucio Bompani; *PSe*: Mario Merlini. *Country*: Italy. *Running time*: 82 min. (m. 2420); Visa n: 35883 (10.18. 1961); *Rating*: V.M.16; *Release dates*: 11.09.1961 (Italy); 06.05.1963 (U.S.A.). *Distribution:* Cineriz (Italy); MGM (U.S.A.); *Domestic gross*: 115,000,000 lire. *Also known as*: *I Married a Werewolf*, *The Ghoul in School*, *Monster Among the Girls* (U.S.A.), *Le Monstre aux filles* (France), *Un hombre lobo en el dormitorio de mujeres* (Spain). *Home video*: Retromedia (DVD, U.S.A.), Alpha Video (DVD, U.S.A.)

A dead girl, horribly mutilated, is found in the woods near a girls' reform school. The official response blames the killing on a pack of wolves, but a friend of the victim, Sandy, finds an anonymous letter which reveals the dead girl as a blackmailer, and her murderer as the person she was blackmailing. When the reform school director, Mr. Swift, shows up with a police inspector to collect the letter, however, it has mysteriously disappeared. Nevertheless, the author of the letter is revealed to be a guy named Whiteman: what is more, it emerges that Whiteman's wife has witnessed the murder. Sandy is attacked by a monster in the woods, and suspicions focus on Julian Olcott, the school's new doctor, who underwent a trial connected to a lycanthropy case. The trail of blood increases, but the monster's true identity is finally unveiled...

Shot in late summer 1961, in about a month around Rome and at Cinecittà Studios, *Lycanthropus* was an attempt at exploiting another key figure in the Gothic after the vampire, in a period where Italian Gothic horror was still trying to find its footing.

However, the erotic element—albeit moderate—is not negligible in Ernesto Gastaldi's script. "If they weren't keeping us separated from men, I would know what this meant," says one of the girls in the female reform school where the story takes place after one of her companions has fainted, thus implying pregnancy[1]; on the other hand, the main reason director Paolo Heusch builds up a suspenseful scene in the dormitory is possibly to show the girls in their nightgowns—strategically left open so as for the viewer to glimpse their breasts. No wonder the American advertising campaign emphasized the female presence in the film, focus-

ing on said scene for the lurid U.S. title *Werewolf in a Girls' Dormitory*. The American version also added a cool rock 'n' roll song to the opening credits, "The Ghoul In School," and a photonovel was published in vol. 2, no. 7 of the Charlton Publications magazine *Horror Monsters* (Winter 1963).

As a result of the clumsy approach to the supernatural that characterized early Italian horror films, the metamorphosis from man to wolf is brought back to (pseudo) scientific territories: a matter of glands, as in the old American horror films of the 1940s featuring mad doctors. There is not a trace of gypsy curses, pentacles and silver bullets in the film: however, the way the theme of lycanthropy is handled is also worth noting for its explicit sexual references. Whereas in the contemporaneous Hammer werewolf epic *The Curse of the Werewolf* (1961, Terence Fisher) the moment in which the transformation starts taking place is identified with puberty, thus implicitly pairing lycanthropy and erotic arousal, Gastaldi openly refers to a sexual dysfunction related to the pituitary gland. Furthermore, the first werewolf attack culminates in a point-of-view shot of the female victim, forced to the ground by the monster, which somehow apes the celebrated POV shot of the rape victim in Akira Kurosawa's *Rashomon* (1950), as the camera frames the tops of trees: then, with a brutal transition, Heusch cuts to the wolfman's claws ripping the woman's skirt open, partially baring her neck and chest.

Most significantly, Gastaldi concocts the plot like a whodunit of sorts—thus predating *The Beast Must Die* (1974, Paul Annett) by over a decade[2]—with a mysterious werewolf on the loose and a list of suspects, and spices it up with references to *The Strange Case of Dr. Jekyll and Mr. Hyde* when it comes to the mystery's solution. Similarly to *Blood and Black Lace*, the story focuses around compromising letters and blackmail, and there are actually two murderers, the werewolf and his accomplice/lover: the latter, like Eva Bartok in Bava's film, dispatches a dangerous witness in order to save her beloved—an example of the way ideas and plot points would turn up again from time to time in the cauldron of Italian genres. What is more,

The evocative Italian poster for Paolo Heusch's *Lycanthropus* (courtesy S. I. Bianchi).

Werewolf in a Girls' Dormitory's perfunctory English setting recalls the German *Krimis*, with its gloomy night exteriors and unwelcoming village pubs. Only one year after *Black Sunday*, it was still difficult for Italian Gothic horror films to find a way towards a more original concept of the Fantastic.

In the credits, Heusch hid under an anglo–Saxon pseudonym, Richard Benson, and so did Gastaldi. *Werewolf in a Girls' Dormitory* marks the first appearance of his favorite a.k.a., Julian Berry. "The origin of 'Julian Berry' is funny," as he explained. "In 1957 I wrote my first science fiction novel and my publisher wanted an

English name on the cover page. At that time, I was sharing a little apartment with an Anglo-Italian named Julian Birri, who worked as an advertising copy writer. As a joke, I used his name, because the book made sly uses of some advertising slogans he had conceived. Well, it so happened that he almost lost his job, because his boss wouldn't believe that he wasn't the real author! [...] In those days in Italy, it was mandatory to sign your films with an English name, because that's the way the producers wanted it."[3]

The cast was a mixed bunch. Top-billed Barbara Lass was a Polish girl who at that time was married to a young film director by the name of Roman Polanski, whom she divorced in 1962 (she later married Karlheinz Böhm, of *Peeping Tom* fame). Carl Schell, the male lead, was Maximilian's brother, while the other German actor in the cast, Curt Lowens, played the titular werewolf. Besides the French-American

Maurice Marsac, the rest of the cast consisted of Italian actors under (often indecipherable) pseudonyms; Bianca Maria Roccatani would become a photonovel star (as Michela Roc), while others were familiar faces in popular cinema such as the ubiquitous Luciano Pigozzi.

Lowens—a former member of the Dutch resistance who ironically was often cast in Nazi roles—had to deal with a rather grotesque make-up, typical of Italian horror films of the period. The man-to-werewolf transformation scenes were made through cross dissolves, starting from full make-up in reverse. "My transformation required a lot of starting and stopping, as the make-up was changed. At each stage, something was done. The hair was removed, or the teeth changed. [...] it was a plaster mask that was put on my face. [...] If you really look at the [werewolf make-up], it's latex from the forehead—where they put the hair—to just

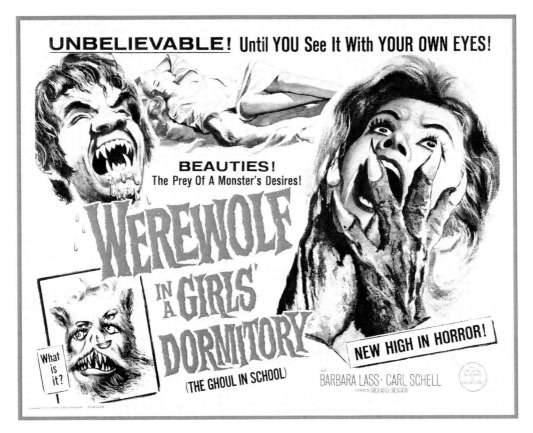

The lurid United States poster for Heusch's film, retitled *Werewolf in a Girls' Dormitory* (courtesy S. I. Bianchi).

below the nose. More latex is added around the eyes. Then they add hair to your neck and the sides separately. Your mouth is almost free but, then I had to wear those werewolf teeth, which were very uncomfortable [...]. The entire make-up process would take about three hours."[4]

After missing his opportunity to play in Otto Preminger's *Exodus* (1960), Lowens got in touch with the Italian producer Tucci through a guy who had a small role in Vittorio De Sica's *Two Women* (*La ciociara*, 1960), in which the German actor played a Luftwaffe officer. As Lowens explains, shooting *Werewolf in a Girls' Dormitory* was a rather chaotic experience, language-wise—a typical occurrence in Italian cinema of the period. "We literally shot in five different languages. Most of the Italian films of this era had actors with different accents, as well as different languages. Carl Schell and I performed well in German. Barbara and Carl acted in French. Maurice Marsac would act in French with Barbara, or English with Carl and me. And the Italians would do their stuff in Italian. The original script was in English, and I tried to stick to English whenever possible. In post-production, when we did the lip-synch and dubbing, I dubbed my own voice."[5]

Paolo Heusch's film career was erratic to say the least. After proving himself as one of Italy's finest assistant directors, he debuted in 1958 with *The Day the Sky Exploded* (*La morte viene dallo spazio*), considered by many as Italy's first science-fiction movie. Most of the film, however, was actually made up of stock footage, recycled and edited by d.o.p. Mario Bava in true Ed Wood manner to get a coherent story. *Lycanthropus* was Heusch's third film as a director; he was then hired by producer Moris Ergas to co-direct *Violent Life* (*Una vita violenta*, 1962, based on Pier Paolo Pasolini's novel of the same name) together with Brunello Rondi, as Ergas wanted a technically experienced filmmaker to help the debuting scriptwriter-turned-director.

Heusch was often called on to co-direct (or to do the whole job) works that were credited to other filmmakers: that was the case with two of the three comedies starring Totò he directed, *Il comandante* (1963), the grim *Whatever Happened to Baby Jane?* parody *Che fine ha fatto Totò*

Baby? (1964), credited solely to producer Ottavio Alessi, and *Totò d'Arabia* (1966), signed by José Antonio de la Loma, which germinated after Heusch showed Totò a screening of *Lawrence of Arabia* (1962, David Lean). He later dabbled in adventure (*Il rinnegato del deserto*, 1965) and heist flicks (*Un colpo da mille miliardi*, 1966), before helming a biopic of Ernesto "Che" Guevara starring Francisco Rabal (*El 'Che' Guevara*, 1968) and the exotic/erotic drama *Incontro d'amore* (1970) starring Laura Antonelli. Heusch's last directorial effort was another work-for-hire, uncredited job: he shot additional scenes for the 1975 re-release of Massimo Dallamano's heavily censored *Venus in Furs* (*Venere in pelliccia/Le malizie di Venere*, 1969). Heusch died in 1982: he was just 58.

Notes

1. This line of dialogue, however, can be heard only in the Italian version, whereas it has been drastically changed—and its meaning softened—in the U.S. dubbing, as follows: "Look, she can't even look at a new man without fainting dead away."
2. Also, as several critics pointed out, the setting in the reform girls school somehow predated Antonio Margheriti's giallo *Naked You Die*, a.k.a. *The Young, the Evil and the Savage* (*Nude...si muore*, 1968).
3. Tim Lucas, "What Are Those Strange Drops of Blood in the Scripts of Ernesto Gastaldi?," *Video Watchdog* 39, May/June 1997, p. 37. It must be noted, however, that even though there is no doubt Gastaldi wrote the film, the production records kept at Rome's State Archive credit the script to Elisa Pezzani and Ottavio Alessi (in the production's budget estimation sheet), whereas other papers at the Ministry credit the story to Gastaldi, Luciano Martino and Ugo Guerra.
4. As for director Paolo Heusch, the actor recalled: "Heusch had a great perception about what he wanted to see and how he wanted to see it. He was easygoing, and tried, very earnestly, to make a good, atmospheric, horror movie." Paul Parla and Charles P. Mitchell, "Werewolf in a Girls' Dormitory: An interview with Curt Lowens," *Ultra Filmfax* 67, June/July 1998, p. 52.
5. Ibid.

1962

The Horrible Dr. Hichcock (*L'orribile segreto del Dr. Hichcock*)

D: Robert Hampton [Riccardo Freda]. S and SC: Julyan Perry [Ernesto Gastaldi]; DOP: Donald Green [Raffaele Masciocchi] (Technicolor); M: Roman Vlad; E: Donna Christie [Ornella Micheli];

PD: Joseph Goodman; ArtD: Frank Smokecocks [Franco Fumagalli]; CO: Inoa Starly [Itala Scandariato]; AD: John M. Farquhar [Giovanni Fago]; C: Anthony Taylor [Antonio Schiavo Lena]; SO: Jackson McGregor [Renato Cadueri]; MU: Bud Steiner [Euclide Santoli]; Hair: Annette Winter. Cast: Barbara Steele (Cynthia Hichcock), Robert Flemyng (Prof. Bernard Hichcock), Montgomery Glenn [Silvano Tranquilli] (Dr. Kurt Lowe), Teresa Fitzgerald [Maria Teresa Vianello] (Margaretha), Harriet White [Harriet White Medin] (Martha, the maid), Al Christianson [Aldo Cristiani], Evar Simpson [Evaristo Signorini], Nat Harley [Giovanni Querel], Neil Robinson (Hospital assistant), Howard Nelson Rubien (Lab specialist). PROD: Louis Mann [Ermanno Donati, Luigi Carpentieri] for Panda Cinematografica; PM: Lou D. Kelly [Livio Maffei]; PS: Charles Law. Country: Italy. Filmed in Villa Perucchetti, Rome. Running time: 84 min. (m. 2422); Visa n: 37710 (06.26.1962); Rating: V.M.18; Release dates: 06.30.1962 (Italy); 12.02.1964 (U.S.A.). Distribution: Warner Bros (Italy); Sigma III Corp. (U.S.A.); Domestic gross: 142,000,000 lire. Also known as: Raptus, The Horrible Secret of Dr. Hichcock, The Secret of Dr. Hichcock, The Terrible Secret of Dr. Hichcock (U.S.A.), The Terror of Dr. Hichcock (U.K.), L'Effroyable secret du Dr. Hichcock (France, 12.09.1964), El horrible secreto del Doctor Hitchcock (Spain). Home video: Video Dimensions (DVD, U.S.A.), Medusa (DVD, Italy).

England, 1885. Renowned surgeon Professor Bernard Hichcock has created a new anesthetic which allows him to operate even in desperate conditions. However, Hichcock also happens to be a necrophile, and uses his invention to "put to sleep" his willing wife, Margaretha, and have sex with her, while pretending that she is dead. One night, though, Hichcock injects her with too much serum, and Margaretha dies. Distraught, the doctor leaves England: he returns twelve years later with a new wife, Cynthia. The woman is welcomed coldly by the doctor's housekeeper Martha (who was an accomplice in the doctor's sex games) and her marriage with Bernard soon seems to collapse under a series of weird events and hints that perhaps Margaretha has returned as a ghost. On the other hand, Hichcock can no longer control his necrophiliac impulses: he eventually discovers that Margaretha is still alive, although insane, and hiding in the house. The doctor then conjures up a deadly plan to restore his first wife's beauty at the expense of Cynthia's life...

Five years after *I Vampiri*, Riccardo Freda's second foray into the Gothic proved to be a turning point in the history of Italian horror cinema. After the first bout of films released in 1960, the thread was stagnating, with only one title (the nondescript *Werewolf in a Girls' Dormitory*) released in 1961. Furthermore, the awkward attempts drawn from the vampire tradition by the likes of Polselli and Regnoli had shown that the *filone* could not rely on a mere reworking of the Anglo-Saxon films but had to find its own steps, as *Black Sunday* had done.

It was thanks to foreign sales that the Gothic returned from the premature burial where it had been confined: by 1962 producers were finding out that, no matter how scarce Italian box-office takings were, their products could easily be sold overseas and make good money. And it was once again Freda who pointed the direction and set a new trend. This time, though, he had learnt his lesson: he hid under the English pseudonym Robert Hampton, while anglicized names were liberally used throughout the credits by cast and crew members as well, leading many critics to actually believe they were watching a British horror film—and enjoying it all the more for that. The box-office returns in its home country were solid, leading Italian distributors to promote Ricardo Blasco's Spanish thriller *Autopsy of a Criminal* (*Autopsia de un criminal*, 1963) as a follow-up to Freda's film, *L'assassino del dott. Hitchkok* [*sic*].

Shot in just two weeks in Villa Perucchetti in Via Pietro Paolo Rubens 21—a huge villa surrounded by a large green spot in the Parioli neighborhood of Rome, which is the current home of the Bulgarian Embassy in Italy—with an English-speaking cast and three small crews working at the same time on different scenes in accordance to Freda's notoriously speedy habits, *The Horrible Dr. Hichcock* marked a neat departure from Hammer-influenced plots, and leaned towards the psychological approach of Roger Corman's Edgar Allan Poe adaptations for AIP. The story features many elements in common with the works of the Baltimore-based writer: the widower who returns with his new wife in the family mansion, where the woman falls prey to rumors and mysterious presences, recalls "Ligeia," while Margaretha's (Maria Teresa Vianello) premature burial and Cynthia's (Barbara Steele) attempted one are a nod to one of Poe's primary obsessions (and a common feature in contemporaneous Gothics). What is more, in a typical Poe-like process, Freda and Gastaldi associate the memory of Hichcock's first wife with the presence of a black cat, Jezebel, who on more than one occasion becomes Margaretha's emanation of sorts (even appearing by her side in the portraits scattered throughout the house), to the point of jumping over her coffin just after the funeral—a Poe moment if ever there was one.

However, the main models of *The Horrible Dr. Hichcock* are exquisitely cinematic, starting with the title, and its reference—barely camouflaged by the deliberately erroneous spelling—to Sir Alfred Hitchcock. The choice of making the film's protagonist a namesake of the Brit filmmaker not just played with Hitchcock's reputation of being a misogynist and a sexphobic, but most of all drew on the enormous popularity that Hitch had gained in Italy: the television series *Alfred Hitchcock Presents*, broadcast on Italian television since January 1959, made him a household name. And, of course, Hitchcock's tongue-in-cheek apparitions as himself as he introduced the episodes turned his face and silhouette into a synonym for the suspenseful and the macabre—even to people who had barely, or never, seen any of his celluloid masterworks.[1]

Ernesto Gastaldi's script for *The Horrible Dr. Hichcock* is a *pot-pourri* of homages, rip-offs and creative reworkings of many, many sources, the most conspicuous being Hitch's *oeuvre*. The main reference here is *Rebecca* (1940), showing how the Italian way to horror preferred melodrama, and can often be traced back to the so-called "female Gothic," which, according to Misha Kavka, "involves the haunting of a woman by another woman (usually a rival, a *doppelgänger*, or a mother) and/or by her own projected sexual fears," and features a female protagonist "who is simultaneously a victim and an investigator of a haunting that is caused by anxieties about transgressive sexuality." Such a haunting may be real or simply paranoid, but as a consequence "the line between the supernatural and the psychological remains permeable, with the result that phantoms must equally

be read as psychological manifestations, while paranoid fears always suggest the possibility of uncanny materialization."[2]

Such a procedure allowed authors to combine the tropes of the nineteenth century haunted house story with the style and themes of 1940s/50s *film noir*. That is what Gastaldi's script does, by centering the story around a haunted house and filling it with paranoia, detection and deviated sexuality galore. *Rebecca*'s sumptuous central part, where Hitch had Joan Fontaine undergo through a series of Sadean humiliations and blunders in the vast De Winter abode, is Gastaldi's inspiration to tell Cynthia's (Barbara Steele) bewilderment inside a huge and strange villa, having to struggle with a hostile housekeeper (Harriet White) clearly specter on *Rebecca*'s Mrs. Danvers and the memory of Hichcock's first wife, Margaretha. The latter, though, is not just the product of an obsession, and more than a true ghost: she is indeed a real, malevolent presence made of flesh and blood, closing the circle and carrying the film from the territory of Gothic melodrama to out-and-out horror.

Freda and Gastaldi unearth other Hitchcockian fetishes as well: the human skull Cynthia discovers in the marriage bed comes from *Under Capricorn* (1949), the poisoned glass of milk followed by the camera in close-up is a nod to *Suspicion* (1941), while Cynthia's poisoning recalls *Notorious* (1946); the complicity between Hichcock and Martha the housekeeper also hints at the one between Claude Rains and his mother in the same film, as well as the quest for the key to open the secret door; the sequence where Cynthia, wandering in the villa, discovers Martha intent on taking care of her insane "sister" (actually Margaretha), seen from behind on a chair, refers to *Psycho*. Last but not least, the funeral under the rain, with the parade of open umbrellas as seen from an aerial shot, is a direct homage to a celebrated sequence in *Foreign Correspondent* (1940).

However, there are as many—and just as patent—references to the Romantic tradition, namely to such works as *Jane Eyre* and *Wuthering Heights*; and by focusing on a heroine persecuted by her own husband, *The Horrible Dr.*

Hichcock also recalls such works as George Cukor's remake of *Gaslight* (1944: the 1940 version had not been released in Italy), *Love from a Stranger* (1937, Rowland V. Lee, and its 1947 remake by Richard Whorf), Douglas Sirk's excellent *Sleep, My Love* (1948) and the more recent *Midnight Lace* (1960, David Miller).[3]

To talk of Postmodernism *avant la lettre* would be risky at least, yet Freda and Gastaldi lay their cinephile cards on the table with a philological cunning that is one step forward compared to the occasional muggings perpetrated by other films of the period, as well as the deftly operated borrowings in Corman's works. Speaking of which, if the use of colored gels and the sequence of Barbara Steele's premature burial seemingly testify to Freda's knowledge of AIP's Poe cycle, the Italian director would angrily reject the comparisons with Corman's films, criticizing their sloppiness as well as Corman's attitude at recycling sets and footage—as Yves Boisset, Freda's assistant on the set of *Roger la Honte* (1966), recalled.[4] Knowing Freda's love for Expressionism, it is also likely that he paid a passing reference to *Nosferatu* in the scene in which the doctor, burning with desire, leans on his wife for a vampire-like kiss, while he grabs her shoulder (and presumably her breast) with his hand, just like the eponymous bloodsucker did in Murnau's masterpiece.

One of *The Horrible Dr. Hichcock*'s outstanding elements is its approach to the supernatural. According to Tzvetan Todorov's famous definition, the fantastic "occupies the duration of the uncertainty ... the fantastic is that hesitation experienced by a person who knows only the laws of nature confronting an apparently supernatural event,"[5] before a choice that will lead the reader to the "uncanny" (that is, psychological realism) or the "marvelous." Freda uses the supernatural and its suggestions as a red herring, just as Alberto De Martino's *The Blancheville Monster* (*Horror*, 1963) and Camillo Mastrocinque's *An Angel for Satan*, where curses, monsters and otherworldly possessions actually have roots in human intrigues—not to speak of the homicidal maniacs of *The Virgin of Nuremberg* (*La vergine di Norimberga*, 1963, Antonio

Margheriti) and *Bloody Pit of Horror*. Yet, the "intrigue" is so deliriously over-the-top—and so far from the usual schemes in order to get inheritances and the like—and deliberately ambiguous (Gastaldi maintains that Freda refused to shoot the last 12 pages of his script, where the characters explained their motivations, thus avoiding to focus on rational explanations) that the film cannot merely be labelled as a mystery of sorts.

This way, *The Horrible Dr. Hichcock* is characterized by a sense of bewilderment and loss that affects the viewer and puts him/her in a state of hesitation which is at the *Fantastique*'s core. Non-Euclidean geometries abound, real surfaces assume unexpected proportions and shapes, the interiors reflect the characters' inner selves and mirror their anxieties, fears and repressed feelings. For instance, the planimetry of Hichcock's mansion is quite unclear and seems to change from scene to scene—a fact no doubt due to the hasty shooting. Yet, the effect of disorientation goes beyond a mere continuity error, when in one scene we see Silvano Tranquilli's character emerging from a window that *should not be there*. Similarly, the underground tunnel that Cynthia walks through by candlelight becomes a boundless, endless path, just like in a nightmare. "I had fun in demolishing and rebuilding the house in order to better lose Barbara Steele and the viewer inside it,"[6] Freda would quip.

Even the passage of time is not quantifiable according to rational parameters. If this is to be expected in a purely supernatural work—as with the never-ending night in Antonio Margheriti's *Castle of Blood*—such an occurrence is decidedly more unsettling when it takes place within a "rational" story. The normal day/night sequence becomes blurred, as in one scene when Cynthia and Kurt are driving back from the theater to Hichcock's house: it should be night, yet the scene takes place in an unequivocal sunlight. What is more, several spaces are arbitrarily associated with a perennial low light or semidarkness, as Hichcock's villa is, so that one is never sure which hour of the day it is. And, last but not least, the chronology of events becomes uncertain and deceitful. As film scholar Glenn

Erickson noted, when Hichcock and Cynthia first arrive at the doctor's mansion, Martha assures the latter that "tomorrow" she will be moving her crazy sister to a mental institute. The following evening, though, Martha claims to have sent her sister away "yesterday."[7] Such incongruences are obviously the result of negligence on the part of the script-girl, disjointed editing, and shooting schedules feverishly browsed in order to reach the expected number of shots for the day. Nevertheless, the result has an undetermined quality that leads to a suggestive complexity which is proper to the realm of Fantasy.

When compared to contemporaneous Italian horror films such as Bava's, *The Horrible Dr. Hichcock* displays a classic filming style: the camera movements and the use of color carry a strong dramatic function, in accordance with a vision of the Gothic as an antagonistic attitude towards realism, seen as a "bourgeois prejudice," to quote Herbert Read.[8] For example, bright red is associated with the doctor's necrophilic pulsions, when Hichcock sneaks into the morgue of his London clinic, where the body of a dead young woman lies covered with a sheet that belies her voluptuous forms. In the ensuing shot/reverse shot of Hichcock and his object of desire, Freda inserts the unreal element of the color red which little by little fills the room, turning Robert Flemyng's face into a horrific mask. Consequently, the abrupt fall of desire, when the doctor is disturbed by a noise which forces him to retrace his steps, is represented by the sudden disappearance of said red light. Similarly, after Hichcock, in a fit of desire, has injected Cynthia with the anesthetic that will slow down her heartbeat, making her just like a dead body under his touch, the woman experiments a hallucinatory vision in which her husband's face appears horribly distorted and bathed in a vivid crimson halo.

If red is the color of insane passion, green is associated with death and decay, and with the moldy dungeons that lead to the family crypt. Freda probably had in mind Poe's short story "The Masque of the Red Death," for the chromatic appearance of the secret alcove where Hichcock consumes his sexual intercourse, character-

ized by black vestments that recall the description of Prince Prospero's seventh room in Poe's tale (whereas Roger Corman's adaptation would follow Bava's lesson in the use of primary colors thanks to Nicolas Roeg's cinematography).

Music is also a vital part of the film's Gothic atmosphere, with elements of experimentation that will later take root. The opening credits of *The Horrible Dr. Hichcock*, on a pitch black background, are accompanied by Roman Vlad's remarkable main theme, which at a certain point abruptly stops. The ensuing silence is broken by a woman's scream. It is a very similar trick to the one in the opening credits of Dario Argento's *Deep Red* (*Profondo rosso*, 1975): the irruption of an external element—represented in Argento's film by a child dirge and the brief Christmas scene that precedes a killing—acts as a preparation for the horrors to come. Pity that such a moment was not featured in the heavily edited U.S. version of the film.

The season of Italian Gothic horror was characterized by the use of the zoom, which became widespread in the movie industry by the end of the 1950s and was soon adopted by many film productions as it saved time and money. Zooming allowed filmmakers to get rid of the more costly dollies and recur to close-ups within the same shot and camera set-up, so as to speed up the shooting and simplify a lot of scenes. By the mid–1960s, the zoom would be a common occurrence in Italian cinema. To check its systematic use it is sufficient to compare two films shot by the same director before and after its appearance: Riccardo Freda was not particularly fond of the zoom lens, and used to criticize Bava for his alleged over-reliance on it, but he himself often recurred to it. In *I Vampiri*, the scene in which Wandisa Guida finds herself in a secret room populated with skeletons features a series of cuts between the terrified actress' close-ups and the human remains. A similar sequence in *The Horrible Dr. Hichcock*—Cynthia discovers a human skull in her own bed, screams in terror and faints—consists of just two shots: a quick zoom-in on the macabre relic and a zoom-out from an extreme close-up of Cynthia's face to a full shot of the woman falling unconscious to the floor.

The zoom provides a much-welcomed short-cut when a filmmaker wants to emphasize a frightening moment: but it is not always a matter of time and money—or sloppiness. The zoom also provides for the corresponding visual element of that tendency to the hyperbole which was one of the main stylistic traits of the Gothic poetics. As observed by Michel Foucault, "the language of terror is dedicated to a boundless expense, even though it only seeks to achieve a single effect."[9] If writers such as Horace Walpole and Ann Radcliffe struggled to produce linguistic archaisms that gave the illusion of a distant past world, the systematic use of the zoom lens in Italian Gothic horror films becomes an unrequired underlining—a tinsel in excess which, when it manifests itself, comments upon its own artificial quality, and therefore emphasizes the detachment from the tale that is being told.

Through the zoom, the *Fantastique* finds a diegetic place as an importune element, unruly and recalcitrant: something that cannot take place peacefully among other objects in the frame, but needs to stand out on its own and as a juxtaposition to them—hence the aforementioned zoom-in on the skull on Cynthia's bed. If Freda's use of the zoom lens was only partially self-aware, Bava would take it to its extremes in *Kill, Baby...Kill!* as well as his 1970s output, where such a stylistic feature is displayed with baroque prodigality.

Also noteworthy is Freda's use of grotesque imagery in Cynthia's nightmare, where the doctor's face appears disfigured by acromegaly—a scene which the director complained had been sabotaged by producers: "it was them, not the censors, who forced me to break the nightmare scene into several pieces. In my version you could see Hichcock's face bloating and gradually transforming [...], I was very disappointed when the producers forced me to edit a series of shots/countershots in what was originally conceived as a sequence shot."[10]

Gastaldi's script also plays a riff on one of Italian Gothic's most recurrent themes: the double. However, in *The Horrible Dr. Hichcock* the splitting takes place in a more subtle way, that is rich with sociological, psychological and psychoanalytic implications. At first glance, the theme of the double seemingly refers to Cynthia, and her position as Margaretha's replacement, echoed by the latter's portraits on the wall. Yet it is Hichcock who actually suffers from a split personality, in the vein of Stevenson's Jekyll/Hyde. An illustrious member of the *haute bourgeoisie*, who in public is dedicated to saving lives, in private he is driven by an irresistible impulse to have sex with the dead. Within a society based on the respect of strict rules of conduct—best exemplified by the party sequence at Hichcock's place, where Margaretha plays the piano for her guests, and the specular sequence at the theater with Hichcock and Cynthia—the doctor's "horrible secret" manifests itself as a violent, spiteful and irrational overturning of the bourgeois life's cornerstones. This way, Hichcock's nuptial bed is seen as a grotesque replica of a mortuary, and the preparation for the coitus has the timings and manners of a funeral wake.

Such duplicity inevitably undermines the bourgeois institution par excellence—family. One of the film's most striking scenes has the doctor—fresh from having resumed his necrophilic habits—sitting in an armchair and distractedly stroking his cat, aloof and almost annoyed by the presence of Cynthia, lost as he is in his own erotic fantasies. Two people in the same room, in two completely different worlds: a slice of Victorian life (and not just that) which is worth a treatise on sociology.

The Sadean element, which deeply pervades Italian Gothic horror, is associated with this portrayal of family. Glenn Erickson emphasized the bizarre conservative nature of the relationship between Hichcock and his first wife Margaretha, who is prone to his wishes as any good wife must be in a society "where women were supposed to want sex not for themselves but only as a way of pleasing their husband/masters"[11]—to the point of fulfilling her husband's necrophilic fantasies. The paradox of a perfect Victorian marriage therefore applies to the secret nature of the bond on which it is based, which replaces traditional wedding practices.

And yet the relationship between Bernard and Margaretha exceeds a mere marital devo-

Besides underlining the film's macabre content, the Italian poster for *The Horrible Dr. Hichcock* (1962) hints at the titular character's secret: necrophilia (courtesy S. I. Bianchi).

tion, and turns out a real sadomasochistic union in which, by the book, the roles are reversed. Margaretha, the slave, the submissive one, becomes the dominant half, so much so that she comes back from the grave and pushes Hichcock to re-sume his old habits. In comparison, the doctor's second wife Cynthia is a true woman-object—or rather a trophy to be confined to the house like a valuable piece of furniture, and all in all a very passive and shallow character indeed.

One of the film's most perverse ironies is that the "revived" Margaretha claims her place next to her husband not as a sexual object but as a mistress, whose role is that of a scopophilic participation. It is a way to see what she was previously not allowed to, unable to be her husband's perfect object of desire: such will be Cynthia, duly murdered in order to provide the doctor with the raw material for his unspeakable dreams. As Foucault suggested, sadomasochism becomes a way to overcome the limitations of the body and achieve an "erotic truth" that transcends sexual pleasure.

The film's dark core, of course, is the "horrible secret" emphasized in the Italian title: necrophilia. A sexual pathology which in earlier Gothic films was just hinted at—see *Black Sunday*—facilitated and amplified by the supernatural dimension of the stories, here comes to the fore and is portrayed with an explicitness that is still rather unsettling today, and which granted the film a V.M.18 rating. It was the first time such a rating was given to a horror film after the entry into force of the new Italian law on censorship in April 1962, which abolished the earlier V.M.16 rating and introduced two new ones, V.M.14 (forbidden to audiences under 14 years old) and V.M.18 (forbidden to minors).[12] Foreign versions were severely trimmed, though: the U.S. cut of *The Horrible Dr. Hichcock* was only 76 minutes long, featured a somehow different edit (such as the opening graveyard scene being turned into a pre-credit prologue) and added fade-outs on most scenes, thus spoiling Freda's pace and atmosphere.[13]

Freda treats Hichcock's paraphilia as if it was an addiction, which makes the doctor a vampire figure *sui generis*, periodically haunted by an irrepressible desire that distorts his features as if he was a drug addict with a monkey on his back. Coherently with his purpose of grounding horror within the individual's mind, in interviews of the period Freda mentioned Krafft-Ebing's *Psychopathia Sexualis* and the historical episode of the killing of Marie-Thérèse Louise of Savoy-Carignan, princess of Lamballe, friend of Marie Antoinette, murdered by the sans-culottes in 1792 and turned into the object of necrophilic practices by her executioners.

It was a bold move. As Gérard Legrand wrote on *Positif*: "Going beyond the threshold of parody as suggested by the title [...], *The Horrible Dr. Hichcock* seems a hymn to necrophilia [...]: the storms, the excesses, the veneer of a modern chirurgical *décor* to cover a stylized *rococo* background, even the photography dominated by fascinating and artificial flashes of color [...], everything warns us that the British "good taste" and the "scary" game of Terence Fisher's characters is irrelevant here."[14] For one thing, the sequence in which Hichcock prepares the anesthetic and then, after a quick glance at his wife, decides to increase the dose to get even closer to the illusion of death, denotes a cinematic shrewdness which is quite far from the system of euphemisms and allusions that were typical of contemporaneous horror films—not to mention the fetishistic quality of Hichcock's alcove, decorated by heavy black velvet drapes and candelabra like a mortuary chamber, and the precious casket where the anesthetic which provides him the key to pleasure is kept.

Freda brilliantly emphasizes the ritual quality of Hichcock's necrophilic practices. "All is ready upstairs," the faithful housekeeper announces before leaving the doctor to his intimacy, and the meticulous preparation of the syringe with anesthetic—visually paired with the similar procedure that Hichcock routinely performs in his clinic—helps anticipate the pleasure to come. With macabre irony, Freda juxtaposes Hichcock's self-imposed celibacy after the overdose that caused Margaretha's apparent death, and his attempt at leading a normal sex life (which presumably leads to impotence or otherwise a Platonic marital *ménage*), with Hichcock's professional failures: after renouncing his miraculous anesthetic, the doctor loses one patient after another on the operating table.

The beast inside cannot be killed, because it gains its strength from the pressure under which society's hypocritical rules hold it subdued—it is our own system of repressions that kills us, as David Punter suggested in *The Literature of Terror*.[15] That is what *The Horrible Dr. Hichcock* captures to perfection, with its protagonist torn between a rational devotion to life and a subterranean dedication to death. If the Gothic literature is essentially erotic in itself, Italian Gothic horror films of the 1960s managed to synthesize such a quality to a much greater extent than other products of that era, because they were able to bring to the screen that "distortion" which—according to Jacques Lacan—is a necessary effect, or a product, of desire.[16]

Notes

1. Hitchcock's name would often be used as a publicity gimmick for such films as *Beyond the Darkness* (*Buio Omega*, 1979) and *Macabre* (*Macabro*, 1980), not to mention the recurring comparison with Dario Argento, which the latter encouraged when appearing as the host of the TV series *Door to Darkness* (*La porta sul buio*, 1973).

2. Misha Kavka, "The Gothic on Screen," in Jerrold E. Hogle, ed., *The Cambridge Companion to Gothic Fiction* (Cambridge: Cambridge University Press, 2002), p. 219.

3. Gastaldi would recycle the husband-planning-to-turn-his-wife-crazy plot in his own *giallo* scripts: take for instance *The Forbidden Photos of a Lady Above Suspicion* (*Le foto proibite di una signora per bene*, 1970, Luciano Ercoli).

4. Poindron, *Riccardo Freda*, p. 376.

5. Tzvetan Todorov, *The Fantastic: A Structural Approach to a Literary Genre* (Ithaca, NY: Cornell University Press, 1975), p. 25.

6. Poindron, *Riccardo Freda*, p. 304.

7. Glenn Erickson, "Women on the Verge of a Gothic Breakdown: Sex, Drugs and Corpses in The Horrible Dr. Hichcock," in Silver and Ursini, *Horror Film Reader*, p. 278 n. 8.

8. Herbert Read, "Foreword," in Varma, *The Gothic Flame*, p. VII.

9. Michel Foucault, *Language to Infinity*, in *Language, Counter-Memory, Practice: Selected Essays and Interviews* (Ithaca, NY: Cornell University Press, 1980), p. 65.

10. Michel Caen and J.C. Romer, "Entretien avec Riccardo Freda," *Midi-Minuit Fantastique* 10–11, Winter 1964–1965, p. 5.

11. Erickson, "Women on the Verge of a Gothic Breakdown," p. 275.

12. Contrarily to what is generally believed, the film was passed with no cuts by the Italian censors (whereas a number of cuts were made when the film was broadcast on RAI-TV for the first time in 1982).

13. Erickson points out the many differences, besides said title credits and the graveyard prologue: "*Horrible* [the U.S. version] has at least one extra off-camera line overdubbed: 'Yes, but you must admit the doctor is a bit strange himself, isn't he?' is added to Margaretha's burial scene [...]. In *Horrible* fades have been imposed on most scenes, retaining most of [...] dialog but dropping entrances and exits [...]. Freda originally cut pointedly from Bernard holding his syringe aloft in the clinic to him identically holding his sex-game syringe later at home; *Horrible* ruins the moment by inserting an unnecessarily literal shot of a homeward-bound carriage in between.

When Bernard dashes into the rainstorm in pursuit of the piano-playing phantom, *Horrible* omits a nice sequence of him returning to the house and confusing a lightning-lit white curtain for the specter, before finding the unconscious Cynthia in the garden. At the conclusion, the young intern's long climb into Hichcock's window is shortened by almost a minute. No key sex scenes are actually missing, but most are abbreviated with the addition of early fadeouts [...]." Erickson, "Women on the Verge of a Gothic Breakdown," p. 277–78 n. 4.

14. Gérard Legrand, "L'Effroyable secret du Dr. Hichcock," *Positif* 53, June 1963, p. 88.

15. David Punter, *The Literature of Terror: A History of Gothic Fictions from 1765 to the Present Day, Vol. 2: The Modern Gothic* (New York: Routledge, 1996), p. 183.

16. Slavoj Žižek, *Looking Awry: An Introduction to Jacques Lacan Through Popular Culture* (Cambridge MA: MIT Press, 1992), p. 12

Slaughter of the Vampires, a.k.a. *Curse of the Blood Ghouls* (*La strage dei vampiri*)

D: Roberto Mauri [Giuseppe Tagliavia]. *S and SC*: Roberto Mauri; *DOP*: Ugo Brunelli (B&W); *M*: Aldo Piga (Ed. Bixio—Sam); *E*: Jenner Menghi; *ArtD*: Giuseppe Ranieri; *CO*: Vilelma Vitaioli; *AD*: Franco Longo; *AC*: Bruno Maestrelli; *SO*: Nino Renda, Fausto Ancillai; *MU*: Carlo Grillo. [*English language version*: Nevada S.P.A.] *Cast*: Walter Brandi [Walter Bigari] (Marquis Wolfgang), Dieter Eppler (The vampire), Graziella Granata (Louise, Wolfgang's wife), Paolo Solvay [Luigi Batzella] (Dr. Nietzsche), Gena Gimmy [Gimmi] (Corinne), Alfredo Rizzo (Manservant), Edda Ferronao (Nietzsche's maid), Maretta Procaccini (Resy), Carla Foscari (Teresa). *PROD*: Mercur Films; *GM*: Dino Sant'Ambrogio; *PS*: Luigi Pinini D'Oliva; *PSe*: Claudio Sinibaldi. *Country*: Italy. Filmed at Castle d'Aquino, Monte San Giovanni Campano (Frosinone). *Running time*: 84 min. (m. 2185); Visa n: 36600 (01.20.1962); *Rating*: V.M.16; *Release dates*: 02.06.1962 (Italy); 06.04.1969 (U.S.A.). *Distribution*: Mercur (Regional, Italy); Pacemaker Pictures/Walter Manley Enterprises (U.S.A.); *Domestic gross*: 36,000,000 lire. *Also known as*: The Slaughter of the Vampires, Curses of the Ghouls (U.S.A.); Le Massacre des vampires (France). *Home video*: Dark Sky Films; Retromedia (DVD, U.S.A.), Sinister (DVD, Italy).

Germany, nineteenth century. The conjugal life of two newlyweds, Marquis Wolfgang and Louise, is perturbed by the arrival of a mysterious nameless stranger, who turns out to be a vampire. The bloodsucker, who hides in the castle's wine cellar, seduces Louise and turns her into his vampire slave. Worried about his wife's declining health, Wolfgang seeks the help of Dr. Nietzsche, who immediately recognizes the symptoms of vampirism but cannot do anything to save Louise.

Meanwhile, the vampire has set his eyes on the housekeeper, Corinne...

Of all the Italian vampire films made between 1960 and 1962, Roberto Mauri's *Slaughter of the Vampires* is the most loyal to the Gothic tradition: the setting is the nineteenth century, the bloodsucker is a charming—at least in the filmmakers' intentions—Dracula surrogate (Dieter Eppler), replete with cloak and canines, his antagonist is a savior *à la* Van Helsing (future film director Luigi Batzella) who claims that "to science must be added the power of faith" and is named Nietzsche—like the philosopher, no less. Mauri draws on the Gothic imagery as made popular by Hammer films, as shown in the opening sequence, where a carriage transporting the vampire (and his coffin) runs at breakneck speed to reach a new safe haven before dawn.

This does not prevent *Slaughter of the Vampires* from veering off decisively from its models, though. The prologue, in which the unnamed vampire flees, leaving his lover exposed to the villagers' wrath (justice will be meted out with sticks and pitchforks) presents us with a monster that is far less untouchable compared to tradition, so much so that he runs screaming from the angry crowd and is ready to abandon his companion without a second thought. What is more, the scene ends with a POV shot of the female vampire, surrounded by a looming mob. It is a neat inversion of clichés which sabotages the classical set-up by adopting the point of view of the monster, who is now menaced rather than menacing: the predator becomes the prey.

Mauri's script portrays the aristocratic vampire as a dark romantic anti-hero who undermines the serenity of Wolfgang's (Walter Brandi) family. He appears as a mysterious, uninvited guest at a nuptial ball and in no time at all seduces Wolfgang's beautiful and repressed wife Louise (Graziella Granata). However, the vampire is not as gallant as others are led to believe: " Ah, if you could but see yourself as you are in my heart, you might then see your real self! In my heart you are not the woman you think you are—you are part of a greater mystery," he somberly whispers to Louise: yet later on we will find out that in the meantime he has put his eyes (and fangs) on the housekeeper (Gena Gimmi), and in the end he even makes an attempt at vampirizing the caretaker's little daughter.

Eppler, however, does not have the necessary appeal, and looks like an unconvincing carbon copy of the vampires as seen in Mexican horror films of the period, with his greased hair, pasty-white face and black circles around his eyes. The story behind the German actor's casting in *Slaughter of the Vampires* is typical of the way the 1960s Italian movie industry worked: Eppler took part in an international Dino De Laurentiis production, and was noticed by Dino's brother (Eppler spoke English and a bit of Italian), who introduced him to several producers. One of them cast Eppler as a police inspector in a thriller that would start production soon, but the actor never heard from the producer again. He showed up in Rome anyway, just to learn that the shooting had been postponed due to lack of funds. Eppler then demanded to be paid just the same. The next day he was called back to the producer's office: another producer would start filming a vampire movie the following day, and needed an actor to play the vampire, who could do the part in Italian.[1]

The vampirization takes place in the nuptial bed, and exudes an explicitly erotic feel. For Lucy's seduction scene as seen in *Horror of Dracula*, Terence Fisher succeeded without even showing the vampire, in four exemplary shots: the woman sitting on the bed, the window where the Count would come in, a close-up of the victim with her neck already marked by the vampire's bite, and then again another shot of the open window, on a landscape swept by a wind which alluded not just to a wild vortex of feelings, but also to the passing of death. Mauri, on the other hand, does not dwell on poetic imagery, but goes for the jugular. Eppler caresses the woman's breasts and pushes his face over them as Klaus Kinski will do in Werner Herzog's *Nosferatu the Vampyre* (*Nosferatu: Phantom der Nacht*, 1979), and the victim moans, sighs and unequivocally raises and lowers her chest in an orgasmic crescendo.

The effects of vampirization immediately affect the marriage. A case in point is the sequence in which Louise wanders at night in the park, where Mauri's camera tracks back, retreating as the woman advances, as if it was intimidated by her erotic frenzy: Louise's gaze lays restless over the treetops beaten by the night breeze, conveying a feverish craving. Another telling scene has Louise sitting in the garden with a blank stare, while beside her the unsuspecting husband is reading her passages from a book. It is a portrait of ordinary marital unhappiness: he, she and the other. An image reiterated later on: Wolfgang is sleeping like a baby in their bed, while his wife is wide awake and alert, waiting for her lover's call. As she will confess to the latter, she now feels disgust for her husband.

As the weak and clumsy Wolfgang, Walter Brandi is perhaps the *filone*'s most unlikely hero: his own wife is seduced under his nose without him noticing, he looks asexual and definitely not virile (starting with the sissy silk nightgown he is wearing in several scenes), he loves books more than action and is eventually bitten by his wife and housekeeper without posing much of a resistance—to the point that he has to resort to those blood transfusions that are usually reserved for female characters. Near the end, Wolfgang is almost impaled by mistake by Dr. Nietzsche, in a comic twist that may or may not be unintentional.

The gore is almost non-existent, mostly because of the lack of budget: when Eppler is transfixed by a stake and turns into a skeleton, Mauri opts for a painless series of cross dissolves. As was customary with contemporaneous Gothic horror films, the entire shooting took place inside a real manor—Castle d'Aquino in Monte San Giovanni Campano, between Rome and Naples: the same location of Luigi Batzella's delirious *Nude for Satan* (*Nuda per Satana*, 1974)—where the cast and crew also stayed during filming. In a 2006 interview, Eppler recalled that *Slaughter of the Vampires* was shot on a shoestring and the actors were not getting paid: a small advance was all the money he ever saw for that film—the producer kept making up excuses whenever he showed up on the set and eventually went bankrupt, a common occurrence at that time.

Mauri's film was released in the United States in 1969, in a truncated 72-minute print, as *Curse of the Blood Ghouls*. Only with the 2007 Dark Sky DVD release American audiences could savor the complete version, whereas the previous Retromedia release was missing about two minutes of footage. However, the Dark Sky transfer was matted and reframed to appeal the 16 × 9 television market.

Roberto Mauri (real name Giuseppe Tagliavia, born in 1924 in Castelvetrano, Sicily), a former actor of B-grade 1950s films, had debuted behind the camera in 1958 with *Vite perdute* (*La legge del mitra*), followed by 1960's *I mafiosi*. In the Sixties Mauri sailed the low waters of genre cinema: period adventure (*Il pirata del diavolo*, 1963), sword-and-sandal (*Gli invincibili fratelli Maciste*, 1964), giallo (*Le notti della violenza*, 1965, which was rejected by the censorship commission for its erotic content), before he specialized in Western with such titles as *Sartana in the Valley of Death* (*Sartana nella valle degli avvoltoi* (1970) and *... e lo chiamarono Spirito Santo* (*And His Name Was Holy Ghost*, 1971). His last film as a director was the sleazy erotic thriller *Le porno killers* (1980).

Note

1. *Dieter Eppler: Interview with the Vampire*, included in the U.S. DVD *Slaughter of the Vampires* (Dark Sky Films). However, in the Italian version Eppler is dubbed by Emilio Cigoli, one of Italy's most famous voice actors (who, among others, dubbed Marlon Brando, John Wayne, Gary Cooper, Clark Gable, Humphrey Bogart, Orson Welles and Vincent Price).

1963

Black Sabbath (I tre volti della paura)

D: Mario Bava. *S*: "The Telephone" based on a short story by Guy De Maupassant (actually F. G. Snyder); "The Wurdalak" based on the novelette *Sem'ya vurdalaka* by Aleksey Tolstoy; "The Drop of Water" based on the story by Ivan Chekhov (actually the short story "Dalle tre alle tre e mezzo" by P. Kettridge [Franco Lucentini]); *SC*: Marcello Fondato, Alberto Bevilacqua, Mario Bava, Ugo Guerra; *DOP*: Ubaldo Terzano; *M*: Roberto Nicolosi (Ed. RCA) (*U.S. version*: Les Baxter; *music coordinator*: Al Simms; *music editor*: Eve Newman); *E*: Mario Serandrei; *AE*: Lina Caterini; *ArtD*: Giorgio Giovannini; *APD*:

Francesco Bronzi; *SD*: Riccardo Dominici; *SE*: Eugenio Bava (Sculptor: masks and faces—uncredited); *CO*: Tina Loriedo Grani; *C*: Mario Mancini; *AC*: Enrico Fontana; *MU*: Otello Fava; *Hair*: Renata Magnanti; *SO*: Mario Messina (*U.S. version*: Alfred R. Bird, Ernest Reichert, Kay Rose); *Mix*: Fausto Ancillai, Nino Renda; *SS*: Priscilla Contardi. *Cast*: "The Telephone": Michéle Mercier (Rosy), Lydia Alfonsi (Mary). *Uncredited*: Milo Quesada (Frank Rainer). "The Wurdalak": Boris Karloff (Gorka), Mark Damon (Vladimire d'Urfe), Susy Andersen (Sdenka), Massimo Righi (Pietro), Rica [Rika] Dialina (Maria), Glauco Onorato (Giorgio). "The Drop of Water": Jacqueline Pierreux (Helen Chester), Milly Monti (The Maid), Harriet White Medin (Miss Perkins, the neighbor), Gustavo De Nardo (Police Inspector). *Uncredited*: Alessandro Tedeschi (Coroner). *PROD*: Salvatore Billitteri and Paolo Mercuri for Galatea Film—Emmepi (Rome)/Lyre Film (Paris); *PM*: Paolo Mercuri; *PS*: Armando Govoni; *ADM*: Franco Grifeo. *Country*: Italy/France. Filmed at Titanus Farnesina Studios (Rome). *Running time*: 93 min. (m. 2556); Visa n: 40988 (08.12.1963); *Rating*: V.M.14; *Release dates*: 08.17.1963 (Italy); 05.06.1964 (U.S.A.). *Distribution:* Warner (Italy); AIP (U.S.A.); *Domestic gross*: 103,500,000 lire. *Also known as*: *The Three Faces of Fear*, *The Three Faces of Terror*, *Les Trois visages de la peur* (France, 11.17.1965), *Die drei Gesichter der Furcht* (West Germany, 08.21.1964), *Las tres caras del miedo* (Spain, 12.06.1965). *Home video*: Kino (Blu-Ray/DVD, U.S.A.), Arrow (Blue-Ray/DVD, U.K.).

"The Telephone": Rosy, a Parisian call-girl, is frightened by a mysterious persecutor who keeps making threatening phone calls on her number; she believes the voice belongs to her pimp, Frank, whom she had jailed with her testimony, and who apparently escaped from prison. Rosy invites a female friend, Mary, to stay. It turns out that Mary is actually the caller... "The Wurdalak": Russia, nineteenth century. Vladimire, a young nobleman on the way home, finds a beheaded corpse with a knife plunged into its heart. He stops at a farmhouse inhabited by the elderly Gorka and his family and learns that the region is plagued by the wurdalak, a vampire who feeds on the blood of its beloved ones. It turns out that Gorka too has been bitten, and he spreads the contagion to his family members... "The Drop of Water": a nurse, Helen Chester, is called to a large house to prepare the body of an elderly medium who recently passed away. Helen steals a valuable ring from the dead woman, but soon she is tormented by her vengeful spirit...

Once the first wave of Italian horror films dried up, the movies produced from 1963 onwards often resorted to co-production deals, as a way to have access to law benefits or to the so-called *minimo garantito* (guaranteed minimum), that is the sum of money granted in advance by the distributors.

The guaranteed minimum played a fundamental role, as their economical power allowed distributors to steer the producers' choices. On the other hand, foreign co-producers had a mere financial function: they did not play any significant role in the film, other than dictating the choice of several actors and technicians, whose presence was necessary by law in order for the film to be qualified as a co-production according to the Italian law. On the other hand, foreign contributions were sometimes listed even though those names did not have anything to do with the finished picture: this was often the case with screenplay credits (i.e., in Italian-Spanish co-productions). Most often, foreign co-producers were *de facto* distributors, who financed the film in order to be granted its distribution in their own country. One such example was Mario Bava's *Black Sabbath*, produced by Galatea Films with the Paris-based Lyre Films, which was actually a French branch of the Roman production company; another participation came, in the form of a guaranteed minimum, on the part of London's Altavista Film Production.

Although a recurring occurrence in Italian cinema of the period, *Black Sabbath* is an oddity within the realm of the Gothic thread: a horror film anthology. Whereas it was commonplace for producers to concoct omnibus comedies, often with the participation of several renowned filmmakers, Bava's effort would prove as something of a rare bird in the history of Italian horror, where just a handful of titles carried the same structure, the closest chronologically being *Spirits of the Dead* (*Tre passi nel delirio*, 1968).[1]

The choice of the anthology format was no doubt due to the film being a co-production aimed mainly at the U.S. market, where it was distributed by American International Pictures—hence the choice of a title which would recall Bava's previous U.S. hit, *Black Sunday*. The obvious model was AIP's Edgar Allan Poe–

Italian fotobusta for Mario Bava's anthology horror *Black Sabbath*, featuring Boris Karloff and Susy Andersen.

inspired *Tales of Terror* (1962, Roger Corman), which spawned a number of imitations in the States as well, such as Sidney Salkow's mediocre *Twice-Told Tales* (1963), based on Nathaniel Hawthorne's stories. Another influence—perhaps suggested to Bava by his American distributors—was the American anthology TV series *Thriller*, featuring Boris Karloff as the host, a role he would reprise in *Black Sabbath*.

With its three episodes, each quite different in tone, settings and premises, *Black Sabbath* functions not only as an epitome of Italian Gothic's thematic and stylistic points, but it also hints at the future of the genre, its ramifications and developments.

Three different approaches to horror co-exist in the film. First, a segment of pure suspense ("The Telephone") which derives from Bava's early *giallo The Evil Eye*, a.k.a. *The Girl Who Knew Too Much* (*La ragazza che sapeva troppo*, 1963) and thus certifies the Gothic's permeability with the thriller. Second, a period Gothic in the vein of Corman's films ("The Wurdalak"), more attentive to narrative coherence than stylistic digressions. Third, the most free-form and genuinely frightening of the lot, "The Drop of Water." Here, Bava enacts terrorist-like fear tactics, touching raw nerves (such as the hassle caused by the buzzing of a fly and a monotonous drop of water) and deeper fears (a pitch-black corridor, a light that comes and goes) with a rule-breaking ease and an attention to the multi-sensorial quality of horror that predates Dario Argento's *Suspiria* and *Inferno* (1980)—thus turning a typical ghost story into something much more modern and original. This, however, could be savored in its entirety only in the original Italian version, as the American cut of *Black Sabbath* altered the original order by opening the film with *The Drop of Water* and saving *The Wurdalak* for last. Quite a debatable choice, indeed.

Black Sabbath displays an impressive triptych of literary sources: according to the credits, its three episodes are based "on works by Maupassant, Tolstoy and Chekhov." Yet, at a second glance, things appear quite different than they seem.

First of all, "The Telephone" was not inspired by any Guy de Maupassant story, but instead came from the work of a certain F. G. Snyder. It has proven impossible to gather any informations on the elusive F. G. (or Howard, according to other sources) Snyder, whose name appears only on the film's publicity material for foreign audiences: it is likely that Bava (and/or his scriptwriters) plundered one of those short stories with a sting in the tail that could be found as an appendix to Bava's beloved *Gialli Mondadori* paperbacks, such as the one that ten years later would serve as a blueprint for the director's grim crime film *Rabid Dogs* ... unless Snyder was just a fabrication on the part of the scriptwriters. An option which cannot be ruled out, given what happened with the other two episodes.

Although decidedly nobler, "The Wurdalak"'s ascendancy is not as illustrious as one might think, since Aleksey Kostantinovich Tolstoy—the author of the novella *The Family of the Vourdalak*, 1839—was just a cousin of the Count Lev Nikolaevich who wrote *War and Peace*. Bava found Tolstoy's story in the popular anthology *I vampiri tra noi*, published in 1960 by Feltrinelli.

Last, and best, there is no short story by Chekhov titled "The Drop of Water." Bava and his acolytes Alberto Bevilacqua and Marcello Fondato took partial inspiration—especially in the description of the protagonist's squalid apartment and the detail of the leaky faucet—from the short story "Dalle tre alle tre e mezzo" ("From three to half-past three") by a P. Kettridge, included in another very popular anthology of the period, *Storie di fantasmi* ("Ghost Stories"), published by Einaudi in 1960 and edited by the renowned Carlo Fruttero and Franco Lucentini. In spite of appearances, P. Kettridge was very much Italian: behind the pseudonym hid none other than Franco Lucentini himself.[2] Similarly to what happened with contemporary pulp paperbacks, the anthology displayed a fake "original title" (*Ghosts Don't Kill*) and Lucentini was credited as the Italian translator. In the preface to the anthology, Carlo Fruttero wrote with sharp irony: "Harvey, Jacobs and Kettridge seem to belong to the kind of writers who have

only one story within themselves," putting Kettridge alongside William Fryer Harvey and William Wymark Jacobs, included as well in the same anthology respectively with "August Heat" and "The Monkey's Paw."[3]

"The Telephone" moves from a typical "female Gothic" plot—the wife persecuted by her lover/husband—and manipulates it in a surprising way. First, it takes place in the present, and not in a gloomy castle but in a squalid basement. Second, Rosy (Michèle Mercier) is a sexually uninhibited version of the anxious women-in-peril of those early *noir* melodramas, as the story makes it rather clear from the beginning that she is a prostitute. The episode was usually dismissed as the least interesting one, especially by U.S. horror scholars—a fact due in large part to AIP's butchering of *Black Sabbath*, which resulted not only in an alteration of the episodes' original order, but also in a heavy tampering of the segment's content.

Besides its morbid subtext (on which later on), "The Telephone" is interesting for its *mise-en-scène* of suspense, which is conditioned by the claustrophobic setting[4]: the barely sketched story turns into a mocking pulp variation on Jean Cocteau's one-act play *La Voix humaine*. The voyeuristic tension which characterized Italian cinema of the period is synthesized by Bava's almost theoretical abstraction: a beautiful woman alone in her apartment, a telephone, and a menacing voice which seemingly belongs to someone who is spying on her all the time.

The conventions and restrictions of the *huis clos* become pretexts to peep on the heroine's intimacy, as Bava shows Mercier as she is undressing and putting on her nightgown, in a striking voyeuristic crescendo. The results are somewhat disturbing—especially when we realize that the unknown persecutor is actually a woman, Rosy's friend Mary (Lydia Alfonsi). Erotically obsessed with Rosy, Mary enacts menacing phone calls—pretending to be Rosy's ex-lover (and pimp) who just escaped from jail and is looking for vengeance—in order to have the opportunity of sleeping with her.

The U.S. version eliminated the (rather explicit) lesbian undertones, adding a supernatural angle that destroyed the story's point, which

AIP thought excessively "strong" for a mere horror film—further proof of the peculiar "adult" quality of Italian Gothic compared to the more juvenile U.S. counterparts. The episode was heavily edited with several cuts, different dubbing in a few scenes and a newly shot insert of the letter Mary writes while Rosy is asleep.[5]

Although apparently closer to Gothic clichés, "The Wurdalak"[6] actually manages to break more than a few rules, and is miles apart from other vampire films of the period. Bava—who already told a story of vampirism perpetrated along the blood line of an aristocratic family in *Black Sunday*—tells of a patriarchal vampire who does not seduce his victims but uses his absolute power of life and death over the other family members, who are led to obey him against any common sense.

Gorka (Boris Karloff) is a peasant vampire: he has rough manners, is irascible and egotistical, and conceives family relations as a matter of ownership. He is in command, and the others have to follow him to the letter. The vampiric contagion also follows different rules compared to tradition. The undead preys on the beloved ones in order to soothe the loneliness of his state, and another clever detail has Gorka's sons rack their brains to interpret his words: Bava suggests that the vampire cannot lie over his own condition, a fact that gives the proceedings a fairy tale–like quality.

The barbaric world of "The Wurdalak" is based on oppressive hierarchical rules. The family's life revolves around the elderly *pater familias*, who is served and revered as a king; his male progeny follows his every word, no matter how unreasonable (such as killing the family dog because of its annoying growls) without batting an eyelid; the women are passive and obedient. Such a world is much closer to Italy's rural culture, which was prevalent at least until World War II, and was gradually disappearing due to mass emigration to the big cities and the development of industries. This makes the episode much more incisive than its rather static and predictable script would allow for.

To Bava, horror begins and develops within the family, and it accompanies its reestablish-

ment in parallel to its disintegration. The vampire contagion spawned by old Gorka sets in motion a curious process of rebellion and (apparent) emancipation which, while it destroys the whole family, prepares for its reconstruction and strengthening. Maria (Rica Dialina) kills her husband, Giorgio (Glauco Onorato), who was preventing her from opening the door to their little vampire son, while the submissive Sdenka (Susy Andersen) turns into a seductress, by biting the fool Vladimire (Mark Damon) before the eager eyes of Gorka and the other vampires. The scene works as an implicit paraphrase (yet in reverse) of the ritual wedding defloration. An entire family welcomes and covets a new member.

Vladimire—the stranger, the outsider—is little more than a powerless observer. Just like other male figures of Italian Gothic, he has very little of the strong and unblemished hero, and in the end he eventually capitulates before a woman, thus showing his own weakness. With his aristocratic manners and naive romanticism, Vladimire is poles apart from Gorka and his family, who embrace concrete values such as the indissolubility—even after death—of the family ties. Most of Bava's themes would be reprised and developed in Giorgio Ferroni's excellent rendition of Tolstoy's story, *The Night of the Devils*, in a contemporary setting, at the border between Italy and Slovenia.

"The Drop of Water" is at the same time the most literary and idiosyncratic of the triptych. The plot has echoes of Poe's "The Tell-Tale Heart," and moves along the coordinates of a typical ghost story based on retaliation, yet with surprising results. It is *Black Sabbath*'s most original, daring and scary segment, and truly one of Bava's very best efforts.

A remarkable element about *Black Sabbath* is the way the film works on different levels when it comes to frighten the viewer. Whereas "The Telephone" leans on a crescendo of uneasy details—such as the phone ringing over and over—rather than gore, "The Wurdalak" employs a grotesque exhibition of gruesome shock details that come off as unexpected blows below the belt: one such example is the scene where Gorka exhibits a vampire's severed head, drawing it by the hair from a sack like a macabre trophy—a detail which AIP judged too raw for American audiences, thus optically censoring it via a crude frame enlargement.

"The Drop of Water" features a more complex array of tricks in order to tell its story of a vengeance from beyond the grave. The supernatural is announced through a series of acoustic signals that act on both Miss Chester's (Jacqueline Pierreux) subjective perception and the viewer's: the grueling, obsessive drop of water from a leaky faucet and the unnerving buzzing of a fly are the hints of a sensory assault that preludes the shocking appearance of the ghost.

Here, Bava develops one of the central characters of his cinema: the correspondence between human beings and their inanimate doubles, which would play a key role in his *oeuvre*, including *Blood and Black Lace* (the opening sequence), *Kill, Baby…Kill!*, *Hatchet for a Honeymoon* (*Il rosso segno della follia*, 1970) and especially *Lisa and the Devil*. Such a concept is linked to an idea of the uncanny with strong literary roots: Olimpia, the "daughter" of professor Spallanzani loved by Nathaniel in E. T. A. Hoffmann's short story "The Sandman," whom all believe to be a girl while she is actually an automaton. The insistence on mannequins and dolls also hinted at Bava's knowledge of Surrealism: Hans Bellmer's famous dummies, which had been inspired as well by Hoffmann's story, aimed at the same disturbing eroticism as Bava's female dolls, especially in the 1972 film.

"The Drop of Water"'s ghost is not played by a real actress, but is actually a wax dummy (sculpted by Bava's father, Eugenio) whose deformed face displays an obscenely grotesque grin, which gives it "an expression that is cruel and stupid at the same time."[7] It is quite an unsettling sight, the more so because the viewer's perception is caught off-guard. Bava emphasizes the ghost's ubiquity and its inexorability: the former is rendered through the shot-reverse-shot routine—as Miss Chester glimpses the ghost in various parts of her flat—as well as the mutation of the shooting axis, whereas the latter is achieved by placing the dummy on an off-screen dolly which allows it to advance towards the camera as if it was fluctuating in the air. It

was a similar trick as the one employed by Jean Cocteau in *Beauty and the Beast*, in the scene where Josette Day first visits the haunted castle, and later re-used among others by William Castle in *House on Haunted Hill* and *The Tingler* (both 1959).

This way, Bava manipulates the viewer's perception, basing the visual shock on the contradiction between motion and stillness: the specter proceeds unnaturally, sliding towards us, and thus demolishing our basic notions about how a living being should move, in accordance with what Freud wrote in his essay *The Uncanny*, about the "doubts whether an apparently animate being is really alive; or, conversely, whether a lifeless object might not be in fact animate," which Freud refers to "waxwork figures, ingeniously constructed dolls and automata."[8]

The elderly lady's movement is not of this earth. This, combined with the rigidity of her features and posture, makes her a paradoxical entity, in contradiction with the rules of logic and rationality. Whereas horror cinema's typical portrayal of someone who has come back to life unnaturally (a zombie, a mummy) features an emphasis on the transition from stillness to motion, Bava enhances the *revenante*'s rigidity, pushing it to the limit of the ridiculous. The director was well aware that horror—just like laughter—is sparked by a sudden contradiction to our beliefs and expectations. The dummy, in short, is just that—a dummy, with its obscene grimace and its *rigor mortis*. Nevertheless, it is able to appear and disappear at will inside Miss Chester's flat, in such absurd poses as sitting on a rocking chair, with a cat in its lap.

Even the shots in which the specter's hand appears behind Miss Chester avoid playing on the element of threat given by the sudden apparition and the danger of its touch. Here, Bava focuses on the incongruity of the wax hand, which becomes an upsetting element in itself, worthy of the W.F. Harvey–inspired *The Beast with Five Fingers* (1946, Robert Florey). This is emblematic of Bava's habit of turning the horrific into the surreal—or the Surrealistic, for that matter: the severed hand was a recurrent element in Surrealism, as in Alberto Giacometti's "Surrealist table"—which would find its peak in *Shock*, with the sight of the ceramic hand that frightens Daria Nicolodi.

Just as in the latter film, in "The Drop of Water" Bava insisted on the exhausting effect that the daily and the trivial have on all of us—a buzzing fly, a leaky faucet, a noise disturbing the stillness of the night—, thus interpreting horror not just as a sudden shock, but also as psychological wear-and-tear. Bava also focused on the individual's relationship with the environment and the inability to dominate the objects—up to the point of being subjugated by them. This is almost subliminal at first: there is a subtle contradiction between the realistic *fin de siècle* setting in Miss Chester's squalid apartment and the implacable, unexplained and anti-realistic blinking green light that turns the place into a creepy cave of sorts. Another example is the lamp that falls from the ceiling down to the

table when the old lady's dress is placed, as if it had its own vitality: it is the first hint of the "revolt of the objects" against Miss Chester that, again, predates the home apocalypse of *Shock*.

All this is masterfully accompanied by the director's celebrated—often self-deprecatory—humor. While watching these films, it is all-too-obvious that their makers did not take themselves too seriously: by manipulating the Gothic imagery as a set of codes and established rules, scriptwriters and filmmakers belied a natural disenchantment. Without reaching the open derision of Corman's *divertissements* such as *The Raven* (1963), they displayed a similar detachment from their subject matters: that is why Italian Gothic horror films are often in a precarious balance between farce and melo-drama, exaggeration and restlessness.

To Bava, however, irony was also the culmina-

THIS IS THE NIGHT OF THE NIGHTMARE...THE DAY OF THE UNDEAD!

A story that goes beyond the boundries of the Supernatural to the half-world of the living dead. Where a woman's soul inhabits a fly's body, where Vengeance is only a voice and where vampires suck only the blood of those they love the dearest.

AMERICAN INTERNATIONAL presents

BORIS KARLOFF STARRING IN

Black Sabbath

...The most gruesome day in the calendar of the Undead!

IN PATHÉCOLOR

MARK DAMON · MICHELE MERCIER · DIRECTED BY MARIO BAVA · AN AMERICAN INTERNATIONAL PICTURE

The United States poster for *Black Sabbath* featured a headless horseman no doubt inspired by Washington Irving's short story "The Legend of Sleepy Hollow" (Libreria Eleste).

tion of a judicious addition of visual counterpoints, that involve the viewers and upset their expectations. The aforementioned mischievous lamp holder in "The Drop of Water" is an upsetting detail which Bava immediately traces back (through the carelessness with which the maid raises it to its original position) to everyday life, eliciting a liberating smile. On the contrary, the dripping faucet becomes a terrifying element of anxiety. Therefore, as noted by James Silver and Alain Ursini, anything—an image, a detail, a scene prop, a camera cut—"which is used for suspense in one film [...] may be transmuted for comic effect in another [...]. Even the most bizarre images may be used to evoke a *frisson* [...] or laughter."[9] Therefore, the tree branches which frightened the coachman in *Black Sunday* elicit laughter in *Black Sabbath*'s much-discussed epilogue.

Boris Karloff's final monologue, as he is apparently riding a horse in the Russian tundra, still in his Gorka outfit, is accompanied by a zoom-out that reveals the set around him: technicians and prop men are busy running in circles around the actor—who is sitting on a rocking-horse prop—and waving branches, so as to simulate vegetation. All this is accompanied by a score seemingly borrowed from a silent movie farce. This is not just a brilliant metafilmic sting in the tail, though, but also a reflection on the subject matter itself.

At the film's beginning, Bava showed Karloff ·dressed in a contemporary outfit, as the host to the trilogy of horror stories: a similar role to the one the actor had in the TV series *Thriller* (1960–1962) and a recurring convention in TV shows of the period (think of Rod Serling in *The Twilight Zone* and Alfred Hitchcock in *Alfred Hitchcock Presents*), which worked as a filter to the narration. In the prologue, Karloff plays the host with amused participation, establishing a direct dialogue with the audience. The host has a privileged position on both the story and the viewer: he is ironic, yet never ridiculous (although sometimes the unintentional effect might be just that: a case in point is the pompous Criswell introducing Ed Wood's films).

In the ending, Bava again shows Karloff, still wearing his scene costume: by addressing the camera, the actor breaks the fourth wall and abruptly stops the flow of the narration. At this point a final sermon would be expected, drawing a moral conclusion to the stories and closing the circle, which indeed happens. Yet, by revealing the illusion of the set and demystifying Karloff's role—an idea which the director improvised on set on the last day of shooting, after receiving a telegram from AIP which asked him to lighten the episode's scary finale[10]—Bava strips the elderly horror icon of that authority which the audience ascribed him, and which he himself had invested Karloff with in the prologue.

In the end, Bava invites us to laugh at (and with) not only Karloff, but also himself and all of those involved in the film. Furthermore, he asks us to laugh at what all that represents. Movies are useless. They cannot teach any moral. The best they can do is allow us to dream. And at the end of the path there is no lesson to be learned, but only a playful goodbye. A rocking-horse, a few grown men acting like children, and lots of imagination.

Movies are just child's play—played by adults who never grew up.

Notes

1. Other Italian horror anthologies are few and far between indeed: *Two Evil Eyes* (*Due occhi diabolici*, 1990, Dario Argento, George A. Romero), *DeGenerazione* (1994, Vv.Aa.), *The Three Faces of Terror* (*I tre volti del terrore*, 2004, Sergio Stivaletti). Recent years have seen a renaissance of the format in a number of indie efforts, such as *Fantasmi* (2011, Vv.Aa.) and *P.O.E.—Poetry of Eerie* (2011), where 15 directors adapted Poe's stories.

2. The ascendancy was first pointed out by Italian film historian Antonio Bruschini, in Piselli, Morlocchi and Bruschini, *Bizarre sinema!*, p. 39.

3. Carlo Fruttero, "Prefazione," in Carlo Fruttero and Franco Lucentini, eds., *Storie di fantasmi. Racconti del soprannaturale* (Turin: Einaudi, 1960, 1984), p. xv. Giuseppe Lippi later signed several short stories and novels with the pseudonym P. Kettridge, Jr., as a homage to Lucentini.

4. Bava fans will recognize "The Telephone"'s main set as the same apartment as seen in *The Girl Who Knew Too Much*. On the other hand, one of the last scenes in *The Wurdalak* features the same set (the ruined monastery) as seen in the striking sequence of Katia's appearance in *Black Sunday*.

5. For further details, see Tim Lucas, *Mario Bava: All the Colors of the Dark* (Cincinnati, OH, Video Watchdog, 2007), pp. 481–511.

6. Misspelled *I Wurdulak* in the Italian cut of the film:

a typo which Bava himself repeated in a radio interview dated April 1, 1978, during the show *Il terzo orecchio*.

7. Pezzotta, *Mario Bava*, p. 62.
8. Freud, *The Uncanny*, p. 135.
9. Silver and Ursini, "Mario Bava: The Illusion of Reality," pp. 107–108.
10. Faldini and Fofi, *L'avventurosa storia del cinema italiano*, p. 204.

The Blancheville Monster (Horror)

D: Alberto De Martino; *S* and *SC:* Jean Grimaud [Gianni Grimaldi], Gordon Wilson, Jr. [Bruno Corbucci]; *DOP:* Alexander [Alejandro] Ulloa [b&w, VistaVision]; *M:* Francis Clark [Carlo Franci] [and Giuseppe Piccillo, uncredited]; *E:* Otello Colangeli; *PD, SD:* Leonard Bublerg [Antonio Simoni]; *CO:* Henry Steckler [Mario Giorsi]; *AD:* Bruce Stevenson [Michelangelo Panaro]; *C:* Ted Shaw [Silvano Mancini]; *MU:* Arthur Grunher [Romolo De Martino]; *Hair:* Shirley Dryant [Adalgisa Favella]; *SE:* Emilio G. Ruiz. *Cast:* Gérard Tichy (Roderick Blackford/U.S. version: Rodrigue De Blancheville), Leo Anchóriz (Dr. Atwell/Dr. Lerouge), Joan Hills [Ombretta Colli] (Emily De Blancheville/Emily Blackford), Helga Liné (Miss Eleonor/Eleonore), Irán Eory [Elvira Teresa Eory Sidi] (Alice Taylor), Richard Davis [Vanni Materassi] (John Taylor), Frank Moran [Paco Morán] (Alistair), Emily [Emilia] Wolkowicz (Cook), Harry Winter (Gamekeeper). *PROD:* Italo Zingarelli for Film Columbus (Rome), Alberto Aguilera for Llama Film (Madrid); *PM:* Robert Palace [Roberto Palaggi]. *Country:* Italy/Spain. Filmed at the Monastery of Santa María La Real de Valdeiglesias (Spain) and at Cinecittà (Rome). *Running time:* 90 min. (m. 2423); Visa n: 40372 (05.14.1963); *Rating:* V.M.14; *Release date:* 06.06.1963 (Italy). *Distribution:* Titanus (Italy); Compton-Casino Films (U.S.A.), AIP-TV (U.S.A., TV); *Domestic gross:* 87,000,000 lire. *Also known as:* Le Manoir de la terreur (France, 05.20.1966). *Home video:* Alpha Video, Bayview/Retromedia (DVD, U.S.A.).

Scotland, 1884. One week before her 21st birthday, young Emily Blackford returns to her family castle with her friend Alice and her boyfriend, John, after years spent at college. A feeling of doom permeates the manor and its inhabitants. Roderick, Emily's older brother, who is now the lord of the castle after the death of his father, behaves in a mysterious way, and so do Miss Eleanor, the enigmatic housekeeper, and the elusive Dr. Atwell. One night, after hearing inexplicable noises in the tower, Alice wakes up to find Eleonor administering an injection to a creature hidden in the castle's tower. It turns out that the elderly Lord Blackford is still alive, even though horribly disfigured, and that Roderick kept him locked in the manor's keep. The monster has escaped, though, and Emily is in peril: according to a prophecy, as soon as she will turn 21 an atrocious curse will strike the Blackfords, and Roderick believes that the deranged Lord Blackford will attempt to murder his own daughter before she turns that age, in order to save the family. The plot thickens when the disfigured man reappears and hypnotizes Emily: soon she starts having horrible nightmares. As it turns out, the girl is actually the victim of a diabolical plot against her life...

Of all the 1960s Italian Gothic thread, *The Blancheville Monster*—an odd Italian-Spanish co-production—is perhaps the closest to the canons of seventeenth/eighteenth century Gothic literature, which the script by Bruno Corbucci and Gianni Grimaldi[1] follows closely. No wonder it came out in Italy with the self-explanatory title *Horror*—chosen by the producer, Italo Zingarelli.

As usual, Italian publicity ads of the time pretended that the film was based on a Poe story, and even if that is not actually the case, Corbucci and Grimaldi indeed reworked elements from Edgar Allan Poe's "The Fall of the House of Usher": the story features a lord of the castle named Roderick who in one scene faces his sister who had been buried alive and escaped from her tomb. On the other hand, the references to mesmerism are lifted from other Poe stories, namely "A Tale from the Ragged Mountains" and "Some Words with a Mummy," with a typical touch of Italian mastery at forgery. In a scene, in fact, Emily discovers a book by Francis [*sic*, instead of Franz] Anton Mesmer entitled *Hypnotism and Magnetism*, yet Mesmer never wrote a book with such a title: *Ipnotismo e magnetismo* was the title of a manual written in 1903 by Giulio Belfiore, which had popularized Mesmer's theories in Italy.

"At that time, Gothic films were en vogue, such as *The Pit and the Pendulum* and the like," De Martino explained. "Even though, to tell the truth, I was inspired by Hitchcock's films, and I didn't think I was doing the same kind of stuff as Bava or Margheriti. I remember Antonio and I were shooting at the same time: I was making *The Blancheville Monster* and he was directing one of his films, side by side, in the same studio."[2] The Hitchcock reference is not as weird as it sounds, as the film is actually a period mystery where the supernatural element is only a red herring: overall, *The Blancheville Monster* is closer to the Richard Matheson-scripted AIP Poe films of the period than to its Italian contemporaries, as underlined by the emphasis on a sinister male authority figure that was typical of Corman's work, where it was embodied by Vincent Price.

However, *The Blancheville Monster* does not have much to offer other than De Martino's competent direction, atmospheric set-pieces (including the ruined monastery that would often be featured in 1970s Spanish horror films[3]) and Alejandro Ulloa's atmospheric lighting. The opening shot, with the camera panning from an ominous-looking forest beaten by the pouring rain through a castle in the distance (via a very visible *maquette*) synthesizes the film's over-reliance on stereotypes: the Scottish setting (which in the U.S. version turns into Northern France!), the old manor and its ancestral curse, the ambiguous servants, the crypt, the disfigured monster, the young lady walking in her nightgown through dark corridors at night, and the lord of the castle playing the organ.

Such a parade of clichés only heightens the story's predictability, stilted dialogue and mediocre acting: in a largely Iberian cast, the 20-year-old and unknown Ombretta Colli (who would later become a popular singer in her home country, and later a right-wing politician) hides behind the pseudonym Joan Hills—that is, her surname's literal translation. The horrific moments, so to speak, are also quite awkward, with a grotesque-looking monster and naive shock cuts underlined by Carlo Franci's melodramatic score, while the script's idea of a mystery is making every character act ambiguously even when there would be no need. "It became a cult movie and I didn't know about that [...]. But it is just a little film of no importance," De Martino recalled. "The only thing that moves me, when I think about that film, are the masks that you see in the film, which were sculpted by my father."[4]

Italian poster for Alberto De Martino's *The Blancheville Monster*. **Note the reference to Edgar Allan Poe's work (Libreria Eleste).**

The technically proficient De Martino, who had debuted with several sword-and-sandal films in the early 1960s, was one of Italy's most eclectic genre filmmakers of the '60s and '70s. He would try his hand at different genres, with admirable ease: spy films (*The Spy with Ten Faces/Upperseven l'uomo da uccidere*, 1966, and the campy cult *O.K. Connery*, 1967, starring Sean Connery's brother Neil); Spaghetti Westerns (*He Who Shoots First/Django spara per primo*, 1966), war flicks (*Dirty Heroes/Dalle Ardenne all'inferno*, 1967), Eurocrime (*Bandits in Rome/Roma come Chicago*, 1968; *Crime Boss/I familiari delle vittime non saranno avvertiti*, 1972; *Counselor at Crime/Il Consigliori*, 1973) and thrillers (*Carnal Circuit/Femmine insaziabili*, 1969; *The Man with Icy Eyes/L'uomo dagli occhi di ghiaccio*, 1971). In the 1970s De Martino would return to the horror genre with *The Antichrist* (*L'anticristo*, 1974) and *Rain of Fire* (*Holocaust 2000*, 1977) starring Kirk Douglas, inspired respectively by *The Exorcist* (1973) and *The Omen* (1976). His last films in the 1980s belonged to the thriller and fantasy genre as well: *Extrasensorial*, a.k.a. *Blood Link* (1982) starring Michael Moriarty in a dual role as surgically separated Siamese twins, one of whom is a serial killer; the weird Florida-based sci-fi *Miami Golem* (1985); and *Formula for a Murder* (*7 Hyden Park: la casa maledetta*, 1985), the latter two starring David Warbeck.

The Blancheville Monster ended up in the public domain list in the United States, and can be easily found—albeit in poor-quality copies—in the home video market.

Notes

1. The Spanish sources add a scriptwriter (Natividad Zaro) whose contribution to the script, as it often happened in the days of European co-productions, was merely nominal for legal (i.e., tax) reasons.
2. Manlio Gomarasca, "Il cinema è quello che ci fa," in "Fatti di cinema." Controcorrente 3," *Nocturno Dossier* 51, October 2006, p. 15 (Interview with Alberto De Martino). De Martino could well have added the name Dreyer, as the film features the umpteenth "homage" to *Vampyr*, in the scene in which Emily is buried alive—naturally, in a coffin with a glass window.
3. The interiors, on the other hand, were filmed in Rome. The hall of Blackford Castle is the same set-piece as seen that same year in *The Whip and the Body*.
4. Gomarasca, "Il cinema è quello che ci fa," p. 14.

The Ghost (*Lo spettro*)

D: Robert Hampton [Riccardo Freda]. *S:* Robert Davidson [Oreste Biancoli]; *SC:* Robert Davidson, Robert Hampton; *DOP:* Donald Green [Raffaele Masciocchi] (Technicolor); *M:* Franck Wallace [Franco Mannino] (and Francesco De Masi, uncredited); *E:* Donna Christie [Ornella Micheli]; *ArtD:* Sammy Fields [Mario Chiari]; *CO:* Mary McCharty [*sic*] [Marilù Carteny]; *AD:* Silvy Black [Silvana Merli]; *C:* Anthony Taylor [Antonio Schiavo Lena]; *AC:* Piero Servo; *SO:* Cristopher [*sic*] Curtis; [Ernesto Livoli] *MU:* Max Justins [Massimo Giustini]; *Hair:* Charles Seaman [Giancarlo Marin]. *Cast:* Barbara Steele (Margaret Hichcock), Peter Baldwin (Dr. Charles Livingstone), Harriet White [Harriet White Medin] (Kathryn), Leonard G. Elliot [Elio Jotta] (Dr. John Hichcock), Carol Bennet (Woman), Charles [Carlo] Kechler (Chief of Police), Raoul H. Newman [Umberto Raho] (Priest), Reginald Price Anderson (Albert Fisher). *PROD:* Louis Mann [Ermanno Donati, Luigi Carpentieri] for Panda Cinematografica; *PM:* Lou D. Kelly [Livio Maffei]; *PA:* Rommy Deutch [Romolo Germano], Lucky Reed. *Country:* Italy. Filmed in Rome. *Running time:* 100 min. (m. 2790); Visa n: 39641 (02.22.1963); *Rating:* V.M.18; *Release dates:* 03.30.1963 (Italy); 02.18.1965 (U.S.A.). *Distribution:* Dino De Laurentiis (Italy); Magna Pictures Distribution Corporation (U.S.A.); *Domestic gross:* 175,000,000 lire. *Also known as:* Le *Spectre du Professeur Hichcock* (France, 12.09.1964). *Home video:* Alpha Video (DVD, U.S.A.), Artus Film (DVD, France).

Scotland, 1910. Bound to a wheelchair because of a grave disease, the middle-aged Dr. John Hichcock is a regretful sad man. His obsession with the afterlife has Hichcock conduct séances in his mansion to get in touch with the spirits of the dead. He is lovingly taken care of by his wife, Margaret, who is much younger than him, as well as Dr. Livingstone, who administers Hichcock small doses of poison as an experimental treatment to cure his paralysis. However, Margaret and Livingstone are actually lovers, and have concocted a plan to murder Hichcock by poisoning him. They apparently succeed, but soon Margaret is haunted by what appears to be her husband's ghost, and shortly she and Livingstone are at each other's throats. However, it turns out that Hichcock just faked his own death, in order to perform a cruel revenge on his wife and her lover...

One of the recurrent features in Italian horror films of the 1960s was that the stories would take place in secluded, almost claustrophobic settings. Whereas this often happened because of mere budgetary reasons, in the case of Riccardo Freda's *The Ghost* seclusion is a necessary, even fundamental element to the story, in a film characterized by an almost theatrical staging: a reviewer evoked, and rightly so, Jean-Paul Sartre's play *Huis clos*.[1]

Freda's sequel of sorts to *The Horrible Dr. Hichcock* features a main character with the same name (but not the same habits) and Harriet White in her customary role as the menacing housekeeper, but it moves on to equally frightening depths as its predecessor in what is essentially a Gothic reimagining of the typical "scheming lovers" plot of H. G. Clouzot's *Diabolique* (*Les Diaboliques*, 1955).[2] This allows the director to twist the knife even deeper into the institution of marriage, seen as a role play, a pantomime of sorts in which both spouses

The French poster for Riccardo Freda's *The Ghost* underlined it being a sequel of sorts to *The Horrible Dr. Hichcock* (courtesy S. I. Bianchi).

play roles and wear masks which they cannot wait to get rid of. An exemplary moment is the scene in which Margaret (Barbara Steele) holds up her elderly husband (Elio Jotta), escorts him to bed and undresses him like any loving wife would do ... a moment immediately followed by Margaret's feverish, liberating race to the greenhouse, the meeting place where her lover (Peter Baldwin) awaits her.

Even more so than in the director's previous horror films, the supernatural element is evoked only to be eventually denied: the ending gives the right perspective to what has happened before, as in a eighteenth century anamorphosis. To Freda, horror is a Cartesian matter, a theorem to be proved through images: the thesis is the immanence of evil, while the supernatural is only a bogus trick in order to reach the deepest, atavistic fears. "*True* horror is deep-rooted in each one of us from birth," as Freda wrote in an oft-quoted passage of his autobiography *Divoratori di celluloide*, contemptuously rejecting the presence of "carnival-like" monsters in the movies.[3] A statement somehow confirmed by a line of dialogue in *The Horrible Dr. Hichcock* which sounded like a declaration of intents: "So much time wasted trying to analyze the secrets of the soul, while the material part of our beings remains an unknown world."

The opening credits for *The Ghost* are superimposed over a slow tracking shot towards a table where a séance has just ended, while the participants leave and the room is left empty. The shot ends with the close-up of a skull—that is, Freda's vision (or rather, negation) of the afterlife. It is no use to look for the spirit, the director seems to imply: what is left are just bones. If the opening scene is a reminder of Freda's vision, the final shot is a grim punchline that culminates with the sight of a secret door behind which Dr. Hichcock is dying, unbeknownst to all, like a rat. What will be left of him is not even worth seeing: he is damned to disappear from view and from the world, doomed to become what the opening shot implied—no spirit, just bones.

It is one of the grimmest, most nihilistic endings ever committed to film, which rivals some of Freda's most celebrated ones, like that of his

Dante-inspired *The Iron Swordsman*. In *The Horrible Dr. Hichcock* the secret passage was a "forbidden door" which Cynthia should not trespass, as in the most classic fairytales: it was the key to move from one world to the other, from the reassuring order and luxury of the *haute bourgeoisie* to the hidden dimension of Hichcock's dark side, and the threshold between the two realities was a mirror. In *The Ghost*, Freda turns the essence of the secret passage upside down: no more a privileged instrument to reach inaccessible places and reveal secrets, but a blind alley, a street of no return where to end up and die like a wounded animal.

"In Freda's film, fear is so everyday and tangible that it becomes flesh," as Italian film critic Carlo Bocci wrote. "Not even once does *The Ghost* slip into the *epouvante cocasse* of so many horror movies, neither can one be relieved with the apparition of the monster, as every single character in the film *is* a monster."[4]

This leads to an important absence to deal with: that of religion. As observed earlier on, Italian Gothic horror films deprived the vampire myth of its anti–Christian core, which was well in evidence in Hammer productions. On the other hand, the metaphysical element was not even considered in a negative way, as Roger Corman's films did. AIP's Poe cycle was centered on a universe abandoned by the divine mercy, where death—deprived of any promise of transcendence—became a terrible and horrific event, evil acquired a tangible quality in the form of genetic tare, and such dialogue was uttered: "Each man creates his own God for himself—His own Heaven, his own Hell" (*The Masque of the Red Death*, 1964). Whereas in Italian Horror films of the same period the dramatic juxtapositions and the boundaries between good and evil were often blurred and tricky, as exemplified by the recurring theme of the *doppelgänger*.

The Ghost moves one step further. To Freda, there can be no fight between good and evil, because good does not exist in the end. All the characters are evil, abject, diabolical. The film's concept of inner evil is closer to the themes of the subconscious, and therefore it focuses on the torments of the individual instead of the universal fight between good and evil. That is why it does not need any monster. This makes *The Ghost* a much more personal film than *The Horrible Dr. Hichcock*, to the point that Freda can even make his own personal stab at organized religion through the character of Umberto Raho, as a petty and almost caricatural priest who in the end takes leave with a punchline which sounds most sarcastic in the context of its delivery: "I told you, Dr. Hichcock, the Devil is a very real person."

As with *The Horrible Dr. Hichcock*, Freda's use of color has a distinct dramatic flair. That is also the case with framing composition and camera movements: to Freda, the camera becomes an instrument of moral judgment. An example of this is the camera approaching objects and moving away from them at the beginning and end of many sequences in *The Ghost*. Such movements express the fascination and repulsion towards evil and the physical tools with which it is perpetrated: a syringe, a razor, a vial of poison, a glass of gin. "The real protagonists," as Bocci noted, "are the objects that we have seen before the horrible doctor's apparent death: the objects that become the tools of fear and death when the plot thickens. Not one of the privileged objects as seen in the first part of the film escapes its fate of transfiguration. Freda's cold camera keeps framing them from a low angle throughout the film, without a single impulse of sympathy towards any of them: the director's cruelty towards his own creatures adds to the theatrical cruelty—we would be tempted to say, Elizabethan—of the *mise en scène*."[5]

Another noteworthy element is the presence of a *carillon* which has a diegetic function similar to the one in Sergio Leone's *For a Few Dollars More* (*Per qualche dollaro in più*, 1965), as well as the harmonica in *Once Upon a Time in the West* (*C'era una volta il West*, 1968) and Dario Argento's *Deep Red*. The score is credited to "Franck Wallace," which—according to the list of a.k.a.s registered with the performing rights society SIAE as well as other sources such as the Italian magazine *Bianco e Nero* and the *Monthly Film Bulletin*—was the pseudonym of Franco Mannino. Other references suggested that "Franck Wallace" was actually a joint pseudonym for Mannino and Roman Vlad. However, when Beat Records released the soundtrack in 2008, it was discovered that the surviving tapes were attributed to Francesco De Masi, even though he is not credited on the picture. It has been suggested that Freda replaced Mannino's score, as a whole or in part, as he was not happy with it. As a matter of fact, the musical accompaniment is one of the film's many highlights, and the exquisite title theme popped up again and again in other Italian horror films of the period, due to the typical recycling habits of Italian low-budget productions.

The Ghost received a predictable V.M.18 rating by the Italian censors, but no cuts were demanded. When interviewed in 1964 by the French periodical *Midi-Minuit Fantastique*, Freda claimed he was satisfied with the way the Ministerial commission had treated his film. "I didn't have any problems with the censors. Contrary to what one might expect, they proved to be intelligent."[6] Funnily enough, a few years later Freda became a member of the censorship commission: among the films he rejected there were Christian Marquand's *Candy* (1968) and Mario Bava's *Four Times That Night* (*Quante volte...quella notte*, 1969).

Nevertheless, *The Ghost* features one of Italian Gothic's most utterly violent moments: the extraordinary scene where Margaret massacres her lover with a razor, shown through a subjective shot of the man while Barbara Steele savagely wields the weapon towards the camera—a scene later redone by Aristide Massaccesi in *Death Smiles on a Murderer* (*La Morte ha sorriso all'assassino*, 1973). It is a chilling, savage moment which rivals the infamous opening of Bava's *Black Sunday*, and synthesizes Italian Horror's emphasis on gruesomeness. What is more, it underlines the utter weakness of Baldwin's character: like so many male figures of the *filone*, the helpless Dr. Livingstone is destined to be dominated, humiliated, and eventually destroyed by the weaker sex.

Notes

1. Anonymous, "Lo spettro," *Il Nuovo Spettatore Cinematografico* 4, August 1963, p. 80.

2. Despite what some writers have claimed—see Sergio Bissoli, *Gli scrittori dell'orrore* (Collegno: Ferrara Editore, 2007), p. 15—the similarities between *The Ghost* and the pulp novel *La vecchia poltrona* (*I racconti di Dracula* 20, June 1961, by Max Dave, a.k.a. Pino Belli) are minimal.

3. Freda, *Divoratori di celluloide*, p. 86.

4. Carlo Bocci, "Lo spettro," *Il Falcone Maltese* 1, June 1974, p. 40.

5. Ibid.

6. Caen and Romer, "Entretien avec Riccardo Freda," p. 3.

Katarsis, a.k.a. *Sfida al diavolo*

D: Giuseppe Veggezzi. *S* and *SC:* Giuseppe Veggezzi; *DOP:* Mario Parapetti (additional scenes: Angelo Baistrocchi) (B&W); *M:* Berto Pisano (*Ti ho visto* sung by Sonia); *E:* Enzo Alfonsi (1965 version: Piera Bruni); *AE:* Laura Caccianti; *PD:* Andrea Crisanti, Giuseppe Ranieri; *AD:* Paolo Bianchini; *C:* Francesco Attenti; *MU:* Giovanni Amadei; *SO:* Salvatore Gaetano; *W:* Maria Maresca; *SP:* Alfonso Avincola; *SS:* Luciano Lo Schiavo; *Grip:* Giulio Diamanti, Tarcisio Diamanti, Alfonso Grilli; *ChEl:* Alberto Silvestri, Eolo Tramontani, Otello Polletin. *Cast:* Christopher Lee (Lord of the Castle), George [Giorgio] Ardisson (Gugo), Lilly Parker [Vittoria Centroni] (Maga), Anita Dreyer [Anita Cacciolati] (Jenny), Bella Cortez [Alice Paneque] (Frie), Mario Zacarti [Mario Polletin] (Gian), Adriana Ambesi (Castle lady), Piero Vida [Pietro Vidali] (Peo), Eva Gioia, Ulderico Sciarretta (Guardian monk—1965 version), Ettore Ribotta, Sergio Gibello, Pasquale Basile, Sonia [Sonia Scotti], Alma Del Rio (Alma the dancer—1965 version). *PROD:* Fernando Cerqua for I Films della Mangusta (*1965 version:* Ulderico Sciarretta for Eco Film); *PM:* Spartaco Antonucci; *PS:* Oscar Santaniello. *Country:* Italy. Filmed at Odescalchi Castle (Bracciano), Montelibretti and Olimpia Studios (Rome). *Running time:* 87 min. (1963 version)—79 min. (1965 version) (m. 2390/m. 2149); Visa n: 40989 (08.10.1963); *Rating:* V.M.18; *Release date:* 09.09.1963 (Italy). *Distribution:* Mangusta (Regional); *Domestic gross:* unknown.

After a reckless car ride, six wild and immoral youngsters reach an apparently abandoned castle. There, they meet an old man who tells them that he had sold his soul to the devil to preserve forever the beauty of the woman he loved. However, the old man can only hear his beloved's voice, and in order to break his pact with the devil he has to find the woman's body and bury it. The young punks do not believe the old man but decide to help him for kicks. After a long struggle against mysterious forces that hinder their search, eventually they find the beautiful woman's body. At the crowing of the cock, the old man dies, finally in peace, while the castle is devoured by the flames. The young people return to their own world marked by this new experience.

The first and only film directed by the Piacenza-born filmmaker Giuseppe Veggezzi—or Vegezzi, as (mis-?)spelled in several official papers: with Italian bureaucrats, you are never sure—*Katarsis* was one of the most obscure fruits in the season of Italian Gothic. Shot in the spring of 1963 at one of the *filone*'s most recurrent locations—Bracciano's Odescalchi Castle—with a budget of just 46 million *lire* (the shooting schedule also mentions the subtitle *L'orgia*, The Orgy), Veggezzi's film benefitted from the special participation of none other than Christopher Lee, as the only "name" actor in a cast of unknowns (although young lead actor Giorgio Ardisson would later attain a modest fame as one of James Bond's Italian lookalikes), in the midst of his busy 1963 Italian schedule.

The Brit thesp was on the set for only one week, just before moving on to play in Mario Bava's *The Whip and the Body*. Lee never saw the dailies nor the finished product, which might explain the confusing way in which he speaks of Veggezzi's film in his autobiography. "*Katarsis* was very hard for those involved to follow. It seemed to be about drop-outs who find an old man in a castle, who turns into the Devil and seizes them, but no one was ever sure. In its efforts to find itself, the film forked into two films, the sequel being *Faust '63*. I was Faust in the first and Mephistopheles in the other, which must have confused people with the strength to see both."[1]

Actually, what Lee recounts never happened in the first place. There was no sequel to *Katarsis*, and there was no *Faust '63* either. What happened instead was typical of the production dynamics that animated genre cinema, which was becoming more and more hectic, chaotic, fraudulent. Quite simply, *Katarsis* obtained the Ministry's visa in August 1963, but soon afterwards the production company I Films della Mangusta went bankrupt. *Katarsis* was then bought by another society, Eco Film, which proceeded to reedit the film, adding new footage, and distributed it again in 1965 with the title *Sfida al diavolo.* The new version was nine minutes shorter than the previous one (78 minutes compared to 87 minutes), and according to the Ministry of Spectacle, which examined the request to obtain Italian nationality (and the subsequent sum of money granted to all films officially labeled "Italian," according to the 1965 Corona law), "given the irrelevance of the alterations, the film itself cannot be considered other than as authorized by the projection to the public in 1963 under the title *Katarsis*." Unfortunately, the original cut of the film is apparently lost.

The additional footage included a slapdash framing story which can be roughly described as "apostolical *film noir*."[2] Whereas the original *Katarsis* centered on a group of young upper-class punks who spent a night in a haunted castle, in *Sfida al diavolo* a monk named Peo (Piero Vida) goes to a shady nightclub to retrieve incriminating documents and save a friend who had taken refuge in his convent to hide from a gangster from Beirut. There, Peo meets an adipose dancer (Alma Del Rio), and in order to persuade her into giving him the papers, he tells the Faust-like parable which was the film's original core: it turns out that Peo was one of the punks, who had been so affected by the experience that he became a monk (!).

Said additions include Del Rio's cellulitic dance routine—which would not have been out of place in one of the period's erotic "documentaries"—and one of the most awkward product placement cases in Italian film history: the guardian monk who greets the wounded and hunted gangster in the convent hands him a drink from a bottle which has no visible label, saying "Don't pay attention to the bottle: this is real 'Stock '84' brandy. I've been told to buy a cheaper one, but since I drink it myself I don't care about the price." This line was also the object of complaints on the part of the Ministry of Spectacle when *Sfida al diavolo* was resubmitted to the censors, as it emerges from a letter dated October 1965, where the producer claims that the "Brendy"[*sic*]'s label had been expunged from the dialogue—which clearly was not. Last but not least, it is worth pointing out that the guardian monk in said scene is played by Ul-

derico Sciarretta, the production manager of "ECO Film" which took over from the bankrupted "I Film della Mangusta."

Similarly to the earlier examples of Italian Gothic horror, *Katarsis* was set in contemporary Italy, with weird results. The obnoxious young punks, who have fun chasing passing cars and drink whisky straight from the bottle, are a bourgeois variation on Pasolini's street kids ("We were like animals: we liked the taste of blood and uncontrolled violence" as Peo's voice-over recalls), and their savage car ride near the film's beginning recalls the opening sequences of the controversial Pasolini adaptation *Violent Life*. The night orgy in the haunted castle, on the other hand, suspiciously looks like a poor man's version of the bacchanales in the villa at sea as described by *La Dolce Vita*.

However, the tone—even more so in *Sfida al diavolo*—is decidedly moral, or rather moralistic. The orgy turns into a path of purification, accompanied by Peo's pedantic voice-over, while the character of the punk-turned-friar becomes an involuntarily comic reversal of the eponymous devilish monk in Matthew Lewis' celebrated Gothic novel. On the other hand, the film pays reference—quite confusingly indeed, as noted by the perplexed commissioner of the Ministry of Spectacle who gave the project the green light—to German romanticism, with a Faustian pact set in the present.

Lee's presence on screen is minimal, even though he plays a dual role (the old man in the castle and the guy in the car the punks push out of the road), and his acting is understandably on autopilot. What is more, to put it bluntly, Veggezzi's direction veers between the naive and the terrible, save for a few wild surreal moments such as the scene in which the punks discover the lady of the castle (Adriana Ambesi) inside a grandfather clock—a moment worthy of Jean Rollin. The protagonists spend a seemingly endless amount of time—at least twenty minutes in *Sfida al diavolo*, possibily even more in the original version—wandering through dark rooms that lead nowhere, endless spiral staircases and even a maze of transparent glasses that recall amusement park labyrinths. It is just a way to pad a thin story to an acceptable running time, yet it does reveal a way of conceiving the Fantastic not as a source of shock but as a limbo where time and space blur, and in which one can float indefinitely: anxiety and fear come from the loss of spacial coordinates and the discovery (always inconclusive) of new ones replacing the previous.

For all its clumsiness, Veggezzi's film was not devoid of ambitions: the basic story was the pretext for an awkward web of symbols to underline the basic storyline. According to the director's own words, the six punks represent the present, the castle is the subconscious where "the conscience crisis that brings the six to their catharsis" takes place, while Lee's character embodies "interior life, exasperated and turned into an ascetic fanaticism." The less said...

The Italian poster for the 1965 rerelease of *Katarsis* (as *Sfida al diavolo*) emphasized the film's Gothic elements (author's collection).

Notes

1. Lee, *Tall, Dark and Gruesome*, p. 187; Lee, *Lord of Misrule*, p. 207.

2. *Sfida al diavolo*'s ridiculous framing story is not the only example of the hybridization between Gothic and *film noir*, as proven by little-seen films such as *I'll See You in Hell* (*Ti aspetterò all'inferno*, 1960, Piero Regnoli) and *Passport for a Corpse* (*Lasciapassare per il morto*, 1962, Mario Gariazzo). In Regnoli's film the Gothic path is only a red herring, as a seemingly vengeful ghost apparently persecutes a trio of thugs led by John Drew Barrymore, who have taken refuge in a cabin in the woods after a hit, near a mephitic swamp. The atmosphere evoked by Luciano Trasatti's b&w cinematography recalls Val Lewton's RKO pictures, and suggests a supernatural explanation that is eventually replaced by a rational one. *Passport for a Corpse* follows the escape of a criminal (Alberto Lupo) after a heist gone wrong, and is more pertinent to the Fantastic. The plot has the man escape while hiding in a coffin, in a variation on Poe's theme of premature burial (the long sequence where Lupo finds himself locked in a cold room is genuinely unnerving), and the story borders on the metaphysical, due to the presence of Death in the form of a mysterious woman (Linda Christian) that appears to the protagonist throughout the story and eventually welcomes him in the end.

Tomb of Torture (Metempsyco)

D: Anthony Kristye [Antonio Boccacci]. *S:* Anthony Kristye; *SC:* Anthony Kristye, Johnny Seemonell [Giovanni Simonelli]; *DOP:* William Grace [Francesco Campitelli]; *M:* Armando Sciascia (Ed. Vedette); *E:* Jean-Pierre Grasset [Luciano Anconetani]; *AE:* Gaby Vital [Gabriella Vitale]; *SO:* Johnny Harold [Bruno Francisci]; *SE:* Patt Collins (trick photography) [Gaetano Capogrosso]; *C:* William Backman [Giovanni Savelli]; *AC:* Basil Klay [Roberto Gengarelli]; *CO:* House of Werther. *Cast:* Annie Albert [Annie Alberti] (Anna Darnell/Countess Irene), Thony Maky [Adriano Micantoni] (Dr. Darnell), Mark Marian [Marco Mariani] (George Dickson), Elizabeth Queen [Flora Carosello] (Countess Elizabeth), William Gray [Antonio Boccacci] (Raman), Bernard Blay [Bernardo D'Angeli], Emy Eko [Emilia Eco] (Esther), Terry Thompson [Maria Teresa Sonni], Fred Pizzot [Andrea Scotti]. *PROD:* Frank Campitelli [Francesco Campitelli] for Virginia Cinematografica; *PA:* Silvano De Amicis. *Country:* Italy. Filmed at Castle Orsini, Nerola (Rome), Palazzo Borghese, Artena. *Running time:* 88 min. (m. 2404); Visa n: 39769 (03.20.1963); *Rating:* V.M.14; *Release date:* 03.27.1963 (Italy); 07.1966 (U.S.A.). *Distribution:* Filmar (Italy); Trans-Lux Distributing Corporation (U.S.A.); *Domestic gross:* unknown. *Also known as:* Le Manoir maudit (France, 11.12.1963), *Die Bestie von Schloß Monte Christo* (West Germany). *Home video:* Image (DVD, U.S.A.).

Early 1900s. Young Anna is suffering from horrific nightmares in which she is murdered night after night in a torture chamber. It is discovered that she is the reincarnation of Countess Irene, who disappeared twenty years earlier—just before her wedding to a rich Hindu named Raman, who is still searching for her to this day. Anna's father, psychiatrist Dr. Darnell, takes her to the Countess' castle in an attempt to help her. The manor hides a secret, though: a demented monster who is responsible for the abduction, torture and murders of two young girls. Newspaper reporter George Dickson arrives at the place to investigate and falls for Anna. After the girl is abducted by the monster and chained in the castle's chamber of torture, Dickson and Raman must find their way into the crypt, where the mystery of Countess Irene's disappearance will be finally solved...

In the great season of Italian pulp fiction, it was not uncommon that a writer would also try his hand at scriptwriting, or vice versa. Before becoming one of Cinecittà's most prolific screenwriters, Ernesto Gastaldi published a number of crime and sci-fi novels such as *Sangue in tasca* (1957, as James Duffy), *Brivido sulla schiena* (1957, as Freddy Foster) and *Tempo zero* (1960, as Julian Berry). Another similar case was that of Giovanni Simonelli, the son of director Giorgio Simonelli, who wrote cheap pulp novels under the pseudonym Art Mitchell—such as *10 bare e un sepolcro* ("10 Coffins and a Grave"), a supernatural reworking of *Ten Little Indians* published in *I Racconti di Dracula* n. 3, February 1960—as well as film scripts under the more transparent a.k.a. Johnny Seemonell.

The results, however, were not just undistinguished but mostly undistinguishable, as with *Metempsyco*, the first and last film directed by the elusive Antonio Boccacci (or Boccaci, according to some sources). Under the imperscrutable pseudonym Anthony Kristye, the same he is credited with in the film, Boccacci had churned out a number of cheap paperback mystery novels in the late 1950s, such as *Vendetta e sangue* ("Vengeance and Blood") and *La ragnatela* ("The Cobweb").

Metempsyco is in many ways the celluloid equivalent of those pulp fiction novels concocted by Simonelli, Boccacci and others, as well as the adults-only *fotoromanzi* (photonovels) of the period: it is a supernaturally spiced murder mystery of sorts, replete with Italian Gothic horror's favorite themes, namely reincarnation (hence the Italian title, no doubt chosen because it sounded a bit like *Psycho*), a vengeful ghost and a *doppelgänger*. Not content, Simonelli and Boccacci throw into the story every kind of cheap horror cliché: a castle with a torture chamber, swarms of rats (actually guinea pigs), secret passages, hooded skeletons and a deformed creature lurking in the surroundings.

Although the attempts at shock effects are ill-advised at the very least, the content was rather outrageous for the period, with cheap sadistic thrills—the aforementioned torture chamber scenes feature plenty of naked legs and a few screaming young girls, a nymphomaniac heroine (a condition that is merely hinted at in the film, however) who goes skinny dipping in the lake, dashes of gore and a grotesque sex-obsessed Quasimodo-like monster, appropriately named "Hugo," who appears too early (and too much, given the atrocious make-up) in the film. No wonder the Italian tagline featured the vital question: "Sesso o terrore?" ("Sex or Terror?").

Boccacci is no Bava, though, a fact that is patent to the audience as from the opening credits, with a montage of crudely animated cut-out stills—a sleeping woman, a hand carrying a lamp, an armor, a skull—that suggests a proximity with the period's horror photonovels rather than contemporaneous Gothics. Besides the director' habit for crude zooms, the production's haphazard quality is best summed up by the sight of the Countess' "painting" of whom the young heroine is found out to be the reincarnation: allegedly unable to find any cheap and good painter, Boccacci had to make do with ... an enlarged photograph of actress Annie Alberti.

As usual, the locations are more interesting that what actually happens—very little indeed,

it must be added—in them. The dilapidated manor where the story takes place is Castle Orsini in Nerola, near Rome, while the interiors were shot in another oft-used location, the labyrinthine Palazzo Borghese in Artena. To stress the *fotoromanzi* connection, the obscure cast was led by Annie Alberti, a minor photonovel star of the early 1960s. Alberti often appeared in the infamous *Killing*, and later on she became the protagonist of the adults-only French photoroman *Baby Colt*, published in 1968 and directed by her husband Gérard Landry. As for the other cast members, Emy Eco (one of the two nosy girls at the beginning, and very active in Italy as a dubbing artist) is the sister of novelist Umberto Eco, the author of *The Name of the Rose*. Boccacci himself, billed as "William Gray," plays an unlikely turban-wearing hindu who looks like he has just stepped out of an Emilio Salgari novel.

The result is as unlikely as the director's

The United States poster for *Tomb of Torture* featured a rather different monster than the one appearing in the film (author's collection).

Anglo-Saxon pseudonym, which patently hints at Agatha Christie, but is bogged down by misspellings and vowels at random. Even more astonishing, however, is the alias used by actress Flora Carosello, a chuckle-inducing "Elizabeth Queen." Armando Sciascia's cool score pushes such clichés to the point of self-parody—not that it was necessary, as shown by the opening sequence in which two girls sneak into the castle and are brutally murdered, or Anna's nightmare featuring a moving armor brandishing a huge sword and an ugly monster peeping out of a sarcophagus. Said armor conceals the murderer's identity in what has to be one of Italian Gothic's most laughably outlandish ideas.

Nevertheless, for all its shortcomings, the film—which passed absolutely unnoticed in Italy and whose box-office takings were so scarce that there is no actual record of them—was picked up for distribution in the United States in 1965 by Richard Gordon, who was hoping to score again as he had done with *The Playgirls and the Vampire*, and released by Trans-Lux Distributing on a double bill—"Twice the thrills! Twice the chills!!"—with the German vampire film *Cave of the Living Dead* (*Der Fluch der grünen Augen*, 1964, Ákos Ráthonyi). The tagline ("Creatures who kill AGAIN, AGAIN and AGAIN!!") promised more than the film could possibly deliver, but the poster featured a memorably sleazy portrait of the monster, albeit with an unlikely set of feline fangs, plus a semi-naked woman chained to a St. Andrew's cross in a crypt.

Boccacci's film was later picked up by Four Star for television broadcasting.

The Virgin of Nuremberg, a.k.a. *Horror Castle (La vergine di Norimberga)*

D: Anthony Dawson [Antonio Margheriti]. *S*: based on the novel *La vergine di Norimberga* by Frank Bogart [Maddalena Gui]; *SC*: Anthony Dawson, Edmund Greville [Edmond T. Gréville], Gastad Green [Renato Vicario]; *DOP*: Richard Palton [Riccardo Pallottini] (Ultrapanoramic, Eastmancolor); *M*: Riz Ortolani, conducted by the author (Ed. North-South); *E*: Angel Coly [Otello Colangeli]; *PD, ArtD*: Henry Daring [Riccardo Dominici]; *CO*: James Lyon [Riccardo Dominici]; *AD*: Bertrand Blier [and Ruggero Deodato, uncredited]; *C*: George

Henry [Filippo Carta]; *AC*: John Baxter [Gianni Modica]; *SE*: Anthony Matthews [Antonio Margheriti]; *SO*: Albert Griffiths [Alberto Bartolomei]; *MU*: Joseph Hunter [Franco Di Girolamo]; *AMU*: Walter Roy [Walter Cossu]; *Hair*: Lilian Moore [Anna Cristofani]; *W*: Peggy Bronson [Antonietta Piredda], Sandra Weber [Irma Tonnini]; *SS*: Eve Marie Koltay [*U.S. version*: Richard MacNamara] *Cast*: Rossana Podestà (Mary Hunter), Georges Rivière (Max Hunter), Christopher Lee (Erich), Jim Dolen (John Selby), Lucile St. Simon (Victim), Luigi Severini (The Doctor), Anny Degli Uberti (Frau Marta), Luciana Milone (Trude), Consalvo Dell'Arti, Mirko Valentin (Max's father). *PROD*: Marco Vicario for Atlantica Cinematografica; *PM*: Fred Holliday [Natalino Vicario]; Jim Murray [Sante Chimirri]; *PS*: Steve Melville [Gianni Di Stolfo]. *Country*: Italy. Filmed at Incir-De Paolis Studios (Rome), Villa Sciarra (Rome). *Running time*: 83 min. (m. 2287); Visa n: 40904 (08.03.1963); *Rating*: V.M.14; *Release dates*: 08.15.1963 (Italy); 01.10.1965 (U.S.A.). *Distribution*: Atlantica Cinematografica (Italy); Zodiac Films (U.S.A.); *Domestic gross*: 125,000,000 lire. *Also known as*: Terror Castle, La Vierge de Nuremberg (France, 02.03.1965), The Castle of Terror (U.K.), Die Gruft der Lebenden Leichen, Das Schloss des Grauens (West Germany, 05.15.1964), El justiciero rojo (Spain). *Home video*: Shriek Show (DVD, U.S.A.).

Mary Hunter and her husband Max are staying at Max's family castle in Germany. One night the young woman awakens to the sound of a woman's scream, and much to her horror she finds a dead body inside a torture device in the manor's crypt. Max convinces Mary that it was just a bad dream, but she remains suspicious: Max behaves strangely, and the disfigured servant, Erich, is an ominous presence as well. It turns out there really is a malevolent presence hiding in the castle, who abducts and tortures young women: Max's father, an ex–SS officer gone mad after he was submitted to horrific experiments by the Nazis after an unsuccessful attempt at killing Hitler...

Antonio Margheriti's first horror film released in Italy, *The Virgin of Nuremberg* was actually filmed after the director's own *Castle of Blood*, as Margheriti himself explained, giving an idea of the hectic days of Italian genre cinema back then. "We made that film in order to exploit *Castle of Blood*'s production values— we used to go on that way, recycling over and over."[1] However, despite being submitted to the censorship commission a couple of months earlier, *The Virgin of Nuremberg* was released almost immediately, in mid–August 1963, whereas *Castle of Blood* had to wait until February 1964.

The film can also be seen as a *fil rouge* between Italian Gothic horror and the country's contemporaneous popular literature. In the early 1900s, the Gothic and the Fantastic developed through either *feuilletons* or magazines such as *La Domenica del Corriere*.[2] A similar

Lurid Italian sleeve of the KKK paperback novel *La vergine di Norimberga*, upon which Antonio Margheriti's film was based (author's collection).

role, sixty years later, would be played by the rise of horror paperbacks, comics and photonovels: the aforementioned Edizioni KKK and *I Racconti di Dracula* as well as similar series with such explicit titles as *Terrore* ("Terror"). Released in the newsstands circuit in 20,000 to 25,000 copies each, with attractive and alluring illustrated covers, these dime-store paperbacks contained badly written novelettes which mixed horror clichés, Gothic stereotypes, cheap eroticism and even cheaper thrills. Passed off as Italian translations of obscure British, French or Teutonic authors, these books were, more prosaically, a genuine, 100 percent made in Italy product. "Original" English titles as indicated in the title page were completely made up, and behind a legion of pseudonyms hid a small bunch of prolific Italian writers, often merely credited as "translators."[3]

Based on the novel *La vergine di Norimberga* by "Frank Bogart" (that is, Maddalena Gui), issue #23 of the KKK series, *The Virgin of Nuremberg* was produced by Marco Vicario—the cofounder of G.E.I., the company which published the KKK paperbacks, in association with his brother Alfonso. No wonder the leading role went to Vicario's own wife, the glamorous Rossana Podestà.[4] On the other hand, the presence of Christopher Lee, in one of his many visits to Italian sets of the period, added a sense of prestigiousness to the whole product. However, Lee does not play the villain, but is relegated to a secondary role (a stretched-out cameo, that is) as a scarred and menacing—yet totally harmless—servant.

The film's straight pulp descendence makes for a few peculiar traits, starting with its present day setting—something that Italian Gothic had already abandoned after the early awkward attempts—which displays a more immediate affinity with contemporaneity, starting with its setting in the present day. "The difficult thing was to start like a classic horror story, and then to move on to the present with a more contemporary approach," as Margheriti recalled when interviewed by Peter Blumenstock.[5] The bouncy, lively jazzy score by Riz Ortolani is perfectly in tone: the feverish contrabass which underlines the opening credits theme would have made Jess Franco smile, and is a noticeable departure from the classical-oriented Gothic scores of the period.

Unlike what he did with the impressive black-and-white of *Castle of Blood*, this time Margheriti employed gaudy colors, courtesy of his customary d.o.p. Riccardo Pallottini: there are lots of garish reds which pop out from the screen, almost as if the film was in 3-D, and the effect in many scenes is that of a lurid pulp novel's cover turned to life. One moment, though—Podestà running in the villa's park, the tree branches appearing before her like claws in a blaze of colored lights—is practically a carbon copy of a similar sequence in Freda's *The Horrible Dr. Hichcock*.

The overall effect is more playful than horrific: an exhibition of sorts, which also serves as a dissimulation—the brighter the colors, the more convincing the illusion of luxury and sumptuousness. Despite the film's pretentions at Gothic grandeur, *The Virgin of Nuremberg* was a rushed production, shot in just three weeks (including special effects photography). Therefore, Margheriti's style is decidedly pragmatic and economical, and his habit of shooting a scene with several cameras is well in evidence. As the director explained, "of course, it limits your possibilities concerning camera movements and composition, because you have to see that no camera is interfering with the others, but it is a good way to cope with very complicated scenes in just a few takes. After that's

done, you just need some intercutting or some filler and all the rest can be done in the editing room."[6]

Such an approach makes for dynamic results at times, as in the sinuous opening sequence, in which Rossana Podestà wakes up, looks out the bedroom window, descends the stairs and finally enters the torture chamber where she discovers a dead woman's body inside the titular device. However, sometimes the expedient results in a certain artificiality: for instance, all the dialogue scenes between two characters are inevitably shot with the usual shot/reverse shot routine, and often come off as boring and predictable.

Yet the Roman filmmaker does not give up his beloved miniatures, with remarkably spectacular results in the scene—absent in the book—where Georges Rivière is trapped in the castle's crypts which the hooded villain floods with the pool water, or the castle corridor catching fire.[7] Elsewhere, Margheriti's miniatures carry a more practical purpose: the shots of the pinnacles and towers of the castle on the Rhine where the story is set belong to a miniature, and are strategically inserted between shots of the Roman villa where the film was shot.

The director was rather pleased with the results: "I changed a few things, tried to insert a war subplot, the surgery, in order to give the story some more sense... [...] Georges Rivière was rather good and the film, for all its modesty, was quite decent, not completely thrown away.... I always tried to save the set-pieces, the special effects, the *mise-en-scène*."[8]

The bulk of the story is a typical Gothic yarn centered on a woman in peril which disposes of the supernatural for a decidedly more earthly menace. Interestingly, though, the mad monster (Mirko Valentin) who inhabits the family castle, kidnapping and torturing all the unfortunate women he can lay his hands on is revealed to be an ex–SS general who took part in a failed plot to kill Der Führer, and as a punishment was tortured and transformed by Hitler's surgeons into a living skull (echoes of Captain America's Red Skull here). The idea of a Nazi-related plot can also be found in such horror flicks of the period as *The Flesh Eaters* (1964,

The Italian poster for *The Virgin of Nuremberg* featured prominently the film's star Rossana Podestà (author's collection).

Jack Curtis) and *The Frozen Dead* (1966, Herbert J. Leder), and later on in Jean Brismée's fascinating moral parable *The Devil's Nightmare* (*La Plus longue nuit du diable*, 1971). However, Margheriti predates by a whole decade the

atrocities of the Nazi-erotic cycle with the flashback scene of the surgery (in black-and-white in order to diminish its gory impact), and the results are decidedly gruesome for the time.

The unbridled sadism of several scenes still

packs a punch, starting with the prologue where Rossana Podestà discovers a dead woman inside the "Virgin of Nuremberg," her eyeballs gouged out; later on the torturer applies a cage containing a rat to a victim's face, and the rodent starts eating the hapless woman's flesh—a scene taken verbatim from the book. However, the script skips the novel's most extreme parts, which are not unworthy of today's *torture porns*: one grotesque highlight in the book has the madman sever a woman's "nerve, at the height of the first dorsal vertebra," before pulling out almost all the bones from her body, leaving only the rib cage and part of the backbone, reducing the poor victim to a shapeless flesh bag—an over-the-top moment that would not have been out of place in *Martyrs* (2008, Pascal Laugier) or *The Human Centipede* (2010, Tom Six).

As for the screenplay, Ernesto Gastaldi denied he was the "Gastad Green" credited as scriptwriter together with Margheriti and Edmund Greville, despite many reference books and websites (including the IMDb) claiming the contrary. ""Gastad Green" was not me, as far as I know. As producers often did with the Spanish co-productions, where they had to put Spanish names into the film even though they actually were not involved, it might be the case that they needed an Italian name, and that either my friend Antonio Margheriti or the producer said "Well, let's use Gastaldi's!"" as the writer himself explained. "However, revisiting the film I had a vague memory of the ending, so my impression was that either I had a chat with Margheriti about the film or I did some sort of supervising. However, the dialogue and the rest are not mine."[9] According to the film's official papers, the man behind the pseudonym "Gastad Green" was actually Renato Vicario, the producer's brother.

For all its violence, *The Virgin of Nuremberg* is not devoid of a much welcomed tongue-in-cheek irony. On paper, the final scene sounds poignant: the servant played by Christopher Lee rushes into the flames to rescue his old master and ends up buried with him under the castle's ruins. At the moment of the final agnition, though, when the ex–Nazi whose face reduced to a horrid skull recognizes his faithful attendant Erich, the scarred servant is apostrophized by the dying monster with the priceless line: "What happened to your face?"

The film was released in the States as *Horror Castle*, to less than raving reviews.[10] The subsequent U.S. home video releases restored a more faithful translation of the original title. The German print, on the other hand, omitted the war flashbacks and even changed typical German names such as Erich and Trude, to disguise the German setting.

Notes

1. Marcello Garofalo, "Le interviste celibi: Antonio Margheriti. L'ingegnere in Cinemascope," *Segnocinema* 84, March/April 1997, p. 7.
2. Created in 1899 by Luigi Albertini as a supplement to Italy's best-selling newspaper *Il Corriere della Sera*, the weekly magazine—which became immensely popular due to its extraordinarily elaborate colored illustrations on the front and back cover (the unmistakable work of the great illustrator and painter Achille Beltrame)—did not just collect the events of the past week, but also short stories and serialized novels, which often dealt with the Fantastic. On *La Domenica del Corriere*, Italian readers got to know the works of Arthur Conan Doyle (*The Hound of the Baskervilles*) and H. G. Wells (*The Flowering of the Strange Orchid*): but the magazine also served as a showcase for Italian authors such as Italo Toscani, Egisto Roggero (*Il vecchio orologio*, The Old Clock, 1900), Virginio Appiani (*Il segreto della morta*, The Dead Woman's Secret, 1901), Giuseppe Tonsi (*Il vampiro*, The Vampire, 1902).
3. Besides novelizations of contemporary horror films—including *The Revenge of Frankenstein* (1958, Terence Fisher), *The Return of Dracula* (1958, Paul Landres) and *The Vampire* (*El vampiro*, 1957, Fernando Mendez)—the series included original, specifically written material. Three years later, with the release of *L'amante gelida* (The Icy Lover) by Lyonel Clayle, the series would become *I Capolavori della Serie KKK. Classici dell'Orrore* ("The Masterpieces of KKK. Horror Classics"): published by G.E.I. (Grandi Edizioni Internazionali, later to become EPI—Edizioni Periodici Italiani), it would run for over 170 issues until 1972. Besides the aforementioned Clayle and O'Neal, the *KKK* paperbacks featured a plethora of exotic names—René Du Car, Roland Graves, Lucien Le Bossu, James Darren, Elizabeth Cronin, Maud Guy, Geremias Gotthelf, Marion Walles, Jean Le Rousse, Mary Sant Paul, Barbara Lee, Jack Cabot, Terence O'Neil, Patty North, Hassan Louvre, Jannet Mills, Stephen Tourjansky, Edgar Mittelholzer, and so on—which were actually ascribable to a quartet of Italian pens: Leonia Celli, Renato Carocci, Maddalena Gui, Laura Toscano. Similarly, *I Racconti di Dracula* were the product of Pino Belli, Libero Samale, Franco Prattico, Gualberto Titta, Giuseppe Paci, Svenio Tozzi, Aldo Crudo, plus future film directors Mario Pinzauti (*2 Magnum 38 per una città di carogne*, 1975) and Marco Masi (*C'era una volta un gangster*, 1969). *I racconti di Dracula* offered such lurid titles as *I*

morti uccidono? (Do Dead Men Kill?), *Femmine dell'al di là* (Females From the Beyond), *L'alito freddo del vampiro* (The Vampire's Cold Breath), *L'organo dei morti* (The Dead Men's Organ)—respectively, issues 1, 7, 52, 73, credited to Max Dave [Pino Belli], Doug Stejner [Sveno Tozzi], George Wallis [Giuseppe Paci], Frank Graegorius [Libero Samale].

4. Margheriti himself recalled Vicario's involvement with horror paperbacks in a 1970 interview with Luigi Cozzi: "(*The Virgin of Nuremberg*) is based on a fairly good book published by Vicario. Yes, Marco Vicario, the director of *Seven Golden Men* [...]." Luigi Cozzi, "Il vampiro in orbita," *Horror* 6, May 1970, p. 27.

5. Peter Blumenstock, "Margheriti—The Wild, Wild Interview," *Video Watchdog* 28, May/June 1995, p. 51.

6. Ibid., p. 49.

7. As for the special effects, Margheriti recalled, "We did them at night. When the rest of the crew went home, I picked some poor guys who were not exactly looking forward to a sleepless night, and we filmed those miniatures [...]." Ibid., p. 51.

8. Garofalo, "Le interviste celibi," p. 7.

9. Ernesto Gastaldi, interviewed in *Il castello del terrore*, a featurette included as an extra on the Italian DVD of the film.

10. The *New York Times* reviewer summarized the film with these words: "Inept horror pic. Rossana Podestà's looks and Christopher Lee's chillpix reputation don't save it. Grind house fate." Murf, "Horror Castle," *New York Times* April 15, 1965.

The Whip and the Body, a.k.a. What, a.k.a. Night Is the Phantom (La frusta e il corpo)

D: John M. Old [Mario Bava]. *S* and *SC*: Julian Berry [Ernesto Gastaldi], Robert Hugo [Ugo Guerra], Martin Hardy [Luciano Martino]; *DOP:* David Hamilton [Ubaldo Terzano] (Technicolor); *M:* Jim Murphy [Carlo Rustichelli], conducted by Pier Luigi Urbini; *E:* Bob King [Renato Cinquini]; *AE:* Kathy Line [Lina Caterini]; *PD:* Dick Grey [Ottavio Scotti]; *CO:* Peg Fax [Anna Maria Palleri]; *SD:* Gus Marrow [Riccardo Dominici]; *AD:* Julian Berry; *2ndAD:* Sergio Martino (uncredited); *C:* Art Balsam [Ubaldo Terzano]; *AC:* Mark Baer; *SO:* Peter Jackson; *B:* Rex McCrea; *MU:* Frank Field [Franco Freda]; *AMU:* Raf Christie [Raffaele Cristini]; *SP:* Robert Schafer; *SS:* Priscilla Hudson [Priscilla Contardi]. *Cast:* Daliah Lavi (Nevenka Menliff), Christopher Lee (Kurt Menliff), Tony Kendall [Luciano Stella] (Christian Menliff), Isli Oberon [Ida Galli] (Katia), Harriet White [Medin] (Giorgia), Dean Ardow [Gustavo De Nardo] (Count Menliff), Alan Collins [Luciano Pigozzi] (Losat), Jacques Herlin (Priest). *PROD:* Vox Film, Leone Film (Rome), Francinor, P.I.P. (France); *PM:* Tom Rhodes [Federico Magnaghi]; *GM:* John Oscar [Elio Scardamaglia]; *UM:* Free Baldwin [Ferdinando Baldi]; *PSe:* Joe M. Seery.

Country: Italy/France. Filmed at Anzio and at Castel Sant'Angelo (Rome). *Running time:* 91 min. (m. 2374); Visa n: 41063 (08.24.1963); *Rating:* V.M.18; *Release dates:* 08.29.1963 (Italy); 12.10.1965 (U.S.A.). *Distribution:* Titanus (Italy); Futuramic Releasing (U.S.A.); *Domestic gross:* 72,000,000 lire. *Also known as:* Le Corps et le fouet (France, 01.26.1966), Der Dämon und die Jungfrau, Der Mörder von Schloß Menliff (West Germany, 06.09.1967), Night Is the Phantom (U.K.). *Homevideo:* Kino (Blu-Ray, U.S.A.), VCI (DVD, U.S.A.), e-m-s (DVD, Germany).

Kurt Menliff arrives at his seaside castle after many years. The black sheep of the Menliff family, he is met with distrust (if not open hatred) by the castle's inhabitants: his invalid father, his younger brother Cristiano, who married Kurt's former lover Nevenka, and the maid Giorgia, whose daughter killed herself because of him. Kurt's arrival soon spreads disorder in the place, and he and Nevenka reprise their sadomasochistic affair. However, one night Kurt is murdered by an unknown hand. After the funeral, though, Nevenka keeps having nightmarish visions of her dead lover, while the Count is assassinated as well. Has Kurt returned as a ghost to exact revenge on his family?

Mario Bava's second Gothic horror film of the year, *The Whip and the Body* was an Italian/French production financed by Luciano Martino and Elio Scardamaglia's Vox Film and based on a script which the opening titles credit to "Julian Berry, Robert Hugo and Martin Hardy"—respectively, Ernesto Gastaldi, Ugo Guerra and Luciano Martino. However, Gastaldi pointed out to this writer: "I surely wrote the script all by myself, but I don't remember whether there was a plotline by Ugo Guerra: that's possible, as Ugo was really a goldmine of ideas. Instead, Luciano Martino had nothing to do with it."[1]

Bava came on board through Guerra, who thought he would be a convenient choice: "I remember Ugo saying, 'Mario can be both photographer and director; that is convenient for us,'" as Gastaldi recalled.[2] Even though Bava took care of the photography, the credited d.o.p. on the film was, as usual, Bava's frequent cameraman Ubaldo Terzano, acting as a front. The director employed for the second time in his career an English pseudonym (the rather self-deprecating John M. Old) after the laughable "John Foam" (the literal English translation of his surname) he had chosen as the d.o.p on *Caltiki, the Immortal Monster*. Bava would re-use the John M. Old alias on his Western *The Road to Fort Alamo* (*La strada per Fort Alamo*, 1964). As for Gastaldi, even though his name (or rather, his pseudonym) can be found in the credits as the assistant director, he never even set foot on the set.[3]

Besides the presence of Christopher Lee, billed as co-star, the female lead was Daliah Lavi, a ravishing Israeli actress who, among other things, had played alongside Kirk Douglas, George Hamilton and Edward G. Robinson in Vincente Minnelli's bitter take on the Italian film industry, *Two Weeks in Another Town*. That same year, Lavi would offer an extraordinary performance in Brunello Rondi's *Il demonio*, as a girl who is believed to be possessed by the devil in rural Southern Italy.

Compared to Bava's previous Gothic efforts, *The Whip and the Body* had no claims on being original, and was probably thought of as a project for the home market consumption, as Gastaldi recalled. With a six-week shooting schedule (plus one for special effects) and a budget of less than 150 million *lire*, it was nonetheless a flop in Italy, with a domestic gross of just 72 million *lire*—no doubt due to its censorship troubles (more on this later). The film was more successful abroad, although poorly represented by an English language version (prepared by Mel Welles) which did not even feature the actors dubbing themselves. In the United States, where it came out in 1965 as *What*, the film soon circulated in a truncated, cheaply processed 77-minute mess of a print (almost identical to the butchered British version, *Night Is the Phantom*) which was best described by Lee as "a picture of opening and closing doors and shadows and funny footfalls and people spinning around and nobody being there."[4]

The storyline featured the now established characters associated with Italian Gothic horror films: a nineteenth century setting (although the producers chose to be unspecific in order to avoid problems on costumes and sets), a morbidly suggestive atmosphere with nods to the *feuilleton*, convenient doses of eroticism and an

emphasis on the female character. All this, however, with an eye to foreign models. As the opening image clearly shows—Christopher Lee galloping towards Castle Menliff is an almost exact replica of the beginning of *The Pit and the Pendulum*, American International Pictures' Corman/Poe cycle was the main model Gastaldi was asked to stick to. "The producers [...] showed me an Italian print of *The Pit and the Pendulum* before I started writing it: 'Give us something like this,' they said."[5]

And yet, the relationship between AIP's Poe films and Italian Gothic horror is a curious one: a game of rebounds and reciprocal influences—of communicating vessels, so to speak. First, both had in common a more disenchanted attitude towards the genre, free from the classical monsters' routine—whose survival was granted by Hammer films—and linked to the inner self. Both displayed an attitude clever enough to grab a Gothic icon such as Poe (with respect to Italy, see *The Blancheville Horror* and especially *Castle of Blood*) in order to shape it and distort it at will—yet they were characterized by a similar taste for the baroque, the mannerism, the delirious as Poe's own stories.

Italian films were similar as well to Corman's works because of the limited budgets, hasty shoots and tight crews. Obviously, there were also precise iconographic and stylistic points of contact, such as the emphasis on the *décor* and set-pieces as an element of anxiety ("The house is the monster" was Corman's answer to Samuel Arkoff's perplexities on the commercial potential of *House of Usher*, which lacked a proper monster) and the repetition of identical situations and images. The sight of ladies in their nightgown moving through dark corridors often evoked by Martin Scorsese about Italian horror films can actually refer to either *House of Usher* or *The Virgin of Nuremberg*, while the multicolored hooded figures of *The Masque of the Red Death* owe a lot to the monochromatic torturers in the opening scene of Bava's debut as well as the pallbearers wearing scarlet hoods in the funeral scene of *The Whip and the Body*.

It was also a matter of commercial strategies. Corman borrowed Barbara Steele as a horror icon after *Black Sunday* for *The Pit and the Pen-*

dulum, whose American trailer openly referred to Bava's film—AIP's biggest hit as a distributor so far. In Italy it was to be the opposite, with *The Pit and the Pendulum* used as a blueprint, as Gastaldi recalled, while Bava cast Mark Damon, the lead in *House of Usher*, for the most Corman-like episode of *Black Sabbath*.

Yet, such a pragmatic film-maker as Corman would have never played with the incongruencies and the limits of the scripts like Bava was used to do. Bava's inventions were often the product of individual craftsmanship and improvisation, whereas the American director relied on a tight organization production-wise, to the point that Richard Matheson, his scriptwriter on many films of the Poe cycle, labeled him—perhaps ungenerously—as a mere "traffic cop."[6] Gastaldi noted how the Sanremese director did not make any changes in regard to the dialogue, plot or characters, but just altered some special effects as described in the script. Yet the way he dealt with the fantastic element of the story in *The Whip and the Body* is particularly interesting, and deserves an in-depth analysis.

According to Tzvetan Todorov's oft-quoted definition, the Fantastic occupies the time span of uncertainty, of the "hesitation" before an event which "cannot be explained by the laws of this same familiar world,"[7] before a choice that will lead the reader either to the "uncanny" (that is, the supernatural explained) or the "marvelous" (that is, the supernatural accepted as just that).

Italian Gothic horror films often took sides in either of these two extremes. Besides those movies where the supernatural element had a central role, there were others where it turned out to be a red herring, such as Freda's *The Horrible Dr. Hichcock* and *The Ghost*, De Martino's *The Blancheville Monster* and Mastrocinque's *An Angel for Satan*. All these films dealt with curses, monsters and possessions which had their roots in earthly intrigues; similarly, the murderous entities of *The Virgin of Nuremberg* and *Bloody Pit of Horror* were decidedly human.

At times, though, a more thought-provoking approach emerged, which in turn revealed the cracks in Todorov's theory and underlined its schematic construction. Such a case is *The Whip and the Body*. The film's peculiar narrative, which continually veers between a ghost story and a murder mystery with a rational explanation, piles up unexplained or obscure passages: examples are the mention of a secret path through which Kurt's father visited his son before being killed, or the muddy footprints that appear on the castle's floor and stairs.

This time it was not, as with *The Horrible Dr. Hichcock*, a matter of pages being torn off the script at the very last minute. The plot had its share of holes. Yet Bava did not worry about tying up the loose ends: on the contrary, he closed the film with an extraordinary directorial *coup de théatre* which further shuffled cards. Unlike the previous apparitions of Kurt's ghost—whom Bava showed with a standard shot/reverse shot routine and always from the point of view of his lover Nevenka (thus emphasizing her subjectivity), in the final scene the director shows the two lovers' deadly embrace, *both in the same shot*, as Nevenka is about to stab Kurt.

As Italian Bava scholar Alberto Pezzotta noted, "This would seem the denial of the theorem, and the evidence of Kurt's 'existence.' Yet immediately afterwards Bava shows us the same scene as seen through the eyes of Cristiano: this time, Nevenka is embracing the void. So then, who was watching the previous scene, when the ghost was visible (which was not a POV shot, mind you)? Bava is not interested in dissolving the ambiguity, or in teaching some lesson about cinema as an illusion. *The Whip and the Body* is a truly Fantastic film precisely because it does not add up and its logic falters: not only and not so much in the plot, but especially in the filming. Contradictions, red herrings [...], misconceptions that the script cannot handle [...]: everything contributes to building a world the laws (or non-laws) of which are quite peculiar."[8]

This way, Todorov's "choice" is denied—or rather, we the audience find ourselves in a position similar to that of the character who is observing Nevenka, yet without any element that might enable us to choose one solution over another. Did Kurt really exist? Or was he just a projection of Nevenka's unsatisfied lust and madness? This is no longer a mere hesitation, but a stalemate, an *impasse*. Well after the words "The End" have appeared on screen, we are still in a position best-described as follows: "Hesitation, doubt, uncertainty, bewilderment are all terms that could equally express such a state, provided it is clear that this is not the state of someone who is undecided between two alternatives, but led to doubt the validity and adequacy of the paradigm of reality itself [...]; this is not the hesitation of someone who stands at a crossroads, but the loss of someone who found himself at a dead end and cannot retrace his own steps."[9]

The Whip and the Body is in many ways the quintessential Gothic film—or rather, it *looks* like it. What immediately strikes the viewer is Bava's use of the landscape and the way it interacts with the characters.

In his treatise *A Philosophical Inquiry into the Origin of Our Ideas of the Sublime and Beautiful* (1757)—one of the key works in the foundation of the aesthetics and poetry of literary Gothic—Edmund Burke pointed out how the Sublime is connected to natural phenomena, whose suggestion is likely to push us "by an irresistible force" towards the world of the imagination and the sensational, where wonder becomes terror. It is commonplace in the Gothic that characters' emotions are highlighted and replicated by natural events.

As he did in *Black Sunday*, with *The Whip and the Body* Mario Bava transposed on film an idea of the landscape that draws on the Romantic and Gothic conception of the Sublime, by blending real exterior locations and studio sets. In both films the landscape conveys a feeling—an emotion connected to terror and pain. In *Black Sunday*'s opening scenes, the crooked branches and brambles, standing between the camera and the carriage on which the two doctors were traveling in the woods, evoked the idea of a hostile and overpowering environment. Similarly, *The Whip and the Body*'s image of the mysterious rider, galloping towards a gloomy castle as darkness falls, perfectly sums up one of the central images of the Romantic iconography.

Nature occasionally assumes anthropomorphic or symbolic shapes: that is the case with the branches which look like skeletal fingers and frighten the coachman in *Black Sunday*, or the tree branch that opens a bedroom window and hisses inside the room like (appropriately) a whip in *The Whip and the Body*. In a similar way, the furious storms that sweep Castle Menliff echo Nevenka's tormented soul and psyche: in the encounter between her and Kurt on the beach, where the two lovers hook up their ancient sadomasochistic bond, Bava elliptically suggests their arising passion by cutting from the lovers to the waves crashing on the shore.

Overall, the landscape in *The Whip and the Body* is a totally imaginary creation, as is typical with Bava. Whereas in *I Vampiri* Bava had sticked a view of the Eiffel Tower by the river Aniene, and reinvented the Saint-Jacques tower as a part of the Du Grand castle, here the director incongruously transported the sight of an Alpine manor (Castle Fenis in Aosta) on a shore—the Tor Caldara beach that Bava also used in *Knives of the Avenger* (*I coltelli del vendicatore*, 1966). In so doing, Bava reproduced, by means of optical tricks, one of those fantastic landscapes dear to such painters as the Mannerist Agostino Tassi (1580–1644), who used to insert realistic details within oneiric contexts. This way, Bava put on film Edmund Burke's celebrated axiom: "No work of art can be great, but as it deceives."[10]

Another element that sets *The Whip and the Body* aside from its American counterparts—as well as much of its Italian contemporaries—is the way Bava used the color palette, which goes far beyond Corman's pop attitude. The arbitrary use of color, as opposed to Freda's dramatic and functional one, is a sign of the modernity of Bava's approach to the Gothic.

First, and most patently, the lighting is not justified by diegetic motives—see also the intermitting light outside the window of the nurse's apartment in "The Drop of Water," or the silhouettes that walk along the village alleys in *Kill, Baby...Kill!*—but responds to unpredictable laws. In *Hercules in the Haunted World* Bava framed the Sibyl behind a curtain of moving beads, bombarded with multi-colored lights (green, blue and yellow), to symbolize her essence, suspended between two worlds. In a

Italian poster for Mario Bava's *The Whip and the Body* (author's collection).

pioneering essay on the director, Alain Silver and James Ursini pointed out how the use of primary colors was an expedient to externalize and emphasized the characters' dilemma about the indistinguishability of reality and illusion.[11] However, this is not always true: on the contrary, more often than not the alternance of primary colors is released from the original meaning as pointed out by Silver and Ursini, and does not obey any rule, if not the director's own whim.

That is the case with *The Whip and the Body*. In the scene in which Nevenka hears the cracking of Kurt's whip for the first time and follows its sound throughout the castle, Bava seemingly resorts to colors as a palette of the character's feelings. Daliah Lavi's face is lighted with a violent red that suggests a feverish desire, and which alternates with a deep blue that stands for fear. Yet, as the story moves along, other characters who wander inside Castle Menliff are subjected to the very same treatment, regardless of their emotional state.

Aesthetic and dramatic function become increasingly blurred. As one critic noted, "Colors serve both to give a scene a greater depth as well as creating a dreamlike dimension and a constant tension."[12] This leads to an unreal and schizophrenic world where every sequence and shot becomes an attraction in itself, regardless of who appears or what is happening (or *not* happening) in it. This way, Bava achieves striking, almost abstract effects: in the scene where Nevenka is in bed, the director cuts from the image of the moon surrounded by clouds to Nevenka's (out-of-focus) hair on the pillow. Then the camera moves towards her eyes, which are the only lighted part of her body, "like in a painting by Alberto Martini."[13]

Much has been said and written about *The Whip and the Body*'s sadomasochistic theme, which caused the film plenty of trouble in its native country. The board of censors—to which the film was submitted only 12 days after Bava's other horror film of the year, *Black Sabbath*—gave it a V.M.18 rating ("forbidden to minors") but demanded no cuts. The production company appealed, after making a few cuts, and obtained a more commercially viable V.M. 14. However, this did not prevent *The Whip and the Body* to be seized on October 12, 1963, with charges of obscenity, because of "several sequences that refer to degenerations and anomalies of sexual life." It was eventually released in January 1964. However, the law court of Rome ordered the confiscation of several scenes that were considered "contrary to morality," disposed that the film poster be destroyed and condemned the chief press officer at Titanus to three months on probation.[14]

Besides the required amount of spicing to the recipe—aided enormously by Lavi's extraordinary screen presence—*The Whip and the Body* is one of the most patent examples of the general intolerance towards the institution of marriage, on a par with the more blatant *The Long Hair of Death*. The return of the prodigal son Kurt, who has come back to claim his family property, including his beautiful sister-in-law Nevenka, has turbulent effects on the woman, reviving her dormant desires and anxieties; furthermore, it undermines a family that is stable only in appearance, leaning on a marriage of convenience and devoid of love—that of Nevenka and Cristiano.

Yet, even though she is an adulteress and a murderess, Nevenka is never seen as an utterly negative character, but rather as the victim of a patriarchal family that has forced her to marry someone whom she does not love. Although at Kurt's funeral the priest claims that the deceased has been struck by divine justice, there is hardly a superior force at work in the film—rather, it is a subterranean vein of self-destruction that corrodes the family as a whole.

Compared to the male characters in other Italian Gothic horror films, the Lucifer-like Kurt Menliff is one of the rare examples of a strong male figure who recalls the "cruel fatal man" as embodied in Gothic novels by the titular character in Maturin's *Melmoth the Wanderer* or Father Schedoni in Ann Radcliffe's *The Italian*. "There was something terrible in [Schedoni's] air; something almost superhuman. [...] and his eyes were so piercing that they seemed to penetrate, at a single glance, into the hearts of men, and to read their most secret thoughts," as Radcliffe wrote, a description which fits Lee's imposing screen presence. All this, however, melts like snow under the sun in Gastaldi's script.

Kurt the rebel shows up at Castle Menliff with all the boldness and the contemptuous arrogance of a fallen angel who returns to reclaim his place in heaven, sowing discord and paying back his relatives with the same hatred that had been reserved for him. But his game costs him his life. Kurt's murder, after scarcely half an hour, comes as a shock to the audience, who—given the presence of Christopher Lee—were expecting an all-round villain for the entire duration of the film. It is not simply a nod to Marion Crane's murder in *Psycho* (as in *The Horrible Dr. Hichcock*, Gastaldi was smart in absorbing and reworking Hitchcockian influences), but a real sabotage of the romantic hero character.

The Whip and the Body moves along in a seemingly contradictory manner, with an apparent subservience towards the romantic trappings of the story and its actual disruption of them. Since the opening credits, in Gothic golden letters on a scarlet silk curtain, accompanied by Carlo Rustichelli's sumptuous main theme, Bava's film seems to stick with a turgid *rétro* Romanticism. Such was also Gastaldi's impression: "The movie disappointed me a lot," he confessed to Luigi Cozzi in a 1970 interview. "I was thinking about a story in terms of a psychological nightmare, in the style of Clouzot's films, but Bava saw in it a baroque and decadent drama, and emphasized such tones beyond belief."[15]

Bava collects the basic elements of the Gothic novel—the galloping rider, the forces of nature as a mirror of the characters' emotions, etc.—and employs languid tracking shots so as to isolate single elements of the scene: a case in point is the dagger that Giorgia's (Harriet White) daughter had used to kill herself under Kurt's influence, which is kept under a glass case and will become the weapon of Kurt's murder. Yet sometimes these symbolic objects—the dagger as an instrument of revenge, the vase of red roses connected to Kurt's apparitions—get the upper hand over the characters and the plot, and dominate the scenes and the story with an effect of abstraction from the narration.[16]

However, Bava's was not quite a post-modern reflection as Sergio Leone's would be with the founding elements of the Western. Bava was never a cinephile, and his was mostly an aesthetic challenge: as a film-maker, he enjoyed cultivating the taste for experimentation, chisel, visual mockery. Add to that a detachment which grew from the awareness that what he was doing meant absolutely nothing: he did not have the presumption of believing otherwise. That is why Bava's less successful films are those where the centrality of the story is unavoidable, such as his Westerns. Similarly, the least interesting parts in his horror films are usually the expository sequences (such as the conversation between Giacomo Rossi-Stuart and Piero Lulli in *Kill, Baby...Kill!*), where the director was restrained by the need to give room to dialogue.

True, the script for *The Whip and the Body* is pegged at outdated clichés, such as a hand that suddenly pops up onscreen and leans on a character's shoulder from behind, and it draws a lot from the overall atmosphere of Corman's films. Nevertheless, Bava was not deluding himself that he could frighten the viewer by showing muddy footprints or playing hide-and-seek with Kurt's ghost. Understandably, he focused his attention on something else, by amplifying the subjective and inner dimension of fear: a case in point is Kurt's ghastly hand which, distorted by a wide angle lens, literally fills the screen from Nevenka's point of view.

This makes *The Whip and the Body* the first Italian Gothic horror film centered on the ghosts of the subconscious, an anticipation of the so-called "paranoid texts" that would characterize so much Gothic cinema to come, including Bava's final masterpiece *Shock*.

Notes

1. Ernesto Gastaldi, email interview, March 2011.
2. Lucas, "What Are Those Strange Drops of Blood," p. 38.
3. Ernesto Gastaldi, email interview, July 2014.
4. Michael Parry, "CoF interviews Christopher Lee, Part 3," *Castle of Frankenstein* 12, 1968, pp. 30–31.
5. Lucas, "What Are Those Strange Drops of Blood," p. 38.
6. Tom Weaver and Michael Brunas, "Quoth Matheson, "Nevermore!,"" *Fangoria* 90, February 1990, p. 16.
7. Todorov, *The Fantastic*, p. 25.
8. Pezzotta, *Mario Bava*, p. 66.
9. Lucio Lugnani, "Per una delimitazione del "genere," in Remo Ceserani, Lucio Lugnani, Gianluigi Goggi, Carla Benedetti and Elisabetta Scarano, eds., *La narrazione fantastica* (Pisa: Nistri-Lischi, 1983), pp. 72–73.
10. Edmund Burke, *A Philosophical Inquiry into the Origin of Our Ideas of the Sublime and Beautiful* (New York: Digireads.com, 2009), p. 42. As with other Italian Gothic Horror outings, the film's castle is actually a mosaic of different locations. A few exteriors (the drawbridge and the inner court) surprisingly come from a famous yet almost unrecognizable location: Castel Sant' Angelo in Rome. Similarly, the studio interiors of Castle Menliff—mostly the same as seen in Margheriti's *Castle of Blood*—are inexorably broken by scenic and color elements that divide them into incongruous portions, thus creating perspectives and niches which seem to belong to contiguous yet impervious dimensions.
11. Silver and Ursini, "Mario Bava: the Illusion of Reality," p. 95 ss.
12. Di Chiara, *I tre volti della paura*, p. 159.
13. Pezzotta, *Mario Bava*, p. 66.
14. Alessio Di Rocco, "Visto in censura: La frusta e il corpo," *Nocturno Cinema* 94, June 2010, p. 81.
15. Luigi Cozzi, "Così dolce ... così perverso... Intervista con Ernesto Gastaldi," *Horror* 5, April 1970, p. 56.
16. One extraordinarily bewildering sequence in *The Whip and the Body* is a case in point: while Cristiano and Katia are debating whether Kurt is dead or not, as Pezzotta notes, "from a pedantic shot/reverse shot of the two characters talking, the director cuts to a vase of red roses (while the dialogue continues off-screen), and moves around it for about 180 degrees, before returning to the actors, now in the background, who are still exchanging fundamental bits of dialogue: but in the meantime the viewer's—and the director's—attention has long gone." Pezzotta, *Mario Bava*, p. 64.

1964

Castle of Blood (Danza macabra)

D: Anthony M. Dawson [Antonio Margheriti] (and Sergio Corbucci, uncredited). *S:* "based on a story by Edgar Allan Poe"; *SC:* Jean Grimaud [Gianni Grimaldi], Gordon Wilson, Jr. [Bruno Corbucci]; *DOP:* Richard Kramer [Riccardo Pallottini] (B&W); *M:* Riz Ortolani; *E:* Otel Langhel [Otello Colangeli]; *PD:* Warner Scott [Ottavio Scotti]; *AD:* Roger Drake [Ruggero Deodato], *SE:* Anthony Matthews [Antonio Margheriti]; *SS:* Eva Koltay. *Cast:* Barbara Steele (Elisabeth Blackwood), Georges Rivière (Alan Foster), Margaret Robsham [Margrete Robsahm] (Julia), Henry Kruger [Arturo Dominici] (Dr. Carmus), Montgomery Glenn [Silvano Tranquilli] (Edgar Allan Poe), Sylvia Sorent [Sylvia Sorrente] (Elsi), Phil Karson, John Peters, Ben Steffen [Benito Stefanelli] (William), Johnny Walters [Giovanni Cianfriglia] (Killer), Merry Powers [Miranda Poggi], Raul H. Newman, [Umberto Raho] (Lord Thomas Blackwood). *PROD:* Franco Belotti, Walter Zarghetta for Era Cinematografica (Rome), Leo Lax Films (Paris) (*U.S. version:* Frank Belty [Leo Lax], Walter Sarah [Marco Vicario]); *GM:* Giovanni Addessi; *PM:* Al Givens [Alfonso Donati]; *PS:* Charles Smith [Giancarlo Sambucini]. *Country:* Italy/France. Filmed at Castle Bolsena (Viterbo); *Running time:* 90 min. (m. 2431); Visa n: 40624 (06.25.1963); *Rating:* V.M.18; *Release dates:* 02.27.1964 (Italy); 07.29.1964 (U.S.A.). *Distribution:* Globe International Film (Italy); Woolner Brothers Pictures, Inc. (U.S.A.); *Domestic gross:* 100,680,000 lire. *Also known as:* The Castle of Terror, Coffin of Terror, Dimensions in Death, Danse Macabre (France, 04.14.1965). *Home video:* Image (DVD, U.S.A.), Sinister Film (DVD, Italy).

Journalist Alan Foster challenges Edgar Allan Poe on the authenticity of his stories, which leads to him accepting a bet from Lord Blackwood to spend the night in a haunted castle on All Souls' Eve. Ghosts of the murdered inhabitants appear to him throughout the night, re-enacting the events that lead to their deaths. It transpires that they feed on the blood of the living visitors in order to maintain their existence. Blackwood's sister Elisabeth is also one of the ghosts, as she had been murdered by her husband. Elisabeth and Alan fall in love, and the woman tries to save his life from the bloodthirsty undead...

The idea of making a low-budget horror movie came to Sergio Corbucci when producer Giovanni Addessi commissioned him a film which would re-use the Medieval sets of Corbucci's period comedy *Il monaco di Monza*, also produced by Addessi and starring Totò. Corbucci, who was supposed to direct the film himself, asked his brother Bruno and Gianni Grimaldi (that is, "Gordon Wilson, Jr.," and "Jean Grimaud") to write the script. Then, when it came to start the movie, Corbucci found himself in a conflicting schedule, having to direct another film. He then called on his good friend Antonio Margheriti.

The presence of Barbara Steele was one of the film's assets. According to Ruggero Deodato, who was Margheriti's a.d. on the set, "since she had just done Fellini's *8½*, Barbara wanted to keep her distance from the horror genre. It was I who persuaded her, because we were friends. I had first met her at Demofilo Fidani's place [...]. She was so nice, she made me crazy. When I paid her a visit or brought her cats back, whenever Fellini stopped by—he used to visit his actresses every morning—Barbara had me hide under the bed."[1]

When interviewed about *Castle of Blood*, Margheriti used to minimize the film's merits, with a self-criticizing attitude that recalled Bava's, claiming that it was "even more boring" after all those years. "I remembered it well, just like that, and unfortunately it's got all the limits of a film done in too much of a hurry, perhaps even scripted in a hurry: we had to shoot everything in a few days, because then the workers would come and dismantle the sets [...]. When today we rediscover and screen these things of the past, I don't think they're good in themselves—they may be good to those of us who experienced them back in our own time."[2]

Having to work on a tight schedule, Margheriti perfected his technique of using several cameras at once: "In order to manage in keeping the shooting schedule within fifteen days, I shot with the same method as in television, by using up to four cameras at once. One was placed on tracks, another one on a dolly, and so on. I had a camera with three lenses, and after a line of dialogue my a.d. used to pat on the cameraman's shoulder, so that he would change the lens and do a close-up [...]. This way I was able to get many fragments which nevertheless were easier to edit together."[3]

However, to finish the film on time Margheriti had to call Sergio Corbucci for help. "Sergio came on the set only once, and gave me a hand shooting one scene, or else we'd have gone half-a-day behind schedule. [...] While I was shooting the bit of the serpent's head being cut, he was above, doing the scene where the couple is in the room, and then the "macho" enters," Margheriti explained, referring to the scene in which Giovanni Cianfriglia kills Barbara Steele and her lover.

Castle of Blood features the most typical traits of the Italian Gothic film—starting with its overt (but fake) literary lineage. According to the credits, *Castle of Blood* is based on a—non-existing—short story by none other than Edgar Allan Poe. The Poe connection goes further: the two scriptwriters conjectured Poe's journey to England (which never happened) and turned him into a character in the film itself, as played by Silvano Tranquilli: an expedient that had already been used by such writers as Manly Wade Wellman ("When It Was Moonlight") and John Dickson Carr ("The Gentleman from Paris," which was made into a film in 1951's *The Man with a Cloak*) and that later became a staple in mystery literature—think of Philip José Farmer, Nicholas Meyer and Harold Schechter's novels starring Poe—and film (Francis Ford Coppola's *Twixt*, 2011, and James McTeigue's *The Raven*, 2012). However, Corbucci and Grimaldi manage to slip in another Poe reference: the name Lord Blackwood (the character played by Umberto Raho) recalls Poe's satirical short story "How to Write a Blackwood Article."

No doubt Corbucci and Grimaldi were trying to cash in on the then very popular AIP Poe adaptations directed by Roger Corman. According to film scholar Chris Fujiwara, "It is, above all, the use of *décor* in Margheriti's film that recalls Corman: the emphasis on the prolonged and repeated examination of the sets; the ritual predictability of the settings—dining room, ballroom, bedroom, staircase, study, crypt. Furthermore, the casting of Barbara Steele in the role of Blackwood's sister, Elisabeth, links *Castle of Blood* as much to Corman's *The Pit and the Pendulum*, in which her character is also called Elizabeth (though with a "z" and not an

"s"), as to the films she had made with Bava and Freda."[4]

Poe as a character brings to the screen the mythical halo of the *maudit* writer and his obsessions: on the other hand, he clashes with the Italian Gothic's typical pragmatism. In the opening sequence we find Poe in a tavern, reciting the final paragraphs of one of his most celebrated tales, "Berenice"—another short story anthologized in Feltrinelli's volume *I vampiri tra noi*—before pointing out to journalist Alan Foster (Georges Rivière), who complimented him for the wisdom of his writings, that he is just like Alan—a reporter. That is, a mere observer of reality, powerless and defenseless against the horrors which he witnesses, as Foster will be as well. Such interpretation is not as far-fetched as it might sound: according to Poe scholar Carlo Bordoni, "when Poe writes about a supernatural theme, he always does it with special attention, by presenting the cause to the reader in a discursive, almost diary-like form, thus underlining the aspect of documentary evidence, of unusual experience, mysterious but no less justifiable on a rational level."[5]

Edgar Allan Poe would return several times in Italian Gothic films, mostly as a commercial gimmick and sometimes just as a vague reference: it is a sign of a sensibility that is closer to the psychological (or "everyday," as Italo Calvino labeled it) Fantastic, characteristic of the late nineteenth century, than to its previous, "visionary" incarnations.[6] In *Castle of Blood*, Poe sheds light on a contradictory vision of the fantastic: he is at the same time the (apocryphal) source of the story *and* a character. Thus, according to Corbucci and Grimaldi's game, he depicts himself and his *oeuvre* within one of his own stories, as is the case with the aforementioned reference to "Berenice." But Poe, as we have seen, claims himself to be just a reporter, and in the final scene he sadly observes: "When I'll tell this story, no one will believe me."

It is a punchline that causes the film to fold in on itself: the story Poe will tell is the one we have just seen. And since said story features the supernatural, it follows that all other Poe tales are not fiction, but mere transpositions of the existing. Without even being aware of it, Cor-

Moody Mexican poster for Antonio Margheriti's *Castle of Blood* (1964) (author's collection).

bucci, Grimaldi and Margheriti end the film on a thought-provoking enigma.

Besides being a ghost story, *Castle of Blood* is also a vampire tale, although the film's bloodthirsty undead, who need blood to maintain their suspended non-life, are a far cry from the typical Victorian specters, and are much more genuinely menacing and terrifying because of that.

Despite Margheriti's cost-saving methods, *Castle of Blood* retains several scenes of undoubted horrific power, such as the skeleton which starts breathing in the crypt (a special effect done by the director himself, who labelled it "terrible"), and Rivière's desperate escape from the undead, which are still rather effective today. Others, such as the "breathing" painting, betray the haste in which the movie was made. "The portrait of the woman, who in our intentions had to look as if it was practically breathing, became a ridiculous thing, tremendous, almost like a flag in the wind," Margheriti

recalled, bemusedly. "Here, these are just the things where we take a fall, failing to reach the desired result by a little.... I was given an old optical printer, one of those that operated in the water ... my a.d. told me: "Well, you know, it's the light...." "What light? (*laughs*) Looks like she's swimming!" I remember I got angry even then because of that special effect."[7]

And yet, the film's core is not horror but eroticism. A typical situation of the Gothic *filone* requires that a living person fall in love with a dead one, or vice versa: in this sense, *Castle of Blood* follows a similar path as *The Long Hair of Death*, *Terror in the Crypt* and *La vendetta di Lady Morgan* (1965, Massimo Pupillo). However, unlike the pale specters that obsessed Poe's characters, such love is often not platonic at all, with all the paradoxes and anxieties that follow. According to Alberto Pezzotta, "eros [...] has to do with, and even seems consubstantial, to the passing of a threshold: the one between the living and the dead, between the real and the supernatural."[8] That is why in *Castle of Blood* Elisabeth proclaims: "I live only when I love." Elisabeth is a "queen bee," more ethereal but no less voracious than Marina Vlady in Marco Ferreri's *The Conjugal Bed*. She is a man-eater that only through her due punishment—death—can become a romantic heroine, without losing her characteristics nor giving up on her sexuality.

Margheriti's emphasis on eroticism is also evident in one of the film's most famous scenes, where Julia (Margrete Robsahm) makes a pass at Elisabeth, who responds in horror "I love men, do you understand? Men!" Although the topic of lesbianism is a recurrent one in Italian Gothic, *Castle of Blood* is the first to explicitly portray it on screen with the aforementioned scene, possibly one of the reasons that earned the film a V.M.18 rating ("for the sadism that permeates the whole picture and for the sensuality [*sic*] of several scenes") and, according to Margheriti, caused quite a scandal when the film opened in Rome.[9] Yet, even though the emphasis on eroticism is a required element (so much so that the more daring French cut featured actress Sylvia Sorrente in a nude scene), Margheriti's film is remarkable for its portrayal of the heroine: Elisabeth Blackwood is a more faceted character than usual, as her psychological and behavioral splitting is not a consequence of hypnosis or coercion.

The way Elisabeth greets Foster, teasing him about his manhood and dropping not-so-veiled allusions to the possibility of spending the night together, makes her immediately appear as a seductress—therefore dangerous, and surely a liar, according to the typical notion of woman in an inhibited society. Soon, though, we find out that Elisabeth is sincerely in love with Foster, thus becoming a positive character. Later on, however, we will discover that, just like the undead who inhabit the castle, she feeds on human blood. Yet, for love—and here is a further reversal—she is willing to sacrifice herself and make her beloved escape. In Elisabeth many contradictory traits live together without apparent friction: she is at the same time a woman-monster and a romantic heroine, thus emerging as one of the most complex and enig-

matic female characters in Italian Gothic horror.

On the other hand, the male hero is eroded as the film moves along. Initially an active character, purposeful and bold, Foster—who accepts without hesitation the bet as proposed by Lord Blackwood, as he is convinced of the non-existence of the supernatural—becomes a passive spectator, fearful and trembling, whose manly bravado cracks with a trifle: "Must I have to give you courage—a woman?" Elisabeth teases him. Powerless against past events that unroll before his eyes, in the end Foster—in a curious reversal of narrative roles—assumes the position normally reserved to the damsel-in-distress: it is up to Elisabeth to save him from the other bloodthirsty undead, in a plot twist later recycled verbatim in Massimo Pupillo's *La vendetta di Lady Morgan*. Foster's failure is ideological (as was that of his predecessor Carmus), economic, diegetic. Soon the reporter's rational conventions are demolished by the evidence of a supernatural dimension, and in the end he loses the bet (and his life with it), thus failing across the board in his "institutional" task, so to speak.

On the other hand, Dr. Carmus—who decapitates a snake in the presence of Foster and shows him the severed head's twitchings in order to prove his theory about the permanence of the vital instinct beyond death—is just a deluded soul, a victim like the reptile he just killed. What is more, he is further proof that Italian Gothic was simply not interested in the theme of progress and science as a Promethean challenge to God, which was central to American Horror.

Despite its plethora of menacing ghosts, *Castle of Blood*'s most ruthless character is a living person: Lord Blackwood (Umberto Raho, rigged with a thin mustache *à la* Vincent Price), the absent lord of the castle who pulls the strings of the story by playing with the lives of the unfortunates who accept his bets. Blackwood (whose true family name, as Foster discovers, is the more ominous Blackblood[10]) is a further development—although not as blatant—of the Gothic's Sadean villains such as Dr. Hichcock, and a figure worthy of an Ambrose Bierce story. "He's as sadistic as his grand-father," as Carmus defines him, recalling the an-cestor's custom of hanging his enemies to the trees in the park: an anticipation of the vicious habits of the bloodthirsty titular character in Bava's *Baron Blood* (*Gli orrori del castello di Norimberga*, 1972)—and near the end Foster actually sees the old victims hanging from the branches, just like in Bava's film the castle bas-tions fill up with corpses. Blackwood survives because his attitude towards the supernatural is pragmatic: he accepts its existence and turns it in his favor, instead of being dazzled by it like the aforementioned "reporters." Blackwood takes advantage of his castle's curse to bet sums he will never lose, and in the last sequence he cynically takes—like he presumably did with Foster's predecessors—the payment from the dead man's pockets.

One of *Castle of Blood*'s most fascinating as-pects is the concept of time that is at its core. An apparently linear situation (a night spent in a haunted castle) unveils a metaphysical dimen-sion which circularly, and obsessively, repeats itself like a loop. In Margheriti's film, the past and the present coexist within the same space: this way, Foster can be the witness of events that took place ten years earlier. The Blackwood manor is a sort of crossroads of space and time, within which characters are pushed by a force that condemns them to an eternal repetition of their own acts. Previous lives (and deaths) are staged again and again in the same places, like contrails of a past whose effects remain and affect the present: rather than the retaliations in Dante's *Inferno*, the result is a meditation on time and the eternal return which recalls either Julio Cortázar's stories (such as *The Other Sky*, where the protagonist finds himself from Bue-nos Aires' art-deco Güemes gallery in 1928 to nineteenth century Paris), Adolfo Bioy Casares' celebrated *The Invention of Morel* or, for a more cinematic comparison, Alain Resnais' *Last Year at Marienbad* (*L'Année dernière à Marienbad*, 1961).

According to Fujiwara, "Foster is a journalist, that is, he deals in the commodification of time. The time of Foster's journalism is no less a cycle of eternal recurrence than the time inside the castle—or, for that matter, the time of Italian genre cinema. Asked by Elisabeth to inform her about life outside, Foster replies, "Well, there's nothing new. People are born and others die every day, business seems as usual. In fact the world goes on and remains the same. You haven't missed anything while staying here in your own world." A few moments later, he adds, "To be honest, I've been very lonely." His soli-tude is the counterpart and the meaning of the unchanging, abyssal time-space of London, a chronotope bound to the commodity form of the reproducibility of experience, in which there is no possibility of a direct experience, but only one more repetition of the same."[11]

Castle of Blood's central theme focuses on the typical dichotomy between the rational and the irrational. At first, reason is represented by Fos-ter—the reporter, the hero; then, once Foster has come in contact with the afterlife, it is the turn of his predecessor, Dr. Carmus (Arturo Dominici). Carmus' loss in the bet, even before Foster's, also marks the defeat of reason: the in-ability to explain and reduce the supernatural to physical terms, measurable and demonstrable empirically. The only solution is to become re-porters—that is, accepting its existence and re-port its record, like Poe does. It is up to Carmus himself to assume such a task, leading Foster from one room (and one time) to the next, like a Virgil with his own Dante, with surreal ef-fects: the duo's peregrinations in the haunted castle bring to mind the visions of the Hôtel des Folies Dramatiques in *The Blood of a Poet*.

Faced with visions of the past, Foster gets stuck, unable to intervene: if one of the recur-ring clichés in films and literature focusing on time paradoxes is the prohibition of meddling in the past, otherwise disastrous effects will fol-low, here the impossibility is even physical. *Cas-tle of Blood*'s central part, in which Carmus shows Foster the past events that took place in the Blackwood manor, also works as a *mise en abyme* of the relationship between the viewer and the film. Just like an audience watching a movie, Foster can look but not act: his partici-pation is only emotional, and marks the hero's gradual embrace of the sensorial dimension—the only thing that will make him live beyond physical life, as Carmus revealed. In the end, after his death, Foster will remain in balance on the threshold of both worlds: his lifeless body is impaled on the outside of the castle, unreachable by the undead vampires but also separated from the living, while his spirit and senses are still active: from now on he too, just like Elisabeth, will live only when he loves.

The film's disappointing box-office results were one of the factors that led Margheriti to remake it in color, in 1970, as *Web of the Spider*, starring Anthony Franciosa, Michèle Mercier and Klaus Kinski. The director would comment: "It was stupid to remake it, because the color cinematography destroyed everything: the atmosphere, the tension. I always tried to do my horror films in B&W. Even today, I'm still convinced that the only way of making a really scary horror film, with that kind of disturbing atmosphere and suspense, is to shoot it in B&W."[12]

Notes

1. Manlio Gomarasca, "Monsieur Cannibal. Il cinema di Ruggero Deodato," *Nocturno Dossier* 73, August 2008, p. 11. Incidentally, several sources (including IMDb) list the renowned stage and film actor Salvo Randone in the cast, as Lester the coachman. This is obviously not true: given that said coachman (who is on screen for a handful of seconds) does not look like Randone at all, the thought that a famous actor like Randone—who had just played major part in such prestigious films as Francesco Rosi's *Hands Over the City* (*Le mani sulla città*, 1962) would accept a blink-and-you'll-miss-it role in a low-budget film, with no close-ups nor dialogue lines, is simply ridiculous.

2. Garofalo, "Le interviste celibi," p. 2.

3. Paolo Fazzini, *Gli artigiani dell'orrore. Mezzo secolo di brividi dagli anni '50 ad oggi* (Rome: Un mondo a parte, 2004), p. 51.

4. Chris Fujiwara, "Margheriti, 'Danse macabre' et l'intensité," in Frank Lafond, ed., *Cauchemars Italiens. Volume 1: Le cinéma fantastique* (Pris: L'Harmattan, 2011), p. 53.

5. Carlo Bordoni, *Del soprannaturale nel romanzo fantastico* (Cosenza: Pellegrini, 2004), p. 82.

6. Italo Calvino, ed., *Fantastic Tales: Visionary and Everyday* (New York: Penguin, 2001, 2009).

7. Garofalo, "Le interviste celibi," p. 2.

8. Pezzotta, "Doppi di noi stessi," p. 30.

9. Blumenstock, "Margheriti—The Wild, Wild Interview," p. 47.

10. As Fujiwara notes, "In any case, "Lord Blackwood" is another fake; as Foster learns, the family name was formerly Blackblood, before it was changed to obscure the source of the family's fortune (the first Lord Blackblood was a hangman). Thus the question of origin, of the orig-

inal name, is folded into the text of the film." Fujiwara, "Margheriti, 'Danse macabre' et l'intensité," p. 56.

11. Ibid.

12. Blumenstock, "Margheriti—The Wild, Wild Interview," p. 45.

Castle of the Living Dead (*Il castello dei morti vivi*)

D: Warren Kiefer. *S* and *SC*: Warren Kiefer; *C:* Aldo Tonti (B&W); *M*: Angelo Francesco Lavagnino, conducted by Carlo Savina (Ed. C.A.M.); *E:* Mario Serandrei; *PD*: Carlo Gentili; *MU*: Guglielmo Bonotti; *AD*: Fritz [Frederick] Muller; *2nd AD*: Michael Reeves; *C*: Luigi Kuveiller; *SO*: Fiorenzo Magli. *Cast*: Christopher Lee (Count Drago), Gaia Germani (Laura), Philippe Leroy (Eric), Mirko Valentin (Sandro), Donald Sutherland (Sgt. Paul/ The witch/The old man), Renato Terra Caizzi (Policeman), Antonio De Martino [Anthony Martin] (Nick), Luciano Pigozzi (Dart), Ennio Antonelli (Gianni), Jacques Stany (Bruno), Luigi Bonos (Marc). *PROD*: Paul Maslansky for Serena Film (Rome), Filmsonor (Paris); *PM*: Renato Dandi; *PS*: Antonio Girasante. *Country*: Italy/France. Filmed at Orsini-Odescalchi Castle, Bracciano and at Bomarzo. *Running time*: 90 min. (m. 2700); *Visa n*: 43311 (06.27. 1964); *Rating*: not rated; *Release dates*: 08.05.1964 (Italy); 1965 (U.S.A.). *Distribution:* Cineriz (Italy); Woolner Brothers Pictures, Inc. (U.S.A., theatrical), AIP-TV (U.S.A., TV); *Domestic gross*: 103,500,000 lire. *Also known as: Crypt of Horror, Le château des morts vivants* (France), *The Castle of the Living Dead* (U.S.A.—TV print). *Home video*: Sinister Cinema (DVD-R, U.S.A.), Passworld (DVD, Italy).

France, early nineteenth century. After the Napoleonic wars, a small traveling theatrical company, specialized in staging a macabre comedy featuring Harlequin in public squares, is invited at the castle of Count Drago to run through their act. The company is joined by a Napoleonic officer on the run, Eric, who falls for the prima donna, Laura. On the way to the castle the group meets an old witch who warns them about the "castle of the living dead," and prophesies death for someone among them. The eerie Count warmly welcomes the company, but the troupe leader, Bruno, falls dead during his stage act, apparently by accident: it turns out, however, that Drago has perfected a drug that can instantly embalm any form of animal life, and needs new victims to add to his macabre collection of "living dead" statues. However, one member of the company, the diminutive Nick, discovers the truth, and tries to stop Drago from killing his fellow troupe members...

When he arrived in Rome, Warren Kiefer

had left everything he had—a job, a wife, a child—behind. What he had, was a dream. As one friend said of him, "he had a romantic concept of the writer's life and a naive fancy that just over the horizon was the Promised Land." As opposed to those pilgrims that moved to America looking for a promised land, Kiefer—born in New Jersey in 1929—followed the opposite trail. His Promised Land turned out to be Italy—better still, Cinecittà. Kiefer wanted to be in the movies, and found a niche in the U.S.–based community that inhabited the so-called "Hollywood on the Tiber," savoring the delights of *La Dolce Vita* and trying to make some money in the process.

Dreamers are lucky. They need to be. And luck, to the 34 year-old Warren, came in the guise of a fellow American, the 30-year-old, New York–born Paul Maslansky. He and Kiefer met at the Cinecittà tank, where the latter was shooting additional footage for a documentary about oil in Libya, while Maslansky was the production manager on the hokey Irving Allen epic *The Long Ships* (1964, Jack Cardiff), which was being shot in the Cinecittà studios.[1] They liked each other, got along well, and talked about making a movie together, in Italy. According to Maslansky, Kiefer had married again at that time, with a beautiful American woman named Ann-Marie. His former self—Kiefer the businessman, trying to make ends meet and struggling to be a writer—had been left behind, and so his first wife and son. The new Kiefer, the writer and filmmaker, was born.

That is how *Castle of the Living Dead* germinated. Kiefer provided a script about a bunch of street comedians who, in the early nineteenth century, are summoned to the castle of a nobleman who has perfected a rather unnerving embalming method and is looking for human beings to add to his collection; Maslansky acted as producer. "We both wanted to make a feature, and Rome was a good place then to try. We each put up $10,000, plus my script" Kiefer recalled. "With those elements we contacted Chris Lee for 10 working days, and shot the film in five weeks at a splendid old castle overlooking Lake Bracciano,"[2] that is Castle Odescalchi. A few scenes—which would pro-

vide for the film's most memorable images—were shot at the Parco dei Mostri, Bomarzo, about a hour's drive from Rome.

All in all, it was just another little B-movie, a hit-and-run job that would provide both director and producer with quick cash. And yet, *Castle of the Living Dead* has gained a one-of-a-kind controversial status, partly because of its own merits, and partly for reasons that are either coincidental, paradoxical, unfathomable, or just plain absurd.

Example? As of today, many sources wrongly state that *Castle of the Living Dead* was directed by an elusive Italian filmmaker named Lorenzo Sabatini, and that Warren Kiefer was just a pseudonym, while it is quite the opposite. The name Lorenzo Sabatini was made up by Kiefer himself, paying homage to an Italian mannerist painter of the sixteenth century. The reason? It was economically convenient for Warren to pass off as an Italian citizen, and for the film to receive subsidies according to Italian cinema laws.

But it was not the only compromise the director had to go through in order to have the film financed and distributed. "Angelo Rizzoli's Cineriz came up with the main financing, and qualified the film as an official Italo-French co-production. This complicated my credit because to receive state subsidies, an Italian director was required," as Kiefer would later explain. "Thus, the Italian version of the film carried me only as scriptwriter and story originator, listing "Herbert Wise" as the director. "Wise" was an American-sounding pseudonym registered in Italy by my first A.D., Luciano Ricci. In my Cineriz contract, however, my name had to appear full card, last credit, as sole director on ALL other versions."[3]

A comparison between different prints of the film confirms Kiefer's words. On the Italian language DVD, immediately after the title, a card says "un film di Warren Kiefer" ("a film by..."), but in the end another card says "regia di Herbert Wise" ("directed by..."). Whereas on the English language print, the screenplay and direction are credited to Warren Kiefer, while Maslansky is listed as the co-scriptwriter. The name "Herbert Wise" does not appear, nor does

Italian fotobusta for Warren Kiefer's *Castle of the Living Dead* (1964). Note that the direction is credited to "Herbert Wise" and Kiefer's name does not appear (author's collection).

Luciano Ricci. It must be noted, however, that *Castle*'s assistant director Frederick Muller is adamant that Ricci never showed up on the set.

However, as discussed earlier, it was a common practice for Italian filmmakers to use foreign pseudonyms. That is why many started thinking that the name "Warren Kiefer" might actually refer to an Italian filmmaker. Where the devil cannot put his head, he puts his tail: according to a publicity article on a movie magazine at the time of *Castle*'s release, the directors were "two young Italian filmmakers, Luciano Ricci and 32-year-old Lorenzo Sabatini, born in Florence." Perhaps the unknown writer simply took this bit from the film's press kit, or just made it up. However, hence came the notion that Sabatini was an Italian director born in 1932, whose pseudonym was Warren Kiefer, which can be found on Italian film dictionaries and reference books.[4] Such an error would spread incontrollably throughout the years.

At the time of the film's release, however, Italian reviewers usually did not seem to care

who the director really was. One ill-advised, unnamed film critic even identified Herbert Wise with Riccardo Freda: "Bomarzo is one of Central Italy's architectural wonders [...] Freda degraded it to the setting of a bad vampire movie [...]. Clumsily directed by the filmmaker, who this time is hiding under the fraudulent pseudonym Herbert Wise (previously it had been Robert Hampton), Philippe Leroy and Gaia Germani try their best to look terrorized [...]."[5] The one exception was the reviewer on *La Stampa*, who wrote: "Signed by Herbert Wise, the pseudonym of Italian Luciano Ricci (such mysteries are typical of French-Italian co-productions) the film was actually directed by an American, Warren Kiefer, who also wrote the story and screenplay."[6]

Castle of the Living Dead was shot in 24 days on a cost which Kiefer recalled as approximately $135,000 dollars ($116,000 according to an article on the *Daily American*,[7] while Maslansky's approximation was $125,000). Maslansky and Kiefer managed to average four minutes of film on the screen each day: an impressive achievement, even though not uncommon in the realm of the Italian B-movie industry, considering that Freda shot *I Vampiri* in 12 days. Each night after shooting they hurried to Rome to watch the rushes of the day's filming, select what they wanted and be on the set the following day at 7 a.m.

The dynamic duo devised all sort of speed-up techniques, no doubt benefiting from shooting most of the film on one location. They devised a floor plan of the Odescalchi castle so as to shoot in one room and then in the next; a second set was ready to go at all times so that as soon as one scene was completed the next would be ready (the same in case something would not work on the first set); filming most scenes in one take and getting three different shots (close-up, medium, long) at the same time. To save time, Maslansky and Kiefer gave up their idea of recording an original sound track. "Changes in the cast which brought in several non–English speaking actors made this impossible, and even if it hadn't the acoustics of the castle would have, said Kiefer. And getting original sound wouldn't have been as time-saving as the moviemakers at first thought."[8]

Another mystery surrounding *Castle of the Living Dead* centers on the entity of the contribution to the finished film on the part of a then unknown, nineteen-year-old Brit by the name of Michael Reeves, who had become friends with Maslansky on the Yugoslavian set of *The Long Ships*, where the former worked as production assistant. Struck by the young man's enthusiasm, Maslansky hired him on *Castle of the Living Dead*. Reeves would make his own debut as a director the following year, on another Maslansky-produced little horror movie shot in Italy and starring (well, not quite so) Barbara Steele, *The She Beast (Il lago di Satana,* 1966).

During the years, Reeves' work on *Castle of the Living Dead* has been wildly overpraised. Italian prints of the film do not even credit Reeves' name, who is listed as a.d. with Fritz [Frederick] Muller on the American International Television English language print. Nevertheless, rumors that Reeves had been the true director all along would soon spread. In his cel-

ebrated piece *In Memoriam Michael Reeves,*[9] written soon after the young filmmaker's premature death, Robin Wood claimed that Reeves had shot all the sequences at the Parco dei Mostri; according to others, Kiefer fell ill after nine days and Reeves took over the whole production. On the revised edition of his classic book on English Gothic cinema *A New Heritage of Horror*, David Pirie writes: "Maslansky corrected this for me while I was writing the first edition of *Heritage*, explaining it was quite untrue. Reeves remained on the second unit for the entire picture, but the work he was doing with a scratch crew turned out so much better than Kiefer's that his contribution was enlarged and he was allowed to make some additions to the script, including the introduction of a rather Bergmanesque dwarf."[10]

However, this contradicts what Maslansky stated in a 1999 interview, that the dwarf character was planned since the beginning: hoping to find an English-language speaking little person for their film, Kiefer and Maslansky flew to England to visit Billy Barty's circus, but to no avail. One night they went to see a Lindsay Anderson Royal Court production of *Spoon River Anthology*, where they spotted an incredibly talented young man, tall, lanky and with a prominent Adam's apple, who played five or six roles in the play. They paid him a visit backstage and asked him if he wanted to make a horror movie in Italy for 50 bucks a week. The young thesp accepted. That's how Warren met one of his closest friends, Donald Sutherland, who would pay homage to him by naming Kiefer one of the twins his girlfriend Shirley Douglas gave birth to a couple of years later. Sutherland would later picture the director as "a lovely cigar-smoking whiskey-drinking mystery-writing rogue of a man."

According to film historian Benjamin Halligan, "Back in Rome, Maslansky had advertised for an actor of restricted growth for the role of the dwarf and fifteen arrived outside his flat on the morning of the audition. The first was called up (from the flat window) and, after four storeys of stairs and a disconcerting amount of time later, Anthony Martin arrived in a state of some physical exhaustion. Maslansky was mortified and to save further embarrassment awarded Martin the part. Martin, a tobacconist and part-time actor, would go on to appear in Corman's *The Masque of the Red Death*, *Horror Hospital*, *Vampire Circus* (as Skip Martin) and *Fellini's Casanova* among many other uncredited roles."[11] Like Kiefer, he was eventually credited with an Italian pseudonym, Antonio De Martino.

While it is true that Jim Duncan's piece in the *Daily American* mentions "a second unit under the two assistant directors filming less important action while the main crew was at work on another scene," conceived in order to create a speed-up technique, Kiefer's assistant director Frederick Muller was adamant with this writer that all the film was shot by Kiefer without Reeves ever being present. Kiefer himself, in a 1990 letter to U.S. film critic Steven Johnson, stated that "Michael Reeves hung around as an unpaid gofer during the production and had nothing whatever to do with the direction or anything else. He was English, rich and bright, and later went on to make one or two films with his own money before dying of a drug overdose."

It is likely Maslansky asked Reeves to film a few missing shots without the cast being present (for instance, a carriage riding in the woods). As Halligan puts it in his book on Michael Reeves, "Mike oversaw some pick-ups, cutaways and, once principal photography was complete, missing shots. In some circumstances this would have been considered "Second Unit" material—but nothing that would ultimately make for any discernable authorial imprint on the finished film."[12] Later on, Reeves would initially talk up his involvement in *Castle of the Living Dead* but, as Halligan recalls, "only occasionally referred to this period as one of "some rewriting" on a script that was being made by a director friend."[13]

In his book on Mario Bava, *All the Colors of the Dark*, Tim Lucas reports Luciano Pigozzi's assertion that Bava actually worked on *Castle of the Living Dead*:

"'Another time, he [Bava] was up on the mountain, and asked for three or four white sheets— I don't know what for—and he painted. The scenery was very bad, but after he made the special effects ... my God! You could see a ship, all the time making with this special glass, and you see the ship on this postcard—and he put it very close to the water, and you could see this ship going up and down, up and down, and afterward, it disappeared.'

"Which film was this?

"'It was, it was ... *Il castello dei morti vivi. The Castle of the Living Dead.*'

"Bava worked on that film, too?

"'Yeah. He came to make that scene, that special effect.'"[14]

However, there are no scenes featuring ships at all in the film, as the story does not even take place by the sea—nor is there any such scene in the original script. Lucas' assumptions that "Bava's effect appeared on the periphery of a scene and would only be visible when the film was shown in its correct 1:85 ratio," or that perhaps it did not make the final cut, do not hold. Occam's razor suggests that Pigozzi simply got confused with another film on which Bava took care of the special effects, especially since the actor's vague memories are contradicted by other participants in the film. When asked about Bava's contribution to *Castle of the Living Dead*, Frederick Muller has no hesitation whatsoever. "Certainly I don't remember Mario Bava coming to the set ever. And I should know because a few years later I produced a film directed by Mario Bava. No, this is pure invention.... I wonder why people make such things up."[15]

Lucas also states that Kiefer was a pseudonym for Lorenzo Sabatini, and further develops Pirie's and Wood's theory that Michael Reeves shot a portion of the film, with ill-advised conclusions. "Reeves' specific contributions to the film would appear to include the scenes involving Dart, such as the gallows skit, the tavern fight, the scaling of the castle wall to Laura's bedroom window, and his death-by-scythe. [...] Another patently obvious Reeves contribution is the film's opening narration [...] which shows an attention to historical timing extremely uncharacteristic of Italian horror, and strongly parallels the opening narration of his final, and finest, film (*Witchfinder General*)."[16]

The film's Italian-language script, conserved

at Rome's CSC, titled *Il castello dei morti vivi—House of Blood* (almost 200 pages long and with a stamp dated April 13, 1964) could be misleading. First of all, it includes a voice-over (absent from the final film) of the dwarf Dart (who will become Pic in Italian language prints) which gives the proceedings an almost picaresque tone. It also further dismisses Maslansky's confidences to Pirie, as the dwarf was obviously a central character since the very beginning.

The script—which is very precise in specifying camera movements and angles in almost every scene—displays a number of differences from the final film. All the scenes set in Bomarzo are missing, and the action takes place almost entirely in the castle. What is more, the old hag who lives in the "Mouth of Hell," played in the film by Donald Sutherland, is absent. According to Frederick Muller, this was an embryonic version of the script, whereas the ones given on the set already included the scenes at the Parco dei Mostri as well as Sutherland's second character. It must be excluded, then, that Kiefer improvised new scenes during shooting: it is likely that he and Maslansky visited Bomarzo while scouting locations, and that the director added a few more scenes in a last-minute rewriting before shooting started in order to take advantage of such a fascinating set. Muller also confirms that all the scenes in Bomarzo were shot by Kiefer alone.[17]

The script also contradicts Mel Welles' assertions, as reported by Halligan: "During post-synch in Fono Roma, a furious Lee discovered that there was no soundtrack at all, and that all the continuity sheets had been mislaid. Fireworks ensued, but Paul [Maslansky] won him over and the film was dubbed in its entirety as well as possible. [...] Mel Welles, who oversaw the post-synching, claims the lost continuity sheets was partly a ruse to improve the dialogue."[18] Yet what can be read in the script is virtually identical to what can be heard in the finished film.

Other differences are the names of a number of characters (Count Drago is named Baron Ippo, his servant Hans is called Fausto) and, most remarkably, the ending, which is much more humorous—and better—than the definitive one. After Baron Ippo has accidentally impaled himself on the sword held by one of his human statues, the dumb Sergent Pogue and his colleague show up and arrest Laura and Eric, the two surviving actors, for the baron's murder; then (while outside Dart helps the prisoners escape) Pogue and his companion drink a toast with the Baron's cognac, unaware that it is actually the embalming fluid, thus getting immediately petrified.

Beautifully photographed by Aldo Tonti and starring Christopher Lee (looking less bored than in his other Italian forays of the period), Philippe Leroy and Gaia Germani, plus a few Italian character actors (including Luciano Pigozzi and Ennio Antonelli), *Castle of the Living Dead* was a modest success in Italy and a rather profitable entry in the U.S. horror market. However, as Kiefer stated, "the dividend for me on *Castle* became my enduring friendship with Don Sutherland." The debuting Canadian actor slept at Kiefer's home during shooting and played two roles in the movie: the dumb, self-important sergeant Pogue and an ugly old witch, in keeping with the mood of the film. Some sources claim Sutherland played a third role, that of an old man: however, this writer has not been able to spot it in the film. Good luck!

As Steven Johnson brilliantly synthesized in an in-depth essay on the film,[19] *Castle of the Living Dead* shares several stock characters (or "masks") with seventeenth and eighteenth century "*Commedia dell'Arte*": the protagonists are specialized in a variation of a classic seventeenth century performance starring Harlequin, who tricks his own executioner into hanging himself in Harlequin's place, and the plot itself unrolls as a variation of a classical *Commedia* play. Philippe Leroy and Gaia Germani embody the figures of Harlequin and Columbine beyond their theatrical roles, the fool Sergeant Pogue is reminiscent of the fearful and pompous Captain and the awkward Hans (Mirko Valentin) is the *zanni*, the antagonist's servant whom Kiefer brings back to the original demonic figure it used to be, while Count Drago is a more malevolent and less luxurious *Pantalone*, the hero's elderly antagonist.

At the center of the story there are two opposing male figures (the evil Count Drago and the clever hero Eric) fighting over a woman, and in the end Drago suffers the inevitable comeuppance, as he accidentally ends up petrified as his own human statues: a bizarre accident which recalls Harlequin's play at the film's beginning, where the hangman falls victim of his own instrument. It is no wonder that Kiefer revealed that he had originally written *Castle of the Living Dead* as a comedy of terrors, but Italian financers asked him to play it straight, making it into a "fairy tale for grown-ups."[20]

The differences with contemporaneous Italian horror films are evident in the description of the main female character. Gaia Germani's Laura is a shallow presence, who passively suffers the hero's advances as well as the villain's attentions, and in the end, while the two are contending for her, stays aphasic into a corner, leaving the stage to the men, just like in a *commedia*. She is definitely not on a par with Italian Gothic's evil queens.

The morbid elements are also reduced to a minimum: necrophilia is barely hinted at and soon forgotten. "You should never grow old, you should stay ... you should stay like this forever" Drago tells Laura, to which she replies: "Every young woman wishes that, sir. To be old and ugly is what we all fear." When we later discover the Count's bride, embalmed in the nuptial bed in the act of observing her own beauty at the mirror for eternity, it almost looks like Kiefer is going to predate the necrophiliac *amour fou* at the center of Mario Bava's *Lisa and the Devil*. However, Drago's purpose is merely aesthetic, instead of erotic: to recreate a personal theater whose players are all embalmed, a wax museum of sorts in the vein of *House of Wax*, and where he is the only director and audience.

What is more, despite being set in a typical Gothic mansion, *Castle of the Living Dead* is sunny and airy, unlike its contemporaries. The fact that the film's unlikely savant is a dwarf gives it a fairylike quality that is especially evident in the scenes set in Bomarzo, easily the most memorable ones: the game of hide-and-seek between Pic and the gigantic Hans under-

lines Kiefer's taste for the grotesque and his playful approach to the genre.

On the other hand, one thing in common with Italian Gothic horror films is the conception of space. Not simply because of its Italian locations, but because of the inventive way Kiefer combines them, elaborating the concept of "vastness" in his own way. When Luciano Pigozzi and Anthony Martin are seen wandering through the castle's crypts only to emerge from the Ogre's mouth in Bomarzo, it is as if they were entering another dimension, unexplained and impossible to reconcile with the film's own topography and logic. This opens the way for a peculiar conception of the Fantastic, which is one of the most remarkable things about Kiefer's film.

Although the *Daily American* announced the director's next film as a Western called *The Outrider*, to be shot in Libya in November '64 and co-produced by Kiefer himself, the project never materialized. Without a doubt, the American film-maker was a victim of the industry crisis that since 1963 displayed the economical fragility of many small production companies which specialized in low-budget flicks. As film historian Simone Venturini wrote, "the extreme fragmentation of production companies, the increased production costs, cinema's progressive loss of centrality compared to other entertainment activities and the companies' recurring economical speculations"[21] were all factors that made many small fish sink in the troubled sea that was the Italian movie industry of the period.

Kiefer's subsequent works were mostly screenplays for other directors, which were basically comprised into the Western genre, which he had always loved. In 1950 Kiefer had written a short story on Billy the Kid, and eventually tried his hand at it as a novelist, with *Outlaw* (1989). While he is credited as the co-scriptwriter for *Beyond the Law* (*Al di là della legge*, 1967), starring Lee Van Cleef and Lionel Stander and directed by Giorgio Stegani,[22] there is no trace of him in the credits of the little-known *Sunscorched* (*Jessy non perdona.... Uccide* a.k.a. *Tierra de fuego*, 1965), directed by and starring Mark Stevens and Mario Adorf, which he nevertheless claimed as being based on his own script.[23] Another Kiefer-penned western was the dreadful *The Last Rebel* (1971, Denys McCoy), starring former football star Joe Namath and Jack Elam and graced by an unbelievable rock score by Ashton, Gardner and Dyke, featuring keyboardist Jon Lord of Deep Purple fame.

In his correspondence with Steven Johnson, Kiefer claimed having directed "half a dozen films after *Castle*" and having scripted "perhaps twenty more," adding that "all this work was done in Italy and various Italian directors got the credit (because under Italian subsidy laws the producer could only collect if the film was signed by an Italian) while I got the paychecks." This makes things even more cloudy, as Kiefer's official output as a director includes only two more titles: the idiosyncratic *film noir Defeat of the Mafia* (*Scacco alla mafia*, shot in late 1968 but released in late 1970) and the erotic *Juliette De Sade* (*Mademoiselle De Sade e i suoi vizi*, shot in 1969 but released in Italy in late 1971[24]), a spurious adaptation of De Sade's work. It may well be that the number of films he scripted and directed was a creative addition on Kiefer's part. After all, reading his own bio on his novel *The Lingala Code* makes one suspect that the author had the same creative knack for mixing fact and fiction regarding his own life as he had for his novels.[25]

Warren Kiefer's subsequent efforts behind the camera were nowhere near as successful as *Castle*. Conversely, they remain barely seen as of today. He eventually moved to Argentina in the early 1970s, where he started a successful career as a novelist. He died of a massive heart attack in Buenos Aires, in 1995.

Notes

1. Warren Kiefer, letter to Steven Johnson, July 24, 1989. Kiefer shot a documentary for Esso in Libya, but it is likely that his experience in Africa also comprised a trip to the Congo, as his 1972 novel *The Lingala Code*— set in the period after the killing of Patrice Lumumba— opens with Kiefer's statement that "The Congo background is represented substantially as it was during the author's time there."

2. Ibid.

3. Ibid.

4. See Roberto Poppi and Mario Pecorari, *Dizionario del cinema italiano. I film (1960–1969)* (Rome: Gremese, 1993); Roberto Poppi, *Dizionario del cinema italiano. I registi* (Rome: Gremese, 2002).

5. Anonymous, "Il vampiro di Bomarzo," *La Notte*, August 8, 1964.

6. Anonymous, "Dracula si rinnova: da vampiro a imbalsamatore," *La Stampa*, August 6, 1964.

7. Jim Duncan, "Horror-For-Fun Pays Off," *Daily American* August 30–31, 1964.

8. Ibid.

9. Robin Wood, "In Memoriam Michael Reeves," *Movie* 17, Winter 1969/1970.

10. Pirie, *A New Heritage of Horror*, p. 168.

11. Email to the author, November 2011.

12. Benjamin Halligan, *Michael Reeves* (Manchester: Manchester University Press, 2003), p. 41.

13. Ibid.

14. Lucas, *Mario Bava*, p. 575.

15. Email to the author, July 2010. Muller was production manager on the additional scenes Bava shot for Alfredo Leone on what would become *The House of Exorcism*.

16. Lucas, *Mario Bava*, p. 575.

17. Email to the author, January 2012.

18. Halligan, *Michael Reeves*, pp. 40–41.

19. Steven Johnson, "Italian American Reconciliation: Waking 'Castle of the Living Dead,'" *Delirious—The Fantasy Film Magazine* 5, 1991.

20. Duncan, "Horror-For-Fun Pays Off."

21. Venturini, *Galatea Spa (1952–1965)*, p. 30.

22. The film's opening titles credit the story to Warren D. Kiefer and the screenplay to "Mino Roli, Giorgio Stegani, Fernando di Leo and Warren D. Kiefer."

23. In a letter to Steven Johnson dated March 1, 1990, Kiefer mentions "two westerns with Lee Van Cleef and Lionel Stander, another with Mark Stevens and Mario Adorf."

24. The film was released in the United Kingdom as *Heterosexual*, in 1970.

25. In his bio for *The Lingala Code*, Kiefer claimed that he had served active duty with the Marines during the Korean War, whereas in fact he was only in the Marine Corps for a few weeks before being discharged for medical reasons. Another misinformation in the bio has Kiefer claiming that he studied at Andover, a private prep school for boys, whereas he was educated at the University of New Mexico, and the University of Maryland.

The Hyena of London (*La jena di Londra*)

D: Henry Wilson [Luigi Mangini]. *S and SC*: Henry Wilson; *DOP:* Hugh Griffith [Guglielmo Mancori]; *M:* Frank Mason [Francesco De Masi]; *E:* John Alen; *ArtD:* Gabriel Kriss [Gabriele Crisanti]; *SD*: Al Merik [Franco Colli]; *AD:* Frank Bhandy [Franco Baldanello]; *C:* Craig Mark [Mario Sbrenna]: *MU:* Landry Manuel [Leandro Marini]; *SO:* Mario Sisti; *SS:* Robert Grand [Roberto Giandalia]. *Cast*: Bernard Price [Giotto Tempestini] (Dr. Edward Dalton), Diana Martin [Patrizia Del Frae] (Muriel), Tony Kendall [Luciano Stella] (Henry), Denise Clar [Ilona Drasch] (Margie, the housekeeper), Claude

Dantes (Elisabeth), Alan Collins [Luciano Pigozzi] (Peter, the caretaker), John Mathews [Giovanni Tomaino] (Chris, the butler), Thomas Walton [Luigi Rossi] (Inspector O'Connor), James Harrison [Angelo Dessy] (Dr. Anthony Finney), Anthony Wright [Gino Rumor] (Quayle), William Burke [Attilio Dottesio] (Police Official Brown), Robert Burton [Mario Milita] (John Reed), Felix De Artal, Annie Benson [Anita Todesco] (Margaret), Tony Wise. *PROD*: Giuliano Simonetti for Geosfilm (Rome); *AP*: Thomas Walton [Gino Rossi]; *PS*: Henry Boley [Enrico Bologna]; *PA*: John Bread [Agostino Pane]. *Country*: Italy. Filmed at Villa Perucchetti, Rome. *Running time*: 79 min. (m. 2680); Visa n: 42977 (05. 20.1964); *Rating*: V.M.14; *Release dates*: 06.23.1964 (Italy); 1966 (U.S.A.). *Distribution*: Geosfilm (Italy, Regional); Walter Manley Enterprises (U.S.A.); *Domestic gross*: 44,000,000 lire. *Home video*: Sinister Cinema (DVD-r, U.S.A.).

London, December 1883. A savage murderer named Martin Bauer, also known as the "Hyena of London," is executed on the gallows. However, a few days later his coffin is found empty. Just when peace seems to have finally returned, a new series of brutal murders start again in the nearby village of Bradford. The victims are all young women, and Scotland Yard has no doubt in recognizing the hand of the "Hyena"—but how could that be, if the monster is dead? Meanwhile, strange things are going on at the house of the renowned Dr. Edward Dawson, whose daughter Muriel is secretly in love with the young and penniless Henry. The suspects include Dawson's colleague Dr. Finney, an alcoholic who is staying at the doctor's house for some mysterious experiments and seems to be hiding a secret, a scheming butler and his lover, the caretaker's wife. The key to the mystery, however, lies in Dr. Edward's secret experiments, which involve injecting fluid from the dead man's brain into another individual...

An obscure item in its home country, where it performed with modest results on the regional distribution circuits, *The Hyena of London* was picked up for U.S. distribution in 1966 by Walter Manley Enterprises and eventually resurfaced on home video via a public domain label. A weird destiny for one of Italian Gothic horror's most schizophrenic oddities: Luigi Mangini's film assembles together a number of Gothic stereotypes, yet it is mainly noticeable for actually being a whodunnit in disguise, in which the supernatural element works as a red herring within a murder mystery plot.

Much of the running time is wasted around a chain of killings that are apparently being committed by a serial killer who seemingly returned from the grave, yet it is all too evident that the solution must be quite different. However, for its final twist Mangini's script draws—with curious results—from *The Strange Case of Dr. Jekyll and Mr. Hyde*, by linking the mystery's solution to a split personality case. Nevertheless, all this is squeezed into a last-minute para-scientific explanation which blatantly rips off both Curt Siodmak's novel *Donovan's Brain* (adapted to film no fewer than three times) and Hammer's *Frankenstein* cycle, albeit in a totally unconvincing way. The solution to the mystery also sweeps away the morbid incestuous implications in the relationship between two of the main characters (namely, Dr. Edward and his daughter), a common theme in contemporaneous Italian Gothics. The erotic content, however, is rather lame.

The same can be said of the stereotyped Victorian setting: working on a shoestring budget, Mangini has to make do as he can: a handful of old London postcards in the prologue make up for the real thing—and luckily for him, Italians do not know enough about British geography to notice that the West Yorkshire town of Bradford is not nearly a "small village," nor is it so close to London as the film pretends it to be. Attentive viewers will notice that the villa where most of the action takes place is Villa Perucchetti in Rome's Monti Parioli district, the same one featured in *The Horrible Dr. Hichcock*. Also, the tunnel at the film's beginning, through which Bauer is accompanied by the guards before the execution, is the same that Barbara Steele explored in Freda's film.

Compared to other Italian horror films of the period, the atmosphere is more clichéd, with foggy cemeteries and unlikely period details (the costumes are especially slapdash), while the murders are elliptically filmed, with a heavy emphasis on menacing shadows and several surprising POV shots, *giallo*-style, of the murderer in action. Yet, for all the film's shortcomings, Mangini manages to come up with a few atmospheric shots and keeps the camera moving resulting in plenty of tracking shots.

As customary, the whole cast hides behind Anglo-Saxon pseudonyms, starting with the stage actor Giotto Tempestini as "Bernard Price."[1] Besides working for the big and the small screen, Tempestini (1917–2009) was also an appreciated voice actor who took part in many radio dramas in the immediate–World War II years. A trio of Mario Bava regulars—a young Luciano Stella, fresh from his role in *The Whip and the Body, Blood and Black Lace*'s Claude Dantes and the unmistakable Luciano Pigozzi—share the spotlights, while a beardless Attilio Dottesio pops up briefly. Francesco De Masi's score is recycled from *The Ghost*.

Director Luigi Mangini (Rome, 1921–1991), here sporting the pseudonym "Henry Wilson" and often credited in reference books with the diminutive "Gino" Mangini, was a former screenwriter who claimed to have written over 100 scripts, a number that must be drastically toned down. Among his credits, which cover many genres, are *Totò all'inferno* (1955, Camillo Mastrocinque), *David e Golia* (1960, Ferdinando Baldi) and *Atlas in the Land of the Cyclops* (*Maciste nella terra dei ciclopi*, 1962, Antonio Leonviola). Mangini debuted behind the camera in 1963, co-directing with Piero Ghione the political documentary on Russia *Dagli zar alla bandiera rossa*. His directorial output consists of six films overall: besides *The Hyena of London,* he made a pair of nondescript *film noir* efforts (*Fango sulla metropoli*, 1967, starring Giancarlo Giannini, and *I diamanti che nessuno voleva rubare*, 1968); the western *Bastardo, vamos a matar* (1971) and the juvenile comedy *Abbasso tutti, viva noi* (1974). His last screen credit is Gabriele Crisanti's shockumentary *Mondo cane 2000: l'incredibile*

Italian poster for the obscure *Hyena of London* (author's collection).

(1988), for which he wrote the story and screenplay.

Note

1. Not to be confused (as IMDb does) with the English-born stage actor Bernard Ashley Price (1925–

2000) who played minor roles in English television series such as *The Canal Children* and *Doctor Who.*

The Long Hair of Death (*I lunghi capelli della morte*)

D: Anthony Dawson [Antonio Margheriti]. *S:* Julian Berry [Ernesto Gastaldi]; *SC:* Robert Bohr [Tonino Valerii], Anthony Dawson; *DOP:* Richard Thierry [Riccardo Pallottini] (B&W); *M:* Evirust [Carlo Rustichelli]; *E:* Mark Sirandrews [Mario Serandrei]; *ArtD:* George Greenwood [Giorgio Giovannini]; *SD:* Henry Fraser [Enrico Fiorentini]; *CO:* Humphrey Patterson [Ugo Pericoli]; *AD:* Bob Parks [Roberto Pariante], Guy Farrell [Gaetano Fruscella]; *C:* Humbert Tennberg [Ubaldo Terzano]; *MU:* Edmund Stroll [Euclide Santoli]; *Hair:* Florence Clark [Itala Cambi]; *SO:* John Tamblyn [Giulio Tagliacozzo]; *SS:* Eva Koltay. *Cast:* Barbara Steele (Helen Karnstein/Mary Karnstein), George [Giorgio] Ardisson (Kurt Humboldt), Halina Zalewska (Elizabeth Karnstein), Robert Rains [Umberto Raho] (Von Klage), Laureen Nuyen [Laura Nucci] (Grumalda), Jean Rafferty [Giuliano Raffaelli] (Count Humboldt), John Carey [Nello Pazzafini] (Monk), Jeffrey Darcey (Messenger). *PROD:* Felice Testa Gay for Cinegai (Rome); *PM:* Fred Dexter [Ferruccio De Martino]; *UM:* Paul Meredith [Paolo Mercuri], Dean Morris [Arduino Mercuri]. *Country:* Italy. Filmed at Cinecittà (Rome) and at Castle Massimo, Arsoli (Rome). *Running time:* 100 min. (m. 2775); Visa n: 44461 (12.29.1964); *Rating:* V.M.14; *Release date:* 12.30.1964 (Italy). *Distribution:* Unidis (Italy); *Domestic gross:* 321,000,000 lire. *Also known as:* La Sorcière sanglante (France, 08.08.1970) Hævnens flammer (Denmark). Home video: East West Entertainment (DVD, U.S.A.—double feature w/*Terror-Creatures from the Grave*), Midnight Choir (DVD, U.S.A.—double feature w/*An Angel for Satan*), Raro (DVD, Italy), Artus (DVD, France).

Towards the end of the 16th century, Adele Karnstein is accused of having murdered Count Franz Humboldt and is burned at the stake. Her little daughter Elizabeth is brought up to the castle and, upon reaching adulthood, is forced to marry Kurt Humboldt, who is actually the real murderer. The curse uttered by the unfortunate Adele becomes true: an epidemic of plague is raging in the land and Count Humboldt, Kurt's father, dies after the sudden appearance of a woman whom he recognizes as Mary, Adele's eldest daughter whom he seduced and killed years before. Kurt falls for the unknown woman and, along with her, plans to kill Elizabeth. His wife disappears, however, while everyone in the castle keeps referring to her as if she were still alive. Kurt, who
feels haunted by Elizabeth's ghost, is driven to terror and madness. Eventually he discovers that Elizabeth is alive while Mary is actually a ghost, who came back to exact revenge in her mother's name. Kurt is locked and gagged inside a wicker figure, to be burned in the garden of the castle during a party...

The past as a crushing weight as well as a dynamic force that occurs again in the present, opening coffins and unmasking the guilty and their sins, shaking up consciences and claiming a price to be paid by the living, is a common element to many Italian Gothic horror flicks. Antonio Margheriti's third foray in the genre, *The Long Hair of Death*, is particularly significant in this sense. Set in a remote past, in a gloomy realm where lust and corruption rule, the film focuses on a punishment that is both individual (striking the unfaithful husband and murderer Kurt Humboldt) and collective, with a plague outbreak that hits the village.

As in *Terror in the Crypt*, the script was the result of teamwork by Ernesto Gastaldi and Tonino Valerii (who reprised the title from their earlier effort) and had an equally hasty genesis. In an interview with Tim Lucas in *Video Watchdog*, Gastaldi recalled: "Valerii tried to direct that film, but the producer didn't want him because, at that time, he hadn't directed any movies. Antonio was called when the script was finished, and we met only once, so that I could explain some details to him. He didn't change the script and I never went on the set."[1]

The story focuses on the idea of the female body as a simulacrum of a terrible and vengeful presence (the reincarnated Adele Karnstein, who was burned at the stake for a crime she did not commit), but moves further by totally destroying the dichotomy between the damsel-in-distress and the *belle dame sans merci.*

Here, Barbara Steele plays a bewitching conspirator who is also an avenging angel, and the script ingeniously plays on the scheme conceived by Mary and her lover Kurt in order to get rid of the latter's wife, Elizabeth. The main influence, of course, is *Diabolique*, as the story focuses on the ambiguity of Elizabeth's effective or presumed death. The apparently deceased woman is continually evoked by other characters or objects that bear traces of her presence, just like Paul Meurisse in H. G. Clouzot's masterpiece. However, even though the audience is immediately aware that Mary is actually a reincarnated *revenante*, *The Long Hair of Death* maintains the point of view of the scheming husband, as a horror reworking of sorts of Pietro Germi's *Divorce, Italian Style* (*Divorzio all'italiana*, 1961).

On the other hand, the final twist borrows the shock ending from *The Pit and the Pendulum*, when Barbara Steele is trapped in the iron maiden. "Yes, of course!" Gastaldi confirmed. "*The Pit and the Pendulum* was a big influence on Italian horror films. Everybody borrowed from it."[2] Nevertheless the final scene surprisingly predates the mocking epilogue of Robin Hardy's *The Wicker Man* (1973) as well. Still, another memory of the *commedia all'italiana* comes to mind: the scheming Kurt, for all his cruelty, meets a fate that is as grimly hilarious as the one reserved to Alberto Sordi as the husband who is planning to kill his wife with disastrous results in Dino Risi's *The Widower* (*Il vedovo*, 1959). All in all, it is a testament to the disenchanted, mordant vision of marriage that characterized the Gothic, Italian style, and which is emphasized by the dialogue.

"You are my wife, Elizabeth!" "You have not yet possessed me. What if I refuse?" "You can't refuse, for I am your master!" can be heard in an explicit exchange between Kurt and Elizabeth. Under its horrific glaze, *The Long Hair of Death* is the story of female rebellion against patriarchy and male prevarications which turn women into designated victims—again, a nod to melodrama's unfortunate heroines. The opening scene has Mary give herself to the elderly Count Humboldt only to save her mother, yet her sacrifice will be vain; what is more, her sister is forced to marry the Count's son, who had her mother executed. Mary's supernatural revenge thus acquires further significance when compared to other Gothic films of the period, and takes on an apocalyptic feel which is a one-of-a-kind moment in the *filone*: Steele's resurrection from the grave takes place on the last night of the century, while an excerpt from John's Revelations is recited.

Even though the result is not quite as strong as *Castle of Blood*, the film still has its moments—namely the memorably horrific sight of an apparently reanimated corpse whose chest is actually infested by rats, that cause it to wriggle and "breathe." Customarily, Margheriti shoots many scenes with several cameras at once: this technique becomes an added factor of unpredictability, as it allows the director to capture a gesture or a momentary grimace, while the frequent use of hand-held shots heightens the irrational element of the story, as in the scene where Kurt comes across hints of the presence of his supposedly deceased wife.

Technically, *The Long Hair of Death* is constantly competent and stylish, thanks to Riccardo Pallottini's accomplished b&w cinematography, which benefits from the presence of Ubaldo Terzano (Bava's frequent collaborator) as the camera operator, under the a.k.a. Humbert Tennberg. Most of the shooting took place at Castle Massimo in Arsoli, with its unmistakable labyrinthine park, in just three weeks, and one cannot help thinking that the film's most patent stylistic bit—the two-minute long take in the scene where the nurse brings young Elizabeth to visit her mother's grave—had less an aesthetic function than a time-saving one.

Margheriti, however, was not too keen on the film. "I don't like that one too much. I don't like the story. The screenplay we had was very badly written and a lot of things were not really fixed in it. On the set, a lot of things turned out to be stupid or impossible, so we had to invent a lot and improvise every day. [...] There was hardly any time to think, to invent, or write something down properly, because we had to shoot, shoot and shoot."[3]

Notes

1. Lucas, "What Are Those Strange Drops of Blood," p. 41.
2. Ibid.
3. Blumenstock, "Margheriti—The Wild, Wild Interview," p. 49.

"Il passo" (from the film *Amori pericolosi*)

D: Giulio Questi. *S* and *SC:* Giulio Questi; *DOP:* Leonida Barboni (B&W); *M:* Ivan Vandor (Ed.

RCA); *E*: Franco Arcalli; *AD*: Rinaldo Ricci; *C*: Elio Polacchi; *PD*: Luigi Scaccianoce; *SD*: Ermanno Manco; *CO*: Marilù Carteny. *Cast*: Juliette Mayniel (Isabelle); Frank Wolff (Captain Gerard Garnier), Graziella Granata (Jeanine); Piero Morgia (Jacques). *PROD*: Moris Ergas for Fulco Film/Zebra; *PM*: Carlo Murzilli. *Country*: Italy/France. *Filmed at*: Cinecittà (Rome); *Running time*: 34 min.; Visa n. 43279 (6.26.1964); *Rating*: V.M.18; *Release date*: 08.14.1964 (Italy). *Distribution:* Cineriz (Italy); *Domestic gross*: 48,300,000 lire.

France, 1912. A military officer, Captain Gerard Garnier, is obsessed by the sound produced by his wife Isabelle's orthopedic shoe, which the woman has to wear since she became lame after a horse-riding accident. Garnier, who does not love his wife and married her just because of her social status and wealth, has an affair with the maid, Jeanine, and the two are planning to get rid of Isabelle by poisoning her. The plan succeeds, but before dying Isabelle repeatedly shoots Jeanine in the leg. Jeanine takes Isabelle's place as the lady of the house, but Garnier will have to live with another lame woman...

"If your wife's step is too heavy don't kill her—another woman will come who will have the same step—if this step is inside you" ominously announces the opening line of Giulio Questi's "Il passo." As part of *Amori pericolosi*, an anthology feature film about "dangerous loves" (as the Italian title translates) produced by Moris Ergas—the other episodes being Carlo Lizzani's *La ronda* and Alfredo Giannetti's *Il generale*—Questi's short film is perhaps the most surprising and idiosyncratic example of the way Italian Gothic overflew and contaminated *auteur* cinema, predating the works of Damiano Damiani, Elio Petri and Federico Fellini—or rather, how filmmakers outside of genres used themes and suggestions from the Gothic to explore more personal territories. As Questi himself recalled, "'Il Passo' made a great impression on the people of the movie industry because it was original, outside of any current canon: a cross between Buñuel's cinema and refined, decadent atmospheres *à la* Cocteau. It was a morbid, sick little film."[1]

The short story, scripted by Questi himself, draws on elements of Edgar Allan Poe's psychopathological Gothic to convey a macabre, darkly humored moral fable reminiscent of Grand Guignol, and riddled with symbols, by exploring a man's obsession over the sound of his wife's lame steps—an obvious nod to "The Tell-Tale Heart"—which leads to murder and a very bitter retaliation in the end.

But there is more than that. The setting, in a luxurious, mysterious villa; the opposite female characters (the faithful wife/victim and the scheming lover); the themes of sin and guilt; and most of all the weak male figure(s), all are typical Italian Gothic staples. Here, they are conjured up for a meditation on the nature of male desire as well as the relationship of mutual dominion between the sexes: in a reversal of roles, the lord of the house (Frank Wolff) is destined to become a mere puppet, at the mercy of his lover's wishes. In another interesting variation on the theme of the "designed victim," the meek, unhappy wife (Juliette Mayniel) eventually turns into her husband's tormentor, with a vengeance that will have its effects after her own death on both her scheming murderers: the surviving woman (Graziella Granata) is subject to a transformation—physical, social and psychological—that turns her into the mirror image of her victim.

The female body becomes once again an object of attraction and repulsion (see the emphasis on Jeanine's bare feet as opposed to Isabelle's orthopedic shoe, which the former ritualistically slips on the latter's foot), as the two opposites merge into one; however, the new lady of the house finds herself another, younger lover (Garnier's young orderly, Jacques [Piero Morgia]), to satisfy her sexual needs that her husband cannot fulfill any longer: Garnier's obsession with the woman's lame step and orthopedic shoe—a typical Buñuelian detail if ever there was one: the obvious reference is *The Criminal Life of Archibaldo de la Cruz* (*Ensayo de un crimen*, 1955)—is also a metaphor of his impotence, while Questi manages to add a biting social commentary in the depiction of the relationship between the protagonists.

All this is rendered in a rarefied manner: just four characters, a quick dramatic progression and a meticulous attention to detail. But it is the style that marks "Il passo"'s approach to the material, which goes through a radical stylistic reinvention of the subject matter. Questi opens the film as if it were a straight Gothic tale, with the aforementioned line and an atmospheric, otherworldly sideways tracking shot of the villa's exteriors at night as seen through the surrounding woods, to the sound of Ivan Vandor's creepy score. However, though, he and ace editor Franco "Kim" Arcalli (possibly Italy's most brilliant editor of the 1960s and 1970s, and a sort of *auteur* himself) immediately conjure up a symbol-ridden oneiric scene. Garnier dreams he is making love to his mistress Jeanine, when he is interrupted by an ominous sound which grows louder and louder: he wanders through the house in search of its source until he is so frightened by it that he eventually hides in a laundry room amidst blinding white clothings; he finally locks himself up in another room where he first glimpses an orthopedic shoe in the middle of a room, and then his wife Isabelle giving him an accusatory stare. The man kneels down behind the woman and starts tying her corset, while elsewhere the other woman laughs…

It is an extraordinary opening, lit and edited in a decidedly experimental style—quick, disorienting cuts between close-ups and long shots, suggestive camera movements, expressionistic sound and overexposed lighting—that owes much to the French *Nouvelle Vague*, and puts *Il passo* apart from its Gothic contemporaries, while in the meantime exploring the genre's stylistic potential for a more mature and self-conscious narration.

Questi and Arcalli maintain this stylistic tension throughout the film, thanks to the frequent use of hand-held camera, and are immensely aided by Leonida Barboni's truly extraordinary lighting and cinematography. Especially outstanding is the sequence where Wolff recalls his past encounter with his future wife in a dilapidated church, rendered through a subjective shot of the man wandering through the ruins and the echoes of past voices that eventually materialize in a flashback, when Gerard is seen proposing marriage to Isabelle. The actors are also top notch, and Granata exudes a proud sensuality (already exploited in *Slaughter of the Vampires*, where she played an unsatisfied wife) that makes her one of the most impressive female characters in Italian cinema of the period—a time when Italian films, and especially anthologies, were literally obsessed with the theme of the eternal feminine.

However, *Amori pericolosi* passed unnoticed at the box-office and soon disappeared from sight. Critics were not that kind either, although they partially salvaged Questi's segment. The renowned Alberto Abruzzese wrote: "The episode conveys an old and decrepit theme with a formal refinement that is between a mannered decadence and a misunderstood naturalism."[2] Stylistical experimentation, in the way Questi conceived it, was not particularly appreciated by Italian critics of the period, which were also not too keen on the film's self-defined "Grand Guignol" quality.

After decades of obscurity, *Il passo* was rediscovered at the 66th edition of the Venice Festival in 2009 through the retrospective section "Italian Cinema Rediscovered." Questi, one of the most peculiar and interesting personalities of 1960s and 1970s Italian cinema, would go on to make his feature film debut in 1967 with the Sadean spaghetti Western *If You Live Shoot*, a.k.a. *Django Kill!* (*Se sei vivo spara*). His sparse career as a director included such genre-defying works as *Death Laid an Egg* (*La morte ha fatto l'uovo*, 1968) and *Arcana* (1972)—all with Arcalli as co-writer and editor—as well as a few TV movies, made in the early 1980s, that contained strong Gothic elements such as *L'uomo della sabbia* ("The Sandman") and *Vampirismus*, inspired respectively by E.T.A. Hoffmann's stories. He passed away in 2014.

Arcalli, perhaps Italian cinema's most brilliant editor, died at age 49 in 1978, while working on the script of Sergio Leone's *Once Upon a Time in America* (1984): among his editing credits are Bernardo Bertolucci's best films, including *The Conformist* (*Il conformista*, 1970), *Last Tango In Paris* (*Ultimo tango a Parigi*, 1972) and *1900* (*Novecento*, 1976).

Notes

1. Giulio Questi with Domenico Monetti and Luca Pallanch, *Se non ricordo male* (Soveria Mannelli: Rubbettino, 2014), p. 114.

2. Alberto Abruzzese, "Amori pericolosi," *Cinema 60* 45, September 1964, pp. 61–62.

Terror in the Crypt, a.k.a. *Crypt of the Vampire (La cripta e l'incubo)*

D: Thomas Miller [Camillo Mastrocinque]. *S:* based on Joseph Sheridan Le Fanu's novel *Carmilla*; *SC:* Robert Bohr [Tonino Valerii], Julian Berry [Ernesto Gastaldi]; *DOP:* Julio Ortas (B&W, panoramic, Vistavision), Giuseppe Aquari (uncredited); *M:* Herbert Buckman [Carlo Savina], conducted by James Munshin [Carlo Savina]; *E:* Herbert Markle [Roberto Cinquini]; *C:* Noel Lardner [Emilio Giannini]; *AC:* Charles Sundberg [Angelo Lannutti]; *AE:* Judy Marlow [Mirella Marino]; *AD:* Robert Bohr; *PD/SD:* Demos Filos [Demofilo Fidani]; *APD:* Remy Villar [Renato Minnesi]; *CO:* Milose [Mila Vitelli Valenza]; *MU:* Joe Carlin [Emilio Trani]; *Hair:* Stephan Carlin [Stefano Trani]; *SO:* Ferdinand Larkin [Fernando Pescetelli]; *SS:* Piper Samson [Paola Salvadori]; *DubD:* Mario Colli. *Cast:* Christopher Lee (Count Ludwig Karnstein), Audry Amber [Adriana Ambesi] (Laura Karnstein), Ursula Davis [Pier Anna Quaglia] (Ljuba/Sheena), José Campos (Friedrich Klauss), Véra Valmont (Annette), Cicely Clayton [Carla Calò] (Ljuba's mother), Vera Conjiù [Nela Conju] (Rowena), José Villasante (Cedric the butler), Angel Midlin [Angelo Midlino] (The hunchback), Bill Curtis [José Cortés], James Brightman; *uncredited:* John Karlsen (Franz Karnstein), Ignazio Balsamo, Lee Campos, Benito Carif, Angela Minervini (Tilde), Rafael Vaquero. *PROD:* William Mulligan [Marco Mariani] for MEC Cinematografica (Rome), Hispamer Films (Madrid); *PM:* Hector Corey [Otello Cocchi]; *PS:* Marcel Harrods [Marcello Lucchetti]; *PSe:* Heinz Bishop [Ezio Ranzini]. *Country:* Italy/Spain. Filmed at Castle Piccolomini, Balsorano (Aquila). *Running time:* 82 min. (m. 2329); Visa n: 42808 (04/22/1964); *Rating:* V.M.14; *Release date:* 05.27.1964 (Italy); 1965 (U.S.A., TV). *Distribution:* MEC (Italy, Regional); AIP-TV (U.S.A., TV). *Domestic gross:* 69,541,000. *Also known as:* La maldición de los Karnstein (Spain: 08/01/1966); La crypte du vampire (France: 09/22/1965—80 min.); Ein Toter hing am Glockenseil (West Germany: 03/03/1967—85 min.); Crypt of Horror (U.K.: 1965—84 min.). *Home video:* Image (DVD, U.S.A.—as *Crypt of the Vampire*).

Baron Von Karnstein, who lives with his daughter Laura in a solitary castle in the mountains, has become obsessed with the idea that Laura is the reincarnation of a vampire, Sheena, who placed a curse on the family several centuries earlier. After a noblewoman and her daughter are involved in a minor accident with their coach near the castle, the elderly lady suggests that the girl, Ljuba, stays at castle Karnstein for a while to recover after the accident. Ljuba and Laura become friends, and perhaps more than just that.

Meanwhile, horrible murders start taking place in the neighboring countryside, and all the victims are drained of blood. Baron Karnstein's suspicions seem to be confirmed...

Among Italian Gothic films about female vampires, *Terror in the Crypt* deserves a place of its own. Joseph Thomas Sheridan Le Fanu's novel *Carmilla*, published in 1872, had already been the inspiration for Carl Theodor Dreyer's *Vampyr* and had been adapted just a few years earlier, in a contemporary setting, by Roger Vadim as *Blood and Roses (Et mourir de plaisir*, 1960). The idea to draw on Le Fanu's original probably came to Tonino Valerii and Ernesto Gastaldi after reading the horror anthology *I vampiri tra noi*, which featured a preface by Vadim and was very popular at that time.

The original script was written in just three days, according to Valerii; Gastaldi says it was nailed in a mere 24 hours. "While chatting with a producer, Tonino Valerii and I told him the story of the film—we had just a tiny little sheet. We caught his interest, and he told us he would produce the film, but he needed the script at once, because he wanted to start shooting in a few days, for economical reasons. Lying shamelessly, I told him that the script was ready, and he happily told us that he would wait for us the next morning in his office with the screenplay, so that we would read it together. So, Tonino and I spent the night writing the script on my terrace, with Mara Maryl providing coffee."[1] The working title was *La maledizione dei Karnstein* (The Curse of the Karnsteins)—the same as the official screenplay deposited at the CSC library in Rome, as well as the one mentioned by Christopher Lee in his autobiography.[2]

Initially, the film was supposed to be directed by Antonio Margheriti, who would later film *The Long Hair of Death*. "The producer liked the result and gave it to Antonio, who invited us at his home on the Appia Antica. Antonio, Valerii and I worked on the script for several afternoons, filling some scenes, correcting others and meeting the director's needs," as Gastaldi recalls.[3] Eventually, due to Margheriti's commitments, the directorial chair was eventually taken by Camillo Mastrocinque (1901–1969), an elderly veteran of comedies who had often worked with Totò on such titles as *Siamo uomini o caporali* (1955), *Totò, lascia o raddoppia?* (1956) and *La banda degli onesti* (1956), and who hid as was customary behind a foreign pseudonym, Thomas Miller. Mastrocinque's name was suggested by the agent Liliana Biancini (the ex-wife of producer Dario Sabatello) who was trying to help the 63-year old director find new assignments. As with most Italian Gothics of the period, *Terror in the Crypt* was not shot in the studio but on an existing natural set, in and around the Castle Piccolomini in Balsorano, in the central region of Abruzzo: cast and crew also accommodated in the 15th century manor in order to cut costs.

Terror in the Crypt is a case in point when it comes to analyze the easiness and lack of diffidence on the part of Italian scriptwriters and filmmakers when adapting (or, more properly, reworking) the Anglo-Saxon Gothic canon. Valerii and Gastaldi retained many elements from *Carmilla*: the opening situation, with young Laura being secluded in a lost castle in the mountains with her father; the warm yet ambiguous friendship that develops between the two young women; the character of the old tramp who sells amulets; and the final desecration of the vampire's grave.

Other parts of Le Fanu's story were either expunged or radically changed. For instance, the long tale of old general Spielsdorf, which occupies the last third of the book, is completely missing: the evocation of a masquerade ball in which an unknown countess had entrusted the General with the care of her daughter Millarca—that is, Carmilla—would later be faithfully reprised in Hammer's *The Vampire Lovers* (1970, Roy Ward Baker). On the other hand, Laura's father, Count Ludwig von Karnstein, first described by Le Fanu

The Italian poster for *Terror in the Crypt* crudely enhanced the film's erotic element (author's collection).

as "the kindest man on earth, but growing old" is brought to the screen in a decidedly different, and more ambiguous, incarnation: he is much younger, visibly nervous (notice the cigarettes he chain-smokes with his mouthpiece), wears brocade robes and has not bid farewell to the pleasures of the flesh, as shown by his affair with the housekeeper-lover Annette (Véra Valmont) he regularly visits in her room after midnight. A transformation heightened by the choice of hiring for the role the then 42-year-old Christopher Lee. The British actor's imposing and alluring screen presence gives new meaning to such dialogue exchanges as "Why don't you marry me?" "You could be my daughter" "Then adopt me" which make explicit the incestuous undercurrent that can only be guessed in Le Fanu's novel.

However, several crucial plot points are entirely the product of the two scriptwriters. First of all, there is the choice of structuring the film along a red herring that deceives the viewer on the real identity of the vampire: the opening sequence, shown through a point-of-view shot, in which the young Tilde (Angela Minervini) is attacked and killed in the woods, as well as the murders of Rowena (Nela Conju) and Annette, are all elements which display a patent stylistic proximity with the nascent Italian thriller.

Furthermore, the script introduces a subplot involving the young restorer Friedrich Klauss (José Campos) who has been summoned to the castle to reconstruct an old portrait of Sheena Karnstein: besides the predictable romantic implication, it becomes an essential element in the story. In *Carmilla* the character of the restorer's son appears briefly in Chapter 5, when he is seen bringing to the castle the old paintings that have been restored to their original conditions; among the paintings there is Mircalla's:

"I remembered it; it was a small picture, about a foot and a half high, and nearly square, without a frame; but it was so blackened by age that I could not make it out.

"The artist now produced it, with evident pride. It was quite beautiful; it was startling; it seemed to live. It was the effigy of Carmilla!"

In *Terror in the Crypt* the mysterious portrait—a common presence in Italian Gothic horror films of the period—becomes the key element in a sort of mystery-like detection, as the original painting is discovered to be hidden under another one—an idea which predates both *Deep Red* and Pupi Avati's *The House with the Laughing Windows* (*La casa dalle finestre*

che ridono, 1976). Another example of narrative cannibalism, so to speak, is the scene where Friedrich is startled to see another figure down the hall, whom he discover to be just his own reflection in a mirror. It is a moment almost identical to one in *Castle of Blood*: whereas in Margheriti's film the episode is a starting point in passing to suggest the protagonist's growing unease, here the cheap shock becomes the pretext for the discovery of Sheena Karnstein's hidden portrait.

Most remarkably, then, *Terror in the Crypt* avoids most clichés of the vampire film: there is no trace of oversized pointed fangs, whereas Le Fanu insists on Carmilla's sharp teeth, "long, thin, pointed, like an awl, like a needle." And the vampire's final dissolution is staged in a quite inventive manner, not through the usual crumbling into dust, but with Ljuba's volatilization, shown with no editing cuts via a visual trick *à la* Jean Cocteau: while elsewhere the tomb of her ancestress Sheena is opened and the body is transfixed with a spike through the chest to put the curse to an end, Ljuba falls to the ground and the camera zooms in on Laura's stunned expression, then it zooms back out to a long shot, showing Ljuba's empty robe on the ground—the only sign left of her existence.

The introduction of magic and divination in the story carries the plot in darker and more ambiguous territories compared to the stately literary source. Rowena, Laura's faithful maidservant, is some sort of a witch who practices black magic, performs disturbing rituals and even amputates a dead man's hand in order to turn it into a macabre fetish: a character much closer to Mediterranean mentality, with her mixture of superstition and peasant pragmatism, than to Le Fanu's world. The fact that Valerii and Gastaldi's vision was firmly rooted in Italian folklore as well as in a vision of the Gothic already marked by their cinematic predecessors can also be found in the curse that Sheena casts over the Karnstein family—a further innovation compared to the novel—which positively recalls *Black Sunday*. Bava's debut is openly quoted—or rather, ransacked—in the flashback of the vampire's execution, as well as in the way the script emphasizes the theme of reincarnation, a key feature in the universe of Italian celluloid Gothic.

Finally, and most remarkably, *Terror in the Crypt* overturns the physical characters of the two female protagonists. Laura Karnstein, whom Le Fanu pictures as the typical Victorian damsel-in-distress—blonde, pale, chaste and modest in manner and appearance, devoid of sexual desires and devoted to a naive, soppy romanticism she learned in the books—takes on the Mediterranean features, black raven hair and sensual curvaceous body of Adriana Ambesi. In contrast, Ljuba/Carmilla—whom in the novel is described as follows: "her complexion was rich and brilliant; [...] her eyes large, dark, and lustrous; her hair was quite wonderful, [...] so magnificently thick and long [...] and in colour a rich very dark brown"—has the angelic features of the innocent-looking blonde Ursula Davis, a.k.a. Pier Anna Quaglia.

Which is to say that whereas in *Carmilla*, the vampire is portrayed as "a female prototype, sensual and perturbing, whose sexuality [...] is doubly improductive, being both vampiric and orientated towards the same sex,"[4] Valerii and Gastaldi skillfully stir the waters, by associating to Laura (the victim) all the characteristics that Le Fanu describes as belonging to Carmilla (the vampire), including the sudden mood changes, to the point of having Ljuba utter the words that Laura says in the novel about Carmilla ("Sometimes she looks at me in a way that scares me, then she smiles and places her arms about my neck").

The deceptive game is amplified by Julio Ortas'[5] exquisite lighting, which associates Laura with gloom and Ljuba—a vampire who is not scared of the sun and on the contrary radiates vitality and *joie de vivre*—with open light. What is more, Mastrocinque builds many shots in a specular manner, putting Laura and Ljuba side by side in order to show the two opposites at once. It is a tricky move, and a smart one—at least for the time in which the film was made: most audiences had not even heard of Le Fanu, and were not shrewd enough to see the trap they were being led into.

As a result, it was inevitable to many to associate the voluptuous Laura with vampirism, according to a model that had already been established by Riccardo Freda, Mario Bava and their Gothic disciples. *Terror in the Crypt*'s final twist is even more striking as it sweeps away the supposed duality between the damsel-in-distress and the *belle dame sans merci* by overturning the roles of Ljuba and Laura: if at the climax of *Black Sunday* the audience knew what the hero did not, that the beautiful Katia was actually the evil Asa, and delighted in the titillating notion of evil's alluring face, here the viewer is tricked just like the characters, his moral notions doomed to be tickled and ultimately ridiculed.

In spite of the copious changes to the text, Valerii and Gastaldi captured and amplified the story's sensual power. In *Carmilla* the uncanny takes forms related to sexuality and sin, starting with Laura's shocking pre-pubescent vision (she recalls that when she was six a mysterious visitor penetrated into her bedroom and bit her on the chest), duplicated by the nightmare in which the girl is visited by a feline creature that assumes female form. Also noteworthy is the way Le Fanu alludes to the covert incestuous relationship between the young woman and her widowed father who has secluded her in the castle, not to mention how the writer conveys the exasperated languor of a lazy, mysterious lewdness as well as the idea of a cyclical time (as expressed by Carmilla's recurring appearances through the years) whose inevitability mocks the woman's monthly menstrual cycle: the breaking of the chain will coincide with the sterility of menopause.

While far from reaching Le Fanu's refined allegories, and saddled with its share of clumsy or throwaway moments, *Terror in the Crypt* is noteworthy for its portrayal of sensuality and female desire. As with many other Italian horror films of the period, the supernatural component allows the scriptwriters and the director to push the pedal of transgression: Ljuba's demonic influence justifies the lesbian relationship between her and Laura, which forms the film's core. If Margheriti's *Castle of Blood* was the first Italian Gothic to explicitly address the issue with Margrete Robsahm's infamous attempted seduction of Barbara Steele, Mastrocinque's film develops the theme of female ho-

The flashback of the female vampire's execution in *Terror in the Crypt* openly recalls Black Sunday (author's collection).

mosexuality of Le Fanu's novel as far as censorship would allow.

The Irish novelist lingers on the languorous kisses and caresses from Carmilla:

"She used to place her pretty arms about my neck, draw me to her, and laying her cheek to mine, murmur with her lips near my ear [...]. And when she had spoken such a rhapsody, she would press me more closely in her trembling embrace, and her lips in soft kisses gently glow upon my cheek. [...] From these foolish embraces, which were not of very frequent occurrence, I must allow, I used to wish to extricate myself; but my energies seemed to fail me. [...] I experienced a strange, tumultuous excitement that was pleasurable, ever and anon, mingled with a vague sense of fear and disgust. I had no distinct thoughts about her while such scenes lasted, but I was conscious of a love growing into adoration, and also of abhorrence."

Carmilla's behavior is so explicit that the innocent young girl even asks herself: "What if a boyish lover had found his way into the house, and sought to prosecute his suit in masquerade [...]?"

Le Fanu's vampire undergoes melancholic impulses that result in an occasional reluctance towards the victim:

"Dearest, your little heart is wounded; think me not cruel because I obey the irresistible law of my strength and weakness; if your dear heart is wounded, my wild heart bleeds with yours. In the rapture of my enormous humiliation I live in your warm life, and you shall die—die, sweetly die—into mine. I cannot help it [...]."

Le Fanu even describes the process of vampirization with a crescendo that openly recalls female orgasm:

"Sometimes it was as if warm lips kissed me, and longer and more lovingly as they reached my throat, but there the caress fixed itself. My heart beat faster, my breathing rose and fell rapidly and full drawn; a sobbing, that rose into a sense of strangulation, supervened, and turned into a dreadful convulsion, in which my senses left me and I became unconscious."

Terror in the Crypt faces the displacement of roles caused by the same-sex vampiric aggression in an interesting way. The encounter between Laura and Ljuba, which takes place in a similar manner as the novel (the carriage accident near the castle), abruptly interrupts the blossoming of a romantic idyll between Laura and Friedrich. Soon afterwards, Mastrocinque isolates the two women with a close-up that hints at their complicity: they are already unreachable by the male. "I would like to help you feel less lonely," Friedrich later tells Laura, not noticing that Ljuba has appeared behind his back. "I'm not alone anymore," Laura replies, after exchanging a significant look with her female friend, who steps by her side: once again the male is rejected out of the female world.

When compared to *Blood and Roses*, *Terror in the Crypt* proves all the more surprising. First of all, Vadim transposed the story to contemporary Italy, in a noble estate where the male hero (Mel Ferrer) delighted in feasts and masquerades, including fireworks *La Dolce Vita*–style. What is more, *Blood and Roses* told the story from the point of view of the centuries-old vampire Millarca, who reincarnates in Carmilla and subdues her to her own seductive will: thus, the story oscillated between a psychoanalytic interpretation—underlined by a nightmare sequence which, although beautifully photographed by Claude Renoir, overindulged in the most banally didactic Surrealist touches—and a supernatural one.

However, by shifting the focus of the story on Carmilla and making her a victim, Vadim missed Le Fanu's point, that is a tale told by a victim who is somehow an accomplice of her tormentor, and turned the characters into one-dimensional figures without a will. Mastrocinque's film does not make the same mistake.

Carmilla came out in the middle of a heated debate on the condition of women in Victorian society. *Terror in the Crypt* reflects quite a different outlook on the female body and sexuality: 1960s Italy is hungry with novelties and naked flesh, and torn between desire and guilt. "Beauty carries the seed of evil" a tramp says in a scene: a line which can almost be read as a critical gloss to the genre as a whole.

In Italian horror, lesbianism is not seen as a shattering force (as it was against Victorian orthodoxy in Le Fanu's novel), but as an excuse for voyeurism, and as such is represented with smug, all-male indulgence.[6] Ljuba—just like Julia (*Castle of Blood*) or Harriet (*An Angel for Satan*)—are not viral particles whose apparition is likely to erode the safety of patriarchal society, as will happen in *The Blood Spattered Bride* (*La novia ensangrentada*) the novel's adaptation directed by Vicente Aranda in 1972, which is more attentive to an updating of the discourse about the battle of the sexes within Spain's sexuophobic culture.[7]

In Aranda's film, woman and man are two worlds apart, the surreal apparition of Mircalla (Alexandra Bastedo)—a female vampire/alien worthy of Dalí, half-buried in the sand and wearing a diving mask—shifts the focus from voyeurism to the institution of marriage, the alliance between the two women aims at the male's castration. In *Terror in the Crypt* all this is, quite simply, a comfortable way to satisfy the curiosity of an audience in search of forbidden emotions, which approached horror movies because of their association to the *mise-en scène* of more or less bizarre perversions. Therefore, Valerii, Gastaldi and Mastrocinque get rid of any pretension at a social discourse, and instead capture the pragmatic aspect of the story: "I used to tell Mastrocinque to cut the niceties and get down to sex!"[8] Valerii would later explain. If, as some critics have noted, in Le Fanu's story "it is to disguise her desire for blood that Carmilla wears the mask of love,"[9] in 1970s Italian Gothic it will be the opposite: what in *Terror in the Crypt* is still merely hinted at, will be explicitly portrayed once the already crumbling walls of censorship are breached.

And yet, even if the representation of sapphic desire is devoid of the punitive harshness to be found in Spanish horror films, as well as the laughable Puritan scrap of Hammer's subsequent Le Fanu adaptations such as *The Vampire Lovers* and Jimmy Sangster's obnoxious *Lust for a Vampire* (1971), unnatural passions are nevertheless destined to be punished, and *Terror in the Crypt* is no exception. Yet, the way Mastrocinque's film portrays sensuality is remarkably effective for an unpretentious genre product.

Take the scene of Laura's nightmare: the young woman is sleeping, her face seen in profile, in an overhead shot, while melodious music underlines her silent grace. The camera zooms in on Laura's face, while her hair is caressed by a sudden breeze. The lighting enhances the girl's facial features and her chest which lifts up and down softly, breathing. Then Laura stands upright in bed, waiting—her eyes framed by a shaft of light in the darkness. What was supposed to be a scene depicting unrest and fear becomes strangely perturbing, even provocative—traits which do not thin out as the scene continues, with Ljuba appearing in the bedroom and Laura kneeling down before her in an adoring pose. The scene ends with a shocking close-up of a skull superimposed over Ljuba's face, *à la Psycho*. It is a moment that reworks the representation of the macabre, transforming its meaning: the horrific nightmare becomes the necessary harbinger of seduction, as Laura asks Ljuba to stay with her for the night and the two women disappear behind the bedroom door. The invitation on the part of the victim, as the tradition demands (the vampire cannot enter the victim's room if not by the latter's will) assumes an explicit character of a sexual proffer. Laura's dream predates the wonderful sequence of Daria Nicolodi's erotic fantasy in Mario Bava's *Shock*, if only because it moves from similar assumptions: the exploration of the subconscious and its surrender through tangible phenomena.

Tonino Valerii, who also acted as Mastrocinque's assistant director on the set, claims he personally shot several scenes. "When this elderly gentleman, who had always directed light comedies, such as Totò's films and so on, was given the opportunity to make a vampire film, he felt lost. There were things that made him shudder: hanged men, severed hands with burn-

ing candles over the fingers and so on ... and he made me shoot that stuff!"[10] Valerii claims to have directed the scene with the so-called "Hand of Glory," Ljuba's vampiric kiss as well as the sequence of the tramp hung in the bell tower, with the dog trying to release the body and provoking each time a mournful tolling—a scene which also emphasizes the grotesque quality of Italian Gothic when approaching an imagery closer to Anglo-Saxon horror: see the close-up of the dead man's mutilated limb that accompanies the discovery of the body.

Formally, however, *Terror in the Crypt* is a rather accomplished work, which is somewhat surprising given Mastrocinque's alleged disinterest towards the genre. Besides the aforementioned nightmare scene and Ljuba's final dissolution, another noteworthy moment is the apparition of Tilde's ghost, in which Mastrocinque uses the same trick as the one adopted by Mario Bava in *Black Sabbath*'s "The Drop of Water" episode for the apparition of the horrid old woman: the actress, placed over an offscreen dolly, seemingly slides towards the camera as if she was levitating without touching the floor. Mastrocinque also uses the zoom lenses with prodigality, but not just as a matter of cutting time and costs: not only the zoom often synthesizes two shots into one, but is also a good stylistic resource to close a sequence and move on to the next one. The director would go on to direct one more Gothic, *An Angel for Satan*, starring Barbara Steele.

Terror in the Crypt was released straight to U.S. television by AIP-TV, whereas it played in U.K. theaters as *Crypt of Horror*. The 2012 Retromedia/Image U.S. DVD release presents the film with the title *Crypt of the Vampire*, even though the credits still read *Terror in the Crypt*.

Notes

1. Email interview, January 2014.
2. "We moved down to a Gothic house in Southern Italy to make *Maledizione dei Karnstein*, a confection of elements of Le Fanu's *Carmilla*, and here it was my pleasure to be Count Ludwig von Karnstein, the noble father of a brood of lesbian vampires." Christopher Lee, *Tall, Dark and Gruesome* (Baltimore MD: Midnight Marquee, 1999) p. 187; Christopher Lee, *Lord of Misrule: The Autobiography of Christopher Lee* (London: Orion, 2004), p. 252.

3. Email interview, January 2014.

4. Sandro Melani, "Introduction," in J. Sheridan Le Fanu, *Carmilla* (Venice: Marsilio, 1999), p. 22.

5. Tonino Valerii states that Ortas was the director of photography during principal shooting, except for the first two or three days, when he was temporarily replaced by Giuseppe Aquari, as the Spanish d.o.p. was blocked by bureaucratic snags. According to Valerii, "Ortas was a young mild man, yet very efficient and quite expert with black-and-white cinematography. He was also an excellent connoisseur of the processes of development and printing of the negative, and he knew what to do to get a very effective result despite the lack of means. Every now and then I saw him approach the script girl after a good take, and tell her to write something down. Once I approached in order to listen to what he said. "Forzar hasta dos cientos" ("Force it up to 200"). Later I discovered at the Technicolor lab in Rome that it was a very delicate process that increased the negative's receptive power in situations where there was not enough light on the set." Email interview, July 2010.

6. Pezzotta, "Doppi di noi stessi," p. 30.

7. Puzzlingly, the script of Aranda's film deposited at Rome's CSC library with the title *La sposa insanguinata*, "The Blood Spattered Bride"—a literal translation of the Spanish title (whereas the film came out in Italy as *Un abito da sposa macchiato di sangue*, "A Blood Spattered Wedding Gown")—which bears the date March 23, 1971, has the following line on the front: "Story: Vicente Aranda. Screenplay: Tonino Valerii, Vicente Aranda." The aforementioned line has been added with a stick under the original one, which credited the script solely to Aranda. However, Valerii denies he ever had anything to do with Aranda's film.

8. Tommaso La Selva, *Tonino Valerii: mai temere il Leone* (Milan: Nocturno Libri, 2000), p. 104.

9. Louis Vax, *La natura del fantastico* (Rome: Theoria, 1987), p. 10.

10. Curti, *Il mio nome è Nessuno*, p. 22.

The Vampire of the Opera, a.k.a. *The Monster of the Opera (Il mostro dell'Opera)*

D: Renato Polselli. *S*: Renato Polselli, Ernesto Gastaldi; *SC*: Ernesto Gastaldi, Giuseppe Pellegrini, Renato Polselli; *DOP*: Ugo Brunelli (B&W); *M*: Aldo Piga, conducted by Pier Luigi Urbini; *E*: Otello Colangeli; *PD*: Demofilo Fidani; *SD*: Franco Cuppini; *AD*: Giuseppe Pellegrini, Gennaro Balistrieri; *C*: Sante Achilli; *AC*: Elio Polacchi; *MU*: Gaetano Capgrosso; *SO*: Sandro Ochetti, Enzo Magli; *SP*: Giorgio Bernardini; *SS*: Carla Ioviti; *CHOR*: Marisa and Gianna Ciampiglia [Ciampaglia]. *Cast*: Mark Maryan [Marco Mariani] (Sandro), John McDouglas [Giuseppe Addobbati] (Stefano), Barbara Hawards (Giulia), Albert Archet [Alberto Archetti] (Achille), Carla Cavalli (Aurora), Boris Notarenko, Jody Excell (Yvette), Milena Vukotic (Carlotta), Gaby Black, George Arms, Romy von Simon, Erich Schonbrunner, Cristine Martin, Maureen Verrich, Olga Jala, Renato Montalbano (Tony), Fidelio Gonzáles (Filippo), Vittoria Prada (Rossana). *PROD*: Nord Industrial Film; *GM*: Oscar Brazzi; *PM*: Fernando Anselmetti; *PS*: Fausto Lupi; *PA*: Roberto Bertolini; *PSe*: Alberto Casati. *Country*: Italy. Filmed in Narni. *Running time*: 85 min. (m. 2310); Visa n: 43135 (06.18.1964); *Rating*: V.M.18; *Release date*: 06.30.1964 (Italy). *Distribution:* Nord Industrial (Italy, Regional); *Domestic gross*: unknown. *Also known as:* Il vampiro dell'Opera (working title), L'Orgie des vampires (France, 07.23.1969). *Homevideo*: Artus (DVD, France).

In order to rehearse a new stage production with his dance troupe, Sandro rents an old Opera house that has been closed for many years. However, the elderly caretaker urges Sandro to leave at once, telling him that the place is cursed. As Sandro and his company will soon find out, the theater is inhabited by an undead vampire named Stefano, who keeps a harem of undead female slaves in an extradimensional crypt. When the bloodsucker finds out that the lead dancer, Giulia, is the reincarnation of the woman he once loved and who betrayed him, he starts preying on the ballerinas. On the other hand, Giulia realizes that the horrible nightmares she has been plagued by are becoming real...

The early vampire *filone* started by Renato Polselli's *The Vampire and the Ballerina* soon dried up, even before Hammer put in production the second *Dracula* film starring Christopher Lee: *The Vampire of the Opera*, produced by Oscar Brazzi (Rossano's brother), was released in 1964 but was filmed in 1961. The shooting title was actually *Il vampiro dell'Opera*, the same as the photonovel published in February 1962 in the adults-only *Malia* magazine—two years before Polselli's film eventually came out in theaters. Lack of money caused shooting to proceed in fits and starts, and eventually the film emerged as *Il mostro dell'Opera* ("The Monster of the Opera"), even though lobby cards had been prepared with the earlier title: in the meantime, audiences' interest on Dracula's makeshifts had waned, and the Italian Gothic horror trend had settled on more original territories.

The title changes confirmed how native bloodsuckers did not take root: Dracula worked much better as a trademark on pocket paperbacks than on the silver screen. And if even the charismatic Lee was reduced to a one-

MAC MARYAN
IL VAMPIRO DELL'OPERA

Produzione M.L.F. - Roma · VITTORIA PRADA · BARBARA HOWARD · JOHN MC DOUGLAS · Regia di RENATO POLSELLI

Rare Italian *fotobusta* for Renato Polselli's *The Vampire of the Opera*. Curiously, it features the shooting title *Il vampiro dell'opera*, whereas the film was eventually released, two years after its making, as *Il mostro dell'opera* (author's collection).

dimensional villain with a merely animal presence in *Dracula: Prince of Darkness*, his homemade substitutes were destined to even worse fates. However, Polselli was once again adamant in pursuing an emphasis on eroticism. Even though according to the credits *The Vampire of the Opera* was written once again by the trio formed by Ernesto Gastaldi, Polselli and Giuseppe Pellegrini, Gastaldi claims he had very little to do with the script: "I'm not sure, but I think I wrote only the treatment. I think I also read the script and made some corrections. I was frankly surprised to find my name on the credits."[1]

As the title suggests, the script takes very loose inspiration from Gaston Leroux's *Phantom of the Opera*: the references are limited to the title and the setting, as well as the scene where the vampire (somewhat incongruously named Stefano and played by character actor Giuseppe Addobbati) is watching the company's rehearsals from a box, while the idea of the

bloodsucker's portrait being the key to his destruction is a nod to *The Picture of Dorian Gray*.

Polselli claimed in an interview that for the film he used again the same skeleton as in *The Vampire and the Ballerina*.[2] More significantly, the script recycled the theme of the heroine being the reincarnation of the vampire's beloved woman—something old-hat in Italian vampire films by 1961—albeit with a twist. Despite the vampire having a whole harem of chained vampire brides who "wait every new moon for young blood to reanimate them so that I can kill them again," the misogynist flashback which exposes Stefano's origins, reveals him to be substantially a victim: he was buried alive by his unfaithful lover and vowed to "live to destroy beauty, because your beauty destroyed me many years ago." Which makes the titular vampire close to the one played by Walter Brandi in *The Vampire and the Ballerina*, and a rather passive figure as well, similar to most of Italian Gothic's male characters.

The rest of *The Vampire of the Opera* plays like a variation on Polselli's earlier *The Vampire and the Ballerina* as well as Piero Regnoli's *The Playgirls and the Vampire*—i.e., a pretext for showing scantily clad young women, with a little hint of lesbianism to spice up the proceedings. "Don't you think that a friendship between two women is finer, larger even than love?" a female dancer (whom the protagonist Marco Mariani claims to be "born in the town of Lesbo, in Sappho's province," just in case anyone had any doubt) allusively asks a colleague whom she is making a pass at, while the choreography for the absurd ballet—no *Red Shoes* here, by far—looks more like, as one reviewer put it, "the fever dream of an oversexed choreographer."

Although he has been iconographically borrowed from tradition, with even an excess of elegance—he looks dapper in his tail-coat and black tie with a gardenia in the buttonhole, Polselli's vampire manages to escape the clichés. This, however, is less a result of calculation than—to use a euphemism—the director's idiosyncrasies. *The Vampire of the Opera*'s bloodsucker sleeps in the requisite coffin, but when they open it, the film's human characters only find his empty clothes inside. The casket even becomes an extradimensional threshold of sorts that leads to the crypt where the vampire hides, amidst dry ice aplenty and half-naked female vampires chained to the walls. Another mind-boggling notion that the film offers concerns the vampire's ability to assault only those who are standing still, a pretext for an incredible sequence where the dancers throw themselves into frantic (and uncoordinated) dance steps in order to keep the bloodsucker away, only to eventually collapse exhausted at his mercy.

As for the film's visuals, Polselli doggedly pursues bizarre effects, yet the results display an overwhelming paucity of technique and style. The opening scene, in which a dancer is being chased by the vampire in a succession of set-pieces and which is soon revealed to be a nightmare, puts together a series of effects that should certify its surrealist approach. The vampire attacks the victim with an unlikely pitchfork, the camera takes on unusual angles and at a certain point even turns upside down. Yet the pompous tricks—such as the "invisible force" that the heroine experiences in her dream, and which is represented by a sheet of glass between the actress and the camera[3]—cannot even be compared to the involuntary Dada of those trash epics so beloved by the likes of Ado Kyrou, such as *Horrors of Spider Island* (*Ein Toter hing im Netz*, 1960, Fritz Böttger), as Polselli lacks even the alibi of naive instinct to make up for his irritating pretentiousness. The director's tendency towards over-the-top, gratuitous oddities would reach a point of no return in his later films, especially the infamous *The Reincarnation of Isabel*.

Notes

1. Lucas, "What Are Those Strange Drops of Blood," p. 41.
2. On this occasion, the director came up with one of his not very reliable anecdotes, halfway between self-created myth and reality. "I remember myself, the leading lady and Brazzi going out one night, arm in arm with that skeleton, in the streets of Narni, where we were shooting *The Vampire of the Opera*. All of a sudden we heard a siren: people got scared and called the police." Andolfi, "Renato Polselli tra horror e censura," p. 492.
3. A similar idea (and effect) was employed in Luigi Cozzi's *Paganini Horror* (1989).

1965

Bloody Pit of Horror, a.k.a. *A Tale of Torture (Il boia scarlatto)*

D: Max Hunter [Domenico Massimo Pupillo]. *S and SC:* Robert Nathan [Roberto Natale], Robin McLorin [Romano Migliorini] (*U.S. version:* "Created and conceived by Ralph Zucker and Frank Merle"); *DOP:* John Collins [Luciano Trasatti] (Eastmancolor); *M:* Gino Peguri; *E:* Robert Ardis [Mariano Arditi]; *PD/ArtD:* Frank F. Arnold [Franco Fontana]; *SD:* Richard Goldbert [Franco Calfapietra]; *AD:* Henry Castle [Massimo Castellani]; *C:* Philip Jones [Luigi Carta]; *AC:* James Stone [Danilo Salvadori]; *SE:* Carlo Rambaldi; *SO:* Geoffrey Sellers [Goffredo Salvadori]; *MU:* Alan Trevor [Duilio Scarrozza]; *Hair:* Lucille Gardner [Luisa Maria Garbini]; *DialD:* Dom Leone; *SP:* Herbert Penn [Italo Tonni]; *SS:* Mary Friend [Lina D'Amico]; (*U.S. version—Script adaptation:* Ruth Carter, Cesare Mancini). *Cast:* Mickey Hargitay (Travis Anderson), Walter Brandt [Walter Bigari] (Rick), Louise Barret [Luisa Baratto] (Edith), Ralph Zucker (Dermott, the photographer), Alfred Rice [Alfredo Rizzo] (Daniel Parks), Nik Angel [Nando Angelini] (Perry), Albert Gordon, John Turner [Gino Turini] (Travis' mustached henchman), Robert Messenger [Roberto Messina] (Travis' bald henchman), Barbara Nelly [Barbara Nelli] (Suzy), Moa Tahi (Kinojo), Rita Klein (Nancy), Femi Martin [Femi Benussi] (Annie). *PROD*: Frank Merle [Francesco Merli], Ralph Zucker for M.B.S. Cinematografica (Rome), International Entertainment Corp. (U.S.A.); *EP*: Felix C. Ziffer, J. R. Coolidge; *PM*: Sean Baker [Marino Vaccà]; *PA*: Lewis Lawrence [Luciano Catenacci], Nicholas Prince [Nicola Princigalli]. *Country*: Italy/U.S.A. Filmed at Balsorano Castle, interiors at Palazzo Borghese, Artena. *Running time*: 87 min. (2500m.); Visa n: 45978 (11.10.1965); *Rating*: V.M.18; *Release dates*: 11.28. 1965 (Italy); 05.16.1967 (U.S.A.). *Distribution:* M.B.S. (Italy, Regional); Pacemaker Pictures (U.S.A.); *Domestic gross*: 65,000,000 lire. *Also known as*: Crimson Executioner, Some Virgins for the Hangman, The Castle of Artena, The Red Hangman, The Scarlet Hangman, Virgins for the Hangman (U.S.A.); *Vierges pour le bourreau* (France), *Scarletto—Schloß des Blutes* (West Germany, 07.14.1967). *Home video*: Something Weird/Image (DVD, U.S.A.), Sinister Film (DVD, Italy).

Pulp publisher Daniel Parks and his crew—a writer, a photographer and five female models— sneak into a castle in order to stage a photo shoot for one of their lurid paperback horror novels. The lord of the castle, Travis Anderson, allows them to stay for just one day's work. A retired actor and muscleman who dedicated himself to seclusion and to the narcissistic worshipping of his own body, obsessed with a dream of absolute purity and physical perfection, Anderson goes berserk when Parks' crew starts staging violent and erotic set-ups in the castle's crypts. Hallucinating that he is the reincarnation of the legendary "crimson executioner," a sadistic man who was allegedly executed in the castle's crypts centuries earlier, Travis starts dispatching the intruders one by one, by submitting them to the sadistic devices in his torture chamber. It is up to Rick, the writer, to face Anderson and save Edith from death...

In the early 1960s, the Gothic was so "in" a phenomenon in Italian popular culture that it spawned not only movies, but also paperback novel series and photonovels. The latter (known in Italy as *fotoromanzi*) had surfaced in 1947, when the country was recovering from the destruction and the moral and economic desolation of the war years. Photonovels are very similar to comics in their format which consist of

succession of panels inclusive of speech balloons and captions. The main difference is that photonovel panels are not illustrations but photographs, portraying real people instead of drawn characters. Photonovels were created by Cesare Zavattini and Luciano Pedrocchi, who launched this hybrid form of popular entertainment in *Bolero Film*, the first magazine entirely dedicated to photonovels. The first *fotoromanzi* director, for the magazine *Il mio sogno*, on May 8, 1947, would become a renowned filmmaker: his name was Damiano Damiani.

Most photonovels were simple, melodramatic love stories, usually variations on the same basic plots: however, by the early 1960s the *fotoromanzi* had become a real industry, and publishers were ready to jump on the bandwagon and explore uncharted territories. In newsstands, beside the traditional syrupy *Lancio* photonovels, one could find male-oriented, adults-only stuff such as the series *Malia—I fotoromanzi del brivido*, which debuted in February 1961 and offered Gothic stories with such evocative titles as *L'urlo del vampiro* ("The Vampire's Scream"), *Il castello maledetto* ("The Damned Castle"), *Il risveglio di Dracula* ("Dracula's Awakening"), *Il regno del terrore* ("The Reign of Terror"), *Il vampiro etrusco* ("The Etruscan Vampire"). Conceived by the magazine's editor-in-chief Umberto Paolessi with journalist and writer Giorgio Boschero, these photonovels were photographed in the very same locations as used for the Gothic horror films of the period.

Moreover, as was commonplace for many genre films, horror movies also had their own photonovel version: this happened ever since *I Vampiri* (under the title *Quella che voleva amare*, in *I Vostri Film* 31, August 1958) and *Mill of the Stone Women* (*Super Star* 75, December 1960). Besides proper photonovels, *Malia* also published a number of Italian Gothic films in photonovel form: *The Playgirls and the Vampire, Slaughter of the Vampires, The Vampire of the Opera, Tomb of Torture, Terror-Creatures from the Grave, The Seventh Grave, Nightmare Castle...*

In a smart bit of self-reference, the world of photonovels and pulp magazines was described with tongue-in-cheek irony by Roberto Natale

United States double feature poster for Massimo Pupillo's Gothic horror films *Bloody Pit of Horror* and *Terror-Creatures from the Grave*, released theatrically in the United States by Pacemaker Pictures in May 1967 (courtesy S. I. Bianchi).

and Romano Migliorini in their script for *Bloody Pit of Horror*, where a shabby and somewhat fraudulent acolyte headed by a stingy publisher (Alfredo Rizzo) sneak into a castle for a photoshoot, in order to gather risqué cover art for a series of cheap novels centered on the character of "Skeletrik," a masked sadistic villain. The starting point recalls an episode of Gualtiero Jacopetti and Franco Prosperi's *Mondo cane 2* (1963), about the making of sadistic photonovels, and alludes to the army of writers and publishers who were luring readers by way of naked flesh and cheap thrills—a phenomenon which would later evolve into the out-and-out adult publishing of the following decade—and who were at home in those castles of Lazio that had been converted into film studios.

However, the character of Skeletrik, with the inevitable "K" in the name and a costume in style, is a nod to Magnus & Bunker's comic book *Kriminal*, and curiously predates *Killing*, the adults-only photonovel created the following year by Milan's Ponzoni Editore, which would soon become one of the most controversial publications in the whole *fumetti neri* phenomenon.[1] On the other hand, The Crimson Executioner as played by Mickey Hargitay in the film is the mirror image of Lee Falk's *The Phantom*, one of the main inspirations for the whole wave of Italian superhero films of the mid-to-late Sixties.

As one critic underlined, the comic book connection drips from every single frame of the film. "*Bloody Pit of Horror* is a comic-strip movie, with a story told through a series of scenes, pictures and pacing that are more akin to comics than cinema. Inside the empty spaces, that open continually, immobilizing the story, one would often be tempted to insert a few captions and balloons. [...] Pupillo (and his screenwriters) might have easily "enclosed" inside a gigantic balloon, floating over Mickey Hargitay's hooded head, these fantastic lines: "Mankind is composed of inferior beings, physically crippled, weak and insignificant. I, on the other hand, am different. My body is wonderful, perfect. I hate mankind. You won't die immediately. You will suffer long ... and I will enjoy your screams and torments.""[2]

However, *Bloody Pit of Horror*'s half-serious approach to Italian pulp can also be applied to the Gothic horror film as a whole, especially since the story takes place in the unmistakable Balsorano Castle (whereas the interiors were filmed at Castle Borghese in Artena) and the cast is a parade of familiar faces of the *filone*—from Walter Brandi to Gino Turini, from Barbara Nelli to Alfredo Rizzo, who in the 1970s would start an undistinguished career as a filmmaker, which included a mediocre erotic/Gothic flick, *The Bloodsucker Leads the Dance* (*La sanguisuga conduce la danza*, 1975).

And then—why not?—Massimo Pupillo's second Gothic film in a row—according to the director himself, filming took place immediately after *Terror-Creatures From the Grave*[3]—could be seen as a reflection on the Italian genre industry. Nods to contemporary Italian Gothic abound: the character of the mad and masked tormentor comes from *The Virgin of Nuremberg*, the opening scene hints at *Black Sunday*, the theme of the double is one of the Gothic's recurrent fixations,[4] while the idea of juxtaposing the villain to a group of potential victims (with a predominance of the weaker sex) of questionable morals recalls the earlier Italian vampire films directed by Renato Polselli and Rizzo has an identical role to the one he played in *The Playgirls and the Vampire*.

Pupillo's film gives a good idea of this frantic microcosm, populated by charlatans and scoundrels, where time is money and quality is not an option. What is more, it pointedly (and amusingly) alludes to the incessant erosion of the barriers of censorship and morality—or, to put it in another way, to the inches of naked skin being conquered at the expense of robes and nightgowns. A case in point is the recurring gag of the photographer (producer Ralph Zucker—who, according to Pupillo, also shot some extra footage[5]) who, while setting up a shot of a girl embraced by an armored skeleton (a perfect synthesis of the Gothic and sexy-*noir fumetti* if ever there was one), keeps sliding down her nightshirt's strap, which the girl immediately pulls up. The punchline is also ironic, as after defeating the villain, Rick (Walter Brandt, a.k.a. Walter Brandi, a.k.a. Walter Bigari, the former star of *The Vampire and the Ballerina* and *The Playgirls and the Vampire*) proclaims: "I won't write any more horror stories. The man that said life is stranger than fiction made no mistake!" (the Italian dialogue was even more mordant in its self-deprecation, as Rick concluded instead: "I realized you mustn't play with death and feelings!").

The narrative frame is actually more interesting than the plot itself. Natale and Migliorini accumulate and combine a number of ideas already seen in previous films: *Bloody Pit of Horror* reworks the Gothic's main themes, though applying them—rather than to the female figure seen as a seductive witch/vampire/ghost—to a grotesque bodybuilder, switching gender with decidedly campy results. A good example is the prologue, set in 1648, which shows the Crimson Executioner being executed and is clearly modeled on *Black Sunday*: the same solemn and gloomy atmosphere, the same stentorian voice announcing the Executioner's misdeeds, a torture device of exasperated cruelty, a curse exclaimed before dying. Yet the Virgin—or, as the Italian dubbing misspells it, the *Widow*—of Nuremberg in which the villain is locked looks more like a magician's device, and the overall effect is that of a bad night club act or a cheap Grand Guignol representation: on top of it all, Gino Peguri's score—with its electric guitars, trumpets and a warbling female voice—introduces a lounge tone which is poles apart from the macabre, an effect heightened by Luciano Trasatti's garish colors (in Psychovision, as the U.S. version proudly declares).

Despite the U.S. version opening with the apocryphal line "My vengeance needs blood!" and claiming to be "based on the writings of the Marquis De Sade"—not to mention the 1972 Italian re-release under the title *Io...il Marchese De Sade* (*I...Marquis De Sade*)—, there is actually very little in *Bloody Pit of Horror* that can be labeled as Sadean. The exhibited cruelty towards women is patently tongue-in-cheek, and often demands a smile: the inventive torture instruments that Travis puts to use are actually just clever gimmicks designed to take off the actresses' clothes, while Hargitay's orgasmic frenzy as he jumps from one device to the next

in his torture chamber like a child at a fairground is too over-the-top to be anything but amusing. "That's just a small portion of the torture that awaits you!" the Hungarian actor sneers, after submitting Femi Benussi and Rita Klein to the torments of a rotating cylinder with blades which caused them just a few scratches ... and ripped their shirts at strategic points.

Pupillo's direction is surprisingly lively and mordant, much better than in his film debut. The scene where Moa Tahi is imprisoned on a giant cobweb and menaced by a ridiculous-looking mechanical spider (courtesy of Carlo Rambaldi) exudes a pop and camp spirit which is closer to Magnus & Bunker's comic books such as *Kriminal* and *Satanik*, and perfectly fits Ado Kyrou's oft-quoted saying that creativity's worst enemy is good taste. In the same scene, the sight of Walter Brandt laboriously crawling under a complicated tangle of cords connected to poisoned arrows that could instantly kill him, brings to mind the contemporaneous spy and heist flicks, where similar tricks—threads disguised as unlikely laser beams—hindered the hero's path. But, in a fragrant cultural short circuit, the scene also recalls an absurd variation of the "limbo," an exotic night club act (the actress is wearing a Hawaiian costume...) that would not have been out of place in a sexy documentary such as the *Mondo di notte* series.

On the other hand, Mickey Hargitay's narcissistic displays of muscle have made some critics talk of a homocrotic subtext, similar to that of sword-and-sandal flicks. It is hard to say whether this was intentional. Hargitay's henchmen, dressed in adhesive white-and-blue striped T-shirts and white trousers that make them look like sailors on leave, are a sight worthy of a Tom of Finland drawing (or a Kenneth Anger film), but Hargitay's delirious monologues, as he sprinkles oil all over his bare chest and boasts about his "perfect body," are rather the outpourings of a misanthrope (and misogynist). "He avoided contact with people. Even with me he was distant. I never had a kiss from him," says (at least in the Italian version[6]) Edith, the woman whom he abandoned just before the wedding. Which brings us to one of Italian cinema's main obsessions—sexual impotence.

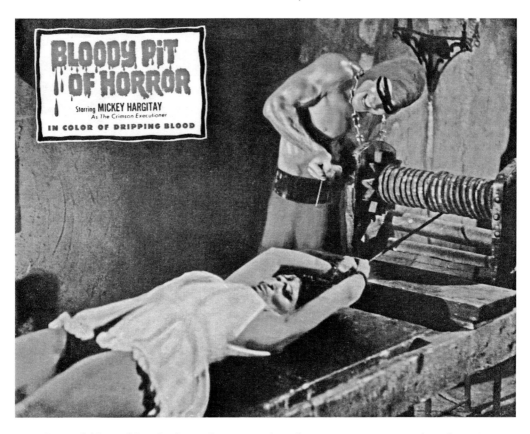

United States lobby card for *Bloody Pit of Horror*, with Mickey Hargitay in action as the sadistic Crimson Executioner (courtesy S. I. Bianchi).

Bloody Pit of Horror came out in the United States in May 1967, on a double-bill with another of Pupillo's Gothic films, *Terror-Creatures from the Grave*.[7] However, it was a heavily edited 74-minute version, with about nine minutes missing (mostly expository scenes of the crew looking around the crypts and the models posing for the shoot, but no extra gore or nudity), the same that popped up again on VHS and DVD over the years. The complete English language version (*A Tale of Torture*) was released on tape by Something Weird Video (whereas the Image Entertainment disc with the title *Bloody Pit of Horror* carries the shorter print, with the deleted scenes included as a supplement).

Notes

1. Starting on March 15, 1966, *Killing* became a *success de scandàle* in Italy. Its novelty was that, unlike *Diabolik*, *Kriminal, Satanik* and the like, it was not a comic book

but a photonovel. Its sexual and gory content were quite strong for the period, and caused its makers a lot of trouble, including a trial for obscenity, which eventually led them to tone down its excesses. *Killing* was published until April 1969, with a total of 62 issues. The director, Rosario Borrelli, was also a well-known character actor in Italian genre cinema of the period, while the mysterious actor who played Killing (always photographed with his face covered by a mask or shown from behind) was eventually revealed to be Aldo Agliata in the 2007 documentary *The Diabolikal Super-Kriminal*, directed by comic book artist and independent film-maker SS-Sunda [Sandro Yassel Spazio]. In recent years *Killing* has been published in the United States by Comicfix, in a three-part miniseries under the title *Sadistik*, by writer/animator Mort Todd, who acquired the rights in 2005.

2. Roberto Guidotti, "I deliri di un sadico narcisista. Il boia scarlatto," in Piselli and Guidotti, *Diva Cinema*, p. 36.

3. Pupillo talked about his involvement with Zucker in a 1993 radio interview with Italian film historian Fabio Melelli, which was included as an extra in the Italian DVD of *5 tombe per un medium*.

4. However, the way the script deals with the theme of the double is subtler than expected, and bears a psychoanalytical explanation: whereas Edith (Luisa Baratto) was the woman Travis (Hargitay) loved in his "previous"

life, the Crimson Executioner whom Travis claims to be a reincarnation of is actually just a dummy with Travis' features.

5. See Merrill Aldighieri and Lucas Balbo's documentary *Mondo Pupillo—Une conversation avec Massimo Pupillo* (2013).

6. The English dialogue is not as explicit in addressing Travis' sexual shortcomings: "He's always been a little strange—even with me. He seems so cold, yet I'm certain that he really loved me," Edith says.

7. The June 14, 1967, issue of *Variety* mentions *Terror Creatures from the Grave* on the bottom of a double bill with *Bloody Pit of Horror* earning $5,000 in release in Providence, Massachusetts. The films had opened in Maryland one month earlier.

Nightmare Castle *(Amanti d'oltretomba)*

D: Allan Grünewald [Mario Caiano]. *S* and *SC*: Mario Caiano, Fabio De Agostini; *DOP*: Enzo Barboni (B&W); *M*: Ennio Morricone; *E*: Renato Cinquini; *PD, SD*: Massimo Tavazzi; *CO*: Mario Giorsi; *AD*: Angelo Sangermano; *C*: Mario Mancini; *SO*: Bernardino Fronzetti; *MU*: Duilio Giustini; *Hair*: Rino Carboni; *SP*: Ermanno Serto; *SS*: Priscilla Contardi. *Cast*: Barbara Steele (Muriel Arrowsmith/ Jenny Arrowsmith), Paul Muller (Dr. Stephen Arrowsmith), Helga Liné (Solange), Lawrence Clift [Marino Masé] (Dr. Derek Joyce), John McDouglas [Giuseppe Addobbati] (Jonathan), Rik Battaglia (David). *PROD*: Mario Caiano for Cinematografica Emmeci; *GM*: Carlo Caiano; *PM*: Pietro Nofri. *Country*: Italy. Filmed at Villa Parisi, Frascati (Rome) and at Incir-De Paolis Studios (Rome). *Running time*: 97 min. (m. 2857); Visa n: 45399 (07.10.1965); *Rating*: V.M.18; *Release dates*: 07.16.1965 (Italy); 07.05.1966 (U.S.A.). *Distribution*: Emmeci (Italy, Regional); Allied Artists Pictures (U.S.A.). *Domestic gross*: 154,000,000 lire. *Also known as*: *Lovers Beyond the Tomb*, *Lovers From Beyond the Tomb*, *The Faceless Monster*; *Orgasmo* (U.S.A.); *Night of the Doomed* (U.K.); *Les Amants d'outre tombe* (France, 06.05.1966); *Amantes de ultratumba* (Mexico); *Die griezel minnaar/Les Amants d'outre-tombe* (Belgium). *Home video*: Severin (DVD, U.S.A.); Alpha Video (DVD, U.S.A.); Retro Media (DVD, U.S.A.—as *The Faceless Monster*); Sinister Film (DVD, Italy).

When he finds out that his wife Muriel has been unfaithful to him, the sadistic Dr. Arrowsmith tortures and murders her and her lover, then removes their hearts from their bodies. Discovering that Muriel has drawn up a new will giving her fortune to her institutionalized sister Jenny, the doctor marries his sister-in-law and brings her to his villa, where Jenny starts experiencing nightmares and hauntings; meanwhile Arrowsmith and his mistress Solange—whom he has rejuvenated through his experiments with

human blood—attempt to murder the woman, to no avail. Young Dr. Joyce, who is in love with Jenny, finds out about Arrowsmith's plans. Eventually, the ghosts of the slain return to exact their bloody revenge...

"The film was born out of my passion for the Gothic genre, and for Barbara Steele, who has a wonderful face—beautiful yet frightening, vampire-like," Mario Caiano said about his 1965 horror film *Nightmare Castle*. "Furthermore, we had to make a low-budget film and my father was the producer. I had just discovered a wonderful villa with a friend of mine, an art director who later won an Academy Award, Bruno Cesari.... We had the main location and the actress, so all I had to do was make up a story, taking inspiration from my childhood fears."[1]

The opening scenes of Caiano's film are a love poem to Barbara Steele: the camera follows and accompanies her moves with sinuous tracking shots, Enzo Barboni's refined lighting caresses her body with lights and shadows, Ennio Morricone's sensuous and macabre *totentanz* celebrates every single gesture she makes, thus emphasizing their seductive nature. The first ten minutes are a hymn to the Goddess of Italian horror: a malicious tracking shot glides forward to show Muriel raising her nightgown and adjusting her stockings, then applying perfume on her neck and between her breasts. Steele is the attraction, not the film.

Nightmare Castle is one of the most accomplished films of the lot in its exploration of eroticism—an ubiquitous and sinuous presence and an irrepressible category in Italian Gothic horror—which earned it a V.M.18 rating from the censors because of its "scenes of blood and ghosts, haunting and obsessive, as well as several sequences of macabre eroticism contraindicated to the particular sensitivity of the younger age." No wonder the original script was entitled *Orgasmo*.

What is particularly memorable about the film is the way Caiano depicts Muriel as a contemptuous *femme fatale* who dominates the male, takes him and rejects him at will: half-drunk, a glass of cognac in hand, she first mocks her husband, teasing his manhood and calling

Italian poster for Mario Caiano's *Nightmare Castle* (author's collection).

and the man who obeys. A theme played by the woman on the piano serves as both a signal and an erotic lure: the manservant—a groom, just like Lady Chatterley's lover, the embodiment of a brute and instinctive masculinity—is just a sex toy to Muriel, as muscle-bound heroes are to the evil vicious queens of the sword-and-sandal genre. It is up to the woman to educate man to pleasure. "I'm going to rid you of your vulgar ways and replace them with other much more subtle and refined," Muriel whispers passionately to her lover; "I don't understand you," he replies; "It doesn't matter," she cuts him short.

As other cursed heroines of Italian Gothic—Nevenka in *The Whip and the Body*, or Elisabeth in *Castle of Blood*—Muriel claims her own independence from the male and her right to satisfy her appetites. The repressive reaction she faces reveals the dark side of marriage as an institution based on abuse, synthesized by the vision of the two lovers chained in a crypt and tortured to death by the husband.

Paul Muller's character in *Nightmare Castle* is one of the Gothic's most patent Sadean epigones: a Machiavellian husband who schemes to lead his wife to madness, worthy of Anton Walbrook in Thorold Dickinson's *Gaslight*. Dr. Arrowsmith draws visible pleasure from the complex para-scientific gadgets that he uses to torture Muriel and the manservant, as well as from dissecting a frog in the film's first scene, as an unequivocal close-up reveals. "You don't know yet how long it takes to die of pain!" he whispers to his victims, even though—in one of the priceless gasps of humor running through the film—

him a "wimp"; then she prepares for the night, waiting to call the virile manservant who will satisfy her cravings.

The disparity between the sexes is immediately clear: it is the woman who calls the shots we see him fill a glass of water before his thirsty wife and then spill it on the floor, in an almost literal replica of a gag seen in *Toto the Sheik* (*Totò sceicco*, 1950, Mario Mattoli), one of Totò's most famous comedies in his home country.

As for its narrative, despite Caiano's claims that he was extraneous to Italian Gothic ("As for Bava, I don't remember watching any of his films, perhaps just *Black Sunday*. I wasn't influenced by his style, anyway I knew he was a great director, even though I never met him personally"[2]), *Nightmare Castle* is the most striking example of how Italian Gothic horror films were the result of a combinatorial narrative. Even though it came out just a mere five years after *Black Sunday*, Caiano's film is truly a summation of situations, characters and narrative patterns that are commonplace in Italian Gothic horror films of the decade. Let us see how, in detail.

1. Dr. Arrowsmith is a hybrid between Dr. Hichcock and the mad doctor of Freda's earlier *I Vampiri*: he plans to kill his second wife and conducts experiments with rejuvenating blood transfusions. 2. His maid (Helga Liné), who regains her youth and beauty through blood transfusions, recalls *I Vampiri*'s Duchess Du Grand and, to a lesser extent, *Mill of the Stone Women*'s Elsie; but she is also the doctor's accomplice in getting rid of the man's wife, like in Freda's diptych (the fact that she is also the doctor's mistress will return in *La vendetta di Lady Morgan* and *The Third Eye*). 3. The stableman (Rik Battaglia) is essentially the same character as the one played by Giovanni Cianfriglia in *Castle of Blood*: same clothes, same narrative function (he is his mistress' lover, with the latter being played by the same actress), same end (he dies on the bridal bed) and even the partially disfigured face which characterizes his post-mortem apparitions. 4. Barbara Steele, as the blonde Jenny, reprises almost literally the role of the *damsel-in-distress* she played in *The Horrible Dr. Hichcock*, while Marino Masé is the young *savant* who in Freda's film was played by Silvano Tranquilli; at the same time, however, Jenny is an instrument of her dead sister Muriel's vengeance, like Katia was of Asa's in *Black Sunday* and Helen Karnstein of her mother's

in *The Long Hair of Death*. All, of course, were played by the British actress. 5. Muriel's vengeful ghost appears in the final scenes with a half-disfigured face, a nod to *Black Sunday*.

That is a sign of the tendency towards self-cannibalism that characterized Italian genre cinema, due also to the frantic production system: in those days the sword-and-sandal cycle was undergoing a similar path. The ultimate effect, of course, would be the end of the commercially exhausted *filone*.

"My love for the genre was born in '43–'44 during the Nazi occupation" Caiano told an interviewer. "I couldn't leave home—curfew started at 4 p.m.—and spent my time in the house's library, reading Edgar Allan Poe's works, which impressed me enormously."[3] Besides Caiano's pseudonym, which pays homage to Poe and German Renaissance incisor Matthias Grünewald—who in his works often portrayed macabre *Totentänze* such as the one that accompanies the credits—the script, by Caiano and Fabio De Agostini,[4] bears strong echoes of "The Tell-Tale Heart," as it reworks the idea of a heart ripped out of a victim's chest and hidden.

What is more, Caiano pushes the theme of the double to exasperated heights. Barbara Steele plays two characters who portray the two extremes of the female universe: Muriel is a ravenous black-haired adulteress, sexually uninhibited, who eventually reappears as a vengeful spirit; Jenny is a helpless blonde, inhibited and restless, the designated victim par excellence. Later on, when Muriel turns up as a ghost, her face is half-covered by the hair which hides her disfigured half—a striking image that symbolizes a yin and a yang, beauty and horror, in the same body, and which also recalls a famous art object: Alberto Giacometti's *Surrealist Table*, a 1933 sculpture which includes a disturbing female severed head, the face half-covered by her hair just like Steele's in Caiano film.

It is not the only unexpected surrealistic moment in the film, and it shows Caiano's accomplished direction, despite *Nightmare Castle* being shot in just eighteen days, under hasty circumstances. Jenny's dream—which features a bleeding plant, transfixed hearts kept in a glass case and a faceless man—is part *Blood and Black*

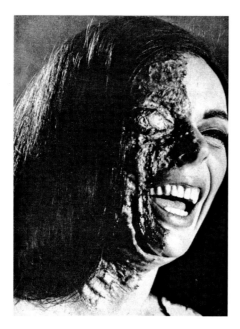

Barbara Steele as the disfigured face of vengeance from beyond the grave in *Nightmare Castle* **(courtesy S. I. Bianchi).**

Lace, part Magritte's famous painting *The Lovers*.

Another impressive idea, which unfortunately Caiano could not develop, regarded the use of color. "Initially the film had to be shot in black-and-white ... and red, but the costs were too high, so I had to abandon the idea," Caiano claimed, explaining that color would be used to great effect in the pounding hearts scene. Enzo Barboni's cinematography is another asset: "To save time, Barboni [...] turned on a 5000W lamp, took the lens out so as to get a scattered light, and put it down in a corner, in order to obtain the peculiar lighting you see in the film."[5] According to Caiano, Morricone's impressive main theme for the film, played by Bruno Nicolai, was recorded in a Roman church on a huge pipe organ.

Caiano, born in Rome (not Naples as some reference books state) in 1933, was the son of producer and distributor Carlo Caiano. After abandoning studies (classical philology and archaeology), Caiano tried to find his way into showbiz in the early '50s, as assistant director to Sergio Grieco. He debuted behind the camera a decade later with a number of sword-and-

sandal pictures before moving on to other genres. The year before directing *Nightmare Castle*, Caiano had helmed a Western, *Bullets Don't Argue* (*Le pistole non discutono*, 1964), starring Rod Cameron and produced by a company named Jolly Film. To cover costs for Caiano's film, Jolly set up another low-budget Western, starring an unknown American actor, Clint Eastwood: Sergio Leone's *A Fistful of Dollars*. The rest, as they say, is history.

Notes

1. Antonio Fabio Familiari, "Intervista a Mario Caiano," in Tentori and Cozzi, *Horror made in Italy*, p. 620.
2. Ibid.
3. Ibid.
4. A former journalist, De Agostini would direct three films, the latter being the Nazi erotic *Red Nights of the Gestapo* (*Le lunghe notti della Gestapo*, 1977).
5. Familiari, "Intervista a Mario Caiano," p. 621.

The Seventh Grave (*La settima tomba*)

D: Finney Cliff [Garibaldi Serra Caracciolo]. *S:* "based on a story by Edmond W. Carloff, Fredrich Mills"; *SC:* Edmond W. Carloff [Alessandro Santini], Fredrich Mills [Antonio Casale], Finney Cliff; *DOP:* Alfred Carbot [Aldo Greci] (B&W); *M:* Leopold Perez [Leopoldo Perez Bonsignore]; *E:* George Maryan [Mariano Arditi]; *PD:* Joseph Ranieri [Giuseppe Ranieri]; *AD:* Paul Sciamann [Antonio Casale]; *AC:* Maurice Flover [Mauro Bergamini]; *SO:* Peter Spad [Pietro Spadoni]; *SP:* Beniamin Curch [Beniamino Curcio]; *MU:* Mary Masterfive [Maria Mastrocinque]; *SS:* Lucy Brown [Isabella Piga]. *Cast:* Stephanie Nelly [Stefania Menchinelli] (Katy), Fernand Angels [Nando Angelini] (Elliot), Armand Warner [Armando Guarnieri] (Inspector Martin Wright/Sir Reginald Thorne), Kateryn Schous [Bruna Baini] (Mary, Jenkins' lover), John Anderson [Antonio Casale] (Jenkins), Germayne Gesny [Germana Dominici] (Betty), Richard Gillies [Ferruccio Viotti] (Pastor Crabbe), John Day [Giovanni Carpanelli a.k.a. Gianni Dei] (Fred, Jenkins' brother), Edward Barret [Calogero Reale] (Patrick), Gordon Mac Winter [Umberto Borsato] (Sir Percival), Jack Murphy [Francesco Molé] (Innkeeper), Robert Sullivan [Marco Kamm] (Stagecoach driver). *PROD:* Felice Falvo, Arturo Giorni, Alessandro Santini for F.G.S. International Pictures; *PM:* Edgard Blondell [Umberto Borsato]; *EP:* F. F. Sandall [Felice Falvo]; *PSe:* Martin Ross [Bruno Burani]; *PS:* Charles Renolds [Cesare Seritti]. *Country:* Italy. Filmed at Balsorano Castle. *Running time:* 77 min. (m. 2112); *Visa n:* 45276 (06.16.1965); *Rating:* v.m.14; *Release date:* 08.18.1965 (Italy). *Distribution:* Meyer Film (Regional); *Domestic gross:* unknown.

Scotland, nineteenth century. A group of strangers—including Jenkins and his brother, who come from America, a parish priest, a colonel and his daughter—are summoned to the Thorne family castle by a notary, Elliot, for the reading of the deceased Sir Reginald's will. Meanwhile, news spreads of an escaped patient from a nearby leper hospital. A huge fortune—the treasure of the infamous pirate Sir Francis Drake, Sir Reginald's ancestor—is believed to be hidden in the castle, and since one of the heirs, Katy, is a psychic, the others decide to conduct a séance in order to get in touch with Drake's spirit and locate the treasure's whereabouts. Soon, though, the caretaker is found hanged in the crypt, while Sir Reginald's body disappears from the crypt. Inspector Wright shows up to investigate, but more murders follow, as an unknown hand is dispatching the heirs one by one, while Katy is abducted. The culprit is Wright, who turns out to be none other than Sir Reginald, who staged his own death in order to continue his demented experiments...

A threadbare-looking coach—no doubt a prop borrowed from some Spaghetti Western set—rides along a country road. A totally incongruous on-screen line specifies: "Old Scotland." The coach stops by a suspiciously bogus sign, "Rooster Inn." The passengers ask for something to eat and some tea. "They look American," the innkeeper tells the waitress. "Bring'em an omelet with smoked bacon." The opening scenes for *The Seventh Grave* are like the sign on the entrance of Hell in Dante's *Inferno*: "Abandon all hope, ye who enter here." Hell, in this particular case, amounts to about seventy-seven minutes of a viewer's life—the price to be paid in order to savor one of Italian Gothic's most elusive titles.

As was commonplace in the frantic days of Italian genre cinema, the rise of a *filone* caused a number of surrogates to pop up like mushrooms in the woods after a rainstorm. And it was not uncommon to stumble upon inedible, if not poisonous, specimens: low-budget flicks, shot on a shoestring by semi-improvised filmmakers, financed by anonymous hit-and-run companies formed specifically for a single productive effort (and destined to bankruptcy—an easy way to avoid paying the creditors)—and intended for limited home circulation.

Even though the Gothic was not a huge

thread—a few dozen titles, compared to the hundreds of Spaghetti Westerns made after the success of Leone's *A Fistful of Dollars*—there were a few such examples. *The Seventh Grave* was produced by F.G.S. International Pictures, a company founded in December 1964 by three associates: Felice Falvo, Arturo Giorni and Alessandro Santini. The latter also wrote the story and screenplay together with director Garibaldi Serra Caracciolo and actor Antonio Casale, who also played one of the main roles (with a ridiculous blonde wig) and acted as assistant director, with three different aliases in order to "pump up" the credits.

Whereas Caracciolo remains some sort of a mystery, having apparently directed just this film and with no other credits nor information about him, both Santini and Casale were recurring names in the realm of genre cinema at its most dilapidated. A former production manager, Santini recycled himself as a filmmaker (of sorts) and directed five (very bad) films, including the Gothic horror oddity *La pelle sotto gli artigli*, 1975), starring Gordon Mitchell as a mad doctor. The slimy-looking Casale was an obscure character actor who appeared in Leone's *The Good, the Bad and the Ugly* (*Il buono, il brutto, il cattivo*, 1966), where he played Bill Carson, the dying man who tells Clint Eastwood the name on the tomb where the gold is buried, and *Duck You, Sucker!* (*Giù la testa*, 1971): he was renamed "Anthony Vernon" (a nod to Howard Vernon, no less!) by Alberto Cavallone, who promoted him as the leading man in a triptych which included *Le salamandre* (1968), *Dal nostro inviato a Copenaghen* (1970) and *Quickly, spari e baci a colazione* (1971). Casale's last screen credit was in Sergio Martino's 1977 Western *A Man Called Blade*.

Another "familiar" face in the cast was that of a very young "John Day" a.k.a. Gianni Dei, a habitué of such cinematic dreck as *Sex of the Witch* (*Il sesso della strega*, 1973), *Giallo a Venezia* (1979) and *Patrick Still Lives*: he plays Casale's younger brother, whose role consists in flirting with a maid in every scene he is in—until he is found dead in a coffin midway through, that is.

Rare Italian fotobusta for the little-seen Gothic oddity *The Seventh Grave* (author's collection).

Shot in just three weeks and a half at the unmistakable Balsorano castle—posing as the Scottish manor where the story takes place—and Olimpia Studios in Rome, between February and March 1965, *The Seventh Grave* cost just 40 million *lire* and disappeared into oblivion after a short theatrical run. A slightly more durable sign of its existence was the photonovel published in the notorious *Malia* series (issue 52, May 1965) just before its release. Although the opening credits display an English language title, it is quite unlikely Caracciolo's film ever went past the boundaries of the *Belpaese*.

In 1968 Fortunato Misiano's Romana Cinematografica, which bought the film after the producer's bankruptcy, vainly tried to obtain the subsidies granted for Italian productions by 1965's Corona law. The Ministerial commission unanimously rejected the application at first instance and on appeal, considering *The Seventh Grave* to be lacking the necessary requisites of "technical eligibility and sufficient artistic, cultural and spectacular qualities," as demanded by the law.

Which is hardly surprising, once seen the film.

The script haphazardly assembles a bunch of Gothic stereotypes around the story of a number of people gathered for the reading of a will (the title refers to the grave where the lord of the castle is buried) which might well be the long-lost treasure of Sir Francis Drake, the pirate (!), hidden somewhere in the manor. Caracciolo and his acolytes do not miss a cliché: the family crypt, a skeleton, spiritism, creaking doors, women in their nightgowns wandering through long dark halls, someone menacingly playing the piano in the middle of the night ... you name it. As for the plot, Santini & Co. clearly saw *The Cat and the Canary* (1927, Paul Leni) one too many times, and it shows, even though the thin story is padded with syrupy romantic interludes between Elliot the notary and Katy the psychic. As for the cast, well, the least said, the better.

If *The Seventh Grave* looks like an awful rendition of the typical "old dark house" thrillers, the leprous villain has something in common with Italian Gothic's mad doctors: once again, the emphasis is on blood transfusions. However, the delirious climax has nothing of the morbidity of Freda's and Caiano's films, but borders on the downright absurd.

If originality is not the film's main asset, what really stands out about *The Seventh Grave* is its overall amateurishness. For one thing, Caracciolo never heard about the 180 degree rule, nor did the script girl have any idea of what continuity means, as cuts often do not match. And it is not over yet. The sets are slapdash, the lighting is passable at best, the dialogue abounds with absurdly inane lines, such as "Now we're going to visit the crypt. There are some wonderful graves in it!"

Abandon all hope, indeed.

Terror-Creatures from the Grave
(5 tombe per un medium)

D: Ralph Zucker [actually Domenico Massimo Pupillo, with additional scenes by Ralph Zucker]. *S and SC:* Robert Nathan [Roberto Natale], Robin McLorin [Romano Migliorini] (*U.S. version—"inspired by Edgar Allan Poe"*); *DOP:* Charles Brown [Carlo Di Palma] (B&W); *M:* Aldo Piga (*U.S. version—"Main theme by Ralph Zucker"*); *E:* Robert Ardis [Mariano Arditi]; *AE:* Mary Andrews; *PD:* Frank Small [Gabriele Crisanti]; *CO:* Serge Selig [Sergio Selli]; *AD:* Nick Berger [Enrico Bergier]; *C:* Albert Farrow [Alberto Spagnoli]; *AC:* Theodore Kelly [Dante Di Palma]; *SO:* Geoffrey Sellers [Goffredo Salvatori]; *MU:* Bud Dexter [Vittorio Biseo]; *SS:* Hilda Wendrow [Ilde Musso] (*English version—Adaptation:* Ruth Carter, Cesare Mancini). *Cast:* Barbara Steele (Clio Hauff), Walter Brandi [Walter Bigari] (Albert Kovacs), Marylin Mitchell [Mirella Maravidi] (Corinna Hauff), Alfred Rice [Alfredo Rizzo] (Dr. Nemek), Richard Garrett [Riccardo Garrone] (Joseph Morgan), Alan Collins [Luciano Pigozzi] (Kurt, the servant), Edward Bell [Ennio Balbo] (Oskar Stinner), Stephen Robinson [Ignazio Dolce], Lewis Czerny [Lucio Zarini], Peter Sarto [Pietro Sartori], Armand Garner [Armando Guarnieri], Tilde Till [Tilde Dall'Aglio] (Louise), René Wolfe [Renato Lupi]. *PROD:* Frank Merle [Francesco Merli], Ralph Zucker, Massimo Pupillo for M.B.S. Cinematografica, G.I.A. Cinematografica, International Entertainment Corp.; *EP:* J. R. Coolidge, Felix C. Ziffer; *PSe:* Lewis Lawrence. *Country:* Italy/ U.S.A.. Filmed at Castel Fusano (Rome). *Running time:* 87 min. (m. 2444); Visa n: 45219 (06.16. 1965); *Rating:* V.M.18; *Release dates:* 06.23.1965 (Italy); 05.16.1967 (U.S.A.). *Distribution:* Selecta

(Italy, Regional); Pacemaker Pictures (U.S.A.); *Domestic gross:* 89,000,000 lire. *Also known as:* Cemetery of the Living Dead, Coffin of Terror, Five Graves for a Medium, Le Cimetière des morts vivants, Cimetière pour morts vivants, Cinq tombes pour un médium (France). *Home video:* Alpha Video (DVD, U.S.A.), East West Entertainment (DVD, U.S.A.—double feature w/ *The Long Hair of Death*), Sinister (DVD, Italy).

Young attorney Albert Kovacs is summoned to the castle of Dr. Jeronimusch Hauff, to settle the estate of its recently deceased owner. There, he finds out that Hauff was a necromancer, who was able to evoke the souls of ancient plague victims. Soon the occupants of the castle begin to die one by one. Kovacs also discovers that Hauff is taking revenge from beyond the grave on those who murdered him, including his unfaithful wife, Clio, through the spirits of invisible plague spreaders. Kovacs and Hauff's daughter Corinne try to escape the deadly curse...

The golden age of Italian horror film marked the arrival in our country of curious individuals in search of fortune like gold diggers in the Far West that was the movie industry of the time. Only, the most important thing was not to grab a piece of land but to get a distribution contract.

That was the case with Ralph Zucker (1920–1982), an American citizen of Jewish origin who had debuted in the 1950s in many roles on the big and small screen (child actor, editor, assistant, associate producer and producer), and who in 1958 tried his luck in Italy. Zucker's name is usually associated with a couple of horror flicks co-produced by the company M.C.S. and starring Walter Bigari (a.k.a. Walter Brandi), *5 tombe per un medium* and *Il boia scarlatto*, both released in Italy in 1965.

Set in the early twentieth century—in the first scenes we are treated to the sight of an early motor vehicle—*5 tombe per un medium* benefits from Barbara Steele's presence as well as an impressive setting—the fascinating Castle Chigi in Castel Fusano, near Rome, which poses as the film's main location. Then, there is Carlo Di Palma's luscious black-and-white cinematography, which gives it a much richer look than expected and makes it one of the most atmospheric Italian horror films.[1] Yet *5 tombe per un*

Barbara Steele's bubblebath scene in *Terror-Creatures from the Grave* **(courtesy S. I. Bianchi).**

medium is far less ambiguous than its contemporaries in the portrayal of the main characters: Steele is a rather bland villainess compared to her other Italian efforts of the period, while Brandi, as the young hero Kovacs, is simply too inept an actor to be convincing in a role that would have required a more impressive screen presence.

Besides the aforementioned references, however, what is interesting in the story is that it is yet another take on the theme of marital infidelity and murder, as the ghost of a man betrayed and murdered by his unfaithful wife seeks revenge from beyond the grave (a sort of reversal of Margheriti's *The Long Hair of Death*). Also worth noting is that Hauff's curse strikes the guilty and the innocent alike: Kovacs as well as the dead man's daughter Corinne (Mirella Maravidi) are involved in the vengeance of the invisible zombies and almost meet their end together with the real culprits. Fire as an element of purification is replaced for once by water, with a salvific final thunderstorm, evoked

by a child's nursery rhyme which, albeit naive ("Remember pure water, pure water will save you"), predates the riddle as a typical *giallo* element. Last but not least, as with other Italian Gothic films of the period, transgression goes as far as censorship allowed: Maravidi's breast is briefly exposed, while Steele has a show-stopping bubblebath scene with water rising just above her nipples.

Despite being a modest success in Italy, *5 tombe per un medium* (literally, *Five Graves for a Medium*, a title which sounds more apt for a Western) was perhaps one of the most popular Italian horror films of the decade abroad, as it was released in a number of different versions for the foreign markets. The U.S. version, entitled *Terror-Creatures from the Grave*, claimed in the credits a non-existent "inspiration" from the tales of Edgar Allan Poe—a detail absent in the other prints. Actually, the script by "Robert Nathan" and "Robin McLorin" (Roberto Natale and Romano Migliorini) gathered a number of typical Gothic elements with curious literary and cinematic references. The "terror creatures" of the U.S. title are the invisible spirits of *monatti*, the servants who in times of plague had to carry away the dead on a handcart in the Middle Ages—a detail perhaps inspired by Alessandro Manzoni's novel *The Betrothed*—and were commonly considered as plague spreaders themselves. The invisible creatures mark their victims with red stains on their faces, like in Corman's *The Masque of the Red Death*, while the sound of the wagon which carries away the dead is a nod to Victor Sjöström's *The Phantom Carriage* (*Körkarlen*, 1921), revisited in a horror key.

The American cut (which opened in Maryland in May 1967 and circulated on a double-bill with Pupillo's *Bloody Pit of Horror*) was littered with gory details that cannot be found in the other versions. The French and Italian cuts begin in the office of notary Morgan (Riccardo Garrone): there, after the notary leaves, his assistant Kovacs (Brandi) receives a letter from Dr. Jeronimusch Hauff, who beckons him to his villa to write his will. On the other hand, *Terror-Creatures from the Grave* opens with a totally different prologue in which a man is frightened by a mysterious presence (a hand appears from behind a window: we will later find out it is one of the *monatti* evoked by the deceased Hauff), leaves his home at night, crosses a deserted square and enters a stable to saddle a horse. The crazed animal kicks the man to death, and the scene ends with a crude zoom in on a close-up of the victim's disfigured face, with the gruesome detail of his partially enucleated left eye.

Later on in the U.S. print, the bizarre suicide of the wheelchair-bound Stinel (Ennio Balbo)—who inserts a sword in a chest of drawers so that the blade protrudes forward, and then throws himself against it on his wheelchair—offers the audience the sight of the dead body's exposed intestines seeping out of his stomach. It is a sop to keep up with the brutality exhibited by Herschell Gordon Lewis' films, which revolutionized the horror genre and shocked the drive-in crowd. What is more, *Terror-Creatures from the Grave* also features the bizarre detail of the purulent hand grabbing hold of Stinel's chair and pulling it backwards. No such thing can be found in the French version, in which Stinel simply hangs himself (as originally envisioned in the script).[2]

The U.S. cut for *Terror-Creatures from the Grave* is also surprising from another point of view: the added scenes emphasize the similarities—impossible to deny, since the scripts were conceived by the same writers—with Mario Bava's *Kill, Baby...Kill!* Tim Lucas underlined the analogy between Stinel's suicide and that of Nadine (Micaela Esdra),[3] who in Bava's film impales her throat on a pointed candlestick. Furthermore, both screenplays are based on a common notion: a vengeance from beyond the grave which strikes one by one those responsible for a murder (Hauff's killing in *Terror-Creatures from the Grave*) or a violent death (Melissa Graps bleeding to death in *Kill, Baby...Kill!*). The two films also employ the same trick to evoke ghosts on screen, as shown by the American prologue with the close-up of a hand (which in the first film belongs to the plague spreader, in Bava's to Melissa) appearing in silhouette behind a glass door, with an identical zoom in to emphasize the event.

An issue long unresolved concerned the identity of the man behind the camera for the film. The Italian credits for *5 tombe per un medium* claim it to be "a film directed by Ralph Zucker," and for a long period Zucker and Massimo Pupillo were thought to be the same person, in one of the typical cases of Italian filmmakers picking up Anglicized names. In a detailed issue published in *Video Watchdog* in 1991,[4] in which he examined the differences between various versions of the film, Alan Upchurch credited the direction to the sole Zucker, based on an interview with Walter Brandi published several years earlier on the French fanzine *Ciné Zine Zone*, in which the actor stated: "Zucker and Pupillo are two different persons. Zucker was a Jew, I don't remember whether American or English. He shot *5 tombe per un medium* and played a role in *Il boia scarlatto*."[5]

When interviewed by French film historian Lucas Balbo a few years later, though, Pupillo—whom some reference books claimed had died in 1982, clearly mistaking him with Zucker—

stated that he let Zucker be credited as director out of indifference towards the results: "Because I didn't care about the film, I let the producer, Ralph Zucker, take the credit. Also we made a deal with M.B.C. for two films—*Terror-Creatures from the Grave* and *Bloody Pit of Horror*—and we didn't want to have the same name on both films. So to please him, I let him sign *Terror-Creatures* and put my name on *Bloody Pit*.... I didn't give a fuck."[6]

The film's co-scriptwriter Roberto Natale confirmed Pupillo to be the director, even though he did not have kind words for him as a film-maker, as he complained about the awkwardness with which he had put on screen some of the script's most disturbing scenes. "There were effects that Pupillo "burned," so to speak. Let me tell you one: you know that, when the *monatti* wagon passes in the film, water dries up ... well, we had Walter Brandi entering a dark room with a candle and hearing a weird noise, *cick ciack, cick ciack*.... He didn't understand, then he turned suddenly, scared, and saw this empty fish tank—since the water was drying up—with just a few goldfish wriggling, half-dead. But if the director frames an establishing shot of someone who enters the room where you can already see the tank and the fish ... well, the story ends, you've ruined the surprise."[7]

Given Bigari's familiarity with both Zucker and Pupillo, the actor's statement that Zucker alone directed the film remains puzzling. The truth lies somewhere in the middle: Zucker actually directed the most violent scenes for the foreign markets, such as the prologue in the U.S. version and the suicide of the wheelchair-bound usurer, in order to tread on the gore and get a more profitable product. Pupillo told Lucas Balbo that Zucker filmed these scenes without him knowing,[8] but this seems highly unlikely, given that Pupillo would claim in another interview: "I never liked violent scenes. In the script, the usurer's suicide was handled fairy well, with the wagon wheel squeaking and the man hanging himself. Yet Zucker wanted something more violent, so I told him "You shoot that one!" So he filmed the bloodiest scene for the foreign market."[9]

However, Pupillo himself boasted about the imaginative special effects included in the original version. "In *Terror-Creatures*, when I needed a thumping heart, I prepared the effect myself without the aid of any specialist. First I bought a pig's heart and a Japanese toy for a dollar. It was a little doll with a rubber ball hand-pump connected to it. When you squeezed the rubber ball, the doll jumped. I inserted this mechanism into the pig heart and it worked perfectly. *Thump, thump. Thump.* The heart would beat as soon as you squeezed the pump." Another scene featured severed hands on display in glass jars under a cabinet, which in the film's climax start moving on their own: actually, the result was reminiscent of the TV series *The Addams Family*. Pupillo, however, explained: "The key special effects scene featured six severed hands which had to move at a precise time. [...] I had the cabinet designed so that six people wearing latex hands could sit behind and protrude their hands through holes. The effect was very successful, and the six people had a lot of fun asking each other to scratch their heads. That's part of the creativity I like in those films. You had to invent a new trick every day."[10]

As for working with Barbara Steele, Pupillo revealed that at first he and his star did not get along at all. "For the first three days of shooting our relationship was quite awful. My cameraman was a young guy named Carlo Di Palma, and Steele's attitude on the set was really disgusting. She posed at the great actress who deigned to do a horror movie. On the fourth day I decided I had had enough and faced her in front of the whole crew. I told her she had not been called to play Shakespeare, but to make a horror film, she had read the script and signed the contract, and I was expecting the utmost cooperation on her part. From then on she was adorable, for the rest of the shooting."[11]

Domenico Massimo Pupillo (born in 1922 in Rodi Garganico, Puglia: most reference books don't even consider his first name[12]) had started his career in movies in the late 1930s through his acquaintance with Fernandel as Marcel Pagnol's assistant. He claimed to have directed about 250 shorts before shooting *Gli amici dell'isola* (1961), a feature film set in Sardinia with non-professional actors. After *Terror-Creatures from the Grave* he would go on to make two more horror films in a row, *Bloody Pit of Horror* and *La vendetta di Lady Morgan*, both also dated 1965.

On the other hand, Zucker never directed another picture, merely covering production roles in a handful of scarcely interesting films, and mostly taking care of the distribution: his name would pop up again a decade later as executive producer on *The Devil's Wedding Night* (*Il plenilunio delle vergini*, 1973, by Luigi Batzella, with a little uncredited help from Aristide Massaccesi), scripted and produced by Bigari.

Notes

1. The talented Carlo Di Palma (1925–2004) was a frequent collaborator of Michelangelo Antonioni, for whom he had conceived the extraordinary desaturated color palette of *Red Desert* (*Deserto rosso*, 1964). Di Palma would also be Antonioni's d.o.p. on 1966's *Blow-Up* and 1982's *Identificazione di una donna*. He also worked with Mario Monicelli and other important Italian filmmakers. In the 1980s, starting with *Hannah and her Sisters* (1986), he became Woody Allen's favorite d.o.p., working on twelve of his films. Di Palma also directed three movies in the 1970s, all starring Monica Vitti, then his partner in life.
2. It gets even more confused when one compares the various prints circulating on DVD and DVD-r in the States. The disc released by Something Weird Video clocks in at 77:30 and includes a very brief nude (courtesy of Mirella Maravidi) absent in the copy released by Sinister Cinema, which on the other hand is over 4 minutes longer (81:4) because of a dialogue scene not included in the SWV version. The Italian videocassette (released in 1999 by Shendene & Moizzi) is another weird hybrid, which includes the same prologue as the French version *and* Stinel's gruesome suicide-by-sword.
3. Lucas, *Mario Bava*, p. 676.
4. Alan Upchurch, "Who Is Ralph Zucker?," *Video Watchdog* 7, September/October 1991.
5. Carlo Piazza, "Walter Brandi—Entretien avec la star du cinéma d'épouvante italien," *Ciné-Zine-Zone* 30, August 1986, p. 10.
6. Lucas Balbo, "I Talked with a Zombie: The Forgotten Horrors of Massimo Pupillo," in Stefan Jaworzyn, ed., *Shock: The Essential Guide to Exploitation Cinema* (London: Titan, 1996), p. 19. Actually the company's name is not M.B.C. but M.B.S. Cinematografica. The company, based in Rome, co-produced the film with another Roman company, G.I.A., and the New York–based International Entertainment Corporation.
7. Davide Pulici, "Intervista allo sceneggiatore Roberto Natale," included in the booklet of the Italian VHS *5 tombe per un medium*.
8. See *Mondo Pupillo—Une conversation avec Massimo Pupillo*.
9. Piselli, Morlocchi and Bruschini, *Bizarre sinema!* p. 96.

10. Balbo, "I Talked with a Zombie," p. 19.
11. 1993 radio interview with Italian film historian Fabio Melelli, included as an extra in the Italian DVD of *5 tombe per un medium*.
12. Most reference books and websites (including IMDb) carry incorrect information about Pupillo's date and place of birth.

La vendetta di Lady Morgan

D: Max Hunter [Domenico Massimo Pupillo]. *S:* Edward Duncan; *SC:* Jean Grimaud [Gianni Grimaldi]; *DOP:* Dan Troy [Oberdan Troiani] (B&W); *M:* Peter O'Milian [Piero Umiliani] (Ed. C.A.M.); *E:* Robert Ardis [Mariano Arditi]; *PD:* Hugh Danger [Ugo Pericoli]; *AD:* Dean Sweet; *C:* Joe Lee; *AC:* Michael Parish; *SO:* Alex Durby; *MU:* Max Justice [Massimo Giustini]; *SS:* Patricia Lane. *Cast:* Gordon Mitchell (Roger), Erika Blanc [Enrica Bianchi Colombatto] (Lilian), Paul Muller (Sir Harald Morgan), Barbara Nelly [Nelli] (Lady Susan Morgan), Michael Forain (Pierre Brissac), Carlo Kechler (Sir Neville Blackhouse), Edith Mac Goven (Terry). *PROD:* Peter Jordan [Franco Belotti] for Morgan Film; *PM:* Thomas Newton; *PS:* Adam Aries. *Country:* Italy. Filmed at Castello Chigi in Castel Fusano (Rome). *Running time:* 88 min. (m. 2465); *Visa n:* 45744 (10.01.1965); *Rating:* V.M.14; *Release date:* 12.16.1965 (Italy). *Distribution:* I.N.D.I.E.F.; *Domestic gross:* 61,000,000 lire. *Also known as:* *Das folterhaus der Lady Morgan* (West Germany, 10.27.1967), *La Vengeance de Lady Morgan* (France). *Home video:* Artus (DVD, France).

Young Susan Morgan, the niece of the wealthy Sir Neville Blackhouse, is about to marry a French architect, Pierre Brissac. On a boat trip to England, however, the young man is cast into the sea: convinced that Pierre is dead, Susan decides to marry the ambiguous Sir Harald. The marriage turns out to be hell for the heiress, because Harald is planning to get rid of his wife and inherit her wealth together with his greedy lover Lilian, Susan's housekeeper, and Roger the butler. Driven to madness, Susan kills herself by jumping off the castle tower. It turns out Pierre has survived, though he suffers from amnesia: after regaining his memory he rushes to Blackhouse castle, only to meet Susan's ghost and learn her sad story. After dying, Susan avenged herself by pushing her three tormentors to death: the assassins have become bloodthirsty vampires. Susan tries to help Pierre escape death at the hands of the undead, but to no avail...

Domenico Massimo Pupillo's third and last horror film, *La vendetta di Lady Morgan*—originally to be titled *La vendetta di Lady Black-*

Italian poster for *La vendetta di Lady Morgan* **(author's collection).**

melodramatic period *feuilleton* with Gothic overtones, as the naive heiress Susan (Barbara Nelli) is seduced, married and driven to madness by her unscrupulous husband (the slimy as ever Paul Muller), who plans to get his hands on the inheritance with his concubine housekeeper (Erika Blanc, in a totally opposite role to the one she would play in Bava's *Kill, Baby...Kill!*). The supernatural angle of the story comes to the fore much later in the film, and allows for a few surprises, amidst a bunch of half-baked or laughable bits: among the latter must be counted the scene where the butler (Gordon Mitchell) descends into the crypt to visit Susan's uncle, who has been imprisoned in the subterranean unbeknownst to his niece, and administers him a good dose of whipping.

The contorted script by Gianni Grimaldi, hiding under his customary Jean Grimaud pseudonym, cannibalizes ideas from *Castle of Blood*: when Susan's former fiancé Pierre (Michael Forain) arrives at the manor—Castle Chigi in Castel Fusano, near Rome, seen also in *Terror-Creatures from the Grave* and later in Fernando di Leo's *Slaughter Hotel* (*La bestia uccide a sangue freddo*, 1971) among others—the woman's specter helps him against the deadly trio formed by Lady Morgan's husband, the housekeeper and the butler, who have turned into the undead. As in Margheriti's film, the ghosts in *La vendetta di Lady Morgan* are far from the traditional Gothic canon. These are tangible presences, apparently impossible to tell from living persons ... so much so that Pierre can finally make love to Susan, in one of Italian

house—is by no means the best, but perhaps the most peculiar of the trio, and undoubtedly the closest to Italian Gothic's most peculiar characteristics.

The first half is neither more nor less than a

Gothic's typical bouts of necrophiliac eroticism. It is not that normality has been broken, anyway: perhaps it never existed in the first place.

As in *Castle of Blood*, the ghosts feed on blood to maintain their undead state: in a surprisingly effective scene Pupillo has Paul Muller, Erika Blanc and Gordon Mitchell throw themselves on the floor to greedily lick the blood trickled from Pierre's wound, thus predating both Udo Kier in Paul Morrissey's *Blood for Dracula* (1973) and the octogenarian Federico Luppi in Guillermo del Toro's *Cronos* (1992).

The ending is unexpectedly grim and downbeat, and gives the film an overall sense of dilapidation and doom. Innocent people once again pay for faults they did not commit, in a punishing fury that knows no limit or rest.

Unlike Pupillo's previous horror films, *La vendetta di Lady Morgan* was not distributed overseas, but only released theatrically in Germany in 1967. As Pupillo commented, "I wasn't interested in making any more horror films and I turned down a lot of propositions. I started in the horror genre because I wanted to get out of documentaries, I wanted to enter the commercial market. In Italy, when you do a certain type of film, you become labelled and you can't do anything else. I remember one day, a producer called me to do a film only because the other producers told him he had to get either Mario Bava or me. When I understood this, I felt dead."[1]

Pupillo's later directorial output was scarce: the western *Django Kills Softly* (*Bill il taciturno*, 1967) and *Love: The Great Unknown* (*L'amore, questo sconosciuto*, 1969), a *mondo*[2] described as a "documentary investigation into sexual deviation, illustrating various aspects of voyeurism, sadism and homosexuality, through sex in the cinema and advertising," whose foreign versions included, according to Pupillo himself, additional hardcore footage shot by the brother of d.o.p. Angelo Filippini.

Disgusted, in his own words, by this type of cinema, Pupillo turned to television, where he would work for the next decade. His last feature was 1981's *Sa Jana*, shot in Sardinia with non-professional actors, which marked a return of sorts to the director's first documentary films. According to Merrill Aldighieri and Lucas Balbo's documentary *Mondo Pupillo—Une conversation avec Massimo Pupillo*, it is likely that Domenico Massimo Pupillo passed away on December 29, 1999—yet no evidence has been found to confirm this so far.

Notes

1. Balbo, "I Talked with a Zombie," p. 20.
2. Pupillo also co-wrote a few *mondo* films: *Primitive Love* (*L'amore primitivo*, 1964) and the infamous *Sweden: Heaven and Hell* (*Svezia inferno e paradiso*, 1967), both directed by Luigi Scattini, and *Taboos of the World* (*I tabù*, 1963) by Romolo Marcellini.

1966

An Angel for Satan (Un angelo per Satana)

D: Camillo Mastrocinque. *S:* based on a novel by Luigi Emmanuele; *SC:* Giuseppe Mangione, Camillo Mastrocinque; *DOP:* Giuseppe Aquari (B&W); *M:* Francesco De Masi; *E:* Gisa Radicchi Levi; *AE:* Marina Sacco; *ArtD:* Alberto Boccianti; *C:* Emilio Giannini; *APD:* Giuseppe Ranieri; *AD:* Stefano Rolla, Fabrizio Gianni; *C:* Giorgio Desideri; *SD:* Camillo Del Signore; *SO:* Fiorenzo Magli; *SS:* Maria Luisa Rosen; *SE:* Antonio Ricci; *MU:* Efrade Titi, Giovanni Morosi; *Hair:* Fausto De Lisio, Giancarlo Malagoli. *Cast:* Barbara Steele (Harriet Montebruno/Belinda), Anthony Steffen [Antonio De Teffé] (Roberto Merigi), Ursula Davis [Pier Anna Quaglia] (Rita), Aldo Berti (Victor), Maureen Melrose [Marina Berti] (Ilda), Vassili Karamenisis (Dario, the teacher), Mario Brega (Carlo Lionesi), Betty Delon, Claudio Gora (Count Montebruno), Halina Zalewska, Antonio Corevi, Livia Rossetti, Antonio Acqua (Gardener), Giovanna Lenzi. *PROD:* Liliana Biancini for Discobolo Film (Rome); *GM:* Giuliano Simonetti; *PS:* Augusto Dolfi; *PSe:* Luigi Anastasi; *PSeA:* Guglielmo Simonetti. *Country:* Italy. Filmed in Lake Bracciano and at Villa Miani (Rome). *Running time:* 90 min. (m. 2522); Visa n: 46866 (04.13.1966); *Rating:* V.M.18; *Release date:* 05.04. 1966 (Italy). *Distribution:* Discobolo Film (Italy, regional); *Domestic gross:* 87,000,000 lire. *Also known as: Un Ange pour Satan* (France, 05.27.1967), *Ein Engel für den Teufel* (West Germany). *Home video:* Midnight Choir (DVD, U.S.A.—double feature w/ *The Long Hair of Death*), Sinister Film (DVD, Italy).

Sculptor Roberto Merighi arrives at a small village, where he has been summoned by the local lord of the castle, Count Montebruno, to restore a statue recovered from the bottom of the nearby lake. According to a legend spread by the superstitious villagers, the statue—which portrays the beautiful Belinda, the Count's ancestress—is believed to bring evil and damnation upon the place. Even though Roberto and Montebruno are skeptical to say the least, the curse soon starts to take effect, or so it seems. The boatmen who accompanied Roberto drown in the lake, while Harriet, the Count's young and beautiful niece who returned to the village after 15 years, is seemingly possessed by the vengeful spirit of Belinda, whom she highly resembles. Harriet seduces her maid Rita, school teacher Dario, a strongman named Carlos and even Victor, the village idiot, leading them to suicide, murder and rape. However, as Roberto finds out, the truth behind Harriet's inexplicable metamorphosis is not supernatural, but the result of a diabolical family plot...

Camillo Mastrocinque's second Gothic horror film in a row is a sort of pulp reworking of Antonio Fogazzaro's novel *Malombra*, which had already been brought to the screen in 1917 by Carmine Gallone and, most impressively, in 1942 by Mario Soldati. The beginning, in which Roberto (Anthony Steffen) arrives by boat, openly echoes the opening of Soldati's film, with Marina di Malombra's arrival to the large and lonely mansion on Lake Como, where her uncle will keep her segregated until the marriage of convenience that has been set up for her.[1]

Other elements seem to have been borrowed from Fogazzaro's novel: a lonely orphan, Harriet (Barbara Steele), a domineering uncle (Claudio Gora), and the spirit of an ancestress whose seemingly supernatural influence causes the heroine's character to abruptly change. Since this is a Gothic horror film, all is declined according to the *filone*'s staples, starting with the *doppelgänger*: Harriet discovers that she is a dead ringer for her ancestress Belinda, whose statue has been fished out of the lake and is being restored by Roberto. The statue itself is an impressive plot element—a variation on the portrait as a remnant of a past evil as seen in *Black Sunday* and *Terror in the Crypt* among others, which also points out at another possi-

ble literary influence, Prosper Mérimée's *La Vénus d'Ille*, later turned into a TV film by Mario and Lamberto Bava (*La Venere d'Ille*, 1978).

Harriet's transformation manifests itself with a sudden sexual aggressiveness, which turns the demure damsel into a nymphomaniac predator, ready to seduce whoever crosses her path, either man or woman. This heightens the typical dichotomy of the Eternal feminine, here incarnated in a single character with a dual personality. Harriet's demeanor changes from scene to scene, dramatically and unpredictably: to quote the Duke of Mantua's famous cynical *aria* in Giuseppe Verdi's *Rigoletto*, "La donna è mobile / qual piuma al vento, / muta d'accento / e di pensiero" ("Woman is fickle / like a feather in the wind, / she changes in voice / and in thought").

Mastrocinque took the seduction scenes as far as censorship of the time allowed, helped by Steele's magnetic screen presence. Here, Harriet becomes the embodiment of woman as a destructive, apocalyptic force—an almost supernatural entity who brings the opposite sex to ruin. She pushes one man to suicide, turns another into a sex maniac and, most significantly, leads a husband and father to burn his whole family alive, in a horrific take on the cliché of woman as a family destroyer as seen in many 1950s melodramas.

In another memorable sequence Harriet faces a brawny villager played by Mario Brega (a recurrent, unmistakable presence in Sergio Leone's westerns and one of Italy's most popular character actors in the '80s due to his work in Carlo Verdone's comedies) and literally has him on her knees. With a whip in hand and a wicked smile, Steele looks like an eighteenth century dominatrix, and the overall atmosphere has a curious resemblance to Tony Richardson's outstanding Jean Genet adaptation, *Mademoiselle* (1966).

Such moments indicate how the Gothic was already a thing of the past, as *An Angel for Satan* pushes the pedal of eroticism and leaves the macabre largely unexplored. The denouement even reveals the supernatural curse to be only the cover for a decidedly earthy, if awkwardly explained, intrigue: as in Freda's diptych *The*

Horrible Dr. Hichcock and *The Ghost*, Satan is much closer than anyone might think and assumes human forms—another sign that the thriller genre was gradually catching on. Yet, in an interesting sting in the tail, even the villain turns out to be manipulated by a woman. Actually, any male character in the film—whether it be the romantic young hero Roberto, the fragile intellectual Dario (Vassili Karis), the rude peasant or the ambiguous Count—is at the mercy of the weaker sex, in a testament to the predominance of the feminine in Italian Gothic.

Even though the script does not fully explore its potential and the pacing drags a little bit, there are a number of strong moments, such as Brega's seduction as well as the dramatic ending, which also vaguely recalls *La Venus d'Ille*. The regional Italian setting—another nod to *Malombra*, perhaps?—is also noteworthy,[2] with its mixture of superstition, morbidity and ignorance. For a director who approached the genre out of necessity, Mastrocinque's direction is surprisingly effective at times—even though a large merit must be given to Giuseppe Aquari's fascinating black-and-white cinematography.

An Angel for Satan would be Mastrocinque's last effort within the Gothic: he would direct three more feature films before his demise in 1969. It was also Barbara Steele's last Italian horror film: that year she also "starred" in Michael Reeves' *The She Beast*, which was shot in Italy and was released in the country the following year. The Brit actress temporarily abandoned show biz after her marriage to screenwriter James Poe—she would return to acting in Jonathan Demme's *Caged Heat* (1974). Steele was again directed by an Italian filmmaker in 2012, when she starred in Gionata Zarantonello's disturbing psycho-thriller *The Butterfly Room*, also featuring Ray Wise, Camille Keaton and Adrienne King.

Notes

1. Incidentally, the slightly transcendental opening image of the hero arriving by boat, already seen in *Mill of the Stone Women*, would also be featured in Pupi Avati's outstanding *The House with the Laughing Windows*.
2. As usual, the setting is a mosaic of different locations, including the familiar-looking Villa Miani (a recurring sight in Italian post-war cinema) posing for Count Montebruno's mansion by the lake—whereas in reality it is not even close to one, being located on the Monte Mario hill in Rome.

But You Were Dead (*La lunga notte di Veronique*)

D: Gianni Vernuccio. *S:* Gianni Vernuccio; *SC:* Enzo Ferraris; *DOP:* Gianni Vernuccio (Eastmancolor); *M:* Giorgio Gaslini (*La ballata di Veronique* sung by Paki & Paki); *E:* Gianni Vernuccio; *ArtD:* Enrico Tovaglieri; *CO:* Giorgio Di Dauli; *SO:* Giovanni Pegoraro; *C:* Alberto Marrama; *AC:* Carlo Petriccioli; *MU:* Gioi Ardessi; *SP:* Mario Coppini; *LT:* Carlo Di Gregorio; *El:* Angelo Marzullo. *Cast:* Alba Rigazzi (Veronica/Veronique D'Ambressac), Alex Morrison [Sandro Luporini] (Giovanni Bernardi/Alberto Anselmi/Young Marco Anselmi), Walter Pozzi (Count Marco Anselmi), Cristina Gaioni (Maria Ferrario, Giovanni's mother), Gianni Rubens, Maria Ardizzone (Denise, the housekeeper), Anna Maria Aveta, Toni Bellani, Egidio Casolari, Licia Lombardi (Nun), Charlie Polesky, Lia Reiner, Marco Righini, Dante Trazzi. *PROD:* Gianni Vernuccio for Mercurfin Italiana; *GM:* Oscar Righini; *PM:* Antonio Bellani; *PSe:* Ivo Gioio. *Country:* Ital. Filmed at Icet-De Paolis Studios (Milan). *Running time:* 91 min. (m. 2700); Visa n: 47648 (09.03.1966); *Rating:* V.M.18; *Release date:* 10.01.1966 (Italy). *Distribution:* Mercurfin (Italy, regional); *Domestic gross:* 61,000,000 lire. *Also known as:* *La longue nuit de Véronique* (France), *Véronique la morte-vivante* (Canada). *Home video:* Cosmo Video (VHS, Italy).

At the hospital where his mother and his alleged father have died after a car accident, Giovanni Bernardi learns from a nurse who collected the woman's last will that the truth about his past lies at Count Marco Anselmi's villa. After a somewhat cold initial reception, the Count invites Giovanni to stay and asks to be called "grandfather." Giovanni learns that his mother, the caretaker's daughter, was the Count's son Alberto's lover, and that he is actually Anselmi's nephew. Staying at the villa, Giovanni is met with hostility by the housekeeper, who eventually becomes his lover: however, he often meets a beautiful strange girl, Veronica, with whom he falls in love. Veronica, though, is actually a ghost. One night Giovanni meets her in the greenhouse, where he ends up killing himself. It turns out that Veronique was the Count's young cousin: when Veronique had been set to marry another man, she and Marco had forged a suicide pact, which only Veronique fulfilled. As the elderly Count now realizes, the events have been a punishment of his own past guilt...

One of the last examples of the Gothic genre—albeit a *sui generis* one—to emerge on the screen in the mid–Sixties, Gianni Vernuccio's *La lunga notte di Veronique* ("Veronique's Long Night," released in the United Kingdom under the title *But You Were Dead*, which gave away the film's point from the start) was a definitely odd sidenote to the by then dying *filone*.

Born in Cairo, Egypt, in 1918, director Gianni Vernuccio moved back to Italy and became an editor at Italy's Istituto Luce: in 1945 he and Massimo Dallamano shot the harrowing images of the bodies of Benito Mussolini and other Fascist hierarchs hung upside down at Piazzale Loreto in Milan. *La lunga notte di Veronique* was the penultimate film in a body of work that counted 15 titles: Vernuccio's previous film, an adaptation of Dino Buzzati's novel *Un amore* (1965), was his best received work by the critics. However, in the mid-to-late 1960s Vernuccio worked mainly for television, as a director of television commercials for *Carosello*.

Financed by a small Milan-based production company, Mercurfin, and filmed entirely in Lombardy, north of the river Po, with a largely unknown cast,[1] *La lunga notte di Veronique* had a marginal distribution in Italy and grossed just over 60 million *lire*. Although marketed as a horror film of sorts, with a tagline stating "Ai margini dell'incubo, in una realtà presente e tangibile torna inesorabile il passato" (At the edge of nightmare, the inexorable past returns in a present and tangible reality"), Vernuccio's film was not interested in the mechanics of fear that were typical of the genre. The director aimed at a supernatural melodrama and rejected any horrific element: therefore, the plot is closer to nineteenth century serial novels, including agnitions, intrigues, doubles, curses and suicidal pacts. Although partially misleading, the aforementioned tagline nevertheless pointed out the film's core: the clash between the present and a haunting past.

Such past, as so often with the Gothic genre, takes the seductive yet deceptive forms of a female ghost. Enzo Ferraris' script centers on a sad spirit who returns to claim the fulfillment of a pact of love and death that had been struck decades earlier, and has vague literary reminiscences: the narrative structure unfolds by juxtaposing past and present, with the former being gradually revealed through flashbacks that hark back in time, and the idea of a cyclical curse is a main theme in the Gothic genre.

Veronique appears throughout the ages: during the war she vainly warns Alberto, the son of her lover, that the Nazis are coming after him, then she haunts Alberto's son Giovanni, and it is eventually revealed that she took her own life in the early 1920s. "It took three generations to seal a pact of love," as the opening line states. On the other hand, the scenes set in World War II, which set the Fantastic element into a precise war setting, hint at a closer reference in time, Tommaso Landolfi's novel *Racconto d'autunno*. What really sets the film apart from its contemporaries is the setting, the peaceful and poisonous modern-day Lombard Brianza, although Vernuccio—who also took care of the cinematography and editing—does not aim at the kind of rural Gothic that will characterize Pupi Avati's films.

For all the differences between *La lunga notte di Veronique* and the horror films of the period, Veronica/Veronique retains the same characters of Italian Gothic *revenants*. She is a definitely carnal presence who appears in full daylight, uses the phone, shows up in the nude and relies on desire rather than fear. Veronique's "vengeance" is eventually revealed to be the romantic lament from a lonely soul who has been abandoned by her lover in the afterlife. Once again the male figures are weak and unreliable, as often seen in Italian Gothic horror, and in a thorough variation on a typical Gothic trick, all the three male protagonists (the young Count, his son and nephew) are played by the same actor.

With a more talented director, the story might have actually worked, but Vernuccio cannot overcome the actors' shortcomings. Nor does he succeed in injecting life into a rather muddled script, bogged down by a subplot concerning the scheming housekeeper, with whom the young Giovanni has an affair.

The film comes alive only during Veronique's apparitions, which are staged with a distinct surreal quality: they are either announced by the sudden lighting of a dark room or are revealed by the ghost's reflection on a car's hood. The effects are often suggestive, such as in the scene where Giovanni sees Veronique hitching a ride on a hearse that incongruously passes on a dirt road in the countryside.

La lunga notte di Veronique is suspended in a languid atmosphere, where even the feelings and plot twists are muffled and sleepy, just barely disturbed by Giorgio Gaslini's score. Overall, this is a pale, bloodless Gothic, exhausted by the same quiet stillness of the Lombard landscape that it portrays.

Note

1. The most familiar name within the cast is Cristina Gaioni, a former mannequin who had won a prize in 1960 as the year's best non protagonist actress for Renato Castellani's *... and the Wild, Wild Women*, a.k.a. *Nella città l'inferno*, and who here appears in a small role as the protagonist's young mother in a couple of flashback scenes.

Kill, Baby...Kill! (Operazione paura)

D: Mario Bava. *S:* Romano Migliorini, Roberto Natale; *SC:* Romano Migliorini, Roberto Natale, Mario Bava; *DOP:* Antonio Rinaldi (Eastmancolor); *M:* Carlo Rustichelli; *E:* Romana Fortini; *SD:* Sandro Dell'Orco; *CO:* Tina Grani; *AD:* Lamberto Bava; *C:* Saverio Diamante; *AC:* Salvatore Caruso; *SO:* Romano Pampaloni, Armando Tarzia; *MU:* Maurizio Giustini; *Hair:* Marisa Laganga; *SE:* Enrico Catalucci (optical effects editor); *SS:* Rosalba Scavia. (*English version: DialD:* Lewis A. Ciannelli). *Cast:* Giacomo Rossi-Stuart (Dr. Paul Eswai), Erika Blanc [Enrica Bianchi Colombatto] (Monica Schuftan), Fabienne Dali (Ruth), Piero Lulli (Insp. Kruger), Max Lawrence [Luciano Catenacci] (Karl, the burgomaster), Micaela Esdra (Nadienne), Franca Dominici (Martha), Giuseppe Addobbati (Innkeeper), Mirella Pamphili [Pompili] (Irina Hollander), Gianna Vivaldi [Giovanna Galletti] (Baroness Graps); *uncredited:* Valerio Valeri (Melissa Graps). *PROD:* Nando Pisani, Luciano Catenacci for F.U.L. Film (Rome); *GM, PS:* Nando Pisani; *UM:* Mario Olivieri. *Country:* Italy. Filmed in Faleria, Fabrica di Roma (Viterbo, Lazio), and Villa Lancelotti, Grottaferrata (Rome), and at Titanus Appia Studios (Rome). *Running time:* 83 min. (m. 2600); Visa n: 47160 (06.07.1966); *Rating:* V.M.14; *Release dates:* 07.08.1966 (Italy); 10.08.1966 (U.S.A.). *Distribution:* I.N.D.I.E.F. (Italy), Europix Consolidated Corp. (U.S.A.); *Domestic gross:* 201,000,000 lire. *Also known as: Curse of the Living Dead* (U.S.A.—reissue), *Curse of the Dead* (U.K.), *Opération peur*

(France), *Die toten Augen* (West Germany, 03.13. 1970). Home video: VCI, Dark Sky, Anchor Bay (DVD, U.S.A.), Sinister (DVD; Italy).

Early twentieth century. Dr. Eswai arrives in the small Carpathian village of Karmingen where a series of inexplicable murders have occurred. Eswai finds out that talismans have been put into the victims' hearts by the local witch, meant to ward off the supernatural source of the deaths. The doctor realizes that the key to the mystery is hidden at the villa of Baroness Graps, an elderly woman whose little daughter Melissa had died years earlier: through the ghost of Melissa, the Baroness is exacting her revenge against the villagers, who caused her child's demise...

Mario Bava's return to Gothic horror, three years after *Black Sabbath* and *The Whip and the Body*, *Kill, Baby...Kill!*, looked like it would be just a modest low-budget horror film. It was financed by a small company named F.U.L. Film and shot—according to Bava—in just 12 days. Gone were the days when Galatea would give Bava an extra week to finish *Black Sunday* with all the care he could put into it. The company which financed Bava's debut, and which had focused on horror films more than any other production house, had experienced a disastrous balance sheet by the end of 1964, with a loss of almost 700 million *lire*. In 1965 Galatea was put under controlled administration and practically disappeared from the market.

The cast was also a far cry from Bava's earlier horror films. No Barbara Steele, no Boris Karloff, no Christopher Lee in sight: the male lead was Giacomo Rossi-Stuart, a 40-year-old Italian actor with a rather undistinguished career in popular cinema, and his co-star was a young actress with the alluring stage name of Erika Blanc, who had only played a handful of roles before. The rest of the cast comprised familiar character actors, such as Giuseppe Addobbati (the titular bloodsucker in Polselli's *The Vampire of the Opera*), Piero Lulli (brother of the great Folco Lulli who co-starred in Henri-Georges Clouzot's *The Wages of Fear*) and Luciano Catenacci (who also acted as producer for F.U.L. films).

Nevertheless, *Kill, Baby...Kill!* marked a turning point in the director's approach to horror. Behind a traditional *ghost story* façade, and

Italian poster for Mario Bava's *Kill, Baby...Kill!* by Averardo Ciriello (courtesy S. I. Bianchi).

despite lesser production values than his earlier Gothic films, Bava's mise-en-scene of the Fantastic and the uncanny proved to be truly revolutionary in more ways than one. The result was not only one of the director's very best efforts, but also a breakthrough work, which would pave the way for the bold stylish freedom of the director's later achievements such as *Bay of Blood* and *Lisa and the Devil*.

Even though it initially seems to draw on the eighteenth century tradition, with Dr. Eswai's (Giacomo Rossi-Stuart) arrival at the village—modeled on the cliché of the lone traveler who arrives at the edge of a no man's land just like Jonathan Harker in *Dracula* or the young heroes in Corman's Poe films—*Kill, Baby...Kill!* soon stands out from the Italian horror films produced in preceding years. Its ghosts arise from the subconscious, and the focus of the story is no longer a female character who is seen as menacing, alluring and diabolical. Despite offering no less than three potentially seductive female characters—the virginal damsel-in-distress (Blanc), the Lolita-esque innkeeper's daughter (Micaela Esdra), the raven-haired witch (Fabienne Dali)—Bava did not dwell on the erotic possibilities of the story, and indeed he dispensed with them in barely concealed haste.

Compared to the increasing degree of morbidity and sexual allusions of contemporary Italian horror, as well as Bava's previous films, *Kill, Baby...Kill!* offers just a brief glimpse of Micaela Esdra's naked back and the sight of Erika Blanc in her nightgown after a nightmare. What is more, although the film's villain turns out once again to be a woman, elderly Baroness Graps (Giovanna Galletti) is a long way from the ageless seducers as seen in *I Vampiri* and *Black Sunday*, who revealed their physical rot and display their decaying flesh only near the film's end, much to the viewer's horror. Graps is a disheveled old woman whose hair resembles the cobwebs that dot her abode and which often act as a veil between the camera and the characters, thus detaching things and persons from our sight, as if they were imprisoned in a painting—just like the one portraying Villa Graps in the film's most celebrated scene.

But there is more. In *Kill, Baby...Kill!* Bava almost completely avoided the usual old-style fear tactics, such as hands snatching someone from behind or windows suddenly opening after a gust of wind. He worked on the filmic representation of the "uncanny" in a way that had never been seen before in Italian Gothic. Shock effects are filmed frontally, with violent zooms on windows behind which we see the features of Melissa: the little girl slides forward to touch the transparent surface that separates her from the characters, as if she was emerging from the other side of a mirror. Bava filmed these scenes backwards, putting Valerio Valeri—his porter's little son who played the dead girl, in one of the film's most exquisite surreal touches—on a cart similar to the one the director used for "The Drop of Water" and driving the cart away from the window where Valeri was leaning.

To give shape to his disquieting little ghost, the Sanremese director further developed the intuition he first used in "The Drop of Water" and in the opening credits of *Blood and Black Lace*, where the main characters are mixed with dummies, and almost indistinguishable from them. The perturbing effect of the scene where Eswai discovers Melissa at Villa Graps, as the girl is sitting in her bedroom and surrounded by dolls, lies in the momentary distraction caused by the ghost's posture, as she is motionless and at first interchangeable with the dolls themselves. What is more, Melissa initially does not appear in full figure, but only as a synecdoche: we get to see her white socks and sandals going down stairs or dangling from an "impossible" swing, her hands pushing on windows, or the famous white ball which at times Melissa even seems to turn into, as if to give it a life of its own.

Just like the old lady in "The Drop of Water," Melissa has the gift of ubiquity, and the power to appear in the most unlikely places, where—according to logic—she should not be. Furthermore, the barriers and distances Bava puts between her and the other characters become increasingly uncertain and unreliable. The effect is disorienting to begin with, as in the scene in which Eswai sees Melissa first at one end of a corridor and then at the opposite. Then it becomes shocking, such as when the burgomaster (Catenacci) opens an old wardrobe and finds himself face the face with the ghost, in close-up, standing *inside* the furniture.

According to Bava scholar Tim Lucas, the film was mostly improvised on set, allegedly on the lines of *Terror-Creatures from the Grave*, also scripted by Roberto Natale and Romano Migliorini. "Both Erika [Blanc] and Lamberto [Bava] corroborate the incredible story that *Operazione paura* was largely a product of improvisation, with the actors inventing their dialogue from rough outlines handed to them in advance of each new camera set-up [...] the screenplay for Bava's film may well have been improvised from the floor plan of the earlier script (of Pupillo's film)."[1]

Even though the similarities between the two films are patent, this theory is refuted by *Kill, Baby...Kill!*'s shooting script (entitled *Le macabre ore della paura*, "The Macabre Hours of Fear," and credited to Robert Christmas and Roman McLioring, that is Roberto Natale and Romano Migliorini, of course), deposited at Rome's Centro Sperimentale di Cinematografia. The script features detailed dialogue and a full storyline, including some of the film's most celebrated scenes. One such example is Dr. Eswai (spelled "Esuei") chasing his *doppelgänger* over and over in the same room, or the seemingly endless spiral staircase that he runs through. However, there are a few important differences between the script and the finished film. For one thing, the surreal fake POV shot from the "invisible swing" which introduces the autopsy in the cemetery morgue was Bava's idea, whereas the script indicates a POV shot of a child moving forward, as if Melissa's ghost was advancing.

Comparing the script to the finished product, it turns out that the screenplay featured ideas that had already been used in Bava's previous films, and which he had discarded in the process of shooting. In *Le macabre ore della paura* Melissa's victims return as zombies, for instance: an allusion to that is the scene in the morgue where the body of Irina Hollander (Mirella Pamphili) seems to reanimate, a detail that remains unexplained in the film. The zom-

bies come back to torment future victims and claim them—in the script, the innkeeper's daughter Nadienne does not see Melissa behind the window, but Irina—just like in *Black Sunday* and "The Wurdalak." Even more, in the script Natale and Migliorini described the zombies as "advancing [...] without apparently moving their legs" like the old lady in "The Drop of Water."

Bava was most likely forced to change the shooting schedule because of the tight budget, as the production ran out of money during filming,[2] but perhaps he just wanted to avoid repetition, or sensed that the duplication of ghosts would be redundant, detracting effectiveness from Melissa' apparitions. Whereas in *Hercules in the Haunted World* Bava had used repetition (which "diminishes the wonder and produces a comic effect"[3]) in the scene in which Hercules throws a boulder after another against his opponents, here he followed the opposite process. A sign, perhaps, that Bava really cared about this little horror film filled with throwaway dialogue, and proof that he could perfectly tell the boundary between fear and ridicule—which perhaps is not enough to make good horror movies, but it usually helps.

Another matter that the CSC script helps to clarify is the time around which *Kill, Baby...Kill!* was actually made. *Le macabre ore della paura* is dated April 5, 1966 (the date when it was deposited at the Ministry of Spectacle), which puts in doubt Lucas' assertions about the film being shot in the month of November 1965[4]: CSC's scripts come from ministerial folders, which were normally delivered by production companies *before* shooting started. Even assuming an exception to the rule, Lucas' assertion that Massimo Pupillo's *La vendetta di Lady Morgan* was filmed immediately after *Kill, Baby...Kill!* cannot be accepted. Shooting for Pupillo's film started on July 26, 1965 (with the title *La vendetta di Lady Blackhouse*), while in September 1965 the film's title was changed into the definitive one: *La vendetta di Lady Morgan* was presented to the Ministerial Censorship Commission on October 1, 1965 and was eventually released on December 16, 1965. Therefore Bava's film is *subsequent* to Pu-

The ghost of little Melissa Graps (played by a boy in drag, Valerio Valeri) in one of its unexpected apparitions in *Kill, Baby...Kill!* (author's collection).

pillo's—a fact proven also by the Ministerial enrollment numbers (3568 for *La vendetta di Lady Morgan*, 3722 for *Kill, Baby...Kill!*) which are chronological.

The way Bava reinvents Italian geography in his films reaches surreal, abstract peaks in *Kill, Baby...Kill!* The Ancient Roman ruins, moss-covered alleys and dilapidated buildings of Faleria, a little village near Viterbo, become an unlikely North-European hamlet, which is Teutonic only in name, whereas the villagers, with

mustaches and berets, look as if they just came out of a realist Italian drama.

Despite the setting being the early 1900, the world of *Kill, Baby...Kill!* is timeless: the opening shots, showing the remains of buildings collapsed under the weight of time (as well as the devastating earthquake of 1942), graft an incongruous memory of Italian Neorealism over a Gothic tissue. A memory which, nonetheless, is transfigured by the music, the camera angles and movements. Bava built a true Fantastic geography by putting together real exteriors and studio sets, and by lighting the former as if they were studio-bound as well. What is more, by having his actors move amidst real ruins and crumbling interiors, in a way that recalls the afterlife scenes in Cocteau's *Orpheus* (1950), the director unveiled the characters' own fleeting nature: they are ghosts, called upon to act out their own play, trapped in a maze in which they mingle and annihilate, as if in a *trompe-l'oeil*— just as it happens to Eswai in one of the film's best scenes.

Bava scholars have pointed out how in *Kill, Baby...Kill!* it is never quite clear what the distances are between Villa Graps, the village, the church and the cemetery: these seem near or far away, varying from scene to scene,[5] similar in fact to *Black Sunday*. Baroness Graps's mansion, connected to an underground crypt which in turn incongruously leads to a door on a precipice, is an Escherian puzzle: it is imposing (and incumbent) when seen from the outside, yet it becomes oppressive in its interiors crammed with dusty relics. Its topography consists solely of a series of interconnected corridors and rooms, whose only access seems to be that endless spiral staircase which Giacomo Rossi-Stuart and then Erika Blanc run through at breakneck speed, while the camera rotates on itself with hypnotic effect. This way, Bava manipulates the audience's spatial perception, by denying a Cartesian center which is usually represented by the huge salon of the villas and manors where evil lurks, from *I Vampiri* and *Black Sunday* onwards.

Whereas the set-pieces and light/shadow games in *The Whip and the Body* pointed to a redefinition of the diegetic space as a means to transcend the barriers between the real and the fantastic, with *Kill, Baby...Kill!* Bava works on the concept of non–Euclidean space. Besides, such space is no longer modeled on the hero/heroine's subjectivity, thus reflecting his or her fears and anxieties (a typical trait of eighteenth century Gothic, usually reprised in the movies—see the scene where Barbara Steele is menaced by colored tree branches in *The Horrible Dr. Hichcock*). On the contrary, here the diegetic space is modeled on (and, more importantly,

by) Melissa's ghost, who has the power to change and reorganize physical space to her liking, as shown by her appearances throughout the film, thus causing in the other characters (and the viewer as well) a sense of displacement.

The fall of space and time barriers is best exemplified by the celebrated scene in which Paul Eswai chases his double along a series of identical rooms. Unsettled by the sight of his own self facing him, he leans against a wall, on a cobweb-covered painting which portrays the villa ... only to find himself trapped in a huge web, *outside* the villa (or *inside* the painting?). Such a payoff was absent in Natale and Migliorini's script, where the scene of the *doppelgänger* is practically identical to the finished film, but ends in a different way: after facing his own double, Eswai falls into a feverish delirium during which, among other things, he "sees" his own burial in a point-of-view scene. Yet an umpteenth variant on *Vampyr*'s most famous scene, which Bava probably judged as an unnecessary verbiage.

In *Kill, Baby...Kill!* Bava reworks the Gothic's recurring features in a subtly subversive way. Take the theme of the double, which assumes grotesque traits in the portrait of Melissa: the little girl, looking serious and posing next to a skull, almost seems a demented version of one of Diego Velázquez' *Meninas*. On the other hand, the *doppelgänger*, deprived of its moral essence, becomes the instrument for a thought-provoking meditation on identity. The scene in which Eswai chases his double in Villa Graps' endless series of rooms, all looking exactly the same, makes him a homologue of Lovecraft's unfortunate *Outsider* or Philip K. Dick's *Impostor*. In the moment when he finally stretches his fingers towards the creature that precedes him, and touches not the "cold and unyielding surface of polished glass" but the shoulder of his own simulacre, Eswai loses the consciousness of his own unrepeatable individuality: for a second, he feels the thrill of being on the wrong side, *on the other side* of the mirror or *inside* the portrait, staring in amazement at his own Dorian Gray.

If Italian Gothic horror was a season of witches, it is precisely in these figures that the deeper ties with the peninsula's folklore and tradition came to the fore. The link between religion, superstition and repression was at the center of Brunello Rondi's extraordinary *Il demonio*, which *Kill, Baby...Kill!* somehow recalls in its portrayal of superstitious rituals akin to the customs of Southern Italy. Those rituals, which had been illustrated with an etnographic pique by Rondi, show up in Bava's film through the character of Ruth, a "witch" who performs a magic ritual on a young girl's body and forces her to use a thorny cilice as an instrument of forced contrition to drive evil away. The fact that Fabienne Dali's character recalls Daliah Lavi in Rondi's groundbreaking, misunderstood film suggests another possible key to understanding *Kill, Baby...Kill!* as a rereading of Gothic themes through Italy's folklore.

Although assembled from a variety of sources, the score—not an original composition by Carlo Rustichelli, who is nevertheless credited as the sole author, but a hybrid comprising music from the CAM archives, including music pieces by Rustichelli, Roman Vlad, Angelo Francesco Lavagnino, Francesco De Masi, Armando Trovajoli[6]—detaches itself from the genre's stylistic features and hints at Serialism, with its bell loops and ethereal sounds, as noted by Pierre Berthomieu.[7] It is a further element that underlines the gap between *Kill, Baby... Kill!* and the Gothic horror films made in Italy till then.

To Bava, *Kill, Baby...Kill!* marked the end of an era. Its box-office receipts werc nondescript, and Bava moved on to other territories, embarking on the De Laurentiis–produced *Danger: Diabolik* (*Diabolik*, 1968). It took several years before he returned to his favorite genre, again with another outstanding work: *Hatchet for the Honeymoon*, shot in 1969 but released theatrically only in 1970.

Notes

1. Lucas, *Mario Bava*, p. 664.
2. Ibid., p. 671.
3. Pezzotta, *Mario Bava*, p. 27.
4. Lucas, *Mario Bava*, p. 668: however, in the cast and credits section (on page 664) shooting is indicated as having taken place on February/March 1966.
5. Pezzotta, *Mario Bava*, p. 57.

6. For an in-depth analysis of the soundtrack, see Lucas, *Mario Bava*, pp. 672–673.
7. Pierre Berthomieu, *La musique de film* (Paris: Klincksieck, 2004), p. 128.

The Murder Clinic, a.k.a. Revenge of the Living Dead (La lama nel corpo)

D: Michael Hamilton [Lionello De Felice]. *S* and *SC:* Julian Berry [Ernesto Gastaldi], Martin Hardy [Luciano Martino]; *DOP:* Marc Lane [Marcello Masciocchi] (Technicolor—Techniscope); *M:* Frank Mason [Francesco De Masi] (Ed. C.A.M.); *E:* Richard Hartley [Alberto Gallitti]; *ArtD:* Walter Parkington [Walter Patriarca]; *CO:* Albert Miller [Alberto Salvatore]; *AD:* Montague Jackson [Roberto Pariante]; *C:* Thomas Rawlins; *SO:* Oliver Scott [Bernardino Fronzetti]; *MU:* Max Huston [Massimo Giustini]; *SS:* Albert Miller. (*English language version:* Lewis A. Ciannelli.) *Cast:* William Berger (Dr. Robert Vance), Françoise Prévost (Gisèle de Brantôme), Mary Young (Lizabeth Vance), Barbara Wilson (Mary), Philippe Hersent (Fred), Grant Laramy [Germano Longo] (Ivan), Harriet White [Medin] (Sheena), Max Dean [Massimo Righi] (Fred), Delphine Maurin [Delfi Mauro] (Laura), Patricia Carr [Rossella Bergamonti] (Ketty), Ann Sherman [Anna Maria Polani] (Janey, first victim), William Gold [Rock Scandurra] (Walter). *PROD:* Elio Scardamaglia, Francesco Scardamaglia, Luciano Martino for Leone Film, Ci.Ti. Cinematografica (Rome), Orphée Productions (Paris); *PM:* Peter Taylor [Piero Lazzari]; *PS:* Paolo Gargano. *Country:* Italy/France. Filmed in Villa Parisi (Francati, Rome). *Running time:* 90 min. (m. 2700); Visa n: 46528 (02.19.1966); *Rating:* V.M.18; *Release date:* 03.17.1966 (Italy); 06.25.1969 (U.S.A.). *Distribution:* Regional (Italy); Europix—Consolidated Corp. (U.S.A.); *Domestic gross:* 96,000,000 lire. *Also known as: Night of Terrors, The Murder Society, The Blade in the Body, Revenge of the Living Dead* (U.S. reissuc); *Les Nuits de l'épouvante* (France, 10.11.1967), *Das Monster auf Schloß Moorley* (West Germany, 06.07.1968). *Home video:* Code Red (DVD, U.S.—as part of the "Six-Pack Volume Two" box-set), Video Bio (VHS, Denmark—English language), MCP Magnetics (VHS, Germany).

Norfolk, England, 1870. Dr. Robert Vance runs a psychiatric clinic where he also resides with his embittered wife, Lizabeth. The place is plagued by a series of violent killings, perpetrated by a hooded maniac. A new nurse, Mary, arrives at the clinic, and soon discovers that something weird is going on. It turns out that Vance is hiding Lizabeth's sister Laura, who was left horribly disfigured after falling into a quicklime pit—an accident perhaps procured by the doctor, who was acquitted at the trial after Lizabeth's deposition. Another patient is killed by the maniac, and a prostitute on the run named Gisèle discovers Vance as he is getting rid of the body. Gisèle attempts to blackmail the doctor, but she too is dispatched by the maniac. Mary discovers her body, but Vance—with whom she is secretly in love—persuades her to help him get rid of it. Mary is then attacked by the maniac, who is confronted by the disfigured Laura...

The Murder Clinic is an early example of the way the Gothic horror thread would mutate and make way for the *giallo* in the following decade. By now the *filone* had been squeezed dry by scriptwriters and filmmakers alike, who realized that its peculiar mixture of excess and transgression would work even better without the supernatural elements it had been carrying along, in order to meet a jaded audience's growing demand for novelties—and the Gothic had never been a box-office winner in the first place.

It had been Bava who led the way, by taking elements from the Krimis and the *fumetti neri* (the violent, sadistic adults-only comic books which were becoming very popular in Italy in the mid–Sixties, such as *Diabolik* and *Kriminal*) and adding a taste for the unlikely and the surreal. With *Blood and Black Lace*, Bava created a world in which anything could happen, just like in the Gothic's ethereal no-man's lands, but with an added *frisson* which female vampires and *revenantes* could no longer give, represented by the film's sadistic and ubiquitous murderer.

In the same period, Gastaldi had spiced Bava's intuitions with a touch of Gothic in his directorial debut *Libido* (1965, co-directed with Vittorio Salerno), one of the very first properly defined *gialli*, as Gastaldi himself proudly claims. The razor-wielding hooded maniac in *The Murder Clinic* was a direct affiliation of Bava's faceless killer, which Ernesto Gastaldi's script (co-authored by Luciano Martino) tried to top in its misogynist attitude towards women. The opening murder, with a mute girl being stalked in the park and dispatched before a backlit fountain, is a patent reminder of *Blood and Black Lace*, even though the violence quota is rather tame when compared to Bava's film, despite it being given a V.M.18 rating by the board of censors.

However, *The Murder Clinic* retained just as many characters that are typical of the Gothic genre, starting from the plethora of English pseudonyms, thus fully justifying its presence in this volume. First of all, the eighteenth century setting—precise to the point of pedantry: "*about* 1870," as the opening line states—in a stereotyped, unlikely England is typically Gothic. So are most plot points: the disfigured female face and the obsession for reconstructing a woman's lost beauty come from Freda's *I Vampiri* as well as Franju's much looted *Eyes Without a Face* (although the make-up work is as crude as ever) while the imperturbable William Berger is given a character with vague "mad doctor" traits. Then there is the theme of the double, with a young bride being haunted by her older sister's horrible fate (only, this time Gastaldi comes up with a grim twist, by turning the designated victim and her guilt into a much more ambiguous figure), and a schizophrenic patient (the usually commendable Massimo Righi) obsessed—à la "The Tell-Tale Heart," by way of Giulio Questi's "Il passo"—with the sound of lame steps on the ceiling. Last but not least, there are plenty of young women in their nightgowns wandering through the sinister villa's dark corridors at night—Italian Gothic horror's most recognizable trademark, as Martin Scorsese once put it.

As was customary within the *filone*, the villa assumes a primary role throughout the film, heightened by its familiar appearance: the main location is Villa Parisi in Frascati, seen also in *Nightmare Castle* and in the same year's *The Third Eye*. Considering that Marcello Masciocchi's cinematography is prodigal with light/shadow effects and lavish colors that recall Freda's diptych, and that Harriet White pops up in her trademark stern housekeeper role, it is not too far from the truth to conclude that *The Murder Clinic* comes out as a sort of reversal of the first *Dr. Hichcock* film which upsets and reverses the three main characters' relationships, to the point of turning the good doctor into a victim.

Too bad the direction is nondescript and the many red herrings—with Berger acting suspiciously all the way through for no other apparent reason than provide viewers with a main suspect—are rather unconvincing: the film only comes alive whenever Françoise Prévost is on-screen as an ill-fated criminal who arrives at the villa after a coach accident reminiscent of *Car-*

milla,[1] exuding an ambiguous erotic fascination which is wasted too early on in the proceedings. She also has one of the film's best lines: "I never look at houses—only the people who live in them."

The Italian poster for the 1971 rerelease of *The Murder Clinic* exploited lead actor William Berger's troubles with the law via the tasteless tagline "William Berger, guilty or innocent?" (author's collection).

Even more than the identity of its hooded maniac, *The Murder Clinic*'s most impenetrable mystery has been the true identity of the filmmaker hidden under the alias "Michael Hamilton," claimed by Italian publicity ads of the period to be "the greatest filmmaker of his time"—no kidding. Although most sources indicate producer Elio Scardamaglia as the man behind the camera, according to Gastaldi the film's real director was actually Lionello De Felice, the author of the short story—a three-page outline—which served as a basis to the script[2] (which according to the credits is based on "the novel *The Murder Clinic* by J. Berry—M. Hardy"). Gastaldi maintained that De Felice abandoned the film near the end of the shooting, when just a few scenes remained to be filmed.[3] Posters and promotional ads bear a producer's credit for Scardamaglia and a separate director's credit for the elusive Hamilton, thus possibly supporting Gastaldi's version.

The Murder Clinic was released in the United States under different titles along the years, including one (*Revenge of the Living Dead*, in 1972) that tried to pass it off as a zombie film. In Italy, after a modest theatrical run in 1966, *The Murder Clinic* was re-released five years later. Not just, as some might think, because of the *giallo* frenzy. On the night of August 5, 1970, William Berger had been arrested during a drug bust: the police had discovered less than a gram of marijuana inside a snuff-box, in the villa Berger had rented in Praiano, on the Amalfi coast (Berger claimed he did not know about the drugs, and that he usually tell people not to bring drugs in the house). Besides the actor, the police arrested his wife Carolyn Lobravico, herself an actress as well, plus seven foreign *capelloni* ("longhairs," as the newspapers contemptuously called the young hippies) who were staying at Berger's in that period.[4] Their hippie lifestyle, long hair and extravagant garments were apparently enough for the judges to label them as "socially reprehensible": Berger and his wife, who was suffering from viral hepatitis, were forcibly transferred to Pozzuoli's hospital for the criminally insane. Carolyn started having severe bellyaches, probably a case of acute peritonitis, but her growingly critical condition was ignored by the place's authorities: when the pain became unbearable and she started to scream, she was even tied up to bed with straps—like it was customary with the mentally ill. Eventually she underwent a useless surgery, before being moved to the "incurable disease" division, where she died on October 14th. Berger could only briefly see Carolyn a few days before her passing away, on October 9th: he was handcuffed and accompanied by police officers. Despite pressures from left-wing newspapers, an autopsy was not performed on Lobravico's body. The case caused a fuss in the United States as well, where Allen Ginsberg headed a committee pleading for Berger's released.

Berger was transferred to Salerno's prison and eventually released in March 1971: the trial ended with him being acquitted due to insufficient evidence.[5] In that period, some unscrupulous distributor had the idea of rereleasing *The Murder Clinic*, with a new tagline: "William Berger colpevole o innocente?" (William Berger, guilty or innocent?). Those were the days of Italian exploitation.

Notes

1. Curiously, as noted by Johan Melle in his blog *Euro Fever*, the man who travels with Gisèle on the coach, played by Philippe Hersent, is portrayed as her escort in the English version, whereas in the German and French ones the dialogue identifies him as her husband.

2. Lucas, "What Are Those Strange Drops of Blood," p. 39.

3. Email interview, December 2013.

4. a.l., "Interprete di "western" in carcere per la droga," *La Stampa*, August 6, 1970. The *capelloni* were Berger's friends from France, Germany, Britain and the States. A few days later, another drug bust ended with the arrest of the British actress Marilyn Lesley Woolhead.

5. a.l., "Assolto l'attore americano Berger rinchiuso in manicomio per la droga," *La Stampa*, March 30, 1971 (the article's title wrongly refers to Berger as being an American actor). The acquittance was confirmed in appeal: see a.l. "William Berger assolto anche in appello dall'accusa di avere detenuto la droga," *La Stampa* February 17, 1972. Berger (with the contribution of psychologist Timothy Wilson) wrote a book about his arrowing experience, *House of the Angels: Love Notes from an Asylum* (New York: Viking, 1974).

The Third Eye (*Il terzo occhio*)

D: James Warren [Mino Guerrini]. *S:* Phil Young [Ermanno Donati], "based on a story by Gilles De

Rais"; *SC*: Dean Craig [Piero Regnoli], James Warren; *DOP*: Sandy Deaves [Alessandro D'Eva] (B&W); *M*: Frank Mason [Francesco De Masi]; *E*: Donna Christie [Ornella Micheli]; *PD*: Samuel Fields [Mario Chiari]; *AD*: Roger Drake [Ruggero Deodato], Ernest Steward; *C*: Joe Gossip [Giovanni Ciarlo]; *SO*: Joseph Delight; *MU*: Julian Laurens [Giuliano Laurenti]; *CO*: Marta De Matteis; *Hair*: Rose Sparkling. *Cast*: Frank [Franco] Nero (Mino), Gioia Pascal (Marta), Diana Sullivan [Erika Blanc—Enrica Bianchi Colombatto] (Daniela/Laura), Olga Sunbeauty [Olga Solbelli] (Mino's mother), Marina Morgan [Marina Meucci] (Dancer at night club), Richard Hillock (Doctor). *Uncredited*: Luciano Foti (Policeman). *PROD*: Louis Mann [Ermanno Donati, Luigi Carpentieri] for Panda Cinematografica; *PM*: Al Given [Alfonso Donati]; *PS*: Joe N. Seery [Sergio Martino]. *Country*: Italy. Filmed at Villa Parisi (Frascati). *Running time*: 90 min. (m. 2700); *Visa n*: 46555 (03.21.1966); *Rating*: V.M.18; *Release date*: 06.11.1966. *Distribution*: Medusa; *Domestic gross*: 72,000,000 lire. *Also known as*: *Le Froid baiser de la mort* (France, 06.02.1971); *Das dritte Auge* (West Germany, 05.26.1971). *Home video*: KSM (DVD, Germany).

Mino is about to marry Laura but his mother, who is morbidly attached to her son, as well as the housekeeper Marta, who is in love with him, are not happy about the wedding. Marta tampers Laura's car, causing her death in an accident, then dispatches Mino's mother, thus becoming the lady of the house. Mino, who is also a taxidermist, embalms the body of his dead girlfriend, and accepts to marry Marta in order to stop his necrophiliac passion, which turns into a homicidal mania, as he murders a stripper whom he picked up at the nightclub and then a prostitute. But one day Laura's twin sister Daniela arrives at the villa...

A former journalist, writer and an accomplished painter, Mino Guerrini (1927–1990) was another of those characters who crossed paths with Italian cinema and eventually followed its decline. Best-known in the artistic world for co-founding in 1947 the avant-garde Marxist movement "Gruppo Forma 1," eventually Guerrini abandoned painting and approached the movie business in the early '50s with Marcello Pagliero's *Vergine moderna* (1954). He became seriously involved with the magical world of Cinecittà in the '60s—first as a scriptwriter, working with such directors as Daniele D'Anza, Ugo Gregoretti (who brought to the screen Guerrini's short stories *I ventenni*

non sono delinquenti in the film *I nuovi angeli*, 1962), Gianni Puccini (*L'attico*, 1963) and ... Mario Bava (*The Girl Who Knew Too Much*). Guerrini's debut as a director came in 1964, with an episode of the omnibus comedy *Amore in quattro dimensioni*, then a few more anthologies followed before Guerrini moved on to other genres.

Released the same year as the spy flick *Killer 77, Alive or Dead* (*Sicario 77, vivo o morto*), *The Third Eye* looks as if it was an unassuming work for a filmmaker who seemed to have already lowered his ambitions to the needs of popular cinema: Guerrini even hid under a pseudonym, as it was commonplace in that period for B-movie directors.[1] The project germinated from a story devised by one of the producers, Ermanno Donati, under the pen name "Phil Young": in another typical Italian Gothic occurrence, the Gilles De Rais reference in the credits was totally made up. Tentatively titled *Il freddo bacio della morte* ("The Cold Kiss of Death"), it went into production in June 1965.

Even though it absorbed themes, pacing and habits of 1960s Italian Gothic—the double, the reliance on melodrama, the use of Anglo-Saxon pseudonyms, even the umpteenth recycling of Francesco De Masi's theme for *The Ghost*—Guerrini's film was definitely moving toward a different direction, thus signalling the end of a phase in the way of conceiving and portraying excess and transgression on screen.

Like Freda did in *The Horrible Dr. Hichcock*, the script by Piero Regnoli and Guerrini himself focused on the necrophiliac mania of the young nobleman Mino (a very young, and wooden, Franco Nero, who, by the time *The Third Eye* came out, was already becoming a star in his home country due to *Django*, released a couple of months prior to Guerrini's film). Mino steals his dead fiancée's body and embalms it, so that he can keep it in his own bed, only to find himself face to face with the dead girl's twin sister, who comes looking for her.

The way Guerrini deals with such a thorny subject matter is surprisingly audacious, and the present-day setting plays quite an appropriate role in it. Mino is an antihero worthy of Poe, just as out of time as his own world is. He prac-

Franco Nero and Gioia Pascal in a scene from Mino Guerrini's *The Third Eye* (Lucas Balbo).

tices taxidermy, and eventually turns into a necrophile, but this does not make him a mere imitation of Norman Bates: it rather reflects Mino's belonging to a decaying and reactionary social order, uncapable of adapting to the present.

The dilapidated villa where Mino lives with his mother and the housekeeper, surrounded by high and unkempt grass, is a powerful symbolic element. It is a relic of a vanished world, which—like Castle Du Grand—is surrounded and menaced by a more and more intrusive present, in a juxtaposition that achieves striking effects. Once the story moves away from Mino's house, the signs of contemporaneity invade the film in all their triviality: car accidents, night clubs, a gas station, the Italian police who pop up near the end. It is as if, once reality is revealed, there is no more room for the Gothic's typical grandeur: what remains is just mean, ugly, banal. Evil included.

Guerrini draws in on a typical melodrama plot, with a tangle of passions that includes Mino's love for a lower-class girl, hindered by his mother (like an updating of Raffaello Mata-

razzo's popular 1951 melodrama *I figli di nessuno*), and the housekeeper's aspiration to climb the social ladder by marrying Mino. All this, however, is veered into the morbid, in a continuous reference and comparison to the present that generates a feeling of discomfort and disgust. In a social contest characterized by female sexual emancipation and women's predatory aggressiveness—take the scene at the night club, where Mino picks up a stripper (future Rai-TV announcer Marina Morgan, displaying a huge pair of nipple covers), a moment which seems almost like something out of a Jess Franco film—the protagonist's abnormality is even more strident.

Whereas in *The Horrible Dr. Hichcock* necrophilia was an aberration cultivated in a repressive context such as the Victorian age, in *The Third Eye* it represents Mino's impossible return to an ideal past where woman is still a passive, helpless presence. On the other hand, the mother figure, as portrayed by the great Olga Solbelli in one of her last film roles, is a teratological figure worthy of *8½*'s uterine pantheon: Mino is pampered and protected from the outside world just as Guido (Marcello Mastroianni) was in the oneiric flashbacks of Fellini's masterpiece. Later on the mother is replaced by Mino's wife and maternal surrogate, the housemaid Marta (Gioia Pascal), thus making explicit the man's unresolved Oedipal complex.

However, Guerrini manages to inject a grim sense of humor into the proceedings, as in the scene where a hooker gets into Mino's car and asks what he would like to do: the young man replies he wants to do just what other men do; the camera cuts and we get to see Mino strangling the woman ... according to Ruggero Deodato, who was his a.d. on the film, Guerrini himself was a rather weird individual, who used to behave quite crazily on the set.[2]

The Third Eye had some trouble when it was submitted to the Board of censors on February 19, 1966: the film was initially rejected (on February 28) since it was considered to be "contrary to the public moral," as the typical formula that accompanied rejections stated. As for the motivation for the rejection, it read as follows: "In addition many scenes of almost full female nudity and excessively graphic intercourses, the film features episodes of necrophilia, close-ups of horrific scenes with blood and brutal violence, presented with real sadism and a protracted insistence which conveys a sense of complacency by part of the makers. All this within a morally harmful story, without any possibility of redemption."

The appeal ended with a demand of cuts on the part of the Commission, for a total amount of 35 seconds. The second part of Morgan's strip scene had to be shortened in the close-ups that showed her naked breasts, together with the scene where "the two lovers, in bed, embrace repeatedly in a lascivious erotic intercourse." The film was finally given a V.M.18 rating, because of its "theme, which illustrates a chain of dark crimes, conceived and executed in a psychopatic atmosphere [sic], as well as the many violent scenes, heightened by their raw and grim realism [...]."

A decade later, Aristide Massaccesi would effectively remake *The Third Eye* in what turned out to be one of "Joe D'Amato"'s most infamous gore-a-thons: *Beyond the Darkness* (*Buio omega*,

1979). Guerrini never returned to horror movies. His following films, the ironic hard-boiled yarn *Murder by Appointment* (*Omicidio per appuntamento*, 1967) and especially the pessimistic *film noir Gangsters '70* (1968), both scripted by his friend Fernando di Leo, were his best works, and truly among Eurocrime's most remarkable efforts. The director's subsequent output would be erratic at best: Franco & Ciccio comedies (*Riuscirà l'avvocato Franco Benenato a sconfiggere il suo acerrimo nemico il pretore Ciccio De Ingras?*, 1971), so-called "Decamerotics"[3] (*Decameron no. 2—Le altre novelle del Boccaccio*, 1972) and the four films in the farcical series devoted to Colonel Buttiglione, starring Jacques Dufilho. Guerrini's last film was a nondescript adventure flick, *The Mines of Kilimanjaro* (*Le miniere del Kilimangiaro*, 1986).

Notes

1. As well as noted directors who dipped in genres, such as Carlo Lizzani, who signed his Western *The Hills Run Red* (*Un fiume di dollari*, 1966) as Lee Beaver.
2. "Regarding *The Third Eye*, I remember that Guerrini was one very weird guy. Crazy, indeed. I had an affair with the script girl and we used to pick him up at his place on the Flaminia road. He had us wait down at the door, then told us to get in, and we found him completely naked. One day we were shooting a scene at Villa Parisi in Frascati, in the bathroom, with Franco Nero and Erika Blanc, and at a certain point he took a dump in front of the whole crew! [...] I called the producers [...] and Ermanno Donati slapped him in the face. Guerrini hated me but I had been imposed by the producers. He was quite the pissed-off type. [...] However, he was talented." Gomarasca, "Monsieur Cannibal," p. 11. Apart from Deodato, another future director was involved in the film: Sergio Martino was the production supervisor, under the pseudonym Joe N. Seery.
3. The "Decamerotics" were lewd, low-budget erotic comedies set in the Middle Age and loosely (or just namely) inspired by the works of Italian poets and writers of the 1300s and 1400s: a very popular *filone* which germinated after the success of Pier Paolo Pasolini's *The Decameron* (*Il Decameron*, 1971), the first episode in Pasolini's "Trilogy of Life," whose following entries—*The Canterbury Tales* (*I racconti di Canterbury*, 1972) and *Arabian Nights* (*Il fiore delle mille e una notte*, 1974)—also produced a number of rip-offs along the same vein.

The Witch (*La strega in amore*)

D: Damiano Damiani. *S:* based on Carlos Fuentes' novelette *Aura*; *SC:* Ugo Liberatore, Damiano Damiani; *DOP:* Leonida Barboni (B&W); *M:* Luis Enriquez Bacalov; *E:* Nino Baragli; *AE:* Rossana Maiuri; *C:* Arturo Zavattini [and Claudio Ragona, uncredited]; *AC*: Sergio Salvati, Gianni Bonivento; *PD*: Luigi Scaccianoce; *ArtD*: Dante Ferretti; *SD*: Francesco Bronzi; *Scene painter*: Angelo Zambon; *CO*: Pier Luigi Pizzi; *ACO*: Silvano Malta; *AD*: Fernando Morandi; *MA*: Franco Fantasia; *CHOR*: Robert Curtis; *SS*: Marcella Rossellini; *SO*: Franco Groppioni; *B*: Armando Bondani; *Mix*: Emilio Rosa; *MU*: Otello Fava; *AMU*: Giuseppe Ferrante; *Hair*: Renata Magnanti; *W*: Maria Castrignano, Mimma Olivieri; *KG*: Mariano Sargenti; *ChEl*: Massimo Massimi; *SE*: Aldo Gasparri, Giuseppe Metalli, Carlo Rambaldi; *PrM*: Aldo De Bonis; *SP*: Divo Cavicchioli. *Cast*: Rosanna Schiaffino (Aura), Richard Johnson (Sergio Logan), Sarah Ferrati (Consuelo Lorente), Gian Maria Volonté (Fabrizio), Margherita Guzzinati (Sergio's ex-girlfriend), Vittorio Venturoli (Dr. Marco Romani), Ivan Rassimov (Third "librarian"), Elisabetta Wilding; uncredited: Ester Carloni (Antique dealer). *NOTE*: Ivan Scratuglia, although credited, does not appear in the film. *PROD*: Alfredo Bini for Arco Film; *PM*: Fernando Franchi; *PS*: Lucio Orlandini, Gilberto Scarpellini; *PSe*: Enzo Ocone, Alfredo Di Santo; *ADM*: Vincenzo Taito. *Country*: Italy. Filmed at Incir-De Paolis Studios (Rome) and on location in Rome. *Running time*: 110 min. (m. 2780); Visa n: 47580 (08.22.1966); *Rating*: V.M.18; *Release dates*: 09.11.1966 (Italy); 08.1969 (U.S.A.). *Distribution*: Cidif (Italy); G.G. Productions (U.S.A.); *Domestic gross*: 203,396,000 lire. *Also known as*: The Witch in Love, Strange Obsession (U.S.A.), *Hexe der Liebe* (West Germany), *Las diabólicas del amor* (Spain). *Home video*: Eclectic DVD (DVD, U.S.A.).

Writer Sergio Logan accepts a job as a librarian and archivist at the mansion of the elderly widow Consuelo Lorente. The woman lives in an old palace in the center of Rome and keeps in her library the memories of her late husband. Sergio meets Consuelo's ravishing daughter Aura, who also lives in the house, and feels irresistibly attracted to her. Sergio cuts all the bridges with the outside world, but he finds out that another man is living in the palace: Fabrizio, Sergio's predecessor both as librarian and Aura's lover. Fabrizio tries to warn him about Aura's true nature, but Sergio accidentally kills him. He is subsequently blackmailed by Aura and Consuelo and forced to remain in the house. Eventually Sergio finds out that Aura and Consuelo are the same person, and that Consuelo is able to regain her youth, although temporarily, through a mysterious potion. Despite his initial repugnance, Sergio seemingly adapts to the situation. Yet, when another candidate as librarian arrives at the house, he feels that his position is in peril. Sergio reacts by tying Consuelo to a gate and burning her alive.

Productively speaking, 1966 marked the swan song in the first phase of Italian Gothic horror. Yet the Italian movie industry started to absorb wider suggestions and influences, and developed a more complex and multifaceted approach, even outside the basin of genre film, towards a matter—the Gothic—that took increasingly vast and indefinable boundaries.

As Fred Botting noted, in the twentieth century, the literary Gothic was "everywhere and nowhere": cinema—which "had sustained Gothic fiction [...] by endlessly filming versions of the classic Gothic novels"—was gradually detaching itself from the initial loyalty to the canons of the genre, and embraced broader and sometimes blurred characters. These were the first signs of "a dispersion and transformation" which would lead to "a diffusion and proliferation of genres and media that are related, often only tenuously, to Gothic."[1]

The properly renewed characters of the Gothic canon became a tool to portray a cultural fragmentation, related to both the family and the individual; to stage disturbing cracks in the boundaries between the single person's inwardness, the social values and concrete reality; to unveil new forms of savagery and monstrosity dealing with contemporary society, through new incarnations of the concepts of "excess" and "transgression," and leading to new kinds of terror and a new irrationality.

One such example is Damiano Damiani's *The Witch,* a film akin to the Gothic but not definable as an out-and-out horror. Damiani took inspiration from *Aura,* a novelette written in 1962 by Carlos Fuentes which Buñuel liked very much, and concocted an atmosphere and storytelling style not dissimilar to Roman Polanski's earlier films, in the attempt to transplant a cultured notion of the Fantastic into contemporary Italy—something truly unprecedented in Italian cinema.

The Witch was born as a vehicle for Rosanna Schiaffino (1939–2009), the wife of producer Alfredo Bini. The gorgeous Genoese actress, after her debut in the mid–'50s, became one of the most idiosyncratic divas in Italian cinema of the following decade, appearing in such diverse films as Vincente Minnelli's *Two Weeks*

Italian poster for Damiano Damiani's stylish exercise in Gothic *The Witch* (courtesy S. I. Bianchi).

in Another Town, Mauro Bolognini's intense drama *La corruzione* (1963) and Alberto Lattuada's grotesque period comedy *La Mandragola* (1965), alongside Totò.

In telling the story of the trap set by the elderly Consuelo Lorente (Sarah Ferrati) for Alpha

male Sergio Logan (Richard Johnson, in the first of his Italian forays in the horror genre), whom the woman first lures in her house and then seduces, hypnotizes, enslaves, by appearing to him under the guise of her own fascinating "daughter" Aura (Schiaffino), Damiani was principally interested in the theme of mad love. The Friulan filmmaker attempted to give a concrete visual form to Fuentes' "magic realism" which the Mexican writer evoked through a complex narrative technique.

Fuentes' novelette encapsulates past, present and future in a single suspended time-frame, through second-person narration and the use of verbal tenses, whereas Damiani's film tries to render Logan's bewilderment by way of a contradictory visual perception, relying on the "suggestion deriving from the audience's inability to perceive reality" as well as their "incapacity to decipher realistic data," as one critic put it.[2] Damiani often has the two women—the elderly Consuelo and the young Aura—appear in the same shot, only to reveal in the end that they are the same person. As the director explained, "it's as if there was a cloud in our character's brain. We leave 'authentic' reality and thus exalt the possibility of an error, which here is the 'double vision' of a single person. It becomes shocking when a psychological fact becomes a realistic one. That's the trick: these are not apparitions, they are two bodies, two different persons."[3]

Damiani and co-scriptor Ugo Liberatore built a new plot around the novelette's ethereal focus: they added events and characters (such as Consuelo's former librarian/slave, Fabrizio, played by an eerie-looking Gian Maria Volonté), and underlined the book's many allusions to magic and witchcraft (such as the herbal potion that the witch drinks to help her metamorphosis, or her ailurophobia). They also tried other ways to evoke Fuentes' idea of a potentially infinite iterativeness in time: between the lines one can sense on the part of the author that same indecision between the supernatural and the rational towards the text which Todorov considered as the key to the Fantastic. As Liberatore summarized: "We couldn't make up our minds whether this was a book on the supernatural or a psychopathological condition of the male character."[4]

This is evident in the finished film. On one hand, the director chose to portray the Fantastic with realistic instruments, highlighting its contradictions when compared to the real world. On the other, he emphasized the symbolical quality of the sets, the lighting, the music. The dark, labyrinthine palace with serpentine corridors where the old witch lives is an out-of-time microcosm, characterized by a space of its own, which resists and defends itself against external agents (the prosaic contemporary Rome as seen in the opening sequences) just like Castle Du Grand did in *I Vampiri*. The show-stopping circular library set, with a spiral staircase in the middle, echoes the whirlpool in which Logan is trapped.

Even Leonida Barboni's extraordinary black-and-white cinematography acquires the same quality: Consuelo's first transformation into Aura is suggested by a sudden shadow that covers the elderly woman's face, emptying it of life, just before the languid sound of a guitar announces her alter ego entering the scene. In a beautifully striking sequence, taken almost verbatim from the book, Aura and her "mother" sit side by side, the first in full light and the second half-immersed in shadows, talking to Logan and moving in unison, thus revealing their complementarity. The duality of the female character is underlined by Luis Bacalov's score, which consists of two main motifs, one with voice and percussions, almost tribal, the other for piano and organ, with baroque overtones.

Damiani's film does not follow Fuentes' iconoclastic discourse, though. In the book, Aura is a paraphrasing of the dichotomy of woman (Mother/whore) according to the Catholic tradition, and at the same time it is a political allegory which leads to a symbolic return of a repressed past. Yet, *The Witch* is full of references to Catholic iconography, but often in a grimly ironic way, such as the angels that Logan pretends he is looking for in the antiquarian shop in one of the film's first scenes, or the image of Logan "crucifying" the dead Fabrizio, in a Christ pose, on the railroad tracks. What is more, Damiani hints at his characters' erotic submission with a mixture of sacred and profane: Fabrizio and Logan wait for Aura to appear like churchgoers waiting for a divine epiphany.

Although Damiani was not interested in making a genre film replete with ghosts and

Grand Guignol, nevertheless *The Witch* features a number of themes and suggestions that recall 1960s Italian Gothic horror—starting, obviously, with the centrality and the role of the female figure, and the theme of obsessive love that moves her. *The Witch* reproduces the duality of woman as a seductress and a monster—the focus of *I Vampiri* and *Black Sunday*, just to name two—in a contemporary setting, and underlies gerontophile implications similar to those featured in Freda's film: this time as well, a repellent old woman sexually craves—and covets—a much younger man.

At first Logan is characterized as a cold womanizer who is used to switching from one conquest to another, as soon as his relationships start to become too serious, while his predecessor (and rival) Fabrizio is the umpteenth love slave of Italian (horror) cinema: a willing victim—as Logan himself will become—who devoted himself to an impossible dream of eternal beauty and exclusive possession. "Fuentes' novel was only a cue," as Damiani explained, "through which I explored a theme which I find very important: the drama of aging, with all it implies on a psychological, human and sexual level."[5] Said drama, however, not only relates to Consuelo, but to Sergio as well.

The film ends—rather abruptly, it must be said—with a fire, less purifying than punishing: Logan escapes the spell and burns Consuelo/Aura alive on an improvised stake. Damiani chose not to keep Fuentes' open ending, in which the librarian—who has discovered that he himself is the double and the reincarnation of the woman's deceased husband—will remain forever linked to Consuelo, awaiting for Aura's "eternal return." In doing so, *The Witch* returns with a critical eye to the ambivalent attitude towards the feminine which is typical of Catholic culture, and an integral part of Italian Gothic: Consuelo is destroyed because she escapes the ideal image of a passionate and exclusive lover—a whore, yet a devout one—in which Logan had deluded himself to imprison her. What is more, whereas Fuentes left his characters with the perpetually renewed miracle of seduction, Damiani ends his film with an emphasis on the all-male anxiety of aging (Sergio

reacts to the danger of a new, younger and possibly sexually attractive librarian, played by a young Ivan Rassimov) and loss.

The Witch was neither a box-office hit nor the critical success its makers had hoped for. Ugo Casiraghi, on *L'Unità*, compared it to Pabst's *Die Herrin von Atlantis*, but overall panned the movie. "There was only one way to shoot such a film: irony. Damiani realized this, in the opening part, which has the tones of a comedy of horrors, and thus manages to amuse the viewer [....]. But then the balance is broken and the film [...] gallops towards decay."[6] To Callisto Cosulich, "The beautiful Rosanna [...] will never be able to compete with Barbara Steele. Nor does Damiani have the skills to become the Dino Buzzati of Italian cinema. The idea of setting a fantastic story in a realistic setting, such as the one—buzzing with life, heat and voices—of today's Rome, was brilliant. Too bad it was left at the stage of a mere idea: that is, an unrealized intuition."[7] *Il Tempo*'s Gian Luigi Rondi, on the other hand, found the film to be too complex, and at times grotesque, redundant and awkward, but praised "the mystery-like atmosphere that surrounds at least the beginning (full of questions, suspense, tension)" as well as the "almost baroque feel with which [Damiani] encased the images, with a round and precious style [...] which undoubtedly proved to be useful to the effects and the atmosphere he wanted to achieve."[8]

With a little more than 200 million *lire* grossed, *The Witch* was a nondescript effort. Damiani would do much better with his subsequent film, *A Bullet for the General* (*Quien sabe?*, 1966), an outstanding political adventure film set during the Mexican revolution and starring Lou Castel, Gian Maria Volonté and Klaus Kinski.

Notes

1. Fred Botting, *Gothic* (London: Routledge, 1996), p. 156.
2. Giacinto Ciaccio, "La strega in amore," in *La Rivista del Cinematografo* 11, November 1966, p. 705.
3. Alberto Pezzotta, *Regia Damiano Damiani* (Pordenone: CEC/Cinemazero 2004), p. 65.
4. Ibid., p. 193. This was the last time Damiani and Liberatore—who had worked together since 1962's *L'isola di Arturo*—collaborated on a project. The follow-

ing year, Liberatore would debut as a director with *Il sesso degli angeli*, a film Damiani was initially attached to as director.

5. Ibid., p. 191.
6. Ugo Casiraghi, *L'Unità*, September 29, 1966.
7. Callisto Cosulich, *ABC*, October 1966.
8. Gian Luigi Rondi, *Il Tempo*, October 20, 1966.

1968

Jekyll (TV miniseries)

D: Giorgio Albertazzi. *S:* based on the novella *The Strange Case of Dr. Jekyll and Mr. Hyde* by Robert Louis Stevenson; *SC:* Ghigo De Chiara, Paolo Levi, Giorgio Albertazzi; *DOP:* Stelvio Massi (B&W); *M:* Gino Marinuzzi, Jr.; *PD:* Luciano Ricceri; *C:* Ezio Altieri. *Cast:* Giorgio Albertazzi (Dr. Henry Jekyll/Mr. Edward Hyde), Massimo Girotti (John Utterson), Claudio Gora (Prof. Hastie Lanyon), Ugo Cardea (Dr. Robert Lévy), Bianca Toccafondi (Paola Poole), Marina Berti (Barbara Utterford), Bob Balchus, Anita Bartolucci, Serena Bennato, Paolo Berretta, Renzo Bianconi, Simona Botti, Sten Braafheid, Penny Brown, Efisio Cabras, Enrico Canestrini, Franco Castellani, Mario Chiocchio, Bruno Cirino, Elvira Cortese, Delia Dalberti, Ruggero Dedaninos, Liana Delbalzo, Sandro Dori, Gianni Elsner, Sergio Fiorentini, Mariella Furgiuele, Armando Furlai, Marco Gagliardo, Bianca Galvani, Fabio Gamma, Olga Gherardi, Orso Maria Guerrini, Maria Marchi, Gianfranco Mari, Simone Mattioli, Gino Nelinti, Jane Pugh, Gino Proclemer, Salvatore Puntillo, Pieranna Quaia [Pier Anna Quaglia], Mario Righetti, Nicoletta Rizzi, Loredana Savelli, Varo Solieri, Gabriele Tozzi. *PROD:* RAI-Radio Televisione Italiana. *Country:* Italy. Filmed in Rome. *Running time:* 250 min.; *Broadcasting date:* February 1969.

Attorney John Utterson finds out by sheer chance that a man by the name of Edward Hyde, who brutally attacked a young girl, has been appointed the sole heir by his friend Henry Jekyll, a renowned biologist. What kind of relationship is there between the scientist and the sadistic young man?

If the mid–Sixties marked the end of the first wave of Italian horror, nevertheless the genre gradually found a cozy niche on the small screen. Made-for-television films or miniseries (called *sceneggiati* in Italy) had been a steady output since the 1950s, thanks to such filmmakers as Anton Luigi Majano, Mario Landi and Daniele D'Anza. Those works were usually based on classic or popular novels and generally

resulted in lengthy, talky scenes filmed on tape in interiors, with the odd exteriors shot on film (which gave the overall results a somehow haphazard look). Their most notable asset was the acting, on the part of such experienced thesps as Gino Cervi, who portrayed Commissioner Maigret in Mario Landi's 1964 miniseries, or Alberto Lupo, who won huge acclaim as Dr. Andrew Manson in Majano's adaptation of A. J. Cronin's *The Citadel*. However, despite the amount of TV movies (a number of which were based on Francis Durbridge's sleepy mysteries), the Fantastic in general and the Gothic in particular were considered unpalatable for the audience.

Then, things suddenly changed. June 1966 saw the first broadcasting on Italian television of Claude Barma's *Belphégor ou le Fantôme du Louvre*, a four-part French miniseries based on the novel of the same name by Arthur Bernède. By skillfully blending mysterious apparitions, references to occultism, an elusive treasure of the Rosicrucian Order, Barma's film offered a modern-day Gothic *feuilleton*, which met with the public' tastes. *Belphégor* was so successful it was broadcast again and again over the years, and RAI, Italy's national public broadcasting company, started producing fantasy-oriented miniseries. Leaving aside Franco Rossi's *The Odyssey* (*L'Odissea*, 1968), a superproduction shot on film and featuring Mario Bava's contribution in the celebrated Cyclops episode, there were a couple of interesting Conan Doyle adaptations, *La valle della paura* and *L'ultimo dei Baskerville* (both 1968), plus the surreal mystery *Geminus* (1969) directed by Luciano Emmer, about a Pagan cult in the catacombs of modern-day Rome.

In February 1969, while the students' protests and their clashes against the armed forces were shaking the country, RAI broadcast the four episodes of Giorgio Albertazzi's *Jekyll*. It was an experimental, thought-provoking work: a cultured rereading of Stevenson's story which was even more significant as Albertazzi—a well-known stage actor whose escapades on the big screen had resulted in such films as Alain Resnais' *Last Year at Marienbad* and Joseph Losey's *Eve* (*Eva*, 1962)—had the nerve to measure himself with television, conceiving an elitist product for the popular media par excellence.

With *Jekyll*, Albertazzi took the Gothic imagery and dropped it into the contemporary world, thus reinventing Stevenson's apologue by means of such current scientific issues as molecular biology, researches on DNA, eugenetics. He also dealt with hot political and philosophical themes, with quotations from Herbert Marcuse's work and references to the hippie movement. Another daring move was giving the film a modern, even futuristic look: the story unfolds amidst bright sunny parks and golf courses, ultramodern labs and cutting-edge architectural complexes, in an often blinding, cold black-and-white.

Albertazzi's Jekyll is the advocate of a new humanism which has to deal with the atom age and the fear of the bomb: "The real danger is man," as a line of dialogue states. He is a guru of sorts who teaches lessons to his students in the park, during sit-ins against the war (the ghost of Vietnam hangs over the story, although the setting is never specified, standing for Western society as a whole)—a modern-day Messiah who eventually falls victim to his own crave for power.

Hyde, on the other hand, is a sinister yet chillingly childish incarnation of Jekyll's out-of-control Id: the actor portrayed him as an overgrown teenager with an unkempt mop and frightening luminescent eyes, a prodigious achievement from d.o.p. (and soon a director himself) Stelvio Massi.

Even though he was somehow limited by television's strict self-regulation dictates, Albertazzi delved into the story's sexual overtones: Hyde's first victim, for instance, is a teenage girl in a miniskirt, and the scene somewhat predates the extraordinary opening of Walerian Borowczyk's underestimated *Dr. Jekyll et les femmes* (1981). Even more surprising is the way Jekyll justifies his suspicious bonding with his "pupil" to his lawyer, Utterson (Massimo Girotti), by implying that he has a homosexual relationship with Hyde.

Jekyll is not an easy viewing experience. It is often ponderous, and filled to the brim with dense dialogue. It was unlike anything that had been seen on television up to that point. Yet it turned out a surprise hit, and paved the way for a number of made-for-TV Gothic films and series in the following decade, including Daniele D'Anza outstanding supernatural mystery *Il segno del comando* (1971).

A Quiet Place in the Country (*Un tranquillo posto di campagna*)

D: Elio Petri. *S:* Tonino Guerra, Elio Petri, based on George Oliver Onions' short story *The Beckoning Fair One*; *SC:* Luciano Vincenzoni, Elio Petri; *DOP:* Luigi Kuveiller (Technicolor—Scope); *M:* Ennio Morricone (Ed. Eureka), executed by Gruppo di Improvvisazione Nuova Consonanza—vocals: Edda Dell'Orso; *E:* Ruggero Mastroianni; *AE:* Adriana Olasio; *PD:* Sergio Canevari; *APD:* Amedeo Fago; *CO:* Franco Carretti (Franco Nero's and Vanessa Redgrave's costumes: Giulio Coltellacci); *AD:* Mario Chiari; *C:* Ubaldo Terzano; *AC:* Nino [Antonio] Annunziata, Michele Picciaredda; *MU:* Antonio Mecacci; *SO:* Mario Bramonti; *Mix:* Emilio Rosa; *SP:* Claudio Patriarca; *CON:* Enzo Ocone; *ACON:* Daniela Corbi; *DubD:* Mario Maldesi; *KG:* Sergio Emidi; *GA:* Sergio Coletta; *Paintings:* Jim Dine. *Cast:* Franco Nero (Leonardo Ferri), Vanessa Redgrave (Flavia), Georges Géret (Attilio), Gabriella Grimaldi [Gabriella Boccardo] (Wanda), Madeleine Damien (Wanda's mother), Rita Calderoni (Egle), Renato Menegatti (Egle's friend), David Maunsell (The psychic), John Francis Lane (Male nurse at asylum), Valerio Ruggeri, Arnaldo Momo (Villager), Costantino De Luca (Villager), Marino Biagiola (Villager), Piero De Franceschi (Villager), Camillo Besenzon (Villager), Renato Lupi, Umberto Di Grazia, Giuseppe Bello, Bruna Simionato, Onofrio Folli, Elena Vicini, Sara Momo (Villager), Otello Cazzola (Villager), Mirta Simionato (Villager), Graziella Simionato (Villager), Giulia Menin (Villager). *PROD:* Alberto Grimaldi for P.E.A. (Rome), Produzioni Associate Delphos, Les Productions Artistes Associés (Paris); *PM:* Gino Millozza; *UM:* Alfredo Petri; *PSe:* Stefano Pegoraro. *Country:* Italy/France. Filmed at Cinecittà Studios. *Running time:* 105 min. (m. 3154); *Visa n:* 52702 (11.13.1968); *Rating:* V.M. 18; *Release dates:* 11.14.1968 (Italy); 08.28.1970 (U.S.A.). *Distribution:* P.E.A.—United Artists (Italy); United Artists (U.S.A.); *Domestic gross:* 387,358,000 lire. *Also known as:* Un coin tranquille à la campagne (France, 08.14.1969), Ein ensamer Platz (West Germany, Berlinale, June 1969). *Home video:* MGM (DVD, U.S.), Koch Media (DVD, Germany, as part of the Elio Petri collection boxset).

Leonardo Ferri, a successful painter who is undergoing a period of professional and personal crisis, moves to an old villa in the countryside. Soon, strange details and events haunt him. On a wall, he finds the time-worn painting of a young girl. A local peasant puts flowers under a wall riddled with bullets. The villa's rooms resound with strange noises, the doors close by themselves, objects fall on the floor on their own. Irresistibly impelled to investigate, Leonardo finds out about Wanda, the young countess who lived in the house with her mother and died during the war, killed during an air raid. Leonardo becomes increasingly obsessed with the dead woman, whom he finds out to have been a nymphomaniac: he convinces himself that not only Wanda's ghost still lives in the house, but that she is attempting to kill his lover, Flavia, out of jealousy. Whether this is true or is just a product of Ferri's imagination is left to the viewer: eventually Leonardo—who thinks he has murdered Flavia—ends up in a mental hospital, where he keeps painting with a renewed inspiration. His works are sold by Flavia, who is alive and well, with great success.

The year 1968—and all that came with it—was a fertile ground for heretic, iconoclastic approaches to the Gothic. The intromission of issues related to the present time and age brought to the variation of styles and icons pertaining to the genre in an allegorical, and at times overtly political, way, thus indicating a growing discomfort with the structures and the different forms of modernity.

One such example is Elio Petri's *A Quiet Place in the Country*—a most unusual example of a Gothic tale imbued with present issues, and preoccupied with such topics as the common man's alienation, as emphasized in the works of philosophers like Herbert Marcuse.

Written by Petri and Tonino Guerra in 1962, and loosely based on George Oliver Onions's story "The Beckoning Fair One," *A Quiet Place in the Country* was eventually filmed with a new script by Petri and Luciano Vincenzoni, and released in 1968. The story, in which a Pop art painter, Leonardo (Franco Nero), who is undergoing a personal and working crisis, rents a villa in the Venetian countryside and becomes obsessed with a ghost that inhabits it, is just a pretext: Petri's aim is to portray the alienation of an artist who is enslaved by the needs of mass

production. And, as David Punter argued in his essay on the Gothic *The Literature of Terror*, he does so with the tools of the genre itself.

Petri's protagonist takes refuge among the ghosts of the romantic culture, yet he is less a romantic hero than an out-and-out victim, tortured and exploited by the Capitalist system he feeds with his successful paintings. Not unlike Edgar Allan Poe's tortured souls, Leonardo ends up a crazed lunatic, who lives in a world of his own: his lover/agent Flavia (played by Nero's real-life lover Vanessa Redgrave) keeps selling his paintings, which are more successful than ever. The fact that Leonardo's descent into madness has finally allowed him to regain his long-lost inspiration is just another biting sting in the tail of Petri's venomous parable. The director bitterly satirizes the way art has become in the modern-day world: there is no place for true artistry in a society where everything is reduced to a commodity.

A Quiet Place in the Country approaches the genre in a highly idiosyncratic way, as the director had done in his satirical sci-fi apologue *The Tenth Victim* (*La decima vittima*, 1965). Petri uses a classic Gothic storyline in an instrumental way which somehow recalls Godard's experiments with genre; at the same time he revisits the Fantastic with a stylistic verve that owes much to contemporary Pop art, immensely aided by Ennio Morricone's outstanding score, executed by his Gruppo di Improvvisazione Nuova Consonanza. The story daringly jumps between past and present, reality and hallucination, with wild abandon: the more puzzling bits give way to typical ghost story material, such as the apparitions of a red-dressed ghost and a séance that preludes to Leonardo's final rampage. The result is a rather puzzling, albeit decidedly fascinating work, definitely not for all tastes.

The overall impression, however, is that the two souls of *A Quiet Place in the Country* hardly blend. Rather surprisingly, given the director's intentions, the ideological part is overtly schematic and didactic, whereas the fantastic scenes are more inspired and genuinely involving. Petri manages to capture the erotic essence of the obsession that is devouring Leo-

Italian poster (designed by Sandro Symeoni) for Elio Petri's contemporary take on the Gothic genre, *A Quiet Place in the Country* (author's collection).

nardo, by portraying his schizoid splitting through the painter's meeting with his own *doppelgänger*, and he juxtaposes the phantoms of eroticism to pornography's commodification of female flesh: porn becomes the symbol of a so-ciety that reduces individual needs to consumer goods. As film critic Tullio Kezich noted, this way the film is able to show Italy's malaise of the period, that is "the crisis of a generation sus-pended between the last echoes of the tragedy of war, the changelessness of the province and the relentless integration of the new cities."[1]

Note

1. Tullio Kezich, *Il Millefilm—Dieci anni al cinema 1967–1977* (Milan: Mondadori, 1983), p. 641.

Run, Psycho, Run *(Più tardi, Claire...più tardi)*

D: Brunello Rondi. *S:* Vittoriano Petrilli; *SC:* Giuseppe Mangione, Vittoriano Petrilli, Brunello Rondi; *DOP:* Carlo Bellero (B&W); *M:* Giovanni Fusco, directed by Bruno Nicolai (soloist flute: Severino Gazzelloni) (ed. C.A.M.); *E:* uncredited; *AE:* Marcella Bevilacqua; *PD, ArtD:* Demofilo Fidani; *CO:* Mila Vitelli; *AD:* Maurizio Mein, Renata Paulucci de' Calboli; *C:* Gaetano Valle; *AC:* Loris Bellero; *SO:* Mario Spadoni, Vittorio De Sisti; *MU:* Eligio Trani; *Hair:* Marisa Fraticelli. *Cast:* Gary Merrill (George Dennison), Elga Andersen (Claire/Ann), George Riviere [Georges Rivière] (Dr. Boyd), Margarita Robles (Lady Florence, George's mother), Adriana Asti (Ruth), Marina Malfatti (George's niece), Rossella Falk (Evelyn, Claire's sister), Tanya Beryll [Tania Béryl] (Sara), Michel Lemoine (Guicciardi, the music teacher), Angela Minervini (Irene), Ivy Holzer (Alberta's friend), Diana Rabito (Party guest), Jeanine Reynaud (Alberta), Francesca Balletta, Juan Cortez, Demofilo Fidani (Prince Demofilo), Cristiano Mauro (Robert), Franco Mauro (Charlie), José Riesgo, José Villasante (Ted, the butler). *Uncredited:* John Karlsen (Parish priest). *PROD:* Gaetano Amata for Bianconero Film; *PM:* Federico Del Fauro; *PS:* Maria Teresa Fera; *PSe:* Marco Gigante; *PA:* Ahmed Haggi; *ADM:* Roberto Tomassetti. *Country:* Italy/France. Filmed at Castello della Castelluccia (Rome) and at the Argentario, Tuscany. *Running time:* 93 min. (m. 2665); *Visa n:* 51864 (06.26.1968); *Rating:* not rated; *Release dates:* 07.1968 (Italy); 11.22.1969 (U.S.A.). *Distribution:* Bianco Nero Film (Regional); *Domestic gross:* unknown. *Home video:* none.

Tuscany, 1912. Claire, the young wife of the retired Judge George Dennison, arrives with her little son Robert at his family villa on Mount Argentario to spend the summer there. However, hatred and jealousy nurture within the household, and after a party both Claire and Robert are murdered. A year later, much to his family's disgust, Dennison returns to the villa with a new fiancée, Ann, who is a dead ringer for Claire and also has a little son. It turns out that Dennison hired the woman to help him unmask the murderer: Ann's presence brings to the surface the greed and mutual animosity among Dennison's relatives. Eventually, Ann discovers the shocking truth about Claire's murder by reading Dennison's secret diary: it was the judge who killed his own wife, who in turn was conspiring to dispatch him with her lover, Dr. Boyd; Dennison plans to kill his whole family as well. Ann reveals the truth to Dennison's relatives, who do not seem to believe her, and protect Dennison with their silence. Ann leaves the place for good.

Born in 1924, Brunello Rondi was—as his elder brother Gian Luigi, one of Italy's most renowned film critics, used to say—a Renaissance man. He was a poet, a philosopher, a musicologist, a film critic and a well-respected playwright: his plays *Il viaggio, La stanza degli ospiti, Gli amanti* (the latter filmed in 1968 by Vittorio De Sica and starring Faye Dunaway and Marcello Mastroianni) were brought to the stage by Italy's most prestigious companies and were favorably received by critics.

Rondi's first steps in the cinema were in the late '40s as a scriptwriter: he worked with the likes of Roberto Rossellini on *Francesco giullare di Dio* (1950), the outstanding *Europa '51* (1952), starring Ingrid Bergman, and the war drama *Era notte a Roma* (1960), Alessandro Blasetti (*Altri tempi*, 1952) and Federico Fellini.

Rondi's collaboration with Fellini was a fruitful and lasting one, starting with *La strada* (1954). Rondi was initially credited as "artistic advisor," a credit which he maintained also on *The Swindle* (*Il bidone*, 1955), *Nights of Cabiria* (*Le notti di Cabiria*, 1957), *La Dolce Vita* (1960) and *8½* (1963). According to Fellini himself, several of *La Dolce Vita*'s most brilliant sequences germinated from Rondi's ideas: the decadent party in the house of a Roman prince, the "miracle" scene and the final orgy with its bitter aftermath on the beach at dawn. Rondi co-wrote Fellini's following films, *Le tentazioni del dottor Antonio* (in *Boccaccio 70*, 1962), *8½*,[1] *Juliet of the Spirits* (*Giulietta degli spiriti*, 1965), the sadly never made *Il viaggio di G. Mastorna* (1965–67), *Fellini—Satyricon* (1969, on which Rondi admitted that his contribution was only nominal), *Orchestra Rehearsal* (*Prova d'orchestra*, 1978) and *City of Women* (*La città delle donne*, 1980).[2]

By the end of the Fifties, Brunello Rondi was a well-known, respected, eclectic intellectual.

He contributed to film magazines, taught acting at Rome's Centro Sperimentale di Cinematografia and even directed a handful of short documentaries. The time for his feature debut as a director came in 1962, when producer Moris Ergas hired him to co-direct *Violent Life*, based on Pier Paolo Pasolini's novel, together with Paolo Heusch. Then came *Il demonio*, a story set in contemporary rural Southern Italy, about a young woman named Purif who is living in a remote mountain village, and whose sexual disinhibition has her fellow countrymen believe she has been possessed by the devil.

Shot during the Second Vatican Council, in a period where the Church was slowly undergoing huge transformations, and released a few months after the death of Pope John XXIII, *Il demonio* was a grim view of a country still plagued with superstition. Rondi drew on the Italian literary tradition: Purif's character brings to mind Giovanni Verga's story *La lupa*. Purif's dark force is a primordial cry against the whole world, starting from her own family, and hers is a rebellion towards society, which the latter vainly tries to stop and cut off through a ritual exorcism. The film clearly predated and inspired Lucio Fulci's *Don't Torture a Duckling* (*Non si sevizia un paperino*, 1972): the character of Purif was a model for Florinda Bolkan's "Maciara," while the local witch doctor Zi' Giuseppe, who should cure Purif but abuses her instead, predated that of Georges Wilson in Fulci's film. On the other hand, an extraordinary scene in which Purif walks crab-like on her back during a hysterical fit predated *The Exorcist*'s infamous "spiderwalk."

When *Il demonio* was shown at the Venice festival, most Italian critics panned the film. One even accused Rondi (himself a Catholic) to have made an anti–Catholic film. A dissenting voice was that of the prestigious Edoardo Bruno, who favorably compared Rondi's vision to that of Buñuel, calling *Il demonio* one of Italy's first examples of cinematic Surrealism: "For the first time, the great Surrealist themes come to the fore in Italian cinema: mad love, violent tirades against the dullest aspects of society, the glossy close search of erotic elements in religion, both pagan and Catholic."[3] Foreign

critics, on the other hand, understood Rondi's approach to eroticism, describing it as a force of traumatizing power.

Il demonio's lack of box-office success halted Rondi's career for a while, though, and his next project suffered a sad fate. In an interview for the daily newspaper *Paese Sera* dated July 1965, Rondi explained his third film as a director, *Più tardi, Claire...più tardi*, to a young interviewer named Dario Argento: "I have no intention of making a mystery, or a horror film, or even a suspense yarn, Hitchcock-style. What really interests me is to grasp with a film set in 1912 the origins of today's disease within the *bourgeoisie*, and to portray its degeneration with extreme violence. I read very few crime novels in my life. And I must say that I do not even like them very much. In my film there is indeed a crime, and an investigation. But it's only a pretext, in a story full of hatred set in the last years of the "Belle Époque," when some kind of false euphoria was decomposing, while one could glimpse the first signs of the impending war, the signs of hatred and the strengthening of class struggle."[4]

Rondi had assembled a composite cast, led by Hollywood has-been Gary Merrill, and featuring German beauty Elga Andersen, future Jess Franco acolytes Michel Lemoine and Janine Reynaud and respected stage actresses such as Adriana Asti and Rossella Falk. However, *Più tardi, Claire...più tardi* was shelved and stayed unreleased for at least a couple of years: it was finally picked up for marginal distribution in summer 1968 (meanwhile Rondi had directed another film, the Antonioni-like drama *Domani non siamo più qui*, 1967, starring Ingrid Thulin) and soon sank without trace. Overseas it was released directly to television as *Run, Psycho, Run* via American International Television (AIP-TV) and was dubbed at the same European dubbing studio where such AIP-TV films like *War of the Monsters* and *The Last Man On Earth* were dubbed. Among the female lead's voices there were those of Carolyn De Fonseca and John Karlsen (who also had a bit role in the film). Gary Merrill did his own dubbing.[5]

Despite Rondi's claims, the plot of *Run, Psycho, Run* clearly shows its Hitchcockian influences: Claire's presence seems to acquire supernatural traits, in a patent nod to Hitchcock's *Rebecca*. Nevertheless, the Gothic elements are very strong. The story plays with the themes of the *doppelgänger* (Claire and Ann are played by the same actress, Elga Andersen) and of past events which haunt the present; the setting is a luxurious yet sinister and hostile-looking villa, whose haunting atmosphere is heightened by Carlo Bellero's sumptuous black-and-white cinematography. On the other hand, the dialogue and character development are definitely closer to art films of the period, and the twist ending is surprisingly grim and pessimistic, in an open refusal of genre clichés.

Exquisitely filmed and featuring a refined score by Giovanni Fusco (with Severino Gazzelloni's soloist flute in evidence), *Run, Psycho, Run* is nonetheless an impressive work, even though the lack of editing credits and several awkward passages (including the sudden presence/absence of first-billed Merrill and said ending) imply serious production problems, which resulted in the film's somewhat disjointed storyline.

Originally, Rondi's intention was to focus on Dennison's disturbed psyche, as shown by a number of "additional scenes" written by the director himself—and probably not filmed in their entirety—which are included in the film's official script kept at the CSC library in Rome.[6] Possibly dissatisfied with the script and willing to push the story towards a more explicit psychopathological dimension, Rondi wanted to thrust the film on a very different direction than the current one.

By examining the aforementioned "additional scenes," it was obvious that Rondi was less interested in the final twist than in the attitude of Dennison's relatives: they are *de facto* accomplices of his crime, and eventually chase away the "intruder" who took Claire's place in order to protect not only the judge, but their own *status quo* as well.

In the unfilmed script, the "horrible secret" of Judge Dennison was at first depicted by Rondi in an extraordinarily daring Buñuelian dream sequence: Dennison finds himself in the middle of an orgy in the woods where all his family and friends are involved, while Lemoine's character (a music teacher) directs the couplings just like a conductor, in front of an ecstatic, applauding crowd. What is more, Rondi had conceived an even more morbid resolution, which dealt with sexual neurosis, voyeurism and scoptophilic tendencies.

The director's own handnotes on the script suggest that part of the scene was shot and edited: it patently recalls *Psycho*, with necrophile suggestions rendered explicit by the sight of Claire's mummified body, wearing a sumptuous evening dress and a line of pearls around her neck, whereas Rondi's ending also featured a delirious monologue which culminated with Dennison's confession of his own impotency and voyeurism: "I was never happy with Claire as other husbands are with their wives.... I always loved to create with my imagination, to invent the deepest pleasures, the most daring situations. My pleasure is in the eyes, in the sight, in the objects. What Claire touched, or who touched her. Because I loved to suffer, I loved to be miserable. I wanted her to betray me, to punish me, but I needed to watch her ... always." Dennison killed Claire because she rebelled to that morbid relationship and threatened to reveal the truth.

It is unlikely that the rest of the scene was shot: probably the money had finished, or Merrill was no longer available. However, none of the aforementioned can be found in the current ending, which recycles several early scenes (with the addition of a voiceover) and reduces the mystery to a banal love triangle. At a certain point Ann discovers a skull with a wig, but it is not quite clear what it is all about. It looks slapdash and badly-mounted.

However, what emerges from the unfilmed scenes would have pushed *Run, Psycho, Run* closer to the morbid atmosphere of *The Horrible Dr. Hichcock*, a film which Rondi's somehow recalls. Just like the eponymous surgeon in Freda's film, *Run, Psycho, Run* is about a respectable member of the upper class who secretly cultivates a "horrible secret," a devouring sexual pathology which is known and protected by Dennison's kin: the caste is willing to do whatever it takes in order to save itself, at all costs. Maybe, with Rondi's additions *Run, Psycho, Run* would have been met by the audience and critics with more enthusiasm. Or maybe not. By the time it came out the interest towards Gothic mysteries had waned, and its thought-provoking approach would have probably passed unnoticed amidst the flood of sex and violence that was starting to fill the screens.

However, it is interesting to spot themes that would prove recurrent in Rondi's subsequent work. One such was that of the family as a viper's nest; similarly, Rondi would often set his following films in a secluded space—a villa, an isle, an asylum, a prison—and juxtapose a single character, usually a woman, with a hostile environment or institution. If *Il demonio*'s Purif was defeated by superstition, Ann is a victim of the "status quo" just as the disturbed "wild girl" (Asti) who lives by herself in the woods near the villa. Both are rejected by a self-sufficient microcosm based on hypocrisy and convenience. There is an extraordinary sequence near the film's beginning where Claire's little child is playing the piano at a party, surrounded by an indifferent, bored audience: the guests are too busy tattling behind each other's backs to pay attention to the poor boy, who is obviously having quite a hard time playing a difficult Bach piece. It is a moment that perfectly captures the film's theme, and shows how Rondi was not just an intelligent scriptwriter, but also quite an accomplished director.

With *Run, Psycho, Run*, Rondi moved further away from Neorealism, and developed the same idea of cinema that he had tried his hand at on *Il demonio*: an attempt at exploring the repressed in relation to society, and characterized by a curiosity towards the irrational, the occult, the paranormal. This led him to such projects as the unfilmed *La sensitiva* (1969), written with Fellini's regular collaborator Tullio Pinelli for producer Maleno Malenotti, and centered on another "witch" figure after *Il demonio*: the heroine (Pinelli and Rondi wrote the role for Silvana Mangano) is not exorcised but psychoanalized, and her neurosis has a sexual origin (as in Rondi's 1972 drama *Valeria dentro e fuori*) and could be cured by motherhood. Rondi also co-scripted *Sortilegio* (1970,

Nardo Bonomi), another paranoid Gothic horror film which mixed nods to *Rosemary's Baby* and references to Aleister Crowley. *Sortilegio* recounted the descent into madness of a woman (Erna Schurer) in the midst of a conjugal crisis: while on vacation with her husband (film director Marco Ferreri in one of his few acting roles) in the countryside, she is the victim of hallucinations or visions that perhaps were induced by a Satanic coven.[7] Unfortunately Bonomi's film is still unreleased to this day.

However, Rondi's directorial output in the 1970s, albeit discontinuous, was often underrated, ignored or even reviled. His last film, 1982's *La voce*, went unnoticed, and Rondi died in 1989. A sad epitaph to the oeuvre of one of Italian cinema's most peculiar and underrated *auteurs*.

Notes

1. Fellini stated that Rondi enthusiastically embraced the project of *8½* when it was only just a vague idea, whereas the other scriptwriters, Tullio Pinelli and Ennio Flaiano were quite perplexed. Federico Fellini and Giovanni Grazzini, *Intervista sul cinema* (Bari: Laterza, 1983, 2004), pp. 126–127.
2. According to Rondi's son Umberto, he also contributed (uncredited) to Fellini's *Ginger e Fred* (1986).
3. Edoardo Bruno, "Realtà e surrealtà ne *Il demonio* di Rondi," in *Filmcritica* 145, May 1964.
4. Dario Argento, "Per Rondi: ancora un tema che scotta," in *Paese Sera*, July 29, 1965.
5. Accordingly, *Run, Psycho, Run* was first shown in the United States on November 2, 1969, on Sacramento's KCRA Channel 3, by Bob Wilkins, as part of his *Seven Arts Theater* show. Another, much more recent broadcast was in September 1984 on New York's Channel 9 (the former WOR-TV) on the 3 a.m. movie called "Nine All Night."
6. The script carries a list of alternate titles: *Il giudice* ("The Judge"), *La grande famiglia* ("The Big Family"), *I forestieri* ("The Strangers"), a Lina Wertmüller–style *Tutto quello che è chiaro o nascosto a casa del nobile Dennison* ("All that is either clear or concealed in the house of the noble Mr. Dennison") and, last and best, *Il piacere negli occhi* ("Pleasure in the Eyes").
7. See Davide Pulici, "Sortilegio: la sceneggiatura," in "Misteri d'Italia 2. Guida ai film rari e scomparsi," *Nocturno Dossier* 58, March 2007.

Spirits of the Dead (*Tre passi nel delirio/ Histoires extraordinaires*)

"Metzengerstein." *D:* Roger Vadim. *S:* based on the short story by Edgar Allan Poe; *SC:* Roger Vadim, Pascal Cousin; *DOP:* Claude Renoir; *M:* Jean Prodromidès; *E:* Hélène Plemiannikov; *AE:*

Catherine Gabrielidis, Claire Giniewski; *PD*: Jean André; *APD*: Jean Forestier; *AD*: Michel Clément, Jean-Michel Lacor, Serge Valin; *C*: Philippe Brun, Alain Douarinou, Wladimir Ivanov, Bernard Noisette; *SS*: Suzanne Durrenberger. *Cast*: Jane Fonda (Countess Frederique de Metzengerstein), Peter Fonda (Baron Wilhelm Berlifitzing), Marlène Alexandre, Georges Douking (Upholsterer), Philippe Lemaire (Philippe), Carla Marlier (Claude), Serge Marquand (Hugues), Marie-Ange Aniès (Courtesan). *Uncredited*: Dennis Berry (Courtier), Jackie Blanchot (Courtier), Audoin de Bardot (Page), Anny Duperey (Courtesan), Andréas Voutsinas (Courtier), James Robertson Justice (Countess' advisor—cut from final print), Françoise Prévost (Countess' friend—cut from final print). *PM*: André Cultet, Ludmilla Goulian. Filmed at Kerousere castle at Sibiel—Finisterre.

"William Wilson." *D:* Louis Malle; *S*: based on the short story by Edgar Allan Poe; *SC*: Louis Malle, Clement Biddle Wood, Daniel Boulanger; *DOP*: Tonino Delli Colli; *M*: Diego Mason; *E*: Franco Arcalli, Suzanne Baron; *AE*: Piera Gabutti; *PD*: Ghislain Uhry; *ArtD*: Carlo Leva; *AD*: Vana Caruso; *C*: Sergio Bergamini; *SS*: Norma Giacchero. *Cast*: Alain Delon (William Wilson), Brigitte Bardot (Giuseppina), Katia Christine (Young girl on the dissection table), Umberto D'Orsi (Hans), Renzo Palmer (Priest), Marco Stefanelli (Wilson as a child), Daniele Vargas (University professor); *uncredited*: Andrea Esterhazy (Officer in the gaming table), Paolo Giusti (William Wilson), John Karlsen (Schoolmaster in yard). *PM*: Thomas Sagone. Filmed in Bergamo Alta, Italy.

"Toby Dammit." *D:* Federico Fellini; *S*: based on the short story by Edgar Allan Poe; *SC*: Federico Fellini, Bernardino Zapponi; *DOP*: Giuseppe Rotunno; *M*: Nino Rota; *E*: Ruggero Mastroianni; *AE*: Vanda Olasio; *PD*: Piero Tosi; *ArtD*: Fabrizio Clerici; *AD*: Eschilo Tarquini [Francesco Aluigi, Liliane Betti—uncredited]; *OE*: Joseph Nathanson; *C*: Giuseppe Maccari; [*AC*: Piero Servo—uncredited]; *SS*: Shaila Rubin. *Cast*: Terence Stamp (Toby Dammit), Salvo Randone (Priest), Annie Tonietti (TV commentator); *uncredited*: Marina Yaru (The Devil), Fabrizio Angeli (One of the Manetti Brothers), Ernesto Colli (One of the Manetti Brothers), Ettore Arena (Rabbi at airport), Federico Boido (Toby's double), Brigitte (Tall girl with the old actor), Paul Cooper (2nd interviewer), Dakar (Black man at airport), Andrea Fantasia (Party producer), Irina Maleeva (Gypsy fortune teller), Marco Messeri (One beatle), Antoni Pietrosi (Actress), Mimmo Poli (Taxi driver/Party guest), Polidor [Ferdinand Guillaume] (Old actor), Alfredo Rizzo (Angry man in car), Giovanni Tarallo (Photographer at airport), Marisa Traversi (Marilù Traversi), Milena Vukotic (TV interviewer), Aleardo Ward (1st interviewer). *PM*:

Thomas Sagone; *GM*: Enzo Provenzale [uncredited]. Filmed at Cinecittà Studios, Rome. *PROD*: Alberto Grimaldi, Raymond Eger for P.E.A. (Rome), Les Films Marceau Cocinor (Paris); *PP*: Enzo Ocone. *Country*: Italy/France. *Running time*: 121 min. (m. 2522); Visa n: 52051 (07.24.1968); *Rating*: V.M.14; *Release dates*: 09.12.1968 (Italy); 07.23.1969 (U.S.A.). *Distribution*: P.E.A. (Italy); AIP (U.S.A.). *Domestic gross*: 512,000,000 lire. *Also known as*: Tales of Mystery and Imagination, Powers of Evil (U.K.). Home video: Arrow (Blu-ray, U.K.), Homevision, Image (DVD, U.S.).

"Metzengerstein": after being rejected by her neighbor Baron Wilhelm, the debauched and promiscuous Countess Federica of Metzengerstein sets his stables on fire, causing the man's death. Soon a black wild horse arrives at Federica's estate, and the woman becomes obsessed with the animal...

"William Wilson": Northern Italy, nineteenth century. A man named William Wilson confesses a murder to a priest: he has killed his own doppelgänger, also named William Wilson...

"Toby Dammit": English actor Toby Dammit arrives in Rome to shoot a Catholic Western produced by the Vatican. The perpetually inebriated Toby is obsessed with the sight of an angelic little girl playing with a ball, whom he believes to be the devil. After he jumps into his new Ferrari for a mad ride in the hills of Rome, Toby's vision turns out to be a macabre omen...

Italian Gothic films of the Sixties had few things in common with Italian fantastic literature of the same period, as proven by a few exceptions: Bava's "The Drop of Water" was based on a (more than passable, indeed) imitation of a typical English ghost story, whereas *The Virgin of Nuremberg* was the adaptation of a lurid pulp paperback novel. Yet it was in the twentieth century that the specificity of Italian *fantastique* emerged with several of the country's major writers, who radically reinvented its themes and style.[1]

Alberto Savinio reworked the ghost story in a surprising way, in the light of psychoanalysis in *La casa ispirata*, 1920–1925; Tommaso Landolfi had his ghosts move within a linguistically refined space, where the deviation from the plausible to the fantastic was minimal, sometimes just a matter of words; Anna Maria Ortese followed the style of eighteenth century *conte philosophique* in *L'iguana*, 1965. These

authors all had in common a conception of the Fantastic in sharp
conflict with the nineteenth-century
tradition, even when it apparently
followed its clichés (see Landolfi's exemplary *Racconto d'autunno*, 1947),
and it was quite distant from proper
Gothic. What is more, their vision
was almost impossible to bring to the
screen without altering its very essence—as evidenced by Catherine
McGilvray's disastrous adaptation of
L'iguana (2004).

And yet there were also figures
who left an indelible mark on Italian
fantasy cinema, and took part in creating a "different" Gothic, by revisiting its stylistic and thematic features in an original, surprising way.
That was the case with Bernardino
Zapponi (1927–2000), a writer, novelist and screenwriter who worked
with the likes of Federico Fellini,
Dario Argento, Paolo Cavara and
Dino Risi among others, bringing a
peculiar sensibility towards the Fantastic in general and the Gothic in
particular.

Zapponi's love for the Gothic
genre emerged in his short story collection *Gobal* (1967), inspired by
E.T.A. Hoffmann, Poe and Dino
Buzzati, where the Roman writer
tried to reshape the Gothic in a contemporary setting. Unsurprisingly,
Zapponi's stories caught the interest
of Federico Fellini (who, just like the
writer, had taken his first steps in the
weekly humorous magazine *Marc'Aurelio*). "Tonight I'm going to bed
happy, because my friend Zapponi
told me some good stories," the filmmaker would tell him.[2]

One of Zapponi's short stories
that most impressed Fellini was *C'è una voce
nella mia vita* ("There is a voice in my life"), an
impressive little sketch which transposed in a
contemporary setting a typical Poe theme, the
sense of guilt at the center of "The Tell-Tale

Italian poster for the Edgar Allan Poe–inspired anthology *Spirits
of the Dead* (author's collection).

Heart." In Zapponi's story, the instrument that
reveals a murder is an everyday innocuous object, the telephone, used to uncanny effect just
like in *Black Sabbath*'s opening segment. So,
when Fellini was involved in a horror movie an-

thology project dedicated to Edgar Allan Poe, produced by Raymond Eger and Alberto Grimaldi, his first choice was Zapponi's short story.

Omnibus comedy films were Italian cinema's most profitable thread of the decade. *Spirits of the Dead* germinated, at least on paper, like a reckless and grim twin of such omnibus films, which brought together renowned filmmakers and stars, and allowed them to indulge in a common theme. This had been the case with *Boccaccio '70*, which Fellini co-directed with Vittorio De Sica, Mario Monicelli and Luchino Visconti, *RoGoPaG* (*Ro.Go.Pa.G.*, 1963, Roberto Rossellini, Jean-Luc Godard, Pier Paolo Pasolini, Ugo Gregoretti), *The Dolls* (*Le bambole*, 1965, Mauro Bolognini, Luigi Comencini, Dino Risi, Franco Rossi), and *The Witches* (*Le streghe*, 1967, Mauro Bolognini, Vittorio De Sica, Pier Paolo Pasolini, Franco Rossi, Luchino Visconti).

Eger and Grimaldi's project of a Poe-inspired anthology was quite ambitious: the names that were initially announced to be involved in it were Visconti, Claude Chabrol, Joseph Losey and Orson Welles. In the end, though, Fellini was joined by Roger Vadim and Louis Malle.

"Metzengerstein," Poe's very first story to be published in 1832 in Philadelphia's *Saturday Courier*, was adapted by Vadim with the same languid approach that characterized *Blood and Roses*. Vadim cast his then-wife Jane Fonda, who had just starred in *Barbarella* (1968), and tried to reinvent her screen presence in a role similar to those played by Barbara Steele in her Italian films: by pushing the pedal on the erotic aspects, Vadim tried to bring Poe's morbid obsessions to the screen, but beside the odd casting of Fonda's brother Peter as her object of desire, the results were disappointingly flat. Malle's episode, based on one of Poe's most celebrated stories, "William Wilson" (published in 1839) was slightly more vital, but no less disappointing. Malle's vision of Poe owed much to Visconti's period dramas such as *Senso* (1954) and *The Leopard* (*Il gattopardo*, 1963), and the choice of the city of Bergamo gave the film an eerie atmosphere, while Alain Delon's turn as the tormented titular character who is persecuted by his own *doppelgänger* was surprisingly effective,

putting to best use the actor's cold and detached beauty. But overall it looked as if Malle had taken the project mostly as a well-paid vacation, or as an excuse for an exercise in style.

Fellini's episode was quite a different story, indeed.

Eventually, due to the reluctance of producers over Zapponi's name, Fellini changed his mind and went back to Poe's original stories as inspiration. After considering "The Scythe of Time" and "The Premature Burial," his choice fell on "Never Bet the Devil Your Head" (1841), subtitled "A Tale with a Moral": definitely not one of Poe's best, it had not even been translated into French by Baudelaire in *Histoires Extraordinaires*, the first collection of Poe's stories published in Europe whose title the film borrowed.

Some parts of "Never Bet the Devil Your Head" looked congenial to Fellini's imagination. Toby's coarse and surreal childhood ("At six months of age, I caught him gnawing a pack of cards. At seven months he was in the consistent habit of catching and kissing the female babies. So he went on, increasing in iniquity [...]. Perhaps the worst of all his vices was a propensity for cursing and swearing, and for backing his profane assertions with bets") seemed apt material for something in the vein of Guido's childhood as evoked in *8½*. In the end, though, the only thing that was left of it was a line in the script when Toby recalls that his own mother smiled while she beat him. Another Fellini-esque trait might have been the hypocritical narrator, who functions as Toby's voice of conscience, but in the end has Toby dug up and sells him for dog's meat.

However, Fellini's choice went beyond the horrific content, as he focused on the moral punchline which Poe sarcastically offered to the reader, "written in capital letters in the title." Fellini and Zapponi took only Poe's macabre ending—the deadly jump that costs Toby his life and the image of the devil carrying away the dead man's severed head—and discarded all the rest.

Much has been written about the Devil as seen by Fellini. In Poe's story he is described as "a little lame old gentleman of venerable aspect.

Jane Fonda and Peter Fonda in Roger Vadim's episode "Metzgengerstein," from the Poe-inspired trilogy *Spirits of the Dead* (Billy Rose Theatre Division, New York Public Library for the Performing Arts, Astor, Lenox and Tilden Foundations).

Nothing could be more reverend than his whole appearance, for he not only had on a full suit of black, but his shirt was perfectly clean, and the collar turned very neatly down over a white cravat, while his hair was parted in front like a girl's." Renowned novelist Goffredo Parise (who had penned the foreword to *Gobal*) offered to play the role, but eventually the Maestro changed his mind, and opted for a totally different interpretation. In his episode *Le ten-*

tazioni del dottor Antonio in *Boccaccio '70*, Satan had the curvaceous feminine shape of Anita Ekberg ("I am the devil" the gigantic Anita claims, as she descends from a billboard, in one of cinema's truly great fantastic moments). In "Toby Dammit," the Devil according to Fellini is an angelic little child with a white ball (played by Marina Yaru), which in the end will be replaced by Toby's head.

The first thing that comes to mind is the little Melissa Graps in Mario Bava's *Kill, Baby... Kill!*, who would become the object of countless references, homages, tributes and plagiarism over the years. Many critics and film historians openly accused Fellini of copying Bava, due also to the latter's answer when asked about the supposed plagiarism: "She is just as in my film, the same. I told Giulietta Masina about it and she shrugged with a smile and said, you know Federico..."[3]

Yet the matter is a little more complicated than that.

Even though Bava and Fellini knew each other since the 1940s, it is widely known that Fellini was no cinephile: he very rarely went to the movies, and it is unlikely that he would "waste" his time with a horror film, albeit one directed by someone of his acquaintance. On the other hand, Bernardino Zapponi had almost certainly seen *Kill, Baby...Kill!*, as he admired Bava to the point that, at the time when he was the editor of the magazine *Il Delatore*, he announced a special issue entirely dedicated to the director—a project which was shelved due to the mag's folding.[4] During the years, Bava scholars pointed out a number of antecedents to the little girl with the ball: Tim Lucas mentioned Susannah York in a scene of John Huston's *Freud* (1962), while Alberto Pezzotta noticed a striking resemblance with the episode "Una donna dolce, dolce" ("A Sweet, Sweet Woman") directed by Mauro Bolognini in the omnibus *La donna è una cosa meravigliosa* (1964: other episodes were directed by Shuntaro Tanikawa and Pino Zac). In said episode, Vittorio Caprioli falls into the river Tevere and dies while playing with a little girl who throws a ball at him. The latter seems a more likely inspiration, given the fact that San-

dra Milo, who played roles in both *8½* and *Juliet of the Spirits*, had a role in the film.[5]

On the other hand, on *Kill, Baby...Kill!* Bava (or his scriptwriters) possibly recalled a famous scene in Fritz Lang's *M* (1931), where a murder committed by the paedophile serial killer (Peter Lorre) is described by metonymy through the little victim's ball rolling unguarded in a field. Bava scholars, on the other hand, did not pay much attention to another possible reference to Bava's work: the unsettling street lamp that descends in the middle of a road during Toby's trip to the Roman hills (the so-called Castelli), which bears a curious affinity with the lamp holder in "The Drop of Water," and was perhaps another homage by Zapponi.

That said, Fellini's devil is only iconographically comparable to Bava's sad little ghost. "Fellini liked contrasts. The devil's ugly? Let's make it beautiful. Is he hideous and evil? We will make it attractive and innocent. It will be a boy—even better, a girl!"[6] as Zapponi recalls in his own book about Fellini. What is more, the writer points out the common inspiration behind *Kill, Baby...Kill!* and "Toby Dammit": the horrors of childhood according to Henry James.

What must be pointed out is what the little girl stands for: the devil. A didactic, emblematic presence in Italian cinema since the early silent era (such as in *Satana*, made in 1912 by Luigi Maggi), the devil had been absent in the 1960s Gothics, if one does not count its iconographical evocation by means of the "Mask of Satan" nailed on Barbara Steele's face in *Black Sunday* or the ill-fated Faustian pact in *Katarsis*. Elsewhere, the Horned One had turned into a harmless, even enjoyable figure, the subject of jokes in parodies such as *Totò al giro d'Italia* or in more sophisticated comedies such as Ettore Scola's *The Devil in Love* (*L'arcidiavolo*, 1966). In Fellini's film, the devil becomes once again a terrifying image, even more so because of its *sui generis* appearance—a fact that underlines the director's peculiar reimagining of his own Catholic background.

It is amazing how Fellini's universe becomes one and the same with Poe's Gothic nightmare, while maintaining a strong individuality. "Poe's horror is mental and still: there is no air, no time, perspectives are deformed, characters do no have bodies, only thoughts," as Zapponi explained. A fantasy world which the director of *8½* populated with his bulimic imagination.

Fellini's choice of setting the story in Italy, between Cinecittà and the Roman Castles area, signed the director's return to the movie industry and the picturesque characters that populated it after the idiosyncratic ghost story *Juliet of the Spirits*. What is more, it underlined how since *La Dolce Vita* Fellini's cinema had portrayed itself as a parade of the horrid and the monstrous, rouged under the tricks and clown-like smiles of a circus' false cheerfulness. Rather than Chaplin's *The Circus*, Fellini's real unconscious model had always been *Freaks*.

In addition to that, "Toby Dammit" reveals the dark and vaguely disturbing side of Italy's Boom, which was slowly emerging from such *sui generis* Gothic films as Damiani's *The Witch*: Fellini's Lazio region is "Papal and felonious [...]; the scenery has the color of blood and wine [...] the smell of donuts and stab wounds," as Zapponi put it: the result was a grotesque rendition of Gothic barbarism, declined to the present day.

Fellini and Zapponi completely distorted Toby's character, who in the story is a shady, not-to-be-trusted jerk, an avid bettor by attitude and habit, "detestably poor." They made him a movie star, admired and pampered, they gave him Terence Stamp's angelic features, they shaped it in such a way as to add him to the ranks of Fellini's typical protagonists. *La Dolce Vita*'s Marcello Rubini (Marcello Mastroianni) was an observer at the edge of the story, a shadow among shadows who lived out of other people's fame: nevertheless he was involved in a world he utterly despised, and where in order to float one had to get dirty and become an accomplice. Toby is just a puppet

without art nor part, even though his strings are not as visible as the ones that moved the characters of Pier Paolo Pasolini's fantasy "Che cosa sono le nuvole?", itself an outstanding segment of an omnibus film, *Capriccio all'italiana* (1968). Toby is exhibited, used, tossed from one set to another, constantly out of focus, confused, inebriated. It is as if the only way for him to interact with (or survive to) the reality he has fallen into is a perennial sensorial alteration.

"Toby's character moves like a POV camera, with no identity whatsoever," as Spanish film scholar Montserrat Hormigos noticed. "The people he meets look either terrified or indifferent to the space occupied by that vampire with no face and body that he is."[8] Toby does not relate to others, except through his passive stare: he registers horror after horror and acts like a filter for the viewer. Compared to Marcello Rubini, he is devoid of any capacity for intellectual analysis. He is stupid, he is dull. He came to Rome just because he was promised a Ferrari, a prize which will also be the instrument of his death. That is his own pact with the devil: the little girl who claims the pledge is only the final user, while everyone else in the story is either an accomplice or an architect of Toby's downfall.

With a brilliant intuition, in the opening

The Devil as an angelic little girl (Marina Yaru) in Federico Fellini's "Toby Dammit," from *Spirits of the Dead* (author's collection).

scene at the airport—almost entirely rendered through Toby's POV shots—Fellini mixed real extras, dummies, people with paper masks representing their faces and two-dimensional full size silhouettes. It was a way to emphasize the narrator's morbid sensibility and his distorted perception of reality—something which in Poe's stories often resolves itself in an initial *excusatio* ("True!—nervous—very, very dreadfully nervous I had been and am [...] The disease had sharpened my senses—not destroyed—not dulled them," "The Tell-Tale Heart"; "I was sick, sick unto death, with that long agony," "The Pit and the Pendulum"; "I am come of a race noted for vigor of fancy and ardor of passion," "Eleonora"). At the same time, though, Fellini moved one step forward the surrealistic vein of Italian horror as represented by Bava's opening parade of men and mannequins during the opening credits of *Blood and Black Lace*. The airport terminal in "Toby Dammit" is a scenery that recalls the idea behind Borges' story *Esse est percipi*: our clothes are full of nothing, we have been replaced by our own shadows, and we are content to attend—to interact is already impossible—, since everything takes place on the shiny and deceptive surface of appearances.

"I only live during the night," Toby confesses. Like Marcello Rubini, he is one of those vampire-like "children of the night" who populate Fellini's cinema in general and *La Dolce Vita* in particular. "Toby Dammit" takes place in one long night which represents an inevitable descent into hell, from the crimson twilight at the Fiumicino airport to the ending at Ariccia bridge—everything is recreated in the studio, as was customary with Fellini. Just one night that expands and deforms dramatically, illuminated by spotlights and neon lights, shop signs and street lamps which pierce the darkness, ripping shreds of hidden truths.

The Faustian Rome that greets and acclaims Toby but demands a pledge from him is an anticipation of *Fellini—Satyricon*'s ancient Rome (which Fellini termed as "science-fiction-like"), as shown by the very first images of its blood-red sky beyond the airport windows. It is a world of vampires and ghosts who live only under (and for) the artificial lights, and whose cheeks are rouged like Paul Morrissey's Dracula in order to hide their decay and degradation.

Nino Rota's extraordinary music score punctuates Toby's descent and functions as an "indirect factor of indictment: it adds a sad note of vulgarity and decrepitude which transcends the various situations and defines the characters and their actions."[9] In the final sequence depicting Toby's mad race, the music is replaced by a mixture of noises, animal verses, screeching tires and engine roars. It is a mechanical requiem for pistons and tires that stands as a grim counterpart to *8½*'s circus march.

Fellini, as Argento would later do in his own Poe rendition (*The Black Cat*, in *Two Evil Eyes*, 1990), stuffs the story with homages to the writer's universe. Terence Stamp—pale, disheveled, sweaty because of his perennial state of alcoholic inebriation—is made-up to look like Poe's portraits (Fellini carried one in his wallet, as Zapponi recalled), and he is dressed like a decadent dandy. His appearance makes him look like a time traveler, an alien fallen to earth, into a present to which he gives in by way of inertia. Fellini cast him after Antonioni had fired him from *Blow-Up* and replaced him with David Hemmings. Stamp was staying in Rome in that period, looking for other work opportunities, and by sheer chance Fellini noticed a photo of him. He was immediately struck by "his extraordinary, angelic face, deeply decadent: the perfect loser dandy, the Dionysiac rock-star, the alcoholic aristocrat rotten from the inside yet still capable of exuding his monumental blond fascination."[10]

Toby's long journey into the night takes place in five distinct stages and brings him in contact with the monsters from his own id: this way, Fellini bypasses the non-filmability of Poe's work by embedding these monsters inside his own imagery. The shot of a hostess' face in a monitor at the Fiumicino terminal is a technologized version of "The Oval Portrait"; the television interviewer (Milena Vukotic) asks Toby whether he has seen the devil in the shape of a black cat; the actor is introduced to his own stunt double (Federico Boido), just as "William Wilson"'s *doppelgänger* shows up in a cowboy hat and boots; later on, the drunk Toby meets an

"ideal woman" who prom-
ises him eternal love: an
appearance which is half
the ghost of *8½*'s Claudia
Cardinale and half Ligeia;
last but not least, the red
Ferrari which is Toby's object of desire is an *up-to-
date* version of the "fiery
colored horse" in "Met-
zengerstein."

Fellini's own universe
perfectly fits this reworking through the prism of
the horror genre. The first
film Federico saw in a theater when he was just six—
and which marked his
imagination so vividly he
once claimed he wanted
to remake a scene of it in
each of his own films—

Terence Stamp as the doomed, eponymous alcoholic British actor in "Toby
Dammit" (Billy Rose Theatre Division, New York Public Library for the
Performing Arts, Astor, Lenox and Tilden Foundations).

was Guido Brignone's *Maciste in Hell* (*Maciste
all'inferno*, 1926). "Toby Dammit" is just that
after all—a descent into hell.

Toby's voiceover, which accompanies us
through the first scene, is a voice from the beyond: in retrospect, the images of the plane
landing—an allegory of the arrival to a hellish
underworld, under a red sky—are perhaps a
nod to Fellini's unfinished project, *Il viaggio di
G. Mastorna*, the story of a man's journey in the
afterlife. Thus, the paparazzi who welcome
Toby poking him with their camera flashes instead of pitchforks can be seen as a devilish version of the photographers who run through Via
Veneto on their Vespas in search of a scoop in
La Dolce Vita. Then, one of the film's most impressive sequences—Dammit's journey from
the airport to the TV studios—is Fellini's per-
fecting his own vision of "cities equal hell," a
theme which definitely took on fantastic/hor-
rific features in his work after *La Dolce Vita*.
Barely sketched in *8½*'s opening—the nightmarish traffic jam where Guido is stuck into
(perhaps an inspiration for Dino Buzzati's extraordinary novelette *Viaggio agli inferni del secolo*, 1966), this idea expanded to encompass
the whole film in *Fellini—Satyricon* and *Roma*

(1972) before the impossible return to the
childhood memories of 1973's *Amarcord*. Yet
Fellini went back to the theme with the studio-
bound Venice in 1976's *Fellini's Casanova*, then
with the eponymous *City of Women*, and eventually—in a summation of his vision and a portrayal of an entire country's degradation—
Cinecittà as seen in *Ginger and Fred* and a
metropolis of antennas in *The Voice of the
Moon* (*La voce della luna*, 1989).

Another extraordinary sequence—the cere-
mony/pantomime of the Italian film awards before a pool that looks like a Chthonian swamp—
echoes the sequence at the Baths of Caracalla
in *La Dolce Vita*, and allows Fellini the umpteenth parade of monsters which were never
that close to damned souls. Then, there is
Toby's frantic last trip, possibly Fellini's reimagining of Kirk Douglas' mad car race through
Rome near the ending of *Two Weeks in Another
Town*: a dizzying escape (again through Dammit's POV) inside another of Fellini's mazes:
closed roads, blind alleys, junctions that do not
take anywhere, illusory escape routes from a
world that finally has shown itself in all its horror, impossible to hide from.

The landscape gradually becomes chaotic

and indecipherable; objects, animal and people emerge from the night and fog—like *Amarcord*'s visions in the mist, but devoid of any poetic inspiration, and frightening in their plain absurdity: an equestrian statue, silhouettes of dogs, waiters, sheets, a flock of sheep that looks like a nod to Buñuel's *The Exterminating Angel* (*El ángel exterminador*, 1962), horrid billboards. As Hormigos put it, "Dammit wants to go back to Rome, to the house of the Father, but he is just a Dyonisus about to be ritually sacrificed— a sacrifice announced by billboards showing images of castrating toothed mouths."[11]

The interrupted bridge over the void that Toby chooses to cross takes a metaphysical meaning: a broken umbilical cord which does not allow Toby's return to the land of the living, the day, the light. Once he realizes that, the only thing left is death—a death which he greets with joy.

"Wait for me!" Toby shouts to the girl before pressing the accelerator.

Notes

1. To quote literature historian Ferdinando Amigoni, "The bestiary of the Fantastic was enriched with unusual specimen, the list of impossible events comprised minimal, specious and disorienting space-time riddles." Amigoni also noted that while the theme of the *doppelgänger* thrived in movies, on paper "it started to look worn, not thin enough to describe the fluctuations of identities and the multiplicity of needs that cohabit in the human psyche." Ferdinando Amigoni, *Fantasmi nel Novecento* (Turin: Bollati Boringhieri, 2004), p. 39.
2. Bernardino Zapponi, *Il mio Fellini* (Venice: Marsilio, 1995), p. 9.
3. Luigi Cozzi, "Intervista a Mario Bava," in *Horror* 13, December 1970/January 1971, p. 101.
4. Alberto Pezzotta, "Sottovalutato? Una leggenda," in Manlio Gomarasca and Davide Pulici, eds., "Genealogia del delitto. Il cinema di Mario e Lamberto Bava," *Nocturno Dossier* 24, July 2004, p. 23.
5. Pier Maria Bocchi and Alberto Pezzotta, *Mauro Bolognini* (Milan: Il Castoro, 2008), p. 85.
6. Zapponi, *Il mio Fellini*, p. 14.
7. Ibid., p. 15.
8. Montserrat Hormigos, "Flores curiosas de la cripta fílmica de Poe," in Antonio José Navarro, ed., *Las sombras del horror. Edgar Allan Poe en el cine* (Madrid: Valdemar, 2009), p. 225.
9. Ibid., p. 224.
10. Federico Fellini and Damien Pettigrew, *Federico Fellini: sono un gran bugiardo* (Rome: Elle U Multimedia, 2003), p. 104.
11. Hormigos, *Flores curiosas de la cripta fílmica de Poe*, p. 229.

1969

La bambola di Satana

D: Ferruccio Casapinta. *S:* Ferruccio Casapinta; *SC:* Giorgio Cristallini, Carlo M. Lori, Ferruccio Casapinta; *Dial:* Alfredo Medori; *DOP:* Francesco Attenni (Telecolor); *M:* Franco Potenza; *E:* Franco Attenni; *PD, SD:* Sandro Dell'Orco; *C:* Vito Brandi; *MU:* Oscar Pacelli, Leandro Marini; *Hair:* Lucia La Porta; *CO:* Giuliana Serano; *SP:* Nicola Bonsanti; *SO:* Giuseppe Mangione; *SOE:* Enzo Di Liberto; *Mix:* Mario Sisti; *DubD:* Lorenzo Artale; *SS:* Margherita Reginato. *Cast:* Erna Schurer [Emma Costantino] (Elizabeth Ballianon), Roland Carey (Jack Seaton), Aurora Batista (Carol), Ettore Ribotta (Paul Reynaud), Lucie [Lucia] Bomez (Claudine), Manlio Salvatori (Edward), Franco Daddi (Mr. Cordova), Beverley Fuller, Eugenio Galadini (Andrea), Giorgio Gennari (Gérard), Domenico Ravenna (Mr. Shinton), Teresa Ronchi (Jeannette), Ivan Giovanni Scratuglia. *PROD:* Cinediorama; *PM:* Carlo Chamblant; *PS:* Giuseppe Frontani; *PSe:* Romolo Salvati; *ADM:* Bruno Sassaroli. *Country:* Italy. Filmed at Castle Borghese, Pratica di Mare and in Abruzzo. *Running time:* 90 min. (m. 2522); Visa n: 53743 (05. 10.1969); *Rating:* V.M.18; *Release date:* 06.12.1969. *Distribution:* Paris Etoile (Regional); *Domestic gross:* 118,009,000 lire. *Also known as:* Satana ha sbagliato una mossa ("Satan did a wrong move"). *Home video:* Dolly (VHS, Italy)

On the death of her uncle Sir Ballianon, young Elizabeth arrives with her boyfriend, Jack Seaton, and a couple of friends to take possession of the castle she has inherited from the deceased. The housekeeper, Miss Carol, warns Elizabeth that the place is haunted, and tries to convince her to sell it to the wealthy Paul Reynaud. During the first nights spent in the manor, Elizabeth is troubled by hallucinatory nightmares: it would seem Carol was right. Truth is, Elizabeth is menaced by a more earthly presence: there is a rich deposit of uranium underneath the castle's basement, which Carol and her mysterious lover want to keep for themselves. They drugged Elizabeth in order to scare her and force her to sell the castle...

Ferruccio Casapinta's only film as a director, *La bambola di Satana* ("Satan's Doll") is an obscure—and deservedly so—addition to the Gothic genre, that looks as if it came out too late for its own good—which was probably the case. The film relies on imagery that, less than a decade after the genre's heyday, was already perceived as obsolete.

As scripted by the director with Giorgio Cristallini and Carlo Lori, the plot is a tiresome reworking of typical pulp novel stuff, a slow-moving murder mystery (with unlikely spy film overtones), spiced with the Gothic's most time-worn clichés (the castle, an inheritance, ghosts, a young lady in peril, a quicksand swamp) plus a pre–Argento black-gloved killer and a few timid erotic sequences.

Nevertheless, despite the heroine's drug-induced erotic "nightmares" (including one in which Erna Schurer is stripped down naked and whipped in a torture chamber by a trio of hooded tormentors) the actress' body is strategically hidden by props or camera angles, that barely a breast can be glimpsed—a decidedly disappointing sight for audiences who were getting used to much more spicy tastes. The results are closer to the period's erotic photonovels, a fact heightened by the opening credits, with black-and-white and color stills to the sound of a cheesy theme, courtesy of Franco Potenza, that sounds more appropriate to a softcore romp than a Gothic horror film.

If the budget is patently on a shoestring, Casapinta shows no directorial flair at all. For a Gothic film, *La bambola di Satana* looks awful. Furthermore, the editing is disjointed at best, with day and night shots alternating within the same scene. Special effects are terrible (with intermittent colored lenses poorly simulating a thunderstorm, not to mention the astonishingly fake pink clouds that surround the castle in the opening scene), zooms abound and the ending features a duel with swords that must be seen to be believed. The sets are almost embarrassing: a restaurant where a group of youngsters are dancing to a juke-box is a poor-looking semi-empty room, yet even more slapdash is the patchwork of several different locations that make for the supposedly French manor where the entire film takes place (which

Italian poster for *La bambola di Satana* (author's collection).

include Castle Borghese in Pomezia), which further hints at production issues.

The director's ineptitude and the film's troubles were best summarized by its leading lady Erna Schurer, the film's *bambola* (no trace of Satan, indeed), who in the '60s took part in many photonovels (including the infamous *Killing*) before ending up in the movies: that year, she also starred in Alberto Cavallone's controversial *Le salamandre*. "It was Casapinta's a.d. who did everything on set, someone who later worked with Tinto Brass. Casapinta was an idiot who couldn't do anything.... I think he had a grant for the film, or something like that—I don't remember. Filming was stopped and then resumed ... it was a troubled shoot, which we did in Abruzzo. However, there were a lot of professionals in the crew: I remember the script girl, Ninni (Margherita) Reginato, who had worked with Pietro Germi. Eventually we finished the film and I still get royalties for TV broadcastings."[1]

Besides Schurer's passable turn in the lead, the cast is badly assembled: former sword-and-sandal *beau* Henri Louis Roland Carey is hopelessly wooden as the hero. The Swiss-French Carey, whose main claim to fame was Riccardo Freda's *The Giants of Thessaly* (*I giganti della Tessaglia*, 1960) where he played Jason, would stay away from the screen for over a decade, focusing on his work as voice actor at Fono Roma. In one of the weirdest comebacks in movie history, the 48-year-old actor showed up again (with a wig) in a quintet of porn flicks directed in 1981/82 by Alexander Borsky, a.k.a. Aristide Massaccesi, namely *Labbra vogliose*, *Sesso acerbo*, *Le porno investigatrici*, *La voglia* and *Super Hard Love*. In the '90s Carey even appeared in Krzystof Kieslowski's austere *Red* (*Trois Couleurs: Rouge*, 1994) as a drug dealer. On the other hand, the Aurora Batista who plays Claudine is *not* the Spanish actress Aurora Bautista.

Note

1. Davide Pulici, "Erna Schurer," in Manlio Gomarasca and Davide Pulici, eds., "Le sorelle di Venere 2," *Nocturno Dossier* 59, June 2007, p. 32.

The Unnaturals—Contronatura, a.k.a. *Schreie in der Nacht*

D: Anthony M. Dawson [Antonio Margheriti]. *S* and *SC*: Antonio Margheriti; *DOP*: Riccardo Pallottini; *M*: Carlo Savina (Ed. C.A.M.); *E*: Otello Colangeli; *AE*: Dante Amatucci; *ArtD*: Fabrizio Frisardi; *C*: Sergio Martinelli; *CO*: Marta Gissi; *MU*: Franco Di Girolamo; *Hair*: Maria Grazia Nardi; *SO*: Giovanni Laureano; *Mix*: Fausto Achilli, Sandro Ochetti, Albes Des Novas; *SS*: Eva Koltay. *Cast*: Joachim Fuchsberger (Ben Taylor), Marianne Koch (Mrs. Vivian Taylor), Helga Anders (Elisabeth), Claudio Camaso [Claudio Volonté] (Alfred Sinclair), Dominique Boschero (Margarete), Alan Collins [Luciano Pigozzi] (Uriah), Marianne Leibl (Herta, Uriah's mother), Giuliano Raffaelli (Archibald Barrett), Marco Morelli (Richard Wright), Gudrun Schmidt (Diana). *Uncredited*: Lella Cattaneo (Party guest), Giuseppe Marrocco (Party guest), Giulio Massimini (Party guest). *PROD*: Antonio Margheriti, Artur Brauner for Super International Pictures, Edo Cinematografica (Rome), C.C.C. Filmkunst (Berlin); *PM*: Nino Masini; *PS*: Franco Ciferri. *Country*: Italy/West Germany. Filmed at Tirrenia Studios. *Running time*: 91 min. (m. 2457); *Visa n*: 54284 (08.20.1969); *Rating*: V.M.18; *Release date*: 09.12.1969. *Distribution*: Paris Etoile (Regional); *Domestic gross*: 287,000,000 lire. *Also known as*: *Screams in the Night*, *Schreie in der Nacht* (West Germany, 05.30.1969), *Contranatura* (Spain). *Home video*: Donau (DVD, Germany)

On a trip to Brighton, where he is expected to deposit papers that will make him the heir of his deceased cousin Richard Wright, the wealthy Archibald Barrett is forced to stop in the middle of nowhere when his car breaks down during a nighttime storm. His traveling companions are his bookkeeper Ben Taylor and his wife, Vivian, Barrett's steward, Alfred Sinclair, and his mistress, Margarete. The five take shelter in a nearby chalet, where a séance is taking place. The house's only inhabitants are the sinister-looking Uriah and his elderly mother, a psychic called Herta. While outside the storm is raging, the woman falls into a trance and reveals the guests' worst secrets: Alfred caused his wife's death after the woman discovered him with Margarete; Vivian was attracted to Richard's wife, Elisabeth, whom she eventually killed; Archibald poisoned his cousin to take possession of his riches and let Ben believe he was guilty; Ben chose not to denounce his own wife for Elisabeth's murder. Eventually it turns out that Uriah and Herta were two servants who had been found guilty and unjustly condemned to death for Wright's murder, and came back from the dead to exact vengeance. The chalet is engulfed by the raging waters of a nearby river: Barrett and his acolytes all die in the flood.

Antonio Margheriti's return to Gothic horror signalled a renewed interest in the genre. In the five years since *The Long Hair of Death*, the director had moved on to such diverse territories as science fiction (the "Gamma One" tetralogy, delivered expressly for the U.S. market), the spy film—*Killers Are Challenged* (*A077 sfida ai killers*, 1966); *Lightning Bolt* (*Operazione Goldman*, 1966)—, the "giallo"—*The Young, the Evil and the Savage* (*Nude si muore*, 1968), originally an aborted Mario Bava project—and eventually the Western, with the grim *Vengeance* (*Joko invoca Dio...e muori*, 1968). Such a trajectory had followed the Gothic's commercial decline in the mid–Sixties, and Margheriti was a particularly attentive filmmaker when it came to eavesdrop on the public's changing tastes.

However, due to the involvement of German producer Artur Brauner, the Roman film-maker was able to return to his favorite territories: a strong Gothic feel would imbue most of his following films in the next few years, which included the impressive Western/horror hybrid *And God Said to Cain* (*E Dio disse a Caino*, 1970), starring Klaus Kinski as an almost supernatural avenger, and *Web of the Spider*, a color remake of his own *Castle of Blood*.

Judging from the cast, *The Unnaturals* (whose shooting title, according to Margheriti, was *Trance*) was mainly aimed at the German market. The film's leads Joachim Fuchsberger and Marianne Koch were very popular in their home country: the former had starred in many Edgar Wallace–inspired *krimis*, while the latter had been one of Germany's most impressive beauties in the 1950s and '60s before embarking in many co-productions with Italy (including *A Fistful of Dollars*). Margheriti added actors of his own choice, though: Luciano Pigozzi, dubbed by many as "the Italian Peter Lorre," was a close friend of the director's, while Claudio Camaso (real name Claudio Volonté, Gian Maria's younger brother) had played the impressive white-dressed and sadistic villain in *Vengeance*.[1]

Shooting took place in Tirrenia studios, Italy's eldest film establishment, set in Tuscany and at that time owned by Carlo Ponti. "He gave me the key and said, "Go and shoot whatever you want"" as Margheriti recalled. "There, I found a soundstage which was full of old decors. That's why the film looks so weird, because we used pieces from the leftover sets of countless other films, from costume dramas to Westerns. The art director was very young and interested in doing new and unusual things, so we used more or less everything we could find to create a really weird, subtle, *avant garde* mixture."[2]

The Unnaturals distances itself from the director's earlier forays into the genre in more than one way. The complex choral structure relies on a very accurate and at times surprising script (penned by Margheriti himself) which recovers and reworks the characters of the typical ghost story, by turning the erotic element into the explicit focus of the story, thanks to the period's more permissive censorship.

The story begins almost like James Whale's *The Old Dark House* (1932), and the idea of travelers finding themselves having to cope with some sort of supernatural judge draws a bit from such omnibus horror stories as Amicus' *Dr. Terror's House of Horrors* (1965). However, although no source is officially credited, Margheriti's true inspiration might well have been a literary one: *Eppure battono alla porta* by Dino Buzzati, a short story originally to be found in Buzzati's 1942 collection *I sette messaggeri* (the story was translated into English for a collection entitled *Catastrophe: The Strange Stories of Dino Buzzati*).[3]

Buzzati's tale takes place on a rainy night, inside a huge decaying house: Maria Gron enters the low dimmed salon, where her family is awaiting her, together with Dr. Martora, an old family friend. The detail of rose petals detaching from a vase at Maria's gentle touch gives immediately the idea of a dilapidated, dying environment. Maria's daughter Georgina tells her that she saw two farmers take away two stone dogs that belonged in the park of Gron's villa. While Maria and the guests discuss the matter, a young man called Massigher comes to inform the family of a danger associated with a nearby river, which is about to overflow due to torrential rain, but Mrs. Gron does not want to hear talk about the river and continues to change the subject. The family and guests start playing cards, but they can hear noises that seem to come from the foundations of the house, which Maria attributes them to the storm. Another warning comes from the farmer, Fred, who is also worried by the water approaching and devouring the land that surrounds the villa, yet the family ignores his words. Finally, the water comes up to the house and enters through an open window, but Mary refuses to leave the place with all her belongings. Everybody stays, still waiting for what will happen next. Suddenly there is a knock at the door.... "Someone knocking? Who could that be?," Martora wonders. "No one," Massigher replies. "There is no one, of course, by now. Yet someone is knocking at the door, and that is positive. A messenger, perhaps, a spirit, a soul, who came over to warn. This is a house of lords. They treat us with respect, sometimes, those from the Otherworld."

Buzzati's story ends abruptly here, an ending which underlines the story's complex, stratified symbolic meanings—revolution as a traumatic cataclysm that sweeps away the past; the bourgeoisie's hypocritical façade of respectability; people's fear of facing reality and the feeble lies upon which they base their frail existence; the confrontation between man's obtuseness and the overwhelming force of Nature, and most of all the thin line between reality as perceived by the senses and the unimaginable, metaphysical truth. Although *The Unnaturals* moves through a different and more explicit path, with vengeful ghosts and people hiding past secrets, the script retains the main elements from Buzzati's story: the secluded house, the rainstorm, the nearby river about to overflow, the weird noises, the eerie image of several people calmly sitting around a table in a room while outside an apocalyptic event is about to take place, and most of all the final reference to an "Otherworld" which is just behind the door, awaiting...

The literary precedent is doubly revealing. First, because it suggests that Margheriti was likely taking his cue from a "highbrow," renowned literary model; second, and even more importantly, because it was an Italian one—neither a throwaway pulp novel like *The Virgin of Nuremberg*, nor an imitation of Anglo-Saxon fiction like *Castle of Blood*, but an example of Italian fantasy literature, which had been thoroughly ignored by the indigenous Gothic cinema.

Another surprising reference, and one which further exposed the filmmaker's intentions, was Friedrich Dürrenmatt's 1956 novel *Traps* a.k.a. *A Dangerous Game* (*Die Panne*), where a traveller, after his car breaks down, is invited for dinner by a former judge, only to be judged by the latter and his colleagues for the sins he has committed in life. Although the similarities with the Swiss writer's novel are only in passing—somebody is forced to take shelter in a secluded house with nightmarish results—the moral center of the story is basically the same: the main characters find themselves as defendants in a moral judgment of sorts, they are judged for their sins by a peculiar jury. It is a trial which leads to a final justice that no real court could impose.

Margheriti builds the film through a composite series of flashbacks that punctuate the story, as the wealthy Barrett (Giuliano Raffaelli) and his companions find refuge in a sinister villa inhabited by the sinister Uriah (Pigozzi) and his elderly psychic mother, and take part in a séance in progress. Like pieces of a puzzle that give an overview of the whole picture only after they are in their proper place, the flashbacks offer a multi-faceted and ever-changing vision of each character, allowing secrets and unconfessable sins to come to the surface. For instance, the bisexual Vivian (Marianne Koch), the unhappy wife of Barrett's lawyer, Taylor (Joachim Fuchsberger), passes through the film from the role of seductress to that of seduced, from victim to murderess: in the framing story we see her blackmailing Margarete (Dominique Boschero) for sexual favors, while in the flashbacks we first find out that she is a neglected (and betrayed) wife, then that she in turn was the victim of the young and ravishing Elisabeth (Helga Anders), who brought forth her re-

German lobby card for Antonio Margheriti's *The Unnaturals—Contronatura*, featuring Joachim Fuchsberger and Marianne Koch (author's collection).

pressed Sapphic tendencies. And there is more: Vivian's attempted seduction of Margarete ends, after one of Italian Gothic's most memorably erotic scenes, in Vivian's deadly fall, whereas the final flashback exposes her as Elisabeth's unpunished slayer.

Overall, *The Unnaturals* is a moral fable for adults, a story of dead people returning to life to judge and punish the living. As such, it ends with a bout of poetic justice: an apocalyptic river of mud wipes out everyone, guilty and innocents alike. "You too are an innocent victim as we once were" says Uriah to Taylor, just before the latter disappears in the mud like the others. Yet the ghost's laughter which greets Taylor's death deletes any remnant of piety.

Margheriti alludes several times to mud as a metaphor for the characters' moral filth, starting with the camera movement that introduces the opening credits, zooming in on a rain-beaten puddle. Water, on the other hand, is seen as a purifying element: it is from the rain on her husband's coat that Vivian discovers his unfaithfulness, while the torrential downpour provokes the final flood.

The *Belle Époque* setting is also in keeping with the story's moral tone, suggesting a sense of waste and implying the end of an era: dancing, gambling, orchestras and champagne, plus overexcited extras who, as reflected in the huge halls' mirrors, are already losing their face and identity, revealing themselves as ghosts similar to those captured by the photographs at *The Shining*'s Overlook Hotel.

For once, Margheriti's typical use of miniatures is not playful: the river of mud that erupts in Uriah's chalet—a sight that recalls the wave of blood in Margheriti's previous sci-fi epic *The Wild, Wild Planet* (*I criminali della galassia*, 1965) and which a number of critics have compared to a similar moment in Kubrick's *The Shining* (1980)—ends the story on an outstanding grim note. The use of color is similarly related to the story's themes: the cinematography—by Margheriti's favorite d.o.p. Riccardo Pallottini—is replete with saturated tints, which amplify the characters' moral abyss and give the idea of a lurid, vulgar world, based on betrayal and abuse.

One of *The Unnaturals*' assets is Margheriti's conviction in staging Gothic clichés. His ghosts—the pale Uriah, who drinks a berry liqueur called "blood," and his mother, who is in a perpetual trance—are not just the umpteenth incarnation of the vengeful and matric *revenant*: they become the exterminating angels of a humanity for which there is no chance of redemption whatsoever.

The way *The Unnaturals* deals with the Fantastic is best exemplified by its final shot: the camera moves with no cuts from the two ghosts to the abyss where all the characters have been swallowed, and then again to the starting point—where now there is no one. It is not only an exquisitely elegant camera movement, but a

deeply significant one, as it represents reason's final defeat to the unknown, the puzzling, the inexplicable.

Another key element in the film is its use of spiritualism—a commonplace in Italian Gothic. Here, far from being simply an ingredient to build up the atmosphere or suggest supernatural red herrings (as in Freda's *The Ghost*), spiritualism becomes the instrument of a *post mortem* justice, which strikes when human justice has proven to be fallacious, if not pernicious. What must be noted, though, is that spiritism is only an apparent instrument to communicate with the afterlife: Uriah and his mother are *already* among the living before the séance even starts. And it is bitterly ironic that such an avid gambler as Barrett—who loves to quip that "whoever invented the table, did it in order to play on it"—finds in a table, the one where the séance takes place, his own nemesis.

Where *The Unnaturals* differs from early 1960s Gothic films is in the frankness with which Margheriti stages eroticism in general and lesbianism in particular. Sexuality—either practiced or dreamed, explicit or unexpressed—becomes the link between all the female characters in the story. After all, it was 1969, *69 année érotique* as a famous song by Serge Gainsbourg defined it: not only the year of the moon landing, the Bel Air massacre and *Easy Rider*, but also the year in which Italy finally savored a loosening of costumes. The first issue of the erotic photonovel *Cinesex* came out, which championed a new vision of eroticism that moved from cinema (the stories on *Cinesex* were photonovel versions of current films) and flooded onto other media. On the other hand, a series of films appeared in theaters which redefined the idea of eroticism in Italian cinema, paving the way for the next decade.

The Unnaturals was deeply imbibed with this new approach towards eroticism, as well as a new-found awareness of the current times. The Italian title itself seemed a wordplay on the term "controcultura" (counterculture), which became "contronatura" (literally, counternature), while the story drew on the new emphasis given to sex, seen here as an instrument of domination, betrayal, social climbing. The voyeuristic component of passion is well in evidence as well, with the recurrent *leitmotif* of naked bodies being spied-upon. Just as we crave what we see, the same happens to the film's characters.

For the occasion, Margheriti's *mise-en-scène* is baroquely complex. The abundance of close-ups and extreme close-ups is exalted by the judicious use of the scope format (a practice taken from Westerns), and is accompanied by a conspicuous use of hand-held shots: this gave greater impact to Margheriti's customary practice of shooting a scene with several cameras at once. Another stylistic trait is the use of wide-angle shots, which enhance the space of the hunting chalet where the séance is taking place, making it incongruously ample, until it ideally coincides with the ballroom where the climactic sequence is set.

Margheriti himself had fun recalling Pallottini's physical feat while shooting the séance scene: the cinematographer was hanging upside down from the ceiling, camera in hand, in order to shoot an acrobatic scene worthy of Sam Raimi. "For the séance, I wanted to shoot the table around which the characters were sitting right from above. Then I wanted the camera to lower down on their hands and faces. Of course there were no flying cameras at that time, so in order to make this movement we hanged cameraman Riccardo Pallottini upside down by his feet and had him slowly descend from the ceiling. This way, he managed to shoot this approaching movement towards the table: then he would bend over backwards and raise the camera and frame the actors' faces."[4]

For the flashbacks Margheriti used a simple yet punchy trick: the camera zooms in on the eyes of the character to whom the flashback refers, and the actor suddenly changes his expression at the very last moment, so that the past and the present seamlessly bind in the same shot.

The editing cuts underline the moral quality of the story. When Alfred bends down to kiss his lover, the next shot has Barrett scoring points at bridge and laying his hand of cards on the table: this way, Margheriti emphasizes Alfred's calculating nature, compares his libido to Barrett's avidity, and combines the two de-

scending movements (of both lovers on the bed, and of the hand laying the cards on the table) through an immediate visual echo. Another similar effect characterizes the homosexual seduction, which is intercut with a fox-hunting scene.

As in Freda's Gothics, in *The Unnaturals* the camera strengthens "the ethical quality and the sense of predestination as well as an irrevocable moral judgment [...], on the other hand, it stands itself as an ethical principle and a moral judge, through the construction of metaphors that highlight and condemn the corruption of the world they portray."[5]

Overall, *The Unnaturals* stands out as Margheriti's greatest achievement in the Gothic genre, and may well be the director's finest film. Although it grossed a modest 170 million *lire* at the Italian box-office (the director claimed he actually lost money on the film[6]) it was the source of inspiration for Mario Colucci's obscure Gothic horror *Something Creeping in the Dark* (*Qualcosa striscia nel buio*, 1971), starring Farley Granger and Lucia Bosé, which ripped off much of its storyline, with a heterogeneous group of characters stuck in an *old dark house* during a rainstorm, and a séance with lethal consequences for most of the people involved.

The Unnaturals was soon championed by younger critics—such as Teo Mora, Marco Giusti and Enrico Ghezzi—who in the early '70s were starting to study Italian genre cinema without the biased attitude of the previous generation. Sadly, as of today the film is not available in the DVD format for English-speaking audiences.

Notes

1. Volonté's career tragically ended in 1977, when the actor stabbed to death an electrician, Vincenzo Mazza, who was trying to stop an argument between Volonté and his ex-wife, Verena Baer, in Rome's central Campo de' Fiori square. After ten days in hiding, Volonté surrendered to the police. Soon after he committed suicide in prison. Margheriti recalled about the cast: "Maybe the only wrong thing about it was the use of Claudio Camaso. That role was written for another actor, but at the very last minute, he couldn't come, so Camaso was hired. At that time, he was living with the female lead, Dominique Boschero. Dear Pigozzi was also in it. He went almost crazy during that film, because I shot scenes lasting 10–15 minutes in one take, with 32 or 33 positions, so he had to remember a lot of dialogue *and* hit the marks.

The poor guy mastered it quite well. I suppose you recognized Joachim Fuchsberger, whom we used to please our German partners. Not a great actor, but very funny and a good face. The old man was played by an Italian guy who worked on cartoons." Blumenstock, "Margheriti—The Wild, Wild Interview," p. 55.

2. Ibid.

3. Dino Buzzati, *Catastrophe: The Strange Stories of Dino Buzzati* (London: Calder and Boyars, 1965); reprinted as *Catastrophe and Other Stories* (London: Calder, 1982).

4. Fazzini, *Gli artigiani dell'orrore*, p. 52.

5. Teo Mora, "Per una definizione del film di fantasmi," *Il Falcone Maltese* 2, July 1974, p. 29.

6. Blumenstock, "Margheriti—The Wild, Wild Interview," p. 55.

Selected Bibliography

On the Gothic Genre in Fiction

Amigoni, Ferdinando. *Fantasmi nel Novecento*. Turin: Bollati Boringhieri, 2004.

Bordoni, Carlo. *Del soprannaturale nel romanzo fantastico*. Cosenza: Pellegrini, 2004.

Botting, Fred. *Gothic*. London: Routledge, 1996.

Burke, Edmund. *A Philosophical Inquiry into the Origin of Our Ideas of the Sublime and Beautiful*. New York: Digireads.com, 2009.

Calvino, Italo, ed. *Fantastic Tales: Visionary and Everyday*. New York: Penguin, 2001, 2009.

Ceserani, Remo, Lucio Lugnani, Gianluigi Goggi, Carla Benedetti, and Elisabetta Scarano, eds. *La narrazione fantastica*. Pisa: Nistri-Lischi, 1983.

Foucault, Michel. *Language, Counter-Memory, Practice: Selected Essays and Interviews*. Ithaca: Cornell University Press, 1980.

Freud, Sigmund. "The Uncanny," in Sigmund Freud, *Writings on Art and Literature*. Redwood City, CA: Stanford University Press, 1997.

Fruttero, Carlo, and Franco Lucentini, eds. *Storie di fantasmi. Racconti del soprannaturale*. Turin: Einaudi, 1960, 1984.

Hogle, Jerrold E., ed. *The Cambridge Companion to Gothic Fiction*. Cambridge: Cambridge University Press, 2002.

Punter, David. *The Literature of Terror: A History of Gothic Fictions from 1765 to the Present Day, Vol. 1: The Gothic Tradition*. New York: Routledge, 1996.

_____. *The Literature of Terror: A History of Gothic Fictions from 1765 to the Present Day, Vol. 2: The Modern Gothic*. New York: Routledge, 1996.

Todorov, Tzvetan. *The Fantastic: A Structural Approach to a Literary Genre*. Ithaca: Cornell University Press, 1975.

Varma, Devendra P. *The Gothic Flame: Being a History of the Gothic Novel in England: Its Origins, Efflorences, Disintegration, and Residuary Influences*. Metuchen, NY: Scarecrow, 1957, 1987.

Vax, Louis. *La natura del fantastico*. Rome: Theoria, 1987.

Žižek, Slavoj. *Looking Awry: An Introduction to Jacques Lacan Through Popular Culture*. Cambridge: MIT Press, 1992.

On Fantastic, Gothic and Horror Cinema

Halligan, Benjamin. *Michael Reeves*. Manchester: Manchester University Press, 2003.

Hardy, Phil, ed. *The Aurum Film Encyclopedia: Horror*. London: Aurum, 1993.

Hogan, David J. *Dark Romance: Sexuality in the Horror Film*. Jefferson, NC: McFarland, 1997.

Leutrat, Jean-Louis. *La vie des fantomes: le fantastique ai cinéma*. Paris: Cahiers du Cinéma—Collection essais, 1995.

Lucas, Tim. *The Video Watchdog Book*. Cincinnati: Video Watchdog, 1992.

McGee, Mark Thomas. *Faster and Furiouser: The Revised and Fattened Fable of American International Pictures*. Jefferson, NC: McFarland, 1996.

Navarro, Antonio José, ed. *Pesadillas en la oscuridad. El cine de terrór gotico*. Madrid: Valdemar, 2010.

Pirie, David. *A New Heritage of Horror: The English Gothic Cinema*. London: I. B. Tauris, 2008.

On Italian Cinema and Italian Gothic Horror

Biographies, Autobiographies, Interview Books

Curti, Roberto. *Il mio nome è Nessuno. Lo spaghetti western secondo Tonino Valerii*. Rome: Un mondo a parte, 2008.

Faldini, Franca, and Goffredo Fofi, eds. *L'avventurosa storia del cinema italiano raccontata dai suoi protagonisti, 1960–1969*. Milan: Feltrinelli, 1981.

Fazzini, Paolo. *Gli artigiani dell'orrore. Mezzo secolo di brividi dagli anni '50 ad oggi*. Rome: Un mondo a parte, 2004.

Fellini, Federico, and Damien Pettigrew. *Federico Fellini: sono un gran bugiardo*. Rome: Elle U Multimedia, 2003.

Fellini, Federico, and Giovanni Grazzini. *Intervista sul cinema*. Bari: Laterza, 1983, 2004.

Freda, Riccardo. *Divoratori di celluloide*. Milan: Edizioni del Mystfest, Il Formichiere, 1981.

Gastaldi, Ernesto. *Voglio entrare nel cinema. Storia di uno che ce l'ha fatta*. Milan: Mondadori, 1991.

La Selva, Tommaso. *Tonino Valerii: mai temere il Leone*. Milan: Nocturno Libri, 2000.

Lee, Christopher. *Lord of Misrule: The Autobiography of Christopher Lee*. London: Orion, 2004.

_____. *Tall, Dark and Gruesome*. Baltimore: Midnight Marquee, 1999.

Poindron, Éric. *Riccardo Freda. Un pirate à la camera*. Lyon: Institute Lumière/Actes Sud, 1994.

Questi, Giulio, Domenico Monetti, and Luca Pallanch. *Se non ricordo male*. Soveria Mannelli: Rubbettino, 2014.

Zapponi, Bernardino. *Il mio Fellini*. Venice: Marsilio, 1995.

Dictionaries, Reference Books and Academic Studies

Acerbo, Gabriele, and Roberto Pisoni, eds. *Kill baby kill!: il cinema di Mario Bava*. Rome: Un mondo a parte, 2007.

Brunetta, Gian Piero. *Storia del cinema italiano dal neorealismo al miracolo economico: 1945–1959*. Rome: Editori Riuniti, 1993.

_____. *Storia del cinema italiano. Il cinema del regime: 1929–1945*. Rome: Editori Riuniti, 1993.

Bruschini, Antonio, and Antonio Tentori. *Operazione paura: i registi del gotico italiano*. Bologna: Puntozero, 1997.

Cozzi, Luigi. *Mario Bava. I mille volti della paura*. Rome: Mondo ignoto, 2001.

Curti, Roberto. *Fantasmi d'amore*. Turin: Lindau, 2011.

D'Agnolo Vallan, Giulia, and Stefano Della Casa. *Mario Bava*. Bellaria: Catalogo del festival Bellaria, 1993.

Della Casa, Stefano. *Riccardo Freda*. Rome: Bulzoni, 1999.

Di Chiara, Francesco. *I tre volti della paura: il cinema horror italiano (1957–1965)*. Ferrara: UniPress, 2009.

Howarth, Troy. *The Haunted World of Mario Bava, Revised and Expanded Edition*. Baltimore: Midnight Marquee, 2014.

Kezich, Tullio. *Il Millefilm—Dieci anni al cinema, 1967–1977*. Milan: Mondadori, 1983.

Koven, Mikel J. *La Dolce Morte: Vernacular Cinema and the Italian Giallo*. Lanham, MD: Scarecrow, 2006.

Lafond, Frank, ed. *Cauchemars Italiens. Volume 1: Le cinéma fantastique*. Paris: L'Harmattan, 2011.

Leutrat, Jean-Louis, ed. *Mario Bava*. Liege: Éditions du Céfal, 1994.

Lucas, Tim. *Mario Bava: All the Colors of the Dark*. Cincinnati: Video Watchdog, 2007.

Martinet, Pascal. *Mario Bava*. Paris: Edilig, 1984.

Pezzotta, Alberto. *Mario Bava*. Milan: Il Castoro, 1995, 2013.

_____. *Regia Damiano Damiani*. Pordenone: CEC/Cinemazero 2004.

Piselli, Stefano, and Roberto Guidotti, eds. *Diva—Cinema 1951–1965*. Florence: Glittering, 1989.

Piselli, Stefano, Riccardo Morlocchi, and Antonio Bruschini. *Bizarre Sinema! Wildest Sexiest Weirdest Sleaziest Films: Horror all'italiana 1957–1979*. Florence: Glittering, 1996.

Poppi, Roberto. *Dizionario del cinema italiano. I registi*. Rome: Gremese, 2002.

_____, and Mario Pecorari. *Dizionario del cinema italiano. I film (1960–1969)*. Rome: Gremese, 1993.

Tentori, Antonio, and Luigi Cozzi, eds. *Horror Made In Italy*. Rome: Profondo Rosso, 2007.

Venturini, Simone. *Galatea Spa (1952–1965): storia di una casa di produzione cinematografica*. Rome: Associazione italiana per le ricerche di storia del cinema, 2001.

Essays in Volumes

Brunetta, Gian Piero. "Cinema muto italiano," in Gian Piero Brunetta, ed., *Storia del cinema mondiale. Vol. III, L'Europa. Le cinematografie nazionali*. Turin: Einaudi, 1999.

Della Casa, Stefano. "Cinema popolare italiano del dopoguerra," in Gian Piero Brunetta, ed., *Storia del cinema mondiale. Vol. III, L'Europa. Le cinematografie nazionali*. Turin: Einaudi, 1999.

Hormigos, Montserrat. "Flores curiosas de la cripta fílmica de Poe," in Antonio José Navarro, ed., *Las sombras del horror. Edgar Allan Poe en el cine*. Madrid: Valdemar, 2009.

Hunt, Leon. "A (Sadistic) Night at the Opera," in Ken Gelder, ed., *The Horror Reader*. New York: Routledge, 2000.

Mora, Teo. "Elegia per una donna vampiro. Il cinema fantastico in Italia 1957–1966," in *Storia del cinema dell'orrore, vol. 2*. Rome: Fanucci, 1978, 2002.

Paniceres, Ruben. "El gotico italiano. Fantastico y ciencia ficcion," in Jesus Palacios and Ruben Paniceres, eds., *Cara a cara. Una mirada al cine de genero italiano*. Gijon: Semana Negra, 2004.

Pezzotta, Alberto. "La cosa in sé. Un percorso nei primi e negli ultimi film," in Stefania Parigi and Alberto Pezzotta, eds., *Il lungo respiro di Brunello Rondi*. Rieti: Edizioni Sabinae, 2010.

Pitassio, Francesco. "L'orribile segreto dell'horror italiano," in Giacomo Manzoli and Guglielmo Pescatore, eds., *L'arte del risparmio: stile e tecnologia. Il cinema a basso costo in Italia negli anni Sessanta*. Rome: Carocci, 2005.

Silver, Alain, and James Ursini. "Mario Bava: The Illusion of Reality," in Alain Silver and James Ursini, eds., *Horror Film Reader*. New York: Limelight, 2000.

Zanotto, Piero. "*Terrore italiano e... cinese*," in *Il film terrifico e galattico*. Turin: Centro Universitario Cinematografico, 1960.

Periodicals: Special Issues

Fassone, Riccardo, ed. "La stagione delle streghe. Guida al gotico italiano." *Nocturno Dossier* 80, March 2009.

Garofalo, Marcello, ed. "Sangue, amore e fantasy." *Segnocinema* 85, May/June 1997.

Monell, Robert. "Riccardo Freda." *European Trash Cinema Special* 2, 1997.

Romero, Javier G., ed. "Antología del cine fantástico italiano." *Quatermass* 7, November 2008.

Gomarasca, Manlio. "Il cinema è quello che ci fa," in "Fatti di cinema. Controcorrente 3." *Nocturno Dossier* 51, October 2006.

_____. "Monsieur Cannibal. Il cinema di Ruggero Deodato." *Nocturno Dossier* 73, August 2008.

_____, and Davide Pulici, eds. "Genealogia del delitto. Il cinema di Mario e Lamberto Bava." *Nocturno Dossier* 24, July 2004.

_____, and _____, eds. "Le sorelle di Venere 2." *Nocturno Dossier* 59, June 2007.

Periodicals: Articles, Reviews, Interviews

Abruzzese, Alberto. "Amori pericolosi." *Cinema 60* 45, September 1964.

Argento, Dario. "Per Rondi: ancora un tema che scotta." *Paese Sera*, July 29, 1965.

Balbo, Lucas. "I Talked with a Zombie: The Forgotten Horrors of Massimo Pupillo," in Stefan Jaworzyn, ed., *Shock: The Essential Guide to Exploitation Cinema*. London: Titan, 1996.

Bernardi, Sandro. "Teoremi della circolarità. L'infinito nel cinema." *Filmcritica* 365–366, June/July 1986.

Blumenstock, Peter. "Margheriti—The Wild, Wild Interview." *Video Watchdog* 28, May/June 1995.

Bocci, Carlo. "Lo spettro." *Il Falcone Maltese* 1, June 1974.

Bruno, Edoardo. "Realtà e surrealtà ne Il demonio di Rondi." *Filmcritica* 145, May 1964.

Caen, Michel, and J.C. Romer. "Entretien avec Ricardo Freda." *Midi-Minuit Fantastique* 10–11, Winter 1964–1965.

Ciaccio, Giacinto. "La strega in amore." *La Rivista del Cinematografo* 11, November 1966.

Cozzi, Luigi. "Così dolce... così perverso... Intervista con Ernesto Gastaldi." *Horror* 5, April 1970.

_____. "Intervista a Mario Bava." *Horror* 13, December 1970/January 1971.

_____. "Il vampiro in orbita." *Horror* 6, May 1970.

Di Rocco, Alessio. "Visto in censura: La frusta e il corpo." *Nocturno Cinema* 94, June 2010.

"Dracula si rinnova: da vampiro a imbalsamatore." *La Stampa*, August 6, 1964.

Duncan, Jim. "Horror-For-Fun Pays Off." *Daily American* August 30–31, 1964.

Fofi, Goffredo. "Terreur in Italie." *Midi-Minuit Fantastique* 7, September 1963.

Garofalo, Marcello. "Le interviste celibi: Antonio Margheriti. L'ingegnere in Cinemascope." *Segnocinema* 84, March/April 1997.

Giani, Renato. "Al vampiro piacquero i decors di Silvagni." *Cinema* 77, December 31, 1951.

Hoveida, Fereydoun. "Les grimaces du démon." *Cahiers du cinéma* 119, 1961.

Johnson, Steven. "Italian American Reconciliation: Waking "Castle of the Living Dead." *Delirious—The Fantasy Film Magazine* 5, 1991.

Legrand, Gérard. "L'Effroyable secret du Dr. Hichcock." *Positif* 53, June 1963.

Lucas, Tim. "Mario Bava's *The Three Faces of Fear*." *Video Watchdog* 5, May/June 1991.

_____. "What Are Those Strange Drops of Blood in the Scripts of Ernesto Gastaldi?" *Video Watchdog* 39, May/June 1997.

Mangravite, Andrew. "Once Upon a Time in the Crypt." *Film Comment* 29, January 1993.

Mora, Teo. "Per una definizione del film di fantasmi." *Il Falcone Maltese* No. 2, July 1974.

Parla, Paul, and Charles P. Mitchell. "Werewolf in a Girl's Dormitory: An Interview with Curt Lowens." *Ultra Filmfax* 67, June 1998.

Parry, Michael. "CoF Interviews Christopher Lee, Part 3." *Castle of Frankenstein* 12, 1968.

Piazza, Carlo. "Walter Brandi—Entretien avec la star du cinéma d'épouvante italien." *Ciné-Zine-Zone* 30, August 1986.

Pulici, Davide. "Sortilegio: la sceneggiatura," in "Misteri d'Italia 2. Guida ai film rari e scomparsi," *Nocturno Dossier* 58, March 2007.

Salza, Giuseppe. "Mario Bava: il brivido sottile di crudeli leggende." *Segnocinema* 13, May 1984.

"Lo spettro." *Il Nuovo Spettatore Cinematografico* 4, August 1963.

TM. "The Mask of Satan (Revenge of the Vampire)." *Monthly Film Bulletin* 408, January 1968.

Totaro, Donato. "A Genealogy of Italian Popular Cinema: the Filone." *Offscreen* vol. 15, no. 11, November 30, 2011.

Upchurch, Alan. "Who Is Ralph Zucker?" *Video Watchdog* 7, September/October 1991.

"Il vampiro di Bomarzo." *La Notte*, August 8, 1964.

Weaver, Tom, and Michael Brunas. "Quoth Matheson, 'Nevermore!'" *Fangoria* 90, February 1990.

Wood, Robin. "In Memoriam Michael Reeves." *Movie* 17, Winter 1969/'70.

Index

Numbers in **_bold italics_** indicate pages with photographs.
Numbers in **bold** indicate main film entries.

Abbasso tutti, viva noi 123
Abbott, Bud 32
Abruzzese, Alberto 127, 203
The Addams Family (TV series) 152
Addessi, Giovanni 109
Addobbati, Giuseppe 136, 159
Adorf, Mario 121
Agliata, Aldo 142
Albertazzi, Giorgio 176, 177
Alberti, Annie 96
Albertini, Luciano 11
Albertini, Luigi 101
Aldighieri, Merrill 142, 155
Alekan, Henri 46
Alessi, Ottavio 68
Alfonsi, Lydia 81
Alfred Hitchcock Presents (TV series) 70, 85, 86
Alighieri, Dante 13, 18, 31, 42, 90, 113, 147
Allen, Woody 153
L'Amante del vampiro see _The Vampire and the Ballerina_
Amanti d'oltretomba see _Nightmare Castle_
Ambesi, Adriana 93, 131
Amici dell'isola, Gli 152
Amigoni, Ferdinando 192, 201
Un Amore 158
Amore in quattro dimensioni 169
Amori pericolosi 125, 126, 127, 203
And God Said to Cain 17, 195
...and the Wild, Wild Women 159
Der Andere 18
Anders, Helga 196
Andersen, Elga 181, 182
Andersen, Susy 82
An Angel for Satan 4, 13, 16, 71, 104, 124, 133, 134, **155–157**
Un Angelo per Satana see _An Angel for Satan_
Anger, Kenneth 141
Anna Goldin, the Last Witch 49
Anno Dracula 34
The Antichrist (1974 film) 88
Antonelli, Ennio 119
Antonelli, Laura 68
Antonioni, Michelangelo 153, 181, 190

Aquari, Giuseppe 135, 157
Arabian Nights 174
Aranda, Vicente 133, 135
Arcalli, Franco "Kim" 126, 127
Arcana 127
Ardisson, Giorgio 92
Argento, Dario 13, 40, 72, 76, 80, 85, 91, 181, 183, 185, 190, 203
Arnaud, Fede 41
L'Assassino del dott. Hitchkok see _Autopsy of a Criminal_
Asti, Adriana 181
Atlas in the Land of the Cyclops 123
Atom Age Vampire **34–37**, 54
L'Attico 169
Aura (novel) 172
Autopsy of a Criminal 69
Avallone, Marcello 17
Avati, Pupi 130, 157, 158

Bacalov, Luis 174
The Bacchantes 53
Baker, Roy Ward 129
Balbo, Ennio 151
Balbo, Lucas 143, 151, 152, 153, 155, 170, 203
Baldi, Ferdinando 123
Baldwin, Peter 90
Balpêtré, Antoine 28
La Bambola di Satana **192–194**
La Banda degli onesti 129
Bandits in Rome 88
Baratto, Luisa 142
Barbarella 186
Barboni, Enzo 143, 146
Barboni, Leonida 127, 174
Barma, Claude 176
Baron Blood 113
Barrymore, John Drew 94
Bartok, Eva 65
Bastardo, vamos a matar 123
Batista, Aurora 194
Battaglia, Rik 145
Batzella, Luigi 77, 78, 153
Baudelaire, Charles 186
Bava, Eugenio 83
Bava, Lamberto 41, 48, 49, 156, 162, 192, 203
Bava, Mario (aka John M. Old) 2, 4,

6, 7, 8, 15, 16, 17, 18, 23, 24, 25, 26, 28, 29, 32, 33, 37–49, 50, 53, 60, 65, 68, 72, 73, 78–86, 91, 92, 96, 102–108, 109, 110, 113, 118, 120, 121, 123, 125, 130, 131, 134, 145, 151, 153, 154, 155, 159–165, 166, 169, 176, 184, 188, 190, 192, 195, 202, 203
Baxter, Les 47
Bay of Blood 33, 161
The Beast Must Die (1974 film) 65
The Beast with Five Fingers 83
Beauty and the Beast (1946 film) 46, 83
"The Beckoning Fair One" (short story) 178
Bedogni, Walter 41
Belfiore, Giulio 86
Bellero, Carlo 182
Bellmer, Hans 83
Belphégor ou le Fantôme du Louvre 176
Beltrame, Achille 101
Benassi, Memo 18
Benussi, Femi 141
"Berenice" (short story) 110
Berger, William 166, 167, 168
Bergman, Ingmar 57, 117
Bergman, Ingrid 180
Bernabei, Domenico 41
Berry, Julian see Gastaldi, Ernesto
Berthomieu, Pierre 165
Bertini, Francesca 27
Bertolucci, Bernardo 127
Between God, the Devil and a Winchester 56
Bevilacqua, Alberto 37, 81
Beyond the Darkness 76, 171
Beyond the Law 120
Bierce, Ambrose 113
Bigari, Walter see Brandi, Walter
Bini, Alfredo 172
Bioy Casares, Adolfo 113
Black Sabbath 4, 37, 46, 50, **78–85**, 104, 134, 159, 185
Black Sunday 4, 6, 7, 13, 14, 16, 17, 22, 27, 29, 34, **37–49**, 52, 63, 66, 69, 75, 79, 82, 85, 91, 103, 105, 130, 131, 132, 140, 141, 145, 156, 159, 161, 164, 175, 188

Blanc, Erika (Enrica Bianchi Co-
lombatto) 154, 155, 161, 162, 164,
171
The Blancheville Monster 7, **86–88**,
103, 104
Blasetti, Alessandro 13, 18, 180
Blood and Black Lace 28, 39, 65, 83,
123, 145, 146, 161, 166, 190
Blood and Roses 128, 133, 186
Blood for Dracula 155, 190
The Blood of a Poet 47, 113
The Blood Spattered Bride 133, 135
The Bloodsucker Leads the Dance
140
Bloody Pit of Horror 6, 71, 104, **137–
143**, 151, 152, 153
Blow-Up 153, 190
Boccacci, Antonio (aka Anthony
Kristye) 95–97
Boccaccio '70 180, 186, 188
Bocci, Carlo 90, 91, 92, 203
Bogart, Frank *see* Gui, Maddalena
Bogart, Humphrey 28, 78
Böhm, Karlheinz 67
Il Boia scarlatto see *Bloody Pit of
Horror*
Boido, Federico 190
Boisset, Yves 71
Bolkan, Florinda 181
Bolognini, Mauro 173, 186, 188, 192
Bordoni, Carlo 110, 114, 201
Borelli, Lydia 27
Borowczyk, Walerian 177
Borrelli, Rosario 142
Borsato, Umberto 62
Boschero, Dominique 194, 196, 199
Boschero, Giorgio 138
Bosé, Lucia (Lucia Borloni) 27, 199
Böttger, Fritz 137
Botting, Fred 172, 175, 201
Bragaglia, Carlo Ludovico 31
Brandi, Walter (Walter Bigari) 54,
57, 59, 62, 64, 77, 78, 136, 140,
150, 151, 152, 153, 203
Brando, Marlon 78
Brass, Tinto 194
Brasseur, Pierre 36
Brauner, Artur 195
Brazzi, Oscar 135, 137
Brazzi, Rossano 135
Brega, Mario 156, 157
Brice, Pierre 151
The Bride of Frankenstein 12
Brismée, Jean 100
Browning, Tod 57
Brunetta, Gian Piero 15, 18, 27, 30,
202
Bruno, Edoardo 181, 183, 203
Bruschini, Antonio 30, 85, 153, 202
Buazzelli, Tino 31
Budden, Julian 14
A Bullet for the General 175
Bullets Don't Argue 146
Buñuel, Luis 126, 172, 181, 182, 192
Burke, Edmund 105, 198, 201
But You Were Dead **157–159**
The Butterfly Room 157
Buzzati, Dino 158, 175, 185, 191,
195, 196, 200

The Cabinet of Dr. Caligari (1920
film) 24
O Caçula do Barulho 27
Caged Heat 157
Caiano, Carlo 146
Caiano, Mario (aka Allan
Grünewald) 6, 143, 144, 145, 146,
149
La Califfa 37
Callegaris, Giampaolo 62
Caltiki, the Immortal Monster 24,
29, 40, 103
Calvino, Italo 110, 114, 201
Camaso, Claudio *see* Volonté, Clau-
dio
Camerini, Mario 17
Cameron, Rod 146
Cammarano, Salvadore 14
Campos, José 130
Canale, Gianna Maria 1, 6, 18, 21,
24, 25, **26**, 27
Candy (1968 film) 91
The Canterbury Tales 171
Il Cappello da prete 12
Caprioli, Vittorio 188
Capuana, Luigi 12, 62
Cardiff, Jack 115
Cardinale, Claudia 191
Carey, Roland 194
Carmilla (novel) 2, 62, 128, 129–
135, 167
Carnal Circuit 88
Carosello, Flora 97
Carpentieri, Luigi 22
Carr, John Dickson 110
Carrel, Dany 51, 52
Casablanca 28
Casale, Antonio 147
Casapinta, Ferruccio 192–194
Caserini, Mario 11
Casiraghi, Ugo 175, 176
Il Caso Haller 18
Castel, Lou 175
Castellani, Renato 159
Castellari, Enzo G. (Enzo Girolami)
56
Il Castello dei morti vivi see *Castle
of the Living Dead*
Castle of Blood 5, 18, 71, 97, 98, 99,
103, **109–114**, 125, 130, 131, 133,
144, 145, 154, 155, 195, 196
The Castle of Otranto (novel) 9, 43,
50
Castle of the Living Dead **114–121**,
203
The Cat and the Canary (1927 film)
148
Catenacci, Luciano 162
*Il Cavaliere misterioso see The Mys-
terious Rider*
Cavallone, Alberto 147, 194
Cavara, Paolo 185
Cave of the Living Dead 97
Cemetery of the Living Dead see
Terror-Creatures from the Grave
C'era una volta un gangster 101
Cervi, Gino 176
Cesari, Bruno 143
Chabrol, Claude 186

"Che cosa sono le nuvole?" (episode
from *Capriccio all'italiana*) 189
Che fine ha fatto Totò Baby? 68
Christian, Linda 94
Christie, Agatha 97
Cianfriglia, Giovanni 110
La Cieca di Sorrento (1953 film) 13
Cigoli, Emilio 78
Cinesex (photonovel) 198
5 tombe per un medium see *Terror-
Creatures from the Grave*
The Circus (1928 film) 189
Circus of Horrors 39
City of Women 180, 191
City Under Siege 56
Cliff, Finney *see* Serra Caracciolo,
Garibaldi
Clouzot, Henri-Georges 89, 108,
125, 159
Cocteau, Jean 46, 47, 81, 83, 126,
130, 164
Colli, Ombretta 87
Collins, Alan *see* Pigozzi, Luciano
Un Colpo da mille miliardi 68
Colucci, Mario 199
Il Comandante 68
I Complessi 54
Conan Doyle, Arthur 39, 101, 176
The Conformist 127
Conju, Nela 130
The Conjugal Bed 54, 112
Connery, Neil 88
Connery, Sean 88
Cooper, Gary 78
Coppola, Francis Ford 110
La Coquille et le clergyman 25
Corbucci, Bruno (aka Gordon Wil-
son, Jr.) 86, 109, 110
Corbucci, Sergio 16, 31, 109, 110
Corman, Roger 39, 46, 50, 69, 71,
72, 80, 84, 87, 90, 103, 104, 105,
108, 110, 118, 151, 161
La Corona di ferro 13
Corridors of Blood 56
La Corruzione 173
Cortázar, Julio 113
Coscia, Marcello 41
Costello, Lou 32
Cosulich, Callisto 175, 176
Counselor at Crime 88
Covert Action 56
Cozzi, Luigi 137
Crabtree, Arthur 39
Crazy Desire 54
Crime Boss 88
*The Criminal Life of Archibaldo de la
Cruz* 126
La Cripta e l'incubo see *Terror in the
Crypt*
Crisanti, Gabriele 123
Cristallini, Giorgio 193
Criswell (Jeron Criswell Konig) 85
Cronin, Archibald Joseph 176
Cronos 155
Crudo, Aldo 62, 101
Crypt of the Vampire see *Terror in
the Crypt*
Cukor, George 71
Cunha, Richard 34

The Curse of Frankenstein 23, 24, 38
Curse of the Blood Ghouls see *Slaughter of the Vampires*
Curse of the Vampire see *The Play-girls and the Vampire*
The Curse of the Werewolf 65
Curtiz, Michael 24, 28
Cushing, Peter 63

Dagli zar alla bandiera rossa 123
Dal nostro inviato a Copenaghen 147
Dali, Fabienne 161, 165
Dallamano, Massimo 68, 158
"Dalle tre alle tre e mezzo" (short story) 81
Damiani, Damiano 8, 17, 126, 138, 171–176, 189, 202
Damon, Mark 82, 104
Danger: Diabolik 165
Daniels, Jonathan 29
D'Annunzio, Gabriele 27
Dante see Alighieri, Dante
Dantes, Claude 123
D'Anza, Daniele 169, 176, 177
Danza macabra see *Castle of Blood*
David e Golia 123
Davis, Ursula see Quaglia, Pier Anna
Dawson, Anthony M. see Margheriti, Antonio
The Day the Sky Exploded 68
Dead Woman's Kiss (1949 film) 13
De Agostini, Fabio 145, 146
Death Laid an Egg 127
Death Smiles on a Murderer 91
The Decameron 171
Decameron no. 2—Le altre novelle del Boccaccio 171
De Concini, Ennio 16, 41
Dee, Sandra 42
Deep Red 72, 91, 130
Defeat of the Mafia 121
De Felice, Lionello (aka Michael Hamilton) 165–168
De Fonseca, Carolyn 181
DeGenerazione 85
Dei, Gianni 147
De La Loma, José Antonio 68
De Laurentiis, Dino 165
Delirium (1972 film) 64
Delon, Alain 186
Del Rio, Alma 93
De Martino, Alberto 7, 16, 42, 43, 71, 86–88, 104
De Martino, Antonio see Martin, Anthony
De Masi, Francesco 91, 123, 165, 169
Demme, Jonathan 157
Il Demonio 103, 165, 181, 183, 203
Demons 5: The Devil's Veil see *La Maschera del demonio* (1989 film)
Deodato, Ruggero 109, 114, 171, 203
De Ossorio, Amando 7, 22
De Palma, Dino 41
De Rais, Gilles 169
De Rita, Massimo 47
De Sica, Vittorio 68, 180, 186
Detective Belli 56
De Toth, André 50, 53

The Devil in Love 188
The Devil's Commandment see *I Vampiri*
The Devil's Nightmare 100
The Devil's Wedding Night 153
Diabolik (comic) 142, 166
Diabolique (1955 film) 89, 124
Dialina, Rica 82
Diamanti che nessuno voleva rubare, I 123
Di Centa, Erika 59
Di Chiara, Francesco 30, 49, 108, 202
Dick, Philip K. 164
Dickinson, Thorold 144
Di Leo, Fernando 121, 154, 171
Di Palma, Carlo 149, 152, 153
Dirty Heroes 88
Divoratori di celluloide (book) 23, 30, 90, 92, 202
Divorce, Italian Style 125
Django 17, 169
Django Kill see *If You Live Shoot*
Django Kills Softly 155
Django the Bastard 17
Dr. Jekyll and Mr. Hyde (1931 film) 24
Dr. Jekyll et les femmes 177
Dr. Terror's House of Horrors 195
La Dolce Vita 26, 28, 41, 42, 93, 115, 133, 180, 189, 190, 191
The Dolls (1965 film) 186
Domani non siamo più qui 181
Dominici, Arturo 113
Donati, Ermanno 22, 169, 171
"Una Donna dolce, dolce" (episode from *La donna è una cosa meravigliosa*) 188
La Donna è una cosa meravigliosa 188
Donovan's Brain (novel) 122
Don't Torture a Duckling 181
Door to Darkness 76
Doré, Gustave 31
Dottesio, Attilio 123
Douglas, Kirk 88, 191
Douglas, Shirley 117
Dracula (1931 film) 57
Dracula A.D. 1972 22
Dracula Cha Cha Cha (novel) 34
Dracula: Prince of Darkness 57, 59, 136
Dreyer, Carl Theodor 11, 24, 30, 50, 62, 88, 128
"The Drop of Water" (episode from *Black Sabbath*) 46, 47, **78–85**, 105, 134, 161, 162, 184, 188
Duck You, Sucker! 147
2 Magnum 38 per una città di carogne 101
Dumas, Alexandre 36, 62
Dunaway, Faye 180
Duncan, Jim 118, 121, 203
Durbridge, Francis 176
Dürrenmatt, Friedrich 196

E lo chiamarono Spirito Santo 78
Eastwood, Clint 146, 147
The Easy Life 33
Easy Rider 198

Eco, Emy 96
Eco, Umberto 96
Eger, Raymond 186
8½ 109, 170, 180, 183, 186, 188, 189, 190, 191
Ekberg, Anita 41, 42, 188
El "Che" Guevara 68
Elam, Jack 121
"Eleonora" (short story) 190
Emmer, Luciano 176
Eppler, Dieter 77, 78
Era notte a Roma 180
Ercole contro il vampiro see *Hercules in the Haunted World*
Ergas, Moris 68, 126
Erickson, Glenn 72, 73, 76
Esdra, Micaela 151, 161
L'Eterna catena 36
Europa '51 180
Eve 176
The Evil Eye (aka *The Girl Who Knew Too Much*) 80, 85
Execution Squad 31
Exodus 60
The Exorcist 88, 181
The Exterminating Angel 192
Extrasensorial (aka *Blood Link*) 88
Eyes Without a Face (1960 film) 34, 36, 50, 166

Falk, Lee 140
Falk, Rossella 181
"The Fall of the House of Usher" (short story) 25, 86
Falvo, Felice 147
Fango sulla metropoli 123
Fantasmi (2011 film) 85
Fantoni, Sergio 36
Farmer, Philip José 110
Faust (1926 film) 22
Faust '63 see *Katarsis*
Fava, Mario see Elio Ippolito Mellino
Fellini, Federico 26, 28, 31, 41, 46, 57, 109, 118, 171, 180, 183–192, 201, 202
Fellini—Satyricon 180, 190, 191
Fellini's Casanova 118, 191
Fernandel (Fernand Joseph Désiré Contandin) 152
Ferraris, Enzo 158
Ferrati, Sarah 173
Ferrer, Mel 133
Ferreri, Marco 54, 112, 183
Ferroni, Giorgio 4, 18, 49–53, 82
Feuillade, Louis 24
Fidani, Demofilo 109
Fiend Without a Face 56
I Figli di nessuno (1951 film) 170
Fisher, Terence 1, 16, 23, 30, 31, 33, 39, 40, 57, 62, 63, 65, 75, 77, 101
A Fistful of Dollars 17, 146, 147, 195
5 Dolls for an August Moon 47
Flaiano, Ennio 183
Flemyng, Robert 72
The Flesh Eaters 99
Florey, Robert 83
"The Flowering of the Strange Orchid" (short story) 101

Fofi, Goffredo 15, 18, 30, 86, 201,
    203
Fogazzaro, Antonio 9, 12, 156
Fonda, Jane 186, 187
Fonda, Peter 186, 187
Fondato, Marcello 81
Fontaine, Joan 70
Forain, Michael 154
*The Forbidden Photos of a Lady
    Above Suspicion* 76
Foreign Correspondent 70
Formula for a Murder 88
Foscolo, Ugo 1
Foucault, Michel 73, 75
Four Times That Night 91
Francesco giullare di Dio 180
Franci, Carlo 87
Franciosa, Anthony 114
Francisci, Pietro 18, 40,
Franco, Jess (Jesús) 39, 99, 170, 181
Franju, Georges 34, 166
Frankenstein (1931 film) 41
I Fratelli Corsi 36
Freaks 189
Freda, Riccardo (aka Robert Hamp-
    ton) 1, 2, 3, 6, 7, 8, 13, 14, 15, 16,
    17, 18, 21–30, 36, 40, 46, 47, 49,
    52, 53, 62, 68–76, 88–92, 99, 104,
    105, 110, 116, 117, 122, 131, 145,
    149, 156, 166, 169, 175, 182, 194,
    198, 199, 202, 203
Il Freddo bacio della morte see *The
    Third Eye*
Freud (1962 film) 188
Freud, Sigmund 27, 30, 45, 49, 63,
    86, 201
The Frozen Dead 100
Frusta, Arrigo (Augusto Sebastiano
    Ferraris) 11
La Frusta e il corpo see *The Whip
    and the Body*
Fruttero, Carlo 11
Fuchsberger, Joachim 195, 196, 197,
    200
Fuentes, Carlos 172, 174, 175
Fugitive Lady 56
Fujiwara, Chris 9, 110, 113, 114
Fulci, Lucio 33, 39, 181
Fusco, Giovanni 182

Gabel, Scilla 50
Gable, Clark 78
Gainsbourg, Serge 198
Gaioni, Cristina 159
Galassi, Angelo 29
Galatea (production company) 40,
    48, 49, 50, 79, 121, 159, 202
Galletti, Giovanna 161
Gallone, Carmine 9, 14, 156
Gangsters '70 171
García Gutiérrez, Antonio 14
Gariazzo, Mario 94
Garrani, Ivo 36
Garrone, Riccardo 151
Garrone, Sergio 17
Gaslight (1940 film) 71, 144
Gaslight (1944 film) 71
Gaslini, Giorgio 159
Gassman, Vittorio 27, 33

Gastaldi, Ernesto (aka Julian Berry)
    1–2, 9, 16, 60, 61, 62, 63, 64, 65, 66,
    68, 70, 71, 73, 76, 95, 101, 102, 103,
    104, 107, 108, 124, 125, 128, 130,
    131, 133, 136, 166, 168, 202, 203
Gautier, Théophile 62
Gazzelloni, Severino 182
Gelosia (1942 film) 12
Geminus 176
Genet, Jean 156
Gentilomo, Giacomo 13, 16, 17
"The Gentleman from Paris" (short
    story) 110
Gerard, Henriette 24
Germani, Gaia 116, 119, 120
Germani, Grmek Sergio 9, 24, 30
Germi, Pietro 125, 194
Ghelli, Nino 31, 33
Ghezzi, Enrico 199
The Ghost **87–92**, 203
Ghosts of Rome 31
Giacometti, Alberto 83, 145
Giallo a Venezia 147
Giannetti, Alfredo 126
Giannini, Giancaro 2, 123
The Giant of Marathon 40
The Giants of Thessaly 194
Gimmi, Gena 77
Ginger e Fred 183, 191
Ginsberg, Allen 168
Un Gioco per Eveline 17
Giolitti, Giovanni 54
Giorni, Arturo 147
Giovannini, Maria 59
Girardot, Annie 41
The Girl Who Knew Too Much see
    The Evil Eye
Girolami, Ennio 56
Girolami, Enzo see Castellari,
    Enzo G
Girolami, Marino 8, 31, 53–56
Girolami, Romolo see Guerrieri,
    Romolo
Girotti, Massimo 177
Giusti, Marco 199
Gloriani, Tina 62
Gobal 185, 187
Godard, Jean-Luc 178, 186
Gogol' Nikolai 4, 40, 41, 42, 43, 48,
    62
The Golden Mass 30
Der Golem (1920 film) 24
Goliath and the Vampires 16
The Good, the Bad and the Ugly 147
Gora, Claudio 156
Gordon, Richard 56, 57, **58**, 60, 97
The Gothic Flame 9, 25, 201
Gragnani, Ugo 63
Granata, Graziella 32, 77, 126, 127
Granger, Farley 199
Green, Gastad see Vicario, Renato
Gregoretti, Ugo 169, 186
Grimaldi, Alberto 186
Grimaldi, Gianni (aka Jean Grimaud)
    86, 110, 111, 154
Grimaldi, Hugo 53
Grimaud, Jean see Grimaldi, Gianni
Guarany 27
Guarracino, Umberto 11

Guerra, Tonino 178
Guerra, Ugo (aka Robert Hugo) 68,
    102
Guerrieri, Romolo (Romolo Giro-
    lami) 56
Guerrini, Mino 168–171
Guest, Val 24
Gui, Maddalena (aka Bogart, Frank)
    98
Guida, Wandisa 29, 72
Gys, Leda 27

Halliday, Bryant 57
Halligan, Benjamin 9, 118, 119, 121,
    201
Hamilton, George 103
Hamilton, Michael see De Felice,
    Lionello
Hammer Films 15, 22, 24, 36, 38,
    40, 41, 50, 52, 56, 57, 59, 65, 69,
    77, 90, 103, 122, 129, 133, 135
Hampton, Robert see Freda, Ric-
    cardo
Hands Over the City 114
Hannah and Her Sisters 153
Hardy, Martin see Martino, Luciano
Hardy, Robin 125
Hargitay, Mickey 6, 140, 141, *142*
Hart, John Davis 53
Harvey, Cy 57
Harvey, William Fryer 81, 83
Hatchet for the Honeymoon 83, 165
The Haunted Strangler 56
Hawthorne, Nathaniel 11, 80
Hayers, Sidney 39
He Who Shoots First 88
Hercules (1958 film) 16, 17, 40
Hercules Against the Moon Men 8, 17
Hercules in the Haunted World 16,
    32, 46, 105, 162
Hercules Unchained 17, 40
Hercules vs. the Giant Warriors 42
Herrin von Atlantis, Die 24, 175
Hersent, Philippe 168
Herter, Gérard 24
Herzog, Werner 77
Heusch, Paolo 1, 64–68, 181
The Hills Run Red 171
Histoires extraordinaires see *Spirits
    of the Dead*
Hitchcock, Alfred 39, 70, 76, 85, 86,
    107, 181, 182
Hoffmann, Ernst Theodor Amadeus
    47, 62, 83, 185
Holden, Lansing C. 24
Honthauer, Ronald 29
Hormigos, Montserrat 189, 192, 202
The Horrible Dr. Hichcock 2, 6, 24,
    28, 29, **68–76**, 89, 90, 91, 99, 104,
    107, 112, 122, 145, 157, 164, 166,
    169, 170, 182
Horror (1963 film) see *The
    Blancheville Monster*
Horror Castle see *The Virgin of
    Nuremberg*
Horror Hospital 118
Horror of Dracula 1, 16, 25, 30, 31,
    38, 40, 41, 57, 60, 61, 62, 63, 77
Horrors of Spider Island 137

Horrors of the Black Museum 39
The Hound of the Baskervilles (1959 film) 39
The Hound of the Baskervilles (novel) 101
The House of Exorcism 121
House of Usher 103, 104
House of Wax (1953 film) 53, 120
The House on Haunted Hill (1959 film) 83
The House with the Laughing Windows 130, 157
Hoveida, Fereydoun 47, 49, 203
"How to Write a Blackwood Article" (short story) 110
Howlers of the Dock 33
Hugo, Robert *see* Guerra, Ugo
Huis clos (play) 89
The Human Centipede 101
Hunter, Max *see* Pupillo, Domenico Massimo
Huston, John 188
The Hyena of London **121–124**

I Was a Teenage Frankenstein 36
Identificazione di una donna 153
If You Live Shoot (aka *Django Kill!*) 127
L'Iguana (1965 novel) 184
L'Iguana (2004 film) 185
I'll See You in Hell 94
Incontro d'amore 68
Inferno (1980 film) 80
The Invention of Morel (novel) 113
Invernizio, Carolina 11, 13, 22
Invincibili fratelli Maciste, Gli 78
Io...il Marchese De Sade see *Bloody Pit of Horror*
The Iron Swordsman 27, 90
L'Isola di Arturo 175

Jacobs, William Wymark 81
Jacopetti, Gualtiero 140
James, Henry 188
Jane Eyre (novel) 70
Jekyll (TV miniseries) **176–177**
La Jena di Londra see *The Hyena of London*
Jenks, Carol 39, 48
Jessy non perdona...Uccide see *Sunscorched*
Johnny Yuma 56
Johnson, Richard 173
Johnson, Steven 9, 118, 119, 121, 203
Jolly Film (company) 47, 146
Jotta, Elio 90
Judgment of Tears see *Dracula Cha Cha Cha*
Juliet of the Spirits 180, 188, 189
Juliette de Sade 121

Kadijevic, Djordje 48
Kardos, László 24
Karis, Vassili (Vassili Karamenisis) 157
Karloff, Boris 41, 79, 80, 82, 85
Karslen, John 181
Katarsis (aka *Sfida al diavolo*) **92–94**, 188

Kavka, Misha 70, 76
Keaton, Camille 157
Kendall, Tony (Luciano Stella) 123
Kezich, Tullio 179, 180, 202
Kiefer, Warren (aka Lorenzo Sabatini) 114–121
Kier, Udo 155
Kill, Baby...Kill! 17, 46, 60, 73, 83, 105, 108, 151, 154, **159–165**, 188
Killer 77, Alive or Dead 169
Killers Are Challenged 195
Killing (photonovel) 96, 140, 142, 194
King, Adrienne 157
Kinski, Klaus 77, 114, 175, 195
KKK (paperback series) 62, 98, 101
Klein, Rita 141
Knives of the Avenger 105
Koch, Marianne 195, 196, *197*
Koscina, Sylva 33
Krafft-Ebing, Richard von 75
Kriminal (comic) 140, 141, 142
Kristye, Anthony *see* Boccacci, Antonio
Kropachyov, Georgi 48
Kurosawa, Akira 65
Kyrou, Ado 137, 141

Labbra vogliose 194
Lacan, Jacques 76, 201
La Lama nel corpo see *The Murder Clinic*
Landi, Mario 176
Landolfi, Tommaso 158, 184, 185
Landres, Paul 101
Landry, Gérard 96
Lang, Fritz 24, 45, 50, 188
Lanza, Mario 31
Lass, Barbara 67
The Last Man on Earth 181
The Last Rebel 121
Last Tango in Paris 127
Last Year at Marienbad 113, 176
Lattuada, Alberto 54, 173
Laugier, Pascal 101
Laura (1944 film) 45
Lautréamont (Isidore Lucien Ducasse) 62
Lavagnino, Massimo Francesco 165
Lawrence of Arabia 68
Lean, David 68
Leaves from Satan's Book 11
Lee, Christopher 1, 16, 32, 33, 38, 60, 92, 93, 94, 98, 101, 102, 103, 107, 108, 115, 119, 128, 130, 134, 135, 159, 202, 203
Le Fanu, Joseph Sheridan 2, 4, 62, 128, 129, 130, 131, 132, 133, 134, 135, 202
Legend of Love 13
Legrand, Gérard 75, 76, 203
Lemoine, Michel 181, 182
Leone, Alfredo 121
Leone, Sergio 17, 48, 53, 91, 108, 127, 146, 147, 156
Leonviola, Antonio 123
Leroux, Gaston 136
Leroy, Philippe 116, 119
Lewis, Al 29

Lewis, Herschell Gordon 151
Lewis, Matthew 12, 93
Lewton, Val 94
Liberatore, Ugo 174, 175, 176
Libido 2, 166
"Ligeia" (short story) 69, 191
Lightning Bolt 195
Lindau, Paul 18
Liné, Helga 145
The Lingala Code 121
Lippi, Giuseppe 85
Lisa and the Devil 47, 83, 120, 161
The Literature of Terror 9, 21, 30, 34, 75, 76, 178, 201
Lizzani, Carlo 126, 171
Lobravico, Carolyn 168
Lollobrigida, Gina 27, 42
Lombardo, Goffredo 23
The Long Hair of Death 4, 14, 46, 107, 111, **124–125**, 128, 145, 149, 150, 155, 195
The Long Ships 115
Lopez, Sylvia 17
Loren, Sophia 42
Loret, Susanne 34
Lori, Carlo 193
Lorre, Peter 188, 195
Losey, Joseph 176, 186
Love from a Stranger (1937 film) 71
Love from a Stranger (1947 film) 71
Love Meetings 42
Love: The Great Unknown 155
Lovecraft, Howard Phillips 41, 164
Lowens, Curt 67, 68, 203
Loy, Mino 2
Lucas, Tim 30, 68, 85, 108, 118, 121, 124, 125, 137, 151, 153, 162, 165, 168, 188, 201
Lucentini, Franco (aka P. Kettridge) 81, 85, 201
Lugosi, Bela 32
Lulli, Folco 159
Lulli, Piero 108, 159
La Luna negra 49
La Lunga notte di Veronique see *But You Were Dead*
Lunghi capelli della morte, I see *The Long Hair of Death*
Lupi, Roldano 12
Lupo, Alberto 34, 36, 37, 54, 94, 176
Luppi, Federico 155
Lust for a Vampire 134
Lust of the Vampire 30
Lutyens, Edwin 25
Lycanthropus see *Werewolf in a Girls' Dormitory*

M 188
Ma l'amor mio non muore! 11
Macabre (1980 film) 76
Le Macabre ore della paura 162
Maciste all'inferno (1926 film) 11, 191
Mademoiselle 156
Maggi, Luigi 11, 188
Magritte, René 146
Majano, Anton Giulio 34–36, 176
Malabimba 57

Malenotti, Maleno 183
Malia—I fotoromanzi del brivido (photonovel) 59, 64, 135, 138, 148
Malle, Louis 186
Malombra (1917 film) 9, 12, 156
Malombra (1942 film) 9, 12, 13, 52, 156
Mamoulian, Rouben 24
A Man Called Blade 147
The Man Who Turned to Stone 24
The Man with a Cloak 110
The Man with Icy Eyes 88
La Mandragola 173
Manfredi, Nino 32
Mangano, Silvana 17, 183
Mangini, Luigi (aka Henry Wilson) 121–123
Mangravite, Andrew 45, 49, 203
Mania 64
Mannino, Franco 91
Manzoni, Alessandro 151
Maravidi, Mirella 150, 153
Marcellini, Romolo 155
Marchesi, Marcello 31, 56
Marcuse, Herbert 178
Margheriti, Antonio (aka Anthony M. Dawson) 4, 5, 8, 14, 15, 17, 46, 71, 86, 97–102, 108, 109–114, 124–125, 128, 130, 131, 150, 154, 194–200, 203
Marquand, Christian 91
Marsac, Maurice 67, 68
Martin, Anthony (aka Skip Martin; Antonio De Martino) 117, 118
Martin, Skip *see* Martin, Anthony
Martini, Alberto (painter) 107
Martino, Luciano (aka Martin Hardy) 68, 102, 166
Martino, Sergio 147, 169, 171
Martyrs 101
Maryl, Mara (Maria Chianetta) 2, 128
La Maschera del demonio (1960 film) see *Black Sunday*
La Maschera del demonio (1989 film) 48, 49
Maschera tragica 11
Masciocchi, Marcello 166
Masé, Marino 145
Masi, Marco 11
Masina, Giulietta 188
The Mask of Satan see *Black Sunday*
Maslansky, Paul 115, 116, 117, 118, 119
The Masque of the Red Death (1964 film) 90, 103, 118, 151
"The Masque of the Red Death" (short story) 11, 72
Massaccesi, Aristide 91, 153, 171, 194
Massi, Stelvio 177
Mastrocinque, Camillo (aka Thomas Miller) 4, 13, 16, 31, 47, 104, 123, 128–135, 155–157
Mastroianni, Marcello 180, 189
Matarazzo, Raffaello 13
Maté Rudolph 30
Matheson, Richard 87, 104, 203
Mattoli, Mario 31, 145
Maturin, Charles Robert 107

Maupassant, Guy de 78, 81
Mauri, Roberto (Giuseppe Tagliavia) 32, 37, 76–78
Mayniel, Juliette 126
McCoy, Denys 121
McGilvray, Catherine 185
McTeigue, James 110
Medin, Gastone 14
Medusa Against the Son of Hercules 16
Melelli, Fabio 142, 153
Melle, Johan 168
Mellino, Elio Ippolito (aka Mario Fava) 37
Melmoth the Wanderer 107
Mendez, Fernando 101
Mercier, Michèle 81, 114
Mérimée, Prosper 156
Merrill, Gary 181, 182
Mesmer, Franz Anton 86
Messalina 38
Metempsyco see *Tomb of Torture*
Metz, Vittorio 56
"Metzengerstein" (episode from *Spirits of the Dead*) 183, 184, 186, **187**
"Metzengerstein" (short story) 186
Meurisse, Paul 125
Meyer, Nicholas 110
Miami Golem 88
Migliorini, Romano 140, 141, 150, 162
The Mill of the Stone Women 4, 16, 22, 49–53, 138, 145, 157
Miller, David 71
Miller, Thomas *see* Mastrocinque, Camillo
Milo, Sandra 188
Milton, John 5
Minervini, Angela 130
The Mines of Kilimanjaro 171
Minnelli, Vincente 34, 103, 172
Il Mio amico Jekyll see *My Friend, Dr. Jekyll*
Miranda, Isa 12, 52
Misiano, Fortunato 148
Mitchell, Gordon 147, 154, 155
Il Monaco di Monza 31, 109
Mondo cane 2 140
Mondo cane 2000: L'incredibile 123
Mondo di notte 141
Mondo Pupillo—Une conversation avec Massimo Pupillo 143, 153,
Monell, Robert 9, 29, 30, 203
Monicelli, Mario 31, 153, 186
"The Monkey's Paw" (short story) 81
The Monster of the Opera see *The Vampire of the Opera*
Montresor, Beni 25, 28, 30
Mora, Teo 9, 30, 63, 64, 199, 200, 202, 203
Morgan, Marina 170, 171
Morgia, Piero 126
Moriarty, Michael 88
Morricone, Ennio 143, 146, 178
Morrissey, Paul 155, 190
Il Mostro dell'Opera see *The Vampire of the Opera*

Il Mostro di Frankenstein 11
Motorizzati, I 47
Il Mulino delle donne di pietra see *The Mill of the Stone Women*
Muller, Frederick 9, 116, 117, 118, 119, 121
Muller, Paul 23, 24, 28, 29, 144, 154
The Munsters (TV series) 29
Murder by Appointment 171
The Murder Clinic **165–168**
"The Murders in the Rue Morgue" (short story) 36
Murnau, Friedrich Wilhelm 22, 41, 71
Mussolini, Benito 12, 158
My Friend, Dr. Jekyll 8, 31, **53–56**
The Mysteries of Udolpho (novel) 6, 12
The Mysterious Rider 27
Mystery of the Wax Museum (1933 film) 24

Nabokov, Vladimir 43
Naked You Die (aka *The Young, the Evil and the Savage*) 68, 195
Namath, Joe 121
The Name of the Rose (novel) 96
Natale, Roberto 16, 138, 141, 150, 152, 153, 162, 164
Nelli, Barbara 140, 154
Nero, Franco 169, **170**, 171, 178
"Never Bet the Devil Your Head" (short story) 186
Newman, Kim 34
Nicolai, Bruno 146
Nicolodi, Daria 84, 134
Nicolosi, Roberto 47
Night Is the Phantom see *The Whip and the Body*
The Night of the Devils 18, 53, 82
Nightmare Castle 6, 138, **143–146**, 166
Nights of Cabiria 180
1900 (1976 film) 127
Nosferatu (1922 film) 24, 31, 41, 71
Nosferatu the Vampyre 77
Nota, Maria 41
Notorious 70
Le Notti della violenza 37, 78
Notti nude 59
Nude for Satan 78
Nuovi angeli, I 169

Odyssey (1968 film) 176
O.K. Connery 88
Old, John M. *see* Bava, Mario
The Old Dark House (1932 film) 195
Olea, Pedro 49
The Omen (1976 film) 88
Once Upon a Time in America 127
Once Upon a Time in the West 91
Onions, George Oliver 41, 177, 178
Onorato, Glauco 82
Opera 40
Operazione paura see *Kill, Baby... Kill!*
Opiate '67 54
Orchestra Rehearsal 180
Orfei, Moira 43

Orpheus (1950 film) 164
L'Orribile segreto del Dr. Hichcock see *The Horrible Dr. Hichcock*
Ortas, Julio 131, 135
Ortese, Anna Maria 184
Ortolani, Riz 99
Oscenità 64
Outlaw (1989 novel) 120
"The Oval Portrait" (short story) 190
Oxilia, Nino 11

P. Kettridge *see* Lucentini, Franco
Pabst, Georg Wilhelm 24, 175
Paganini Horror 137
Pagano, Bartolomeo 11
Pagliero, Marcello 189
Pagnol, Marcel 152
Pallottini, Riccardo 99, 125, 198, 199
Pamphili, Mirella (Mirella Pompili) 162
Paolessi, Umberto 138
Parise, Goffredo 187
Pascal, Gioia *170*, 171
Pasolini, Pier Paolo 42, 46, 68, 93, 171, 181, 186, 189
"Il Passo" (episode from *Amori pericolosi*) 8, 17, *125–127*, 166, 186
Passport for a Corpse 94
Patrick Still Lives 57, 147
La Paura fa 90 31
Pavoni, Pier Ludovico 52
Pedrocchi, Luciano 138
Peeping Tom 39, 67
Peguri, Gino 141
La Pelle sotto gli artigli 147
Petri, Elio 8, 17, 126, 177–180
Pezzotta, Alberto 9, 41, 48, 49, 66, 104, 108, 114, 135, 165, 175, 192, 202
The Phantom (comic) 140, 151
The Phantom Carriage 151
Phantom of the Opera (novel) 136
Photonovels 59, 64, 67, 95, 96, 135, 138, 140, 142, 148, 193, 194, 198
Pichel, Irving 24
The Picture of Dorian Gray (novel) 136
Pierreux, Jacqueline 83
Pietrangeli, Antonio 31
Pigozzi, Luciano (aka Alan Collins) 67, 118, 119, 123, 195, 196, 199
Pilgrimage 30
Le Pillole di Ercole 32
Pinelli, Tullio 183
Pinkus, Gertrud 49
Pinzauti, Mario 17, 101
Piranesi, Giovan Battista 43
Il Pirata del diavolo 78
Pirie, David 15, 8, 59, 60, 117, 118, 119, 121, 201
The Pit and the Pendulum (1961 film) 39, 86, 103, 104, 110, 125
"The Pit and the Pendulum" (short story) 190
Pitagora, Paola 38
Più tardi, Claire ... più tardi see *Run, Psycho, Run*

Planet of the Vampires 37
The Playgirls and the Vampire **56–60**, 97, 137, 138, 140, 141
Podestà, Rossana 98, 99, *100*, 101, 102
Poe, Edgar Allan 11, 12, 25, 36, 39, 50, 62, 69, 70, 71, 72, 79, 82, 85, 86, 87, 90, 94, 103, 104, 109, 110, 111, 113, 126, 145, 149, 150, 161, 169, 178, 183–192, 202
Poe, James 157
P.O.E.—Poetry of Eerie 85
Poggioli, Ferdinando Maria 12
Poindron, Éric 18, 22, 23, 30, 49, 76, 202
Polani, Anna Maria 17
Polanski, Roman 67, 172
Poli, Mimmo 54
Polidori, John 62
La Polizia è al servizio del cittadino? 56
Polselli, Renato 1, 4, 59, 60–64, 69, 135–137, 140, 159
Ponti, Carlo 195
Le Porno investigatrici 194
Le Porno killers 78
Potenza, Franco 193
Powell, Michael 39, 52
Praz, Mario 9
Preminger, Otto 45, 68
Pressburger, Emeric 52
Prévost, Françoise 167
Price, Bernard *see* Tempestini, Giotto
Price, Vincent 78, 87, 112
Primitive Love 155
Prosperi, Franco 140
Prova d'orchestra see *Orchestra Rehearsal*
Psycho 39, 70, 95, 107, 134
Psychopathia Sexualis (essay) 75
Ptushko, Aleksandr 48
Puccini, Gianni 169
Punter, David 4, 9, 21, 30, 34, 75, 76, 178, 201
Pupillo, Domenico Massimo (aka Max Hunter) 6, 111, 112, 137–143, 149–155, 162, 203

Quaglia, Pier Anna (aka Ursula Davis) 131
47 morto che parla 31
The Quatermass Xperiment 24
Quel fantasma di mio marito 31
Questa specie d'amore 37
Questi, Giulio 8, 17, 125–127, 166, 202
Quickly, spari e baci a colazione 147
A Quiet Place in the Country 8, 17, **177–180**

Rabal, Francisco 68
Rabid Dogs 81
Racconti di Dracula, I (paperback series) 62, 92, 95, 98, 101
Racconto d'autunno (novel) 158, 185
Radcliffe, Ann 4, 12, 73, 107
Raffaelli, Giuliano 196
Raho, Umberto 91, 110, 112

Raimi, Sam 199
Rain of Fire 88
Rains, Claude 28, 70
Rambaldi, Carlo 141
Randone, Salvo 114
"Rappaccini's Daughter" (short story) 11
Rapsodia Satanica 11
Rascel, Renato 31, 32
Rashomon 65
Rassimov, Ivan 175
Ráthonyi, Ákos 97
Ravaioli, Isarco 63
The Raven (1963 film) 84
The Raven (2012 film) 110
Read, Herbert 72, 76
Rebecca 70, 182
Red (1994 film) 1994
Red Desert 153
Red Nights of the Gestapo 146
Red Shoes 137
Redgrave, Vanessa 178
Reeves, Michael 117, 118, 121, 157, 201, 203
Regnoli, Piero 23, 56–60, 69, 94, 137, 169
The Reincarnation of Isabel 64
Rémy, Hélène 62, 64
Renoir, Claude 133
Resnais, Alain 113
Return of the Vampire 101
The Revenge of Frankenstein 101
Revenge of the Living Dead see *The Murder Clinic*
Revenge of the Vampire see *Black Sunday*
Reynaud, Janine 181
Reynolds, Debbie 42
Ricci, Luciano (aka Herbert Wise) 115, 116
Richardson, Tony 156
Riethof, Peter 57
Righi, Massimo (aka Max Dean) 28, 166
Ringo, It's Massacre Time 17
Il Rinnegato del deserto 68
Risi, Dino 33, 54, 125, 185, 186
Riuscirà l'avvocato Franco Benenato a sconfiggere il suo acerrimo nemico il pretore Ciccio De Ingras? 171
Riva, Valerio 62
Rivière, Georges 99, 110, 111
Rizzo, Alfredo 57, 60, 140
Rizzoli, Angelo 115
The Road to Fort Alamo 103
Robinson, Bernard 25
Robinson, Edward G. 34, 103
Robsahm, Margrete 112, 131
Roc, Michela (Bianca Maria Roccatani) 67
Rocco, Lyla 59
Rocco and His Brothers 6, 41
Roger La Honte 71
RoGoPaG 186
Rolando, Maria Luisa 62
Roli, Mino 121
Rollin, Jean 39, 93
Roma (1972 film) 191
Rome Against Rome 16

Romero, George A. 85
Rondi, Brunello 48, 88, 103, 165, 180–183, 202, 203
Rondi, Gian Luigi 175, 176, 180
Rosa, Salvator (painter) 9, 43
Rosemary's Baby 183
Rosi, Francesco 114
Rossellini, Roberto 180, 186
Rossi, Franco 176
Rossi-Stuart, Giacomo 108, 159, 161, 164
Rota, Nino 190
Run, Psycho, Run 180–183
Rustichelli, Carlo 107, 165

Sa Jana 155
Sabatini, Lorenzo see Kiefer, Warren
Le Salamandre 147, 194
Salce, Luciano 32, 54
Salerno, Vittorio 166
Salgari, Emilio 96
Salkow, Sidney 80
Salvador, Henri 34
Samale, Libero 101, 102
"The Sandman" (short story) 83, 127
Sangster, Jimmy 134
Santi, Nello 40
Santini, Alessandro 147, 148
Sartana nella valle degli avvoltoi 78
Sartre, Jean-Paul 89
Satana (1912 film) 11, 188
The Satanic Rites of Dracula 22
Satanik (comic) 141, 142
Savinio, Alberto 184
Scardamaglia, Elio 102, 165–168
Scattini, Luigi 155
Schechter, Harold 110
Schell, Carl 67, 68
Schiaffino, Rosanna 172, 173, 175
Schiller, Friedrich 5
Schneider, Romy 37
Schreie in der Nacht see The Unnaturals—Contronatura
Schurer, Erna (Emma Costantino) 183, 193, 194
Sciarretta, Ulderico 93
Sciascia, Armando 97
Scorsese, Martin 103, 166
Scott, Gordon 16
Scott, Walter 4
Seddok "l'erede di Satana" see Atom Age Vampire
Il Segno del comando 177
Le Sei mogli di Barbablù 31
La Sensitiva 183
Serandrei, Mario 41
Serling, Rod 85
Sernas, Jacques 16
Serra Caracciolo, Garibaldi (aka Finney Cliff) 146–149
Sesso acerbo 194
Il Sesso degli angeli 176
Sesso profondo 56
La Settima tomba see The Seventh Grave
The Seven Hills of Rome 31
The Seventh Grave 146–149

Sex of the Witch 147
Sfida al diavolo see Katarsis
She (1935 film) 24
The She Beast 117, 157
She Demons 34
Shelley, Barbara 59
Shelley, Mary 29
The Shining (1980 film) 198
Shock (1977 film) 47, 84, 108, 134
Siamo uomini o caporali 129
Sijöstrom, Rijk 30
Silvagni, Giulio Cesare 25, 30
Silver, Alain 48, 76, 85, 86, 106, 108, 202
Simonelli, Giorgio 31
Simonelli, Giovanni 95
Sins of Rome 27
Siodmak, Curt 122
Six, Tom 101
Sjöström, Victor 151
Slaughter Hotel 154
Slaughter of the Vampires 32, 76–78, 127, 138
Sleep, My Love 71
Snyder, F.G. 81
Soldati, Mario 9, 12, 13, 52, 156
Solomon, Joe 57
Solway, Jerry 57
"Some Words with a Mummy" (short story) 86
Something Creeping in the Dark 199
Sordi, Alberto 54, 125
Sorrente, Sylvia 112
Sortilegio 183, 203
Lo Spettro (1907 film) 11
Lo Spettro (1963 film) see The Ghost
Spirit of Evil see Viy
Spirits of the Dead 79, 183–192
The Spy with Ten Faces 88
SS-Sunda (Sandro Yassel Spazio) 142
Stamp, Terence 189, 190, 191
Stander, Lionel 120, 121
Steele, Barbara 6, 7, 24, 37, 38, 39, 41, 42, 44, 47, 48, 49, 52, 69, 70, 71, 88, 90, 91, 103, 109, 110, 117, 122, 124, 125, 131, 134, 143, 145, 146, 149, 150, 152, 155, 156, 157, 159, 164, 175, 186, 188
Steffen, Anthony (Antonio De Teffé) 156
Stegani, Giorgio 120, 121
Steno (Stefano Vanzina) 8, 30–34
Stevens, Mark 121
Stevenson, Robert Louis 18, 25, 31, 54, 73, 176, 177
Stoker, Bram 1, 31, 57, 64
La Strada 56, 180
La Strada buia see Fugitive Lady
La Strage dei vampiri see Slaughter of the Vampires
The Strange Case of Dr. Jekyll and Mr. Hyde (novel) 18, 25, 34, 65, 73, 122, 176–177
La Strega in amore see The Witch
Strock, Herbert L. 36
Sunscorched (aka Jessy non perdona... Uccide) 120
Sunset Blvd. 27

Super Hard Love 194
Suspicion 70
Suspiria 30, 40, 80
Sutherland, Donald 117, 119
Sutherland, Kiefer 117
Sveto mesto 48
Swanson, Gloria 27
The Sweet Body of Deborah 56
Sweet Deceptions 54
Swindle 180

Taboos of the World 155
Tahi, Moa 141
"A Tale from the Ragged Mountains" (short story) 86
A Tale of Torture see Bloody Pit of Horror
Tales of Terror 80
Tanikawa, Shuntaro 188
Taranto, Nino 31
Tassi, Agostino (painter) 105
"The Telephone" (episode from Black Sabbath) 78, 79, 80, 81, 82, 85
"The Tell-Tale Heart" (short story) 12, 82, 126, 145, 166, 185, 190
Tempestini, Giotto (aka Bernard Price) 123
Tempi duri per i vampiri see Uncle Was a Vampire
Tenebrae 13
The Tenth Victim 178
Terror-Creatures from the Grave 124, 138, 139, 140, 142, 143, 149–153, 162
Terror in the Crypt 1, 2, 4, 16, 60, 111, 124, 128–135, 156
Terzano, Massimo 12
Terzano, Ubaldo 102, 125
Il Terzo occhio see The Third Eye
Testa, Eugenio 11
Theodora, Slave Empress 27
The Third Eye 145, 166, 168–171
The Thousand Eyes of Dr. Mabuse 50
The Three Faces of Terror (2004 film) 85
Thriller (TV series) 80, 85
Thulin, Ingrid 181
The Tingler 83
Tingwell, Charles 59
"Toby Dammit" (episode from Spirits of the Dead) 184–192
Todd, Mort 142
Todorov, Tzvetan 43, 71, 76, 104, 108, 174, 201
Tognazzi, Ugo 37, 47, 49, 54
Tolo, Marilù 42
Tolstoy, Aleksey Kostantinovich 62, 80, 82
Tolstoy, Lev Nikolaevich 81
Tomb of Torture 95–97, 138
Tombolo 53
Torelli, Lucia 41
Totaro, Donato 3, 9, 64, 203
Totò al Giro d'Italia 31, 188
Totò all'inferno 31, 123
Totò cerca casa 31
Totò d'Arabia 68
Totò, lascia o raddoppia? 129

Toto the Sheik 145
Tourneur, Jacques 40
Tranquilli, Silvano 71, 110, 145
Un Tranquillo posto di campagna see *A Quiet Place in the Country*
Traps (novel) 196
Trasatti, Luciano 94, 141
Tre passi nel delirio see *Spirits of the Dead*
Tre volti della paura, I see *Black Sabbath*
Trovajoli, Armando 165
Il Trovatore (1949 film) 14
Truffaut, François 57
Turini, Gino 62, 63, 140
Twice-Told Tales 80
The Twilight Zone (TV series) 85
Twixt 110
Two Evil Eyes 85
Two Weeks in Another Town 34, 103, 172, 173, 191
Two Women 68

Ulloa, Alejandro 87
L'Ultima preda del vampiro see *The Playgirls and the Vampire*
L'Ultimo dei Baskerville 176
Ulysses (1954 film) 17
The Uncanny (essay) 27, 30, 49, 83, 86, 201
Uncle Was a Vampire 8, **30–34**, 54
The Undead 46
Under Capricorn 70
The Unnaturals—Contronatura **194–200**
L'Uomo della sabbia 127
Upchurch, Alan 151, 153, 203
Ursini, James 48, 76, 85, 86, 106, 108, 202

Vadim, Roger 128, 133, 186, 187
Valentin, Mirko 99, 119
Valeri, Valerio 161, *163*
Valeria dentro e fuori 183
Valerii, Tonino 2, 9, 16, 18, 124, 128, 129, 131, 133, 134, 135, 201, 202
La Valle della paura 176
Valmont, Véra 130
Der Vampir von Notre Dame see *Vampiri, I*
The Vampire (1957 film) 101
The Vampire and the Ballerina 1, 6, 54, 59, **60–64**, 135, 136, 137, 141
Vampire Circus 118
The Vampire Lovers 129, 134
The Vampire of the Opera **135–137**, 138, 159
Les Vampires 24
I Vampiri 1, 3, 6, 7, 16, **21–30**, 34, 42, 46, 62, 64, 69, 72, 105, 117, 138, 145, 161, 164, 166, 174, 175

Vampiri tra noi, I 62, 81, 110, 128
Vampirismus 127
Il Vampiro dell'Opera see *The Vampire of the Opera*
Vampyr 24, 50, 62, 88, 128, 164
Van Cleef, Lee 120, 121
Van Nutten, Rik 33
Vandor, Ivan 127
Vari, Giuseppe 16
Varma, Devendra P. 9, 25, 76, 201
Veggezzi, Giuseppe 92–94
Velázquez, Diego 164
Velle, Gaston 2
La Vendetta di Lady Morgan 111, 112, 145, **153–155**, 162, 163
La Venere d'Ille 41, 156
Vengeance 195
La Venus d'Ille (novel) 156
Venus in Furs 68
Verdone, Carlo 156
Verga, Giovanni 9, 181
La Vergine dei veleni 11
La Vergine di Norimberga see *The Virgin of Nuremberg*
Vergine moderna 169
La Verità secondo Satana 64
Vernon, Howard 147
Vernuccio, Gianni 157–159
Vertigine bianca 53
Il Viaggio di G. Mastorna 180, 191
Vianello, Maria Teresa 69
Vianello, Raimondo 54
Vicario, Marco 98, 102
Vicario, Renato (aka Gastad Green) 101
Vida, Piero (Pietro Vidali) 93
Vidali, Enrico 11
Vincenzoni, Luciano 178
Violent Life 68, 93, 181
Violent Rome 56
The Virgin of Nuremberg 8, 71, **97–102**, 103, 104, 140, 184, 196
Visconti, Luchino 6, 41, 186
Vite perdute (La legge del mitra) 78
Vitti, Monica 153
Viy (aka *Spirit of Evil*; 1967 film) 48
"*Viy*" (short story) 4, 40, 42, 62
Vlad, Roman 72, 91, 165
Vlady, Marina 112
La Voce 183
La Voglia 194
The Voice of the Moon 191
Volonté, Claudio (aka Claudio Camaso) 195, 199
Volonté, Gian Maria 174, 175, 195
Volta, Ornella 62
Vukotic, Milena 190

The Wages of Fear (1953 film) 159
Walbrook, Anton 144

Walpole, Horace 73
War of the Monsters 181
Warbeck, David 88
Wayne, John 78
Web of the Spider 18, 114, 195
Welles, Mel 103, 119
Welles, Orson 78, 186
Wellman, Manly Wade 110
Wells, Herbert George 101
Werewolf in a Girls' Dormitory 1, **64–68**, 69, 203
Whale, James 41, 195
What see *The Whip and the Body*
Whatever Happened to Baby Jane? 68
The Whip and the Body 2, 6, 13, 88, 92, **102–108**, 123, 144, 159, 164
White, Harriet (aka Harriet White Medin) 70, 133, 166
The Wicker Man (1973 film) 125
The Widower 125
Wiene, Robert 24
The Wild, Wild Planet 198
Wildon, Gordon, Jr. see Corbucci, Bruno
Wilkinson, June 60
"William Wilson" (episode from *Spirits of the Dead*) 184, 186, 190
Wilson, Georges 181
Wilson, Henry see Mangini, Luigi
Wise, Herbert see Ricci, Luciano
Wise, Ray 157
The Witch 8, 17, **171–176**, 189
The Witches (1967 film) 186
Witchfinder General 118
The Witch's Curse 8, 14, 16
Wolff, Frank 126, 127
The Woman in the Window 45
Wood, Edward D., Jr. 68, 85, Wood, Robin 117, 121, 203
Wordsworth, Richard 24
"The Wurdalak" (episode from *Black Sabbath*) 4, 18, 43, 53, 79, 80, 81, 82, 85, 162
The Wurdalak (novelette) 62, 81
Wuthering Heights (novel) 70

Yershow, Konstantin 48
York, Susannah 188
The Young, the Evil and the Savage see *Naked You Die*
Young, Violent, Dangerous 56

Zac, Pino 188
Zapponi, Bernardino 185, 186, 188, 189, 190, 192, 202
Zarantonello, Gionata 157
Zavattini, Cesare 138
Zingarelli, Italo 86
Zombie Holocaust 56
Zucker, Ralph 140, 142, 149, 151, 152, 153, 203